Management Skills for the New Health Care Supervisor

Third Edition

William Umiker
Adjunct Professor
The Penn State's Milton S. Hershey Medical Center
Hershey, Pennsylvania

AN ASPEN PUBLICATION®
Aspen Publishers, Inc.
Gaithersburg, Maryland
1998

Library of Congress Cataloging-in-Publication Data

Umiker, William O.
Management skills for the new health care supervisor/William
Umiker—3rd ed.
p.   cm.
Includes bibliographical references and index.
ISBN: 0-8342-1091-6
1. Health facilities—Personnel management. 2. Supervision of employees.
I. Title.
[DNLM: 1. Health Facility Administrators. 2. Personnel Management—Methods.
WX 155 U51m 1998]
RA971.35.U526   1998
DNLM/DLC
for Library of Congress
98-8096
CIP

Orders: (800) 638-8437
Customer Service: (800) 234-1660

About Aspen Publishers • For more than 35 years, Aspen has been a leading professional
publisher in a variety of disciplines. Aspen's vast information resources are available in both
print and electronic formats. We are committed to providing the highest quality information
available in the most appropriate format for our customers. Visit Aspen's Internet site for more
information resources, directories, articles, and a searchable version of Aspen's full catalog,
including the most recent publications: **http://www.aspenpub.com**
Aspen Publishers, Inc. • The hallmark of quality in publishing
Member of the worldwide Wolters Kluwer group.

Editorial Services: David A. Uffelman
Library of Congress Catalog Card Number: 98-8096
ISBN: 0-8342-1091-6

Printed in the United States of America

1 2 3 4 5

Table of Contents

Objectives of This Book

MY VISION

I picture the readers of this book returning to their workstations with renewed enthusiasm and confidence. These employees also use this tome as a reference source when they face challenging situations or difficult people.

MISSION STATEMENT

The purpose of this book is to enlighten its readers in the principles and techniques of supervision in the health care setting.

OBJECTIVES

This book will enable you to:

- survive the transition from professional or technical employee to supervisor.
- increase customer satisfaction.
- plan, organize, and delegate work to achieve greater productivity.
- improve policies, position descriptions, and work standards.
- recruit, select, orient, and train new employees more skillfully.
- implement organizational changes and build high-performing teams.
- improve the safety and cope with violence in the workplace.
- enhance your leadership, coaching, counseling, and disciplinary skills.
- cultivate your communication, meeting, and negotiating expertise.
- provide your people with helpful performance feedback.
- cope with cultural diversity, conflict, and problem employees.
- adjust to changes, managed care, and the demands of cost-control.
- encourage creativity, solve problems, and delegate more.
- stimulate staff development and groom a successor.
- make better use of your time and reduce time theft.
- reduce workplace stress and prevent burnout.
- increase your marketability and career development.
- develop an efficient personal network.
- sharpen your workplace political skills.

Foreword

I had the privilege of serving as one of Dr. Umiker's laboratory supervisors before he retired. His book reflects the importance he attributes to sound management principles. It made me recall the firm yet humane and caring manner in which he guided us.

Supervisors know that people problems are the most difficult and frustrating ones. This book is about preventing and solving people problems.

Many supervisors are promoted to supervisory roles with little or no preparation for managerial responsibilities. Even innately skilled leaders encounter situations in which they feel like screaming for help. My confidence, creativity, sense of humor, and respect for others were strengthened by reading this opus.

I particularly recommend this informative and highly readable work to newly appointed supervisors and to laboratorians who contemplate moving up into management. This book will help them avoid the snares and pitfalls that can turn challenges into nightmares.

Experienced supervisors will also find this book valuable if they want to fine-tune their skills in communication, time management, problem solving, motivation, and other critical competencies. The numerous chats and lists of "helpful hints" are very useful.

The book addresses many day-to-day problems as well as broader management issues and will be a valuable "resource manual" for all health care supervisors and professionals.

Wendy George, MT (ASCP), MS, SM
Microbiologist
St. Joseph Hospital and Health Care Center
Lancaster, Pennsylvania

Preface

In the first edition of this book we dealt with concepts. In the second edition we concentrated on the practical aspects of supervision. At the time of the second edition, health care institutions were emphasizing quality assurance and technical advances. Hospitals were the champions of health care, and inpatients received most of the attention. Now, managed care is in vogue. Cost control gets more attention than quality assurance. Outpatient and home care are being featured. Hospitals search for creative ways to fill their beds.

Supervisors are confronted with smaller budgets, fewer professional workers, and more time pressure. Morale has declined markedly in many institutions, and job insecurity adds additional stress to an already stressful environment. In the third edition we have addressed these health care changes and their impact on supervisors.

Every chapter has been updated. You will find the customer, computer, and managed care mentioned frequently throughout the book.

Let me introduce you to our six new chapters:

Chapter 2 (Customer Service) features the impact of managed care and techniques for improving the personnel systems that affect customer service.

Chapter 10 (Safety and Workplace Violence) deals mainly with the increasing problem of violence in health care institutions. We present the essentials of a violence control program. You will learn how to deal with a bomb threat and break up a fight.

Chapter 14 (Rewards and Recognition) describes how to improve your reward and recognition system at a time when financially strapped employers are cutting back on their institutional award programs.

Chapter 25 (Managed Care) features a description of opportunities for professional health care workers in the managed care industry. Those of you who are considering a vocational change may find this chapter eye-opening.

Chapter 36 (Negotiating Skill) emphasizes that health care supervisors must negotiate more than ever before. They must convince administrators that their budgets are realistic. They haggle with vendors. Every time an organizational restructuring or procedural change takes place, supervisors must negotiate task assignments with their employees. Merging of departments and changes in spans of control involve much persuasion or negotiation.

Chapter 40 (Succession Planning) focuses on the need for supervisors to develop a successor so that the supervisors can move up or laterally in the organization. Today's employers want supervisors who can move into new slots on short notice.

Preface to the First Edition

This book was written primarily for health care workers who have no managerial training but who may be, or have been, promoted to supervisory positions. Seasoned first-line and middle managers will also find many practical suggestions for improving their effectiveness.

Managers are judged not only by their personal performance but also by that of their subordinates. This book provides the information that managers need to get the maximum effort and results from staff.

There is not a great deal of theory in this book. Also omitted are discussions of administrative responsibilities such as budget preparation and inventory control. There is only practical advice on getting things done through and with people. You will learn not only what you must do but also exactly how to do it—even the best words to use.

Acknowledgments

When I was a young boy, my parents gave me a radio kit. I put all the parts together, but the radio didn't play. A kind uncle took it all apart and reassembled it, and it worked. The editors at Aspen Publishers did the same thing for this book.

I wish to thank Patricia Rush Miller and Florita A. Gaenzle for their help in my literature searches.

PART I
Planning and Organizing

Chapter 1

Do You Really Want To Be a Supervisor?

- think it over first
- definitions
- two essential facts of supervision
- critical functions of supervision
- essential supervisory skills
- the transition from employee to supervisor
- relationships with subordinates, other supervisors, and your manager
- adjusting to the new routine
- pitfalls
- tips for launching a successful supervisory career

Unfortunately not all health care organizations provide supervisory training on a timely basis to the technical or professional employees they promote to supervisory slots. This compounds the tendency to promote technically skilled employees who have not shown leadership skills or who have little interest in supervision.

Many workers accept such promotions only because of the salary increase or because they feel obligated to do so. Insightful employers and employees know that "doing" skills do not convert easily to "leading" skills.

Promotion to supervisor is a major vocational change if you have never held a leadership position. You must exchange some tasks that you enjoy for others you either dislike or feel uncomfortable doing. It's very likely that you were promoted because of your professional knowledge, technical skills, and seniority, despite the fact that you have had little or no experience as a leader.

Of course, to be offered the supervisory job is flattering. You can use the extra pay. Your family will be proud of you. Yet accepting the position could be a decision you will regret. For one thing, your relationship with former teammates will never be the same. You are now part of "them," not "us." Your daily routine, your interpersonal relationships, and your self-concept all must change. Loyalty must be with management.

A supervisory position separates you from your coworkers. Occasionally you will feel alone. Your decisions and your efforts to enforce policies and rules will not always be popular. These decisions and actions may create adversaries. New peers (ie, supervisors and other managers) may be reluctant to accept you, especially if you continue to identify closely with your old group.

If you have not thought about this role change and have not prepared for it, be especially careful. Weigh the advantages and disadvantages of the change. To help you to think this through, answer the following questions:

- Why do I want to become a supervisor? Is it because I really have no choice or because I need the money very badly?
- Do I want more opportunities to get things done the way I think they should be done?
- Am I prepared to take the risk and to let go of old behavior?
- Will I enjoy instructing people and evaluating their performance?
- How will I react to enforcing policy, counseling, and disciplining others?
- Am I willing to engage in budget preparation and workplace politics?
- Am I ready and willing to learn a lot more about supervision?

Seek the advice of your present supervisor and mentors. You may find it helpful to list the advantages and disadvantages of this new role before you make the choice.

DEFINITIONS

Management is getting things done through people. The term manager is used in both a generic and a titular sense. In the generic sense it refers to any member of the management team, from supervisor to chief executive officer. In the titular sense it describes someone at an organizational level below an executive but above a supervisor. We use the term manager for persons above the rank of supervisor and the term executives for members of top management. A distinguishing characteristic of supervisors is that the people who report to them are not managers or supervisors. The supervisors in this book are all first-line managers.

According to the Taft-Hartley Act of 1947,[1] a supervisor is "any individual having the authority to hire, transfer, suspend, recall, or discipline other employees; or responsibility to direct them, or to adjust their grievances."

The supervisor has been depicted as the person-in-the-middle, beset by the opposing forces of upper management and the workers. Upper management wants work quality, productivity, and low costs. Workers want higher pay, more fringe benefits, and job satisfaction. Although the supervisor's primary loyalty is to the organization and its customers, subordinates expect their supervisors to represent their needs and to be their spokespersons.

Supervisors spend most of their time meeting goals, implementing plans, and enforcing policies. Managers spend most of their time setting goals, planning, and making policies. Supervisors are more likely to be able to fill in for absent workers than are managers. In small departments, supervisors may spend much of their time performing technical or professional work with the people who report to them.

TWO ESSENTIAL FACTS OF SUPERVISION

1. Supervisors need subordinates more than subordinates need supervisors.
2. Supervisors get paid for what their subordinates do, not for what they themselves do.

In the past supervisors were bosses. Today's supervisors must be leaders. They are the primary source of answers, instructions, assistance, and guidance for the employees who report to them. Their primary function is to help their employees get the daily work done. Many employees feel that their supervisors have forgotten this. As a supervisor, you must accept full responsibility for the success or failure of your personnel.

CRITICAL FUNCTIONS OF SUPERVISION

Besides professional and technical duties, a supervisor is responsible for the following five functions:

1. *Planning:* budgets, new methods and procedures, goals and objectives, and continuing education programs.
2. *Organizing:* position descriptions, locations of equipment and workstations, and storage areas.
3. *Directing:* selection and indoctrination of new personnel, schedules, assignments, training, coaching, and resolution of employee grievances.
4. *Controlling:* policies and rules, standards of performance, performance appraisals, quality, safety, cost, inventory controls, counseling, and discipline.
5. *Coordinating:* cooperation with other sections of the department, other departments, and services.

According to Marvin,[2] typical supervisors spend about 40% of their time leading other people and 40% performing technical or professional work. Another 15% of their time is spent training, counseling, and appraising. About 5% is devoted to other tasks.

ESSENTIAL SUPERVISORY SKILLS

First, a supervisor must be technically and professionally competent. Most supervisors help with some technical tasks. In larger units supervisors serve as pinch hitters. In either case, supervisors need professional competency for making decisions and solving problems.

Your influence as a leader must not be limited to the authority granted to you by your employer. Your knowledge and experience give you much more power. Most health care workers promoted to supervisory roles have specific professional or technical competency. This does not mean that they must know more about everything or be technically more proficient than their subordinates, but their expertise must be sufficient to earn the respect of subordinates.

Basic Skills That Every Supervisor Needs

Supervisors need the following leadership skills:

- communication
- motivation
- decision making and problem solving
- delegation
- time management
- career development

The importance of these leadership skills is clear in the comments of some health care supervisors. Wilder[3] reported that laboratory supervisors found the following activities to pose the most difficulties for them:

- preparing letters and memos
- conducting selection and disciplinary interviews
- setting goals for themselves and subordinates
- offering suggestions for work improvement
- delegating authority
- providing data for budgets
- developing job descriptions
- resolving conflicts among subordinates

Effective Supervisors Exhibit the Following Traits

- *Self-confidence.* Good supervisors do not become defensive when criticized. They accept responsibility for their own actions and the actions of their subordinates.
- *Respect for others.* Good supervisors welcome input from all sources and are good listeners. They praise more often than they criticize.

- *Sense of humor.* Competent supervisors can laugh at themselves. They seldom lose their temper.
- *Ability to make decisions.* Effective supervisors make decisions promptly, but not before careful consideration. They do not pass the buck.
- *Flexibility and resiliency.* Good supervisors adjust rapidly to changing situations and demands. They overcome setbacks without becoming bitter.
- *Energy and enthusiasm.* Good supervisors have a strong work ethic. They are optimistic and cheerful, even when under stress.
- *Creativity.* Good supervisors are always thinking about better ways to do things. They encourage others to be innovative.
- *Customer awareness.* Good supervisors know their external and internal customers and strive to exceed these customers' expectations.
- *Quality oriented.* Good supervisors insist on things being done right the first time. They support all quality improvement measures.
- *Empowering.* Good supervisors practice participative management and are great team builders.
- *Risk taking.* Good supervisors are willing to express opinions, encourage creativity, and accept responsibility.

Supervisors from the Point of View of Their Employees

The following is a list of statements that workers make about the supervisors they respect:

- He discusses problems with me and listens to what I have to say.
- She tells the big boss when we do a good job.
- She lets me know how she feels about my work, good or bad.
- I can trust him to go to bat for me.
- He means it when he gives me a compliment, and I know exactly what I did that he liked.
- He is always ready to listen to me.
- She tries to help me do a better job.

THE TRANSITION

Moving into a supervisory position in the department in which you have been working has its advantages and disadvantages. You know the people and the territory. On the other hand, you must establish a new relationship with former buddies and must now identify with management. The transition is easiest if you have:

- been recognized as an informal group leader.
- served in leadership roles, such as chairperson, trainer, or substitute supervisor.

- performed administrative tasks.
- prepared for the promotion through formal educational programs or self-training.

Leading Versus Doing

Your new role requires you to spend more time getting the work done through others and less time doing it yourself. Many new supervisors simply cannot stop doing what they did before their promotion. This is partly because they did those things so well and partly because they were not trained to be supervisors. Some supervisors become frustrated when they realize that they no longer can do everything better than each of their subordinates. Trying to serve as a full-time leader and a full-time worker simultaneously ends in burnout or failure.

Supervisors must maintain enough technical or professional expertise to be able to answer questions and to serve as a source person. They often must pitch in and help with the daily work. Some positions, especially in smaller units or on after-hour shifts, call for hybrid leadership-worker roles.

RELATIONSHIPS WITH SUBORDINATES

As a supervisor you want to be liked by the people you supervise, but you can't continue to be part of the old gang. Strive for their respect rather than their affection. Be firm, fair, and consistent. Develop your managerial skills while maintaining your professional knowledge.

If you previously earned the respect of your teammates, you are off to a good start. On the other hand, if they resent your promotion, or think that someone else deserved it more, or believe that you were selected because of favoritism, you may experience some rough going.

Honeymoon Phase

Right after the promotion, you and your subordinates will make a special effort to cooperate. Your former pals have mixed feelings toward you; this is called the phenomenon of ambivalence. They want to like and trust you, but they resent your control over them. Sure, they congratulate you and say they are happy to have you as their new leader. You reciprocate with equal enthusiasm. You tell them that nothing has changed and that with their help you will correct all the things that have long bothered the group.

During this phase, those at organizational levels above and below you will watch you carefully. Your leadership is being tested.

After the Honeymoon

The honeymoon phase, when everyone cooperates, acts friendly, and conceals problems, lasts about as long as a marital honeymoon. It may give way abruptly to a phase of discomfort when a sensitive problem, such as the need for a reduction in personnel, arises. More often, the honeymoon ends gradually as the new supervisor turns down requests or exhibits ineffectiveness. In their desire to be liked, new supervisors often go too far with the friendship approach. This ultimately hampers their ability to give directions, to criticize work performance, or to make unpleasant decisions. It is necessary to risk friendship to gain respect. Like it or not, you finally realize that you are now one of "them," not one of "us."

Some subordinates take advantage of the supervisor's goodwill; the rest take a wait-and-see attitude. The chronic complainers, cynics, passive-aggressives, and negativists cannot stay silent long. They soon begin to describe all the new boss's weaknesses, compare her unfavorably with her predecessors, and point out how things have been getting worse, not better.

Work should be the primary topic of conversation. This does not rule out casual conversation, but your main job is to ensure that the work is completed. You must enforce orders from your superiors, even when these orders do not seem sensible or fair to you or to your subordinates. You will feel an urge to dissociate yourself from these orders. If you yield to that temptation, however, you will lose the respect of your subordinates. Instead, discuss such an order with your manager and try to change it. At least find out and explain to your people the reasons for the directive. Above all, don't discredit management with statements such as "What do you expect from those idiots?"

If you let your authority go to your head and lower the boom on your charges, they will unite against you. It's essential to meld humility with firmness. Micromanaging is largely one-way communication: no listening and a great deal of ordering. This may occur either because a new supervisor wants to do a good job or because he enjoys the feeling of authority.

Because of all your new supervisory responsibilities, spend less time with former teammates and more with your fellow supervisors. This should extend to time spent in social activities. Others are more likely to charge you with favoritism if you have close social ties with your old buddies. You are also more likely to reveal confidential information while socializing. As a supervisor, you must remember that your words carry more weight. Comments you make about others are more often repeated and get you into hot water.

On the other hand, do not destroy old relationships. The temptation to please management may reduce your sensitivity to your reports. You should take time to continue personal, positive contacts with each person, chiefly during brief encounters at the workbench or during breaks. Don't be afraid to ask questions or solicit the help from them.

RELATIONSHIPS WITH OTHER SUPERVISORS

Your new peers, the other supervisors, will not accept you unless you start meeting with them. These contacts are important for other reasons. Sharing problems and ideas with other supervisors enhances your growth as a supervisor. In the health care industry, there has been too much emphasis on strictly professional growth. We identify with fellow professionals rather than with fellow managers.

Another reason for moving closer to fellow supervisors is the increasing need for coordinating work flows. Sharing equipment and overlapping services requires close cooperation between departments and other units.

RELATIONSHIP WITH YOUR MANAGER

If you have been promoted from the ranks, you already know something about the boss. You know whether he or she prefers to communicate verbally or by memo. You have learned how to interpret the boss's body language, when to stay out of his or her way, and what pleases or displeases him or her. If you are new to the department, learn these things as soon as you can.

Good supervisors help their managers control their time by handling trifles themselves. They give the managers all the necessary information, even if the news is bad. They admit their mistakes and do not make the same mistake twice.

ADJUSTING TO THE NEW ROUTINE

The transition phase consists of preparing for your behavioral changes. This involves enhancing your communication processes, learning how to best get the work completed effectively and efficiently, and applying the right skills at the right time—"situational leadership." Shandler[4] advises new supervisors to find a coach or mentor. He also recommends that they modify their leadership style after learning how their staffers react.

Balance a task-oriented style with people-oriented needs. Model the behavior you want to encourage in others.

PITFALLS

Supervisors should do their best to avoid the following pitfalls:

- Lack of flexibility and judgment in dealing with attitudes, biases, perceptions, emotions, and feelings. Previous experience depended on objective measurement and things one could objectively control and measure. Now the ambience is murky and decisions based on subjective factors.

- Lack of assertiveness. Introverts struggle with leadership roles.
- Unwillingness to pay the price for lonesomeness, fewer peers, and stress.
- Striving to be liked rather than respected.
- Not knowing what superiors expect of them.
- Not maintaining technical and management competence, and thus not staying marketable.
- Withholding important information from peers, subordinates, or superiors.
- Becoming a bottleneck rather than a supporter and expediter.

See Chapter 11 for more on leadership.

TIPS FOR LAUNCHING A SUCCESSFUL SUPERVISORY CAREER

The following advice can help to guarantee success for supervisors:

- Know what is expected of you. Be familiar with your position description.
- Have a personal meeting with each of your employees.
- Build relationships and a personal network.
- Learn to trust your intuition more.
- Be available to help others. Become a great listener.
- Be sensitive to the feelings and wants of the people who report to you.
- Share knowledge and keep your people informed.
- Maintain high ethical and moral standards, especially that of integrity.
- Be willing to ask for help and to ask questions.
- Join professional organizations and go to their meetings.
- Maintain an active self-educational program.
- Insist on and reward good performance.
- Remain calm under stress. Avoid shouting or pouting.
- Display self-confidence.
- Remain fair. Show no favoritism or discrimination.
- Defend your people from hostile people and tormentors.
- Have the courage to make unpopular decisions.

NOTES

1. Taft-Hartley Act of 1947 (Labor-Management Relations Act of 1947), Section 101, Subsection 2(11).
2. P. Marvin, *Executive Time Management* (New York, NY: AMACOM, 1990), 4.

3. R. Wilder, "How One Lab Gauges Job Satisfaction." *Medical Laboratory Observer* 13 (1981): 35–39.

4. D. Shandler, *From Technical Specialist to Supervisor* (Menlo Park, CA: Crisp Publishers, 1993), 13.

RECOMMENDED READING

D. Shandler, *From Technical Specialist to Supervisor* (Menlo Park, CA: Crisp Publishers, 1993).

C.R. McConnell, *The Effective Health Care Supervisor,* 4th ed. (Gaithersburg, MD: Aspen Publishers, Inc., 1998).

J.G. Liebler et al. *Management Principles for Health Professionals,* 3d ed. (Gaithersburg, MD: Aspen Publishers, Inc., 1998).

Chapter 2

Customer Service

- who are our customers and what do they want?
- impact of managed care
- the three essentials of customer service: systems, strategy, and employees
- techniques for improving personnel systems
- designing a customer satisfaction system

WHO ARE OUR CUSTOMERS AND WHAT DO THEY WANT?

"I need a husband. I want Tom Selleck."

widow in retirement home

External health care customers include patients, patients' families and visitors, referring physicians, doctors' offices, blood donors, and third-party payers. Internal customers are nurses, students, trainees, employees, departments, and committees.

There is a difference between needs and wants. Patients are aware of their *wants*. They want quiet, clean rooms with all the conveniences of a first-rate hotel. They want tasty food served on time and still hot. They want painless procedures and no waiting on gurneys or in ready rooms. They want a courteous, attentive, skillful, and professionally looking staff. Most of all, they want to leave the institution alive and feeling better than when they came in. On the other hand, few patients are completely aware of their *needs* for diagnostic tests or therapeutic modalities.

Physicians are not always cognizant of what they should order for their patients until they learn about some new diagnostic or therapeutic procedure. Then they demand it. They certainly want fast and courteous service, and all the latest gadgets.

Insightful care providers find out what their customers must have (needs), what they want, and what they do not want. To stimulate or modify the needs and wants of their customers, health care providers make their customers aware of new services or products as they become available. What they often forget to do is to find out what new services or products their external customers want or need.

IMPACT OF MANAGED CARE

The shift to managed care has already had a major impact on customer service. As a result of mergers, alliances, and restructuring, we must add many new people and interdependent work units to our list of internal customers.

Managed care enrollees are becoming more sophisticated in their knowledge of what is promised and what is delivered. They are more critical of how they are handled, especially concerning real and perceived barriers to their access to medical specialists and expensive procedures.

While all agencies claim that quality and patient satisfaction are still important, the emphasis on cost control and limitation of services is unmistakable.

Managed care has been responsible for staff reductions and the replacing of highly trained personnel by employees who have much less education. Language and cultural differences take their toll on efficiency and productivity. All these factors place a greater burden on health care facilities and increase the need for capable and flexible leaders.

THREE ESSENTIALS OF CUSTOMER SERVICE

Systems

Systems include policies, protocols, procedures, topography of the physical facilities, staffing, operations, work flows, and performance monitoring. Policy statements and procedure manuals provide behavior guidelines, rules, and regulations. Here are five policy tips:

1. Eliminate policies that adversely affect client satisfaction.
2. Review annually.
3. Establish a policy committee or quality circle.
4. Introduce new policies that improve client service (eg, special parking area for blood donors, more convenient locations and times for specimen collections).
5. Consider a new policy for each new service (eg, point of care service).

Later we will discuss policies relating to the topics of personnel selection, orientation and training, reward systems, communication, empowering people, and building teams.

Strategies

Strategy consists of developing a customer-oriented culture. A customer-oriented culture is achieved when every employee understands that good service is expected, that exceptional service is rewarded, and that bad service is not tolerated. Strategy involves statements of vision, values, mission, goals, objectives, and action plans.

Customer feedback is essential to strategy, and we obtain it from multiple sources. These include complaints, suggestions, incident reports, surveys, interdepartmental meetings, cross-functional work groups, task forces, and focus groups.

Employees

Employees are our best customers in that we must satisfy them before we can please other customers.

The five major personnel responsibilities of supervisors are:

1. to find and respond to the needs and wants of their employees;
2. to field the best team;
3. to empower employees to solve problems (Can each of your employees say: "I rarely need anyone else to handle customer problems or questions?");
4. to teach by example; and
5. to insist on good customer service and to monitor it.

TECHNIQUES FOR IMPROVING PERSONNEL SYSTEMS

Position Descriptions

In the Summary Statement of position descriptions, insert the word "customer" (eg, "The major goal of this position is to meet or exceed customer expectations and needs. Our external and internal customers include . . . ").

Modify performance standards to include items on quality and customer service. Here are some examples.

- Is discrete with patient information.
- Accepts night and weekend assignments willingly.

- Uses tact in personal interactions with customers and staff.
- Frequently reports customer comments and suggestions.

Recruiting Process

Your goal is to hire employees who are competent, caring, and turnover resistant. Help the recruiting process by providing your employment department with concise, up-to-date position descriptions. Add the attractive aspects of each job to the position description.

Help your recruiters by recommending the best media for contacting candidates, by answering inquiries about jobs enthusiastically, and by interviewing candidates promptly.

Selection Process

> *Hire for attitude, train for skill.*

The ability to "sell" jobs to candidates is important. The better the candidates, the more other organizations will offer them jobs.

You can learn much about candidates' attitudes by asking questions such as:

- What does superior service mean to you?
- What gives you the most satisfaction at the end of your workday?
- Give me an example of how you made an extra effort to serve a client.

Orientation and Training System

Make certain that new people know who are their external and internal customers. Orient them toward better customer service. Infuse the latest ideas of quality improvement. Emphasize the importance of a "can do" attitude and how it affects performance ratings.

Review work flows and each provider-recipient interface. Alert the new people to questions that customers frequently ask and where the answers can be found. Describe what you regard as proper telephone and electronic etiquette. Introduce them to major customers.

Performance Review and Reward Systems

Refocus performance objectives and appraisals on customer satisfaction. Discuss customer service when reviewing past performance and when formulating objectives for future activities. Encourage objectives such as attending seminars on communication skill or customer service, visiting internal customers, or learning to speak customers' languages.

Tie recognition and reward strategy to customer service. Unfortunately the health care people who have the most client contacts are among the lowest paid, receive the least training, and have the least opportunity for promotion.

Inservice Educational Programs

Topics for all employees should include customer identification, recognition of customer expectations, customer problem solving, new services, and communication skills—especially telephone courtesy.

Topics for employees who contact customers should include, in addition, empathic interactions, listening skill, dealing with complaints, assertiveness, and how to cope with angry people.

Personnel Retention

A great impediment to customer service is the turnover of personnel. Unfortunately the people who provide the most hands-on service have the highest turnover rates.

Note: Each of the above topics is covered in more detail in subsequent chapters.

DESIGNING A CUSTOMER SATISFACTION SYSTEM

Principles of good customer service include the following:

- Treat customers as you would like to be treated.
- Anticipate your customer's needs and wants.
- Hire people who have a caring attitude. Reassign or get rid of those who do not.
- Include customer satisfaction in your orientation and training programs.
- Model good customer service yourself.
- Make customer satisfaction a condition of satisfactory performance.
- Monitor the behavior of your service providers and coach any deficiencies.
- Get frequent feedback from internal and external customers.
- Underpromise and overdeliver.
- Do work right the first time.
- Reward those who make special efforts to please customers.
- Give your people the authority to solve customer complaints.

Address Complaints

Patients are most likely to complain about noise, food, their rooms, waiting, and lack of courtesy. Clients are displeased when:

* they don't get what is expected or promised;
* they have to wait;
* someone is rude, patronizing, or indifferent;
* they get the brush-off or the runaround; or
* someone expresses a "can't do" attitude or hits them with the rule book (eg, "It's our policy").

Regard complaints as suggestions for improving service. This is the least expensive source of customer feedback. Invite additional comments and ask for specific suggestions for better service. Encourage your staff to report complaints and make suggestions for eliminating them. Record these suggestions. Express your appreciation at performance reviews and at the time they are made.

Ask for customer comments and suggestions at every staff meeting. These suggestions need not be elaborate or complicated. In one large hospital, music was piped into the waiting room for visitors, most of whom were waiting for patients undergoing surgery. Results of the study indicated that the self-reported stress levels of the visitors were reduced.[1]

Maintain a comment log. Empower your front line troops to solve customer problems. Most customers are understanding if they feel that providers care about them. So give your people the authority they need.

When faced with a complaint, acknowledge its validity and apologize. Accept responsibility without blaming others. Empathize with them and ask them what they would like done. If they do not respond, make an offer. Thank the person for bringing the matter to your attention. Promise to do what you agreed to do, then do it promptly.

NOTE

1. R.L. Routhieaux and D.A. Tansik, "The Benefits of Music in Hospital Waiting Rooms," *The Health Care Supervisor 16,* no. 2 (1997):31–39.

RECOMMENDED READING

K. Albrecht and R. Zemke, *Service America* (Homewood, IL: Dow Jones-Irwin, 1985).

J. Carlzon, *Moments of Truth* (Cambridge, MA: Ballinger, 1987).

R.Y. Chang and P.K. Kelly, *Satisfying Internal Customers First* (Irving, CA: Richard Chang Publishers, 1994).

W.H. Davidow and B. Uttal, *Total Customer Service* (New York, NY: Harper & Row, 1989).

R.L. Desatnick, *Managing To Keep the Customer* (San Francisco, CA: Jossey-Bass, 1988).

L. Goldzimer, *"I'm First." Your Customer's Message to You* (New York, NY: Rawson, 1989).

W. Umiker, *The Customer-Oriented Laboratory,* 2d ed. (Chicago, IL: ASCP Press, 1997).

Chapter 3

Planning

"Great success in any enterprise comes from a balanced combination of three elements: the mission, the leadership, and the people who make it happen. By far the most important is the mission."[1]

Roger Dawson

Planning is the most fundamental management function, and it logically precedes all other functions. Planning is the projection of actions to reach specific goals. In other words, a plan is a blueprint for the future. It starts with the questions of what and why, then focuses on the how, when, who, and where.

BENEFITS OF PLANNING

Planning ensures that we work effectively and efficiently. It reduces procrastination, ensures continuity, and helps use resources more intelligently.

Planning assists in doing things right the first time, resulting in that great feeling of having everything under control and knowing what to do next.

Planning is proactive. It decreases the need to manage by crisis. It is a prerequisite for practically all important managerial activities—teaching, committee and staff meetings, performance appraisals, employment interviews, and budget preparation.

20

Planning is essential for coping with crises such as fires, natural disasters, strikes, bomb threats, or hostage taking.

CLASSIFICATION OF PLANS

Strategic plans are plans for achieving long-range goals and living up to the expectations expressed in statements of mission and values. Without strategic planning, few visions are realized. *Tactical plans* translate broad strategies into specific objectives and action plans. *Organizational plans* start with a table of organization and include position descriptions, staffing, and channels of communication. *Physical plans* concern topography (eg, the site of a building, the layout of an office, or the location of diagnostic and therapeutic equipment.) *Functional plans* are directed toward major functional units such as nursing service, clinical laboratory, human resources, finance, and clinical services. *Operational plans* deal with systems, work processes, procedures, quality control, safety, and other supportive activities. *Financial plans* address the inflow and outflow of currency, profit and loss, budgets, cost and profit centers, charges, and salaries. *Career planning, time managing, and daily work planning* are also vital forms of planning.

SIX ELEMENTS OF PLANNING

The six elements of planning are (1) vision, (2) mission statement, (3) goals, (4) objectives, (5) strategy, and (6) action plans. Each is discussed in detail below.

VISION

> *"A vision is an image without great detail. It acts*
> *as a flag around which the troops will rally."*[2]
>
> Michael Hammer

Vision and mission statements deal with purpose and alignment. Without these attributes, the energy of an organization scatters rather than focuses. Leaders create a vision around which people rally, and managers marshal the resources to achieve that vision. Vision provides a premise that leaders commit to and dramatize to others. A vision statement should not read like a financial report. It must conjure up a compelling vision that fires people up. Martin Luther King provided the best vision statement with his "I have a dream."

Visions should be clear and exciting and should leave wide latitude to the pursuit of new opportunities. The vision of top management must be broad enough that the vision of the lower echelons of the organization fit within it.[3]

One portion of a vision segment can be aimed at the consumer (eg, "Our vision is to have a fully staffed, high-quality, committed work force. A work force that is efficient and effective in providing the highest quality service in our community"). Another portion can be directed at the employees. For example:

> We visualize an organization staffed by dedicated, enthusiastic, customer-oriented people. People who act as though they were partners. Our people readily adapt to change, seek continuous technical improvements, and exhibit a caring attitude. Our organization is preferred by most patients and admitting physicians. It is the darling of third party payers and a local favorite place of employment.

The vision must be sustained through action. A vision is translated into a mission statement. Goals are enunciated, strategy developed, and action plans constructed.

MISSION STATEMENT

Mission statements proclaim the purpose of an organization or department—the "why." Like visions, mission statements should serve to define the organization and to inspire its employees. Most mission statements are too vague, platitudinous, and quickly forgotten. Most of them cannot pass the "snicker test." Organizations work hard to develop vision and mission statements, then let them become just framed pieces of paper on a wall.

An effective mission statement must be expressed clearly in one paragraph or less and in simple language. When workers participate actively in the formulation of mission statements, they understand why the organization exists and what their work is all about. They will do their best to make the virtual visions come to life.

Some mission statements include the vision, goals, and strategy. They answer the key questions of why (Why does this organization or department exist?), what (What is our goal?), and how (What strategy will we use?). The following is a departmental mission statement that would be appropriate for a small hospital unit. Note that it starts with a goal, adds objectives, and ends with a strategy:

> We seek a service that surpasses the expectations of our clinician customers. We will improve the quality of reported results, shorten turnaround time, reduce costs and promote a spirit of cooperation between our staff, our customers, vendors, and associates in other departments. To accomplish this we will meet weekly to analyze service needs, investigate complaints and suggestions, and explore new methods or equipment. We will make recommendations to management, monitor progress and evaluate results.

Before accepting a mission statement, experienced originators ensure that it answers four critical questions:

1. Do you know where you want to be five years from now?
2. Is it clearly and definitely expressed in one paragraph or less?
3. Is it in language that a tenth grader could understand?
4. Will it be believable to everyone in the organization?[4]

GOALS AND OBJECTIVES

Leaders share their visions and involve their associates in setting goals and objectives. Goals have ends or conclusions, while mission statements usually do not. Employees like things that have conclusions. For example, they usually prefer to work on projects rather than to perform routine work because projects have clear destinations. Everyone knows when they have arrived at the station. Retirees often die shortly after retiring because mentally their goal (end of employment) has been reached . . . and they lack a mission statement that deals with the future.

Targets become more specific when you subdivide goals into objectives. Objectives relate to actions taken to reach a goal. Objectives should be realistic, understandable, measurable, behavioral, achievable, and specific. An objective such as "to reduce inventory costs" is not sufficiently specific. Instead use *"to reduce inventory costs by 10% within 12 months."* Assign priorities to objectives and set a target date. Written objectives get more attention and provide a permanent record.

While there should be some degree of challenge—employees are motivated by achieving difficult but possible tasks—the objectives must be attainable. If a plan has little chance of success, it will frustrate rather than motivate.

Examples of Objectives

- Within 12 months, a repeat morale survey of employees will show an increase in average employee satisfaction rating from the current level of 3 to level 2.
- By the end of the next quarter, we will provide point-of-care testing for all patients in the north wing.

Examples of Objectives for a More Comprehensive Goal for Customer Satisfaction

- Hire employees who are client oriented in addition to being technically or professionally competent and who will remain on board.
- Provide an orientation-training program that stresses client satisfaction.

- Anticipate changes in customers' needs or expectations, and monitor their satisfaction by using multiple feedback sources and techniques.
- Encourage all employees to participate in the planning and execution of new or improved services and in solving customer problems.
- Provide an intensive continuing education program that features client satisfaction.

STRATEGY

Successful organizations build on their existing strengths and eliminate their weaknesses or render them irrelevant. They constantly search for innovative ways to please their customers.

Keys to success include:

- vision, mission, goals, objectives, and action plans;
- support of top management;
- effective and efficient systems, processes, and procedures;
- quality tools and techniques;
- sufficient time; and
- empowered, caring, competent employees.

ACTION PLANS

Typical Steps of an Action Plan

Step 1. Identify the Problem or Need.

Answer the following questions:

- Why is there a need for change? What's wrong with the present service or system?
- What are our strengths and weaknesses and those of our competitors?
- What are the potential gains, losses, or risks of a change?
- Who will be affected? What will it cost?
- What is likely to happen if action is not carried out?

Step 2. Obtain and Analyze Data.

Select a method of collecting information and build a data bank. Be thorough when you collect information. Become familiar with statistical analysis and the use of charts, electronic data interchange, electronic mail, and work-flow automation. Document current deficiencies and opportunities for improvement.

Step 3. Determine the Best Action.

Action plans should answer the questions of:

- What is to be done?
- Why must it be done?
- When should it be started and completed?
- Who is to do it?
- Where is the action to take place?
- How should it be done?

Plan Essentials

A plan should be doable, understandable, comprehensive, cost-effective, approved, and reviewed periodically. Include an executive summary in complex plans. In that summary state how the proposal affects the mission statement and how it will affect service quality and operational costs. Add how you think clients and employees will react to the changes.

Step 4. Carry Out the Plan.

The implementation process includes:
- Identifying resources (eg, people, supplies, equipment, facilities, time, and funds).
- Preparing checklists of important tasks to be performed.
- Assigning tasks, authority, and responsibilities.
- Preparing work schedules.
- Providing necessary training.
- If necessary, formulating new policies, systems, and procedures.

Sequencing and Scheduling of Tasks

Use Gantt diagrams and flowcharts or other logic diagrams to document tasks and to analyze the times required for the work processes. On a chart, chronologically list the tasks to be done on one side opposite the appropriate calendar periods. See Chapter 35 for more on charting.

Budget Preparation

Estimate all costs associated with each task. Build in some slack for inflation or other unanticipated costs. Prepare a cost spreadsheet with tasks listed vertically and cost factors, eg, labor, supplies, listed horizontally, and totaled at the right of each line.

Establish Priorities

Priorities are a vital part of any plan. To avoid frustration, be prepared to modify your priority list. Unexpected interruptions are the rule rather than the exception.

Step 5. Monitor Process, Report Progress, and Make Adjustments.

Formal control is planned control and consists of data gathering and analysis. Informal control consists of the day-by-day observations and meetings with other participants. Informal controls are more proactive than formal ones. Issue periodic status reports for large projects.

Monitoring progress usually leads to tying up some loose ends. These may involve changes in plans, reassignment of tasks, removal of barriers, or seeking additional resources. The earlier a problem is identified, the easier it is to correct.

NOTES

1. R. Dawson, *Secrets of Power Persuasion* (Englewood Cliffs, NJ: Prentice Hall, 1992), 277.
2. M. Hammer and J. Champy, *Re-engineering the Corporation* (New York, NY: Harper, 1993), 155.
3. K. Fisher, *Leading Self-Directed Work Teams: A Guide to Developing New Team Leadership* (New York, NY: McGraw-Hill, 1993), 136.
4. R. Dawson, *Secrets of Power Persuasion*, 278.

Chapter 4

Organizing, Coordinating, and Reengineering

- values
- authority
- unity of command
- span of control
- staffing
- assigning
- the informal organization
- the coordination process
- process reengineering

Organizing is gearing up to carry out decisions made in the planning phase. It concerns delineating tasks and establishing a framework of authority and responsibility for the people who will carry out these tasks. It involves analyzing the workload, distributing it among employees, and coordinating the activities so that work proceeds smoothly.

Supervisors carry out these functions using their delegated authority as shown in tables of organization.

Essential organizational tools include policies, procedures, rules, and position descriptions.

VALUES

Corporate Values

In value statements employers express what they regard as evidence of loyalty, expected behavior, or ethical practice. Organizational cultures are comprised of the values that guide an organization in its daily activities—the sum total of all the ways people are expected to act. As work crosses departmental boundaries (eg, flow of patients moving from unit to unit), inevitable differences in values affect what, how, and when things are done.

27

When corporations or supervisors violate their own values, employees become cynical. They recite past broken promises. They use descriptors like "unfair" or "double-talk."

Personal Values

What we consider ethical and unethical depends on our personal value systems—the things we believe in. Personal values concern what is important regarding work (eg, challenges, tasks, recognition, creativity, authority). They encompass relationships, personal finances, living and recreational activities, hobbies, and entertainment. Others are ambition and desire for fame or owning one's own enterprise. Attitudes reflect our core beliefs and values. Attitudes can change when our beliefs and values change, but that does not happen very often.

AUTHORITY

Authority is delegated or formal power passed on down the hierarchy. Supervisors need this power to carry out their responsibilities. It is axiomatic that people should not be given responsibilities without enough authority to get the job done. Although authority is the power that makes a managerial job a reality, it is relatively weak unless supplemented by powers such as:

- expertise (eg, licensed, certified, knowledgeable, skilled, or experienced),
- credibility (eg, being trusted and respected),
- natural or acquired leadership skill,
- persuasiveness or charisma, and
- influence (eg, whom one knows or is related to).

Ideally the extent of supervisors' authority is expressed in their position descriptions. Some more important activities over which supervisors have variable amounts of authority include the following three categories:

1. Personnel Administration
   - Selecting, orienting, and training new employees
   - Assigning or delegating
   - Scheduling and approving overtime
   - Coaching, counseling, and disciplining
2. Fiscal Administration
   - Selecting or approving purchases of supplies and equipment
   - Selecting vendors
   - Establishing inventory levels

3. Procedures
   - Selecting or modifying methods
   - Enforcing or formulating policies and rules
   - Participating in administrative matters (eg, quality management, safety, and education)

UNITY OF COMMAND

The principle of unity of command originally meant that each employee reported to one and only one superior. Matrix structures and other complex organizational structures have eroded that concept. Now unity of command simply means that for each task that an employee performs he or she is accountable to someone.

SPAN OF CONTROL

Span of control refers to the number of employees who report to a leader. Factors such as computers and autonomous work teams have led management to expand spans of control and to strip away layers of management. The result is that supervisors now find themselves directing more people. Unfortunately, replacing highly qualified personnel by workers who have less education has added an additional burden on these overworked supervisors. This is compounded by the fact that the supervisors have fewer superiors from whom to solicit advice and support.

When the number of people who report to a supervisor is too low, that supervisor often micromanages, much to the discomfort of the people who report to her.

STAFFING

The staffing process starts with human resource planning, recruitment, personnel selection, and orientation of new employees. It continues with training, career development, control, and appraisal of performance. It may lead to promotion, transfer, demotion, or separation.

Avoid staffing with overqualified people; the personnel costs and turnover are excessive. Underqualified candidates may or may not represent good investments. The key factor is whether you can train them without great cost or loss of time. These individuals, when trained, are less likely to be bored with routine tasks, and their turnover rate is lower than that of overly qualified people.

You enhance personnel availability and morale when you can adjust work hours to suit your employees. Health care workers are predominantly women, and many prefer work hours that allow them to take care of their family responsibilities. Part-time employment, flextime, and job-sharing opportunities can be powerful incentives. The use of these staffing strategies also helps provide the needed flexibility in jobs that have peaks and troughs.

ASSIGNING

Assigning and delegating have one thing in common: If they are not done, the supervisor does all the work. Assigned tasks are those described in position descriptions. They are activities ordinarily performed by employees in each particular category, and the employees have limited choice in the specific assignments. A delegated task, on the other hand, involves transfer of a responsibility and authority from supervisor to employee. It is often voluntary. Delegation is discussed in more depth in Chapter 31.

A composite list of qualifications of all your employees is like all the pieces in a set of Tinkertoys®. All the pieces (qualifications) are not used, and some may be missing. Your task is to match the expertise and available work hours to the requirements of your unit.

Supervisors who keep an inventory chart of employees' skills find such charts helpful in assigning backup services. They also use the information when designing educational and cross-training programs.

Supervisors make the specific assignments and ensure that the assignments are carried out. To do this effectively, supervisors must know the following:

- what must be done;
- what equipment and supplies are needed;
- what authority the supervisor has;
- what quality and productivity are needed;
- what the cost constraints are;
- where the tasks are to be performed;
- where supplies and service supports are found;
- where help can be obtained;
- who does what;
- when must work be done (eg, deadlines and turnaround time);
- when changes must be made ;
- how the work is to be performed (eg, methodology);
- how well, fast, and inexpensively work must be done; and
- why the work is done (employees must know how their work affects the big picture).

Supervisors must also match assignment with ability, as described below:

- Make certain that the assignee has sufficient time to finish the work.
- Provide necessary training and experience.

- Explain the assignment without overloading the explanation with trivial details.
- Ask the assignee to repeat the instructions or perform the work under observation to ensure understanding.
- Posit complicated orders in writing.
- Alert assignees to pitfalls or constraints.
- Tell assignees when and how to seek help or to report problems.
- Whenever possible, make holistic assignments, that is, consisting of a complete task. For example, most nurses prefer being responsible for all the nursing care of an individual patient rather than providing only part of that care (eg, passing out medications).

INFORMAL ORGANIZATION

Every organization has an informal network that is not represented in organization charts but is nevertheless powerful. It even has its own communication system—the grapevine.

In addition to unions, there are groups of workers that have no formal power. They negotiate with management and may intimidate or ostracize coworkers. Within formal work groups there are cliques that select informal leaders based on expertise, personality, persuasiveness, or physical power. Sometimes informal and union leaders have more power than the formal leaders.

When members of these informal groups are frustrated or disloyal, they may sabotage equipment, block work flow, start malicious rumors, or inflict physical harm.

Supervisors must be aware of informal networks. They can tap into the grapevine and use it to their advantage. They identify the informal leaders and make special efforts to get along with them.

COORDINATION PROCESS

Coordination is the process of synchronizing activities and participants so that they function smoothly. When coordination fails, conflict and confusion run rampant. *Proactive* coordinating involves activities aimed at anticipating and preventing problems. *Reactive* coordinating consists of regulatory activities aimed at the maintenance of existing structural and functional arrangements and corrective activities that rectify errors after they have occurred.

The more steps and the more gatekeepers involved in a work-flow process, the greater the need for coordination. Joint projects and services that require interdepartmental cooperation also demand coordination.

Breakdowns in coordination are largely due to faulty communication, personality conflicts, turf battles, and job design problems. Other causes include training deficiencies, flawed physical arrangements, conflicts of authority, and lack of appropriate policies or procedures.

Work-flow coordination is eased when each employee interaction is regarded as a customer service with a provider and a service user (customer). Recipients are encouraged to provide positive or negative feedback to the providers and to make suggestions for improving the interactions.

Coordinating Requires Persuasive Ability

The definition of management can be expanded to include not only getting things done through people but also getting things done with people. This addition of "with people" signifies the importance of influencing persons who are neither bosses nor subordinates. These relationships are lateral, or collegial, rather than hierarchical. As organizations grow more complex and more highly specialized, supervisors spend less time with superiors and subordinates and more time with their peers. Peer groups include internal and external customers, vendors, and other outside providers, as well as employees who precede or follow them in work flows.

Most managers and supervisors are involved in both intradepartmental and interdepartmental coordination. The inability to function effectively and efficiently as a coordinator in these relationships can impair careers.

Tools of Coordination

Committees

A major purpose of committees is to increase coordination, but this tool is costly, time consuming, and often ineffective. The strength of committee action comes through a synthesis of divergent viewpoints.[1]

Coordinators

As interdepartmental coordination becomes more important, new coordinating and facilitating roles are established. Coordinators play an important role in quality management, employee safety, risk management, customer service, staff training, and cost containment.

Communication Modalities

Up-to-date tables of organization, policy and procedural manuals, standard operating procedures, computers, memos, reports, and newsletters are important, as are telephones, intercoms, voice mail, and meetings.

Clinical Paths

Critical and clinical paths are special flowcharts that link disparate activities and people to achieve greater efficiency. In medicine they are important in planning, coordination, communication, and evaluation of care. Critical paths represent the activities that take the most time. For inpatient care, a critical path may be initiated at the time of admission and end when patients are discharged. There are also algorithms that guide clinicians through the "if, then" decision-making process.

Better Interdepartmental Coordination

Tips for achieving better interdepartmental coordination are as follows:

- Make service requests direct and clear. Whenever possible, make the requests directly to the person who provides the service.
- Anticipate negative responses, and be ready to respond.
- Get an agreement on date or time of action when the initial request is made.
- Follow up verbal requests with written ones.
- Listen to employees' problems and empathize.
- Seek collaborative (win-win) solutions, but be prepared to compromise.
- Treat people as collaborators. Say "we" instead of "you."
- Place teamwork above competition.
- Be patient and reasonable, not demanding or critical.
- Avoid getting upset or upsetting the other person.
- Eliminate all kidding and sarcasm from your repertoire.
- Get to know your staff and colleagues and their work better.
- Express sincere appreciation for their efforts.

PROCESS REENGINEERING

Process reengineering is a major tool for managers who want to change a system or process or to design a new approach or procedure. Smith[2] defines process reengineering as the redesign of processes and the systems, policies, or structures that support them. The purpose is usually to optimize work flow and productivity. The ultimate goal is increased productivity, reduced costs, improved quality, or greater customer satisfaction.

An example of an operational process is the sequence that begins when a physician writes an order and ends when the patient receives what has been ordered. Process reengineering is not merely modifying flowcharts. It includes abandoning obsolete systems, forming cross-functional teams, amalgamating jobs, discarding old rules and assumptions, introducing new technologies, and creating new principles for task organization.

On a macro level, reengineering concerns downsizing, strategic alliances, decentralization, structural changes, reorganizing, and mergers. On a micro level it deals with quality circles, team building, and operational efficiency.

Successful reengineering requires a leadership style that features participative management, delegation, employee empowerment, and self-directed teams.

Systems or processes are more likely to be the cause of medical service problems and patients' complaints than is employee performance. For example, an audit of hospital inpatients found that the most common complaints were noise, quality of food, temperature and appearance of room, and waiting for admission, discharge, or X-rays. Most of these problems were attributed to faulty processes.[3]

How well departments work together is just as important as the performance of individual departments. This is illustrated in the treatment of patients in emergency departments. In this critical care unit, collaboration of physicians, nurses, laboratory, blood bank, respiratory therapy, radiology, and electrocardiographic services is essential.

Successful reengineering eliminates much of the monitoring, checking, waiting, tracking, and other unproductive work. There is more time for doing real work. In one hospital a cross-functional team cut patient admission waiting time by 17%. Another team at that facility reduced the paperwork process of hiring from an average of 9.5 days to 4.5 days.[4]

Many health care processes are complex and nonlinear and cannot be simplified into a string of quick, sequential tasks. The desired result often requires a high degree of collaboration between individuals and functions.

Processes often are more efficient if they have multiple operational channels. For example, a large emergency department may be more efficient if one section cares for major trauma cases, another handles minor injuries, and a third treats nonsurgical patients.

Selection of the Process To Be Reengineered

A current process may be dysfunctional—things are just not working as they should. There may be chronic problems, frequent breakdowns, excessive loss of time or money (eg, too much waiting in admissions office, slow turnaround time of laboratory or radiology work, difficulties obtaining physician discharge notes, excessive inventory, or breakdown in quality).

Another factor in the selection includes the importance of the process (ie, how seriously are customer service, employee morale, and profitability affected?). Feasibility also enters into the equation. Do we have the wherewithal to accomplish a significant change?

Hospital processes that will receive increasing attention are those that cross departmental lines. These systems involve multiple compartmentalized functions, many different employees, and diverse priorities. Modification of these systems because of their complexity and need for cooperation are the most difficult to modify, but they will pay the greatest dividends in terms of time and money saved. Such a process may be as complicated as the handling of a trauma patient from the time of admission to the time of discharge. It may be as simple as getting a blood transfusion for an outpatient.

Preparation and Implementation

What is the problem and how is it being handled now? Start with customer input. Learn more about what they want or need. Watch them go about their daily routines. For example, laboratorians can make rounds with physicians when they order laboratory tests and when they receive the test results. Talk to customers about your billing process. Visit a physician's office and talk to the office manager or nurse about the ease of requesting services. Talk to your front-line service providers (eg, patient care technicians or phlebotomists, nurses, and others who meet the customers). They can tell you more than consultants or inservice specialists can.

Determine what tasks can be eliminated. Should work be out-sourced? How could technology help?

Visit facilities that have reputations for outstanding service and learn what you can. Consider innovative approaches. Identify and attack assumptions or time-honored practices such as paying suppliers only after they have delivered the goods. Consider eliminating a large inventory storage space to force the use of a just-in-time inventory system.

Identify variables that can be readily measured, and create temporary problem-solving teams to improve a specific metric. For faster action, avoid too many open-ended initiatives. When a team finds itself alone with a specific problem and a deadline, the thinking often comes with startling ease.

Establish a measurement system. These systems include schedules, overhead costs, employee and customer satisfaction gauges, and any conditions that would trigger a variant that would require attention.

Barriers to Reengineering

Barriers relate to cost, time, and risks (to customers, employees, or vendors). There may also be problems of team function or turnover. Outsiders and in-house executives may toss in a few monkey wrenches. New challenges or management initiatives may divert attention from the reengineering efforts.

The two common causes of reengineering failure are the loss of interest and support of top management and the resistance of workers who must implement the initiative. Employees who are not convinced of the need for change or who perceive it as a threat may drag their feet or even refuse to participate.

NOTES

1. B.B. Longest, Jr., *Management Practices for the Health Professional,* 3d ed. (Reston, VA: Reston Publishing, 1984), 179.
2. B. Smith, "Business Process Re-engineering: More than a Buzzword," *HR Focus 71,* no. 1 (1994): 17.
3. R.J. Rollins, "Patient Satisfaction in VA Medical Centers and Private Sector Hospitals," *Health Care Supervisor 12,* no. 3 (1994): 44–50.
4. L. McKenzie, "Cross-functional Teams in Health Care Organizations," *Health Care Supervisor 12,* no. 3 (1994): 1–10.

Chapter 5

Position Descriptions and Performance Standards

- job title and classification
- the summary statement of position descriptions
- required competencies
- reporting relationships
- scope of authority and degrees of independence
- special demands and working environment
- responsibilities, duties, and tasks
- effects of the Americans with Disabilities Act (ADA) on position descriptions
- uses of performance standards
- levels of performance
- the three kinds of standards
- characteristics of a good standard
- a practical approach for preparing standards
- tips and pitfalls in formulating standards

POSITION DESCRIPTIONS

The 1995 standards of the Joint Commission on Accreditation of Healthcare Organizations include job description and performance appraisal guidelines.[1] The Americans with Disabilities Act (ADA) also focuses on these two functions. This focus is designed to prevent discrimination against persons with physical or health concerns.[2]

Job descriptions should be regarded as contracts between employer and employee. In addition, they establish a rational link with performance appraisals.

Because position descriptions define requirements for jobs done in the past and because job responsibilities change rapidly, these documents are out of date a good part of the time. To avoid rapid obsolescence and to provide more flexibility, managers are becoming less specific about assigned tasks, and they substitute general terms such as customer satisfaction and willingness to adjust to change.

A major cause of unsatisfactory performance is that employees simply do not know what is expected of them. Professional athletes seldom have written position descriptions, but they know precisely *what* they must do and *how well* these things must be done. Institutions use position descriptions and work standards to flesh out these two essentials.

Title and Classification

Job titles are important for prestige and self-esteem. Usually a title change is accompanied by a pay raise. Even without pay increases, most recipients appreciate more prestigious titles. In the following list, the title on the right is usually preferred:

Secretary—Administrative assistant
Technician—Specialist
Technologist—Scientist
Director—Vice President
Salesperson—Sales Associate

Positions are classified as salary or hourly (exempt or nonexempt) and as part time or full time. The classification includes job grade and wage range. The position classification may note that an employee is permanently assigned to a particular shift or rotates among shifts. If the employee must occasionally work after hours, take weekend assignments, or be subject to recalls, those requirements should be stated to avoid future disagreements. Verbal promises made prior to hiring are notoriously inaccurate.

Summary Statement

The summary statement—also called "position summary," "umbrella statement," "position purpose or goal," "mission statement," or "function statement"—condenses the responsibilities of the position and is required by the Joint Commission. It may include the goal, reporting channel, and other features of the job. For example:

The incumbent plans, directs and controls a 10-person hematology section of the laboratory. The major goal of this position is to meet or exceed customer expectations. Our customers include patients, patient's families and visitors, clinicians and other care providers, third party payers, teammates, students and trainees, and hospital departments or committees served by our department. The incumbent is also responsible for the teaching of students and new employees. The incumbent performs a wide range of hematological procedures. The incumbent reports to the administrative director of the laboratory.

Required Competencies

Competencies or qualifications describe the requirements of the *job*, not the qualifications of the *job holder*. These competencies include those that the incumbents must have and those you would like them to have. For some positions the list of basic qualifications can be eliminated because they are detailed in the credentialing process. For example, in the position description for a radiologist, the competency requirement may simply be that applicants must be board certified and hold a state license. This eliminates the need for a long list of tasks that radiologists perform.

In addition to educational and experiential requirements, special skills may be required (eg, a medical transcriptionist must be familiar with medical terminology).

Temperament, traits, and personality are important, as are characteristics such as flexibility, ability to adjust to change, and willingness to learn new skills. However, these are very subjective. Justification for including them should be provided in the descriptions of duties and responsibilities.

We want to go beyond technical or professional skills and look for people who are willing to walk the extra mile for customers. To assist in the candidate selection process, describe items of special importance or sensitivity. Express these items in behavioral terms (eg, "Is discrete with patient information." "Shows composure under stress." "Accepts night and weekend assignments." "Recognizes or anticipates needs of customers." "Uses tact in personal interactions with customers and staff.") Inclusion of these "soft skill" items is especially helpful when orienting and training new employees because they express in clear terms the kind of behavior that you expect.

Reporting and Coordinating Relationships

The "reporting relationships" section identifies an incumbent's immediate superior and others to whom he or she is directly accountable. Many employees must work closely with colleagues in other sections of their department, in other departments, and in outside agencies. Radiology and laboratory supervisors must cooperate with personnel in the surgical suite, the emergency department, and critical care units. For example:

The radiology supervisor must establish and maintain close working relationships with admissions, surgical suite, emergency department, special care units and the quality assurance coordinator. He or she advises the technical director of the school for radiology technicians, and frequently consults with the director of hospital information systems.

Scope of Authority

Delineating levels of authority avoids misunderstandings and embarrassment, especially when supervisors undertake disciplinary actions or incur major expenses. Three levels are recommended for each major responsibility. Level 1 (the highest) delegates unlimited power to make decisions and to take action without consulting one's superior. Level 2 has some limitations. For example, a supervisor may be authorized to assign overtime but must inform her manager of the action on the next day. At level 3, a supervisor must obtain approval *before* taking action.

A global statement may suffice in some situations. For example, "the supervisor has the authority to discharge all the responsibilities of the job within the constraints of the law, organizational and departmental policy, and the labor contract. He or she has signing authority for up to $1,000 for instrument repair."

Degrees of Independence

These are important in descriptions of nonsupervisory positions. Pertinent questions include the following:

- Are detailed written instructions always available or only for new or difficult tasks? These instructions may include policy or safety manuals and specific aids such as procedures manuals.
- Does the employee organize his or her daily work and modify it when appropriate or does the supervisor do this?
- Does the incumbent perform any supervisory or administrative functions? If so, to what extent?

Here is one such classification:

- Level 1. No responsibility for directing others.
- Level 2. Performs same kind of work as other members of the work group, but spends about 10% of time serving as trainer, instructor, or resource person.
- Level 3. Rotates as five-person team leader with five other technical employees. Minimal direction from supervisor.

- Level 4. Permanent team leader. Functions include directing, controlling, assigning, and scheduling. Reports to supervisor. No authority to discipline without approval of supervisor.

Special Demands and Working Environment

Working conditions include physical space, temperature extremes, and exposure to infectious agents, chemicals, radiation, and other hazards. The document may describe the type of safety equipment and attire that are used.

Physical demands have assumed new significance with the passage of the ADA (see later) and must be based on current requirements of actual incumbents. Most professional and technical positions make special demands on incumbents. Such demands include absolute integrity and accuracy in reporting observations, discretion with patient information, willingness to alter work schedules, and the ability to work under stress.

Responsibilities, Duties, and Tasks

Match each responsibility with a statement that describes the type of behavior or outcome that identifies successful job performance. These descriptors serve as *performance criteria*. Content validity is thus established because these criteria are based on observable work behavior or results rather than on traits.

Responsibilities describe activities in their broadest sense; tasks describe them in the most specific terms. For example:

Responsibility: "Teach radiology students"

Duty:　　　　 "Provide benchwork instruction for 20 three-hour sessions"

Tasks:　　　　 "Prepare agenda, demonstrate method, grade students."

List responsibilities in order of importance or according to the percentage of time needed.

Subdivisions of duties require more effort and lengthier documents. However, the effort may be worthwhile when detailed instructions are necessary (eg, jobs filled by individuals who have limited cognitive skills or no previous experience).

Select the best descriptive terminology, using action verbs when possible. Consider the clarification of the duty, the self-esteem of the employee, and the effect of the terminology on the salary classification. Consider the following alternatives:

- "Makes visitors feel welcome" is better than "greets people."
- "Evaluates clinical results" is better than "checks records."

- "Establishes controls that prevent release of erroneous information" is better than "sets quality controls."

The following list contains useful verbs for position descriptions:

Apply (current knowledge)	Monitor (work of new employees)
Arrange (meeting room)	Perform (tests)
Calibrate (instruments)	Practice (ethical standards)
Design (new work flow)	Process (specimens)
Determine (suitable methods)	Promote (public relations)
Establish (procedures for)	Recognize (errors)
Evaluate (new techniques)	Record (complaints)
Instruct (orientees)	Report (violations)
Maintain (systems for documenting)	Select (new employees)

Effects of the ADA on Position Descriptions

The ADA protects individuals with physical or mental disabilities that limit major life activities. Included are persons with acquired immunodeficiency syndrome, rehabilitated drug and alcohol abusers, obese persons, and those with cosmetic disfigurement. The law prohibits employers from discriminating against these people when hiring or firing. The law may also be relevant to salary, training, promotion, and any other condition of employment.

This new law has had a major impact on hiring and promotion. People who can otherwise qualify for a job may not be disqualified because they cannot perform tasks that bear only a marginal relationship to a particular job.

The ADA forces employers to make changes in the work environment. For example, the ADA requires that reasonable accommodations be made for physically or mentally challenged employees. Such accommodations may be physical, such as installing ramps, repositioning workstations, widening doors, and installing grab bars in toilet stalls. They may also involve deletions of certain nonessential tasks from position descriptions. An example would be to delete a task performed only occasionally and to assign that task to another employee (eg, if a job calls for occasional driving of a car, that responsibility may be assigned to a coworker; or a driver may be assigned to transport the person with the disability).

Duties must be designated as essential or nonessential. The essential functions of a job are those that, in the employer's judgment, constitute business necessity. If a person cannot carry out essential responsibilities, that person is disqualified for the job. Employers are not required to lower qualification standards tied to the essential functions of a job.

The ADA is concerned with factual determinations of essential functions, such as the percentage of time spent on the function and the consequences of not requiring the incumbent to perform the function. The physical requirements' portion of the position description is critically important in terms of ADA compliance. It must delineate the actual level of physical demands. Information includes kinds and amount of lifting, types of work surfaces, and any auxiliary devices used, such as ladders. Management must indicate whether the physical demand is occasional, frequent, or constant.

PERFORMANCE STANDARDS

A basic job description states only *what* is expected and the necessary qualifications. Performance standards have two cardinal purposes. The first is to inform employees *how well* they must do their work. The second is to simplify performance evaluations, especially if a pay-for-performance strategy is in place. Without performance standards, employee evaluations are highly subjective and can lead to charges of discrimination or favoritism.

All employees like to have the following requests honored, even when they do not articulate them:

- "Tell me exactly what it is that you want me to do."
- "Tell me how well and how fast I must do these things."
- "Show me how to do what I can't do."
- "Tell me how I'm doing."

Position descriptions and performance standards address the first two of these queries directly and lay the foundation for responding to the other two.

Uses of Performance Standards

Performance standards are used for the following reasons:

- To provide guidelines for orienting and training new employees
- To enable employees to appraise their own performance
- To provide a solid basis for performance appraisals, counseling, and disciplinary actions
- To support pay-for-performance and promotion selection strategies
- To identify training and development needs
- To satisfy the requirements of accrediting and licensing agencies
- To avoid charges of discrimination and protect against grievance actions

Levels of Performance

A few organizations have only two levels: "meets standards" and "does not meet standards." Many more use the following three levels:

1. Does not meet expectations (fails)
2. Meets expectations (passes)
3. Exceeds expectations (excels)

A pass-fail level seldom motivates, except for new employees. Adding an "exceeds expectations" or "superior" level introduces challenge and motivation.

Standards for bilevel and trilevel systems are easiest to administer, but five-tiered systems are also popular. Beyond the above three levels, these systems include an additional category: "meets expectations, but needs improvement." The fifth class is derived by splitting the "exceeds expectations" group into "superior" and "outstanding." A supervisor faced with an indignant overachiever who wants to know why he or she is rated as "superior" instead of "outstanding" appreciates the difficulty in using a five-level system.

Importance of Setting Appropriate Levels

A minimum-level standard provides a fail-pass situation. Performance below that level is unacceptable, signaling a need for remedial or administrative action. If this level is set too low, it leads to the acceptance of poor performance and the accumulation of "deadwood." On the other hand, if the level is too high, there may be frustration and loss of self-esteem when standards are not met.

Three Kinds of Standards

Compliance Standards

Compliance standards concern obedience to policies and procedures. They relate to attendance, punctuality, appearance, and so forth. These standards need not be duplicated in position descriptions. Dispose of them with a global statement such as "complies with the conditions of employment described in our Personnel Policy and Procedures Manual."

While you need not duplicate these criteria, variations from what are prescribed in personnel manuals may be necessary. For example, the dress code for patient care technicians or phlebotomists may be more stringent than that for employees who have no patient contact.

Temperament and Interrelationship Standards

Temperament and interrelationship standards pertain to work habits, initiative, creativity, self-development, reliability, and communication skills. These standards rely on "soft data" because they are highly subjective. Most of them can't be tied directly to specific tasks and therefore are presented in a special segment of the position description. Although these traits are often omitted from position descriptions, they usually show up in performance evaluation forms and discussions.

Task Standards

Task standards are based on outcomes and results. They use "hard data," since most of them are objective. Examples are turnaround time, infection rates, and compliance with budget. Task standards have several dimensions:

- Quality (errors, accuracy)
- Productivity (completing daily tasks)
- Timeliness (meeting deadlines)
- Cost-effectiveness (meeting budgets, inventory control)
- Manner of performance (courtesy, cooperation)

Characteristics of a Good Standard

A good standard does the following:

- It describes a level either below which a performance is not acceptable or above which a performance is superior.
- It provides a challenge but is attainable by most incumbents.
- It is results based and quantifiable whenever possible.
- It is specific, objective, and measurable.
- It deals with performance over which the employee has control.
- It excludes imprecise words such as professional, suitable, timely, attitude, and ethical unless these words are accompanied by descriptors.
- It limits the use of absolute terms such as never, always, or 100% to actions that are life threatening or serious in other ways (eg, issuing compatible blood for transfusions).
- It is understood and agreed to by both employee and supervisor.
- It does not discriminate against any member of a group protected by the Equal Employment Opportunity Commission.
- It directly or indirectly benefits customers.

Practical Approach for Preparing Standards

The simplest approach is to list the major duties, then add appropriate descriptors that represent one or more of the five above dimensions. For example:

Task: Answer the telephone.

Standards:

- Provides complete information sought by callers. Ensures that transfer calls are completed. (Quality)

- Keeps lines open by processing calls expeditiously, and avoiding personal calls. (Quantity)

- Answers calls within three rings. (Timeliness)

- Identifies department and self. Asks "how can I help?" (Manner)

- Uses caller's name frequently. (Manner)

- Closes by thanking caller. (Manner)

Do not be discouraged when you must settle for descriptors that are not as precise as you would like. Periodic modifications dictated by experience are a key to success.

Some General Customer-Oriented Performance Standards

Performance standards that apply to an employee's interactions with customers include the following:

- Uses tact in personal interactions.
- Communicates in honest, straightforward manner.
- Reports employee concerns to lab management.
- Reacts constructively to criticism and to changes.
- Maintains high team spirit and morale.
- Interacts in a positive manner.
- Rare complaints from customers or staff.
- Customer information is always kept confidential.

Example of Performance Standards for a Specific Position

Performance standards for the position of phlebotomist or patient care technician are as follows, with rare exception:

- Maintains appearance, dress, and decorum that conform to special lab code.
- Greets patients courteously by introducing self and calling patient by name.
- Explains procedure about to be performed.
- Complies with institutional policies and procedures with special attention to isolation procedures.

Quantification When Applicable and Possible

The introduction of numbers and percentages adds objectivity. Employees get a more accurate description about what is called for. For example, "Answer within three rings" is very precise; "answer courteously" is not.

Percentages indicate the amount of tolerance or the number of errors permitted. This can be important. Consider "answer within three rings 90% of the time" and "correctly cross-match blood 90% of the time." This would be appropriate for the phone rings, but would be completely unacceptable for compatibility testing.

Often it's not possible or advantageous to apply percentages. Objections to their use have been voiced, since one would need to record each episode before percentages could be calculated, converting supervisors into "bean-counters."

There is no interpretive problem with terms like "always," "never," or "without exception," but there is a problem of achievement. Even our best employees slip occasionally. Therefore terms like "with rare exception" are often more appropriate than absolute terms.

The adverbs "generally, ordinarily, and usually" mean over 50%, while "sometimes, seldom, and infrequently" denote occurrences below 50%.

Tips for Formulating Standards

Start by upgrading the position descriptions, particularly the segment on responsibilities. This is the skeleton for the standards. If you have long lists of duties, group them into segments of related topics. Call these key results areas, significant job segments, or some similar title.

For example, for an administrative assistant, all activities that relate to preparing for a meeting can be grouped under meeting preparations. For a nursing unit supervisor, these could consist of the following[3]:

• personnel functions
• financial functions
• operational functions
• patient care functions
• professional growth and development

Use a KISS strategy: Keep It Short and Simple. In health care, new technologies, services, and responsibilities translate into frequent changes in position descriptions. If you spend too much time developing comprehensive standards, you find yourself back at the drawing board. Most authorities believe that only six or seven major responsibilities of professional or technical specialists need descriptors.

Solicit the help of incumbents when deciding what should and should not be included. Incumbents are also helpful when selecting the degree of difficulty for standards. Contrary to what we may expect, employees peg their expectations higher than do their supervisors.

When working on minimum standards, be sure you know what level of performance is acceptable and what is not. If descriptors are too low, you will find you have accumulated deadwood and cannot get rid of it. To use the old quality assurance cliché, "Do it right the first time."

If you subsequently raise those standards, you should negotiate the changes with all the members of the group. Do not forget to raise the same standards for all the other employees who hold that position.

It is helpful to recall what kinds of problems your borderline performers have had or are having. Perhaps they forget a step in a complicated procedure or have difficulty dealing with certain customers. Composing standards based on such practical knowledge gives great standards.

When pondering descriptors for superior levels, watch one of your best employees at work. What does he or she do that makes the difference? These observations give you clues to good indicators.

Pitfalls

Pitfalls in standards formulation include the following:

- The list of responsibilities (duties) is incomplete or too exhaustive.
- Average performance level is used.
- Responsibilities are not under the employee's control.
- A standard is based on invalid or unreliable data.
- Expectations are too low or too high.
- Too few of the standards are based on outcomes or results.
- The supervisor or employee is unwilling to renegotiate the level of a standard.
- There is little or no commitment of the employee. No input from the employee is equally bad.
- There is inadequate monitoring of subsequent performance.

For examples of performance standards, see Exhibits 5–1, 5–2, 5–3, and 5–4.

Exhibit 5–1 Sample Format for Duties and Performance Standards for a Medical Technologist

---

PERFORM ROUTINE BACTERIOLOGY PROCEDURES INCLUDING READING OF PLATES, IDENTIFICATION, AND ANTIBIOTIC SUSCEPTIBILITY TESTING OF SUSPECTED PATHOGENS

a) Cultures must be planted on appropriate media within 15 minutes of receiving the specimens.

b) Stat Gram stains must be prepared and interpreted within 30 minutes of receiving the specimen.

c) Plates must be read and necessary tests set up by 3 PM.

d) Must advise technicians on identification workup of unusual isolates.

e) All procedures in the department must be performed according to laboratory specifications.

f) There shall be no more than three complaints (incident reports) a year from physicians or nursing personnel regarding bacteriology results and procedures.

PERFORM ROUTINE AFB WORK INCLUDING SPECIMEN PROCESSING AND STAINING

a) Process, culture, and prepare smears of specimens within one hour.

b) Interpret stains within 15 minutes, and notify the proper authorities when positive.

Note: The duties are capitalized. The standards follow in lower case.

Source: Reprinted from *Performance Standards for Laboratory Personnel* by W.O. Umiker and S.M. Yohe, p. 99, with permission of Medical Economics, © 1984.

Exhibit 5–2 Sample Format for Coupling of Duties and Performance Standards

Duties	*Standards*
Orient new employees	Submit schedule and agenda to office 1 week before arrival of new hire.
	Notify trainers at least 1 week before arrival of new employees.
	Complete orientation within 5 workdays.
	Return check-off list to office within 1 week of completion.
	Receive favorable evaluations from indoctrinees more than 90 percent of the time.

Exhibit 5–3 Performance Standards for Phlebotomist

Duty: Draws blood from patient, and returns tubes and requests to clinical laboratory.

Standards:
1. Greets patient by introducing self and calling patient by formal name.
2. Verifies correct patient by checking name on requisition form against name on patient's wrist band.
3. Explains procedure to patient.
4. Follows infection prevention instructions in phlebotomist's procedure manual.
5. Performs phlebotomy. No more than three unsuccessful attempts are permitted. Calls supervisor if help is needed.
6. Labels blood tubes immediately after blood is obtained by following procedure in manual.
7. Disposes used needles in accordance with procedure in manual.
8. Returns tubes and requisitions to the blood collection station within the time allowed by supervisor.

Exhibit 5–4 Sample Format of Behaviorally Anchored Performance Standards

---

Meets Expectations	*Exceeds Expectations*	*Fails To Meet Expectations*
Quality assurance Performs required reagent quality control each day; records results, dates, and initials. Notifies supervisor of discrepant results or bad reagents. Changes temperature graphs and charts promptly when needed and makes sure pen and graph are working properly. Performs equipment QC according to predetermined time schedule greater than 90 percent of the time; records dates, initials, and	Consistently performs reagent QC and temperature checks prior to testing. When there will not be enough reagent to last until the next day, assists other shifts by checking extra bottles. Volunteers to do required equipment QC and follows through without reminders. Completes QC records accurately. Notifies supervisor and/or biomedical department of discrepant	Forgets to change temperature charts, or perform temperature of reagent QC, more than twice per year. Does not notify supervisor of equipment or reagent problems or discrepant results. Needs reminder more than once per year to perform scheduled equipment QC. Does not follow established lab safety regulations.

continues

Exhibit 5–4 Sample Format of Behaviorally Anchored Performance Standards

results on proper forms. Notifies supervisor of discrepant results or nonfunctioning equipment. Follows established lab safety regulations.

results or broken equipment after attempting to identify and fix problem. Follows established lab safety regulations and encourages others to do so.

Result reporting

Efficiently and accurately reports results manually and via computer. Always writes neatly and legibly. Forms always include date, technologist's initials, and completion time. No more than 2 uncorrected transcription errors (undiscovered before they go into patient records) per year.

Meets expectations and reports results manually and via computer with no uncorrected transcription errors.

Makes more than 2 uncorrected transcription errors per year. Reports are found to be illegible or incomplete, or lack required information.

Source: Reprinted from *Medical Laboratory Observer,* Vol. 19, pp. 33–39, with permission of Medical Economics, © November 1987.

NOTES

1. *1995 Accreditation Manual for Hospitals,* Vol. 2 (Oakbrook Terrace, IL: *Joint Commission of Healthcare Organizations,* 1994).
2. Americans with Disabilities Act of 1990, U.S. Code, Vol. 42 [USC 12101].
3. L. Berte, *Developing Performance Standards for Hospital Personnel* (Chicago, IL: ASCP Press, 1989), 61.

RECOMMENDED READING

L. Berte, *Developing Performance Standards for Hospital Personnel* (Chicago, IL: ASCP Press, 1989).

R.J. Plachy and S.J. Plachy, *Results-Oriented Job Descriptions* (New York, NY: AMACOM, 1993).

C.M. Chesser et al. "Job Descriptions and Performance Appraisals," *Health Care Supervisor 15,* no. 4 (1997): 1–34.

S.S. Heatherley, "Key Performance Indicators To Assess Laboratory Operations," *Clinical Laboratory Management Review 11,* no. 3 (1997): 164–170.

Chapter 6

Policy Making and Implementation

- importance of policies
- uses of policies
- enforcing policies of upper management
- policies formulated by supervisors
- your policies
- potential problems with policies

Policies are guidelines for reaching goals and controlling behavior. They reflect the mission and values of organizations and are made more specific by procedures and rules. They are more important today because of the propensity for litigation. Legal, moral, and ethical problems, sexual harassment, discrimination, and patients' rights all require reevaluation of current policies.

Unnecessary or vague policies create red tape and Mickey Mouse rules that frustrate employees and supervisors. Poorly worded policies lead to confusion. Inappropriate, ill-conceived, unfair, or illogical policies are obstacles to effective performance and require many exceptions.

The absence of policies results in management by crisis. Managers waste time making the same decisions and answering the same questions repeatedly. Confusion, uncertainty, and conflicts become pervasive.

When practices stray from policies and procedures or when practices turn into unwritten policies, problems arise. Lax adherence to policies may cause legal problems and may endanger staff morale.

Although there are always legal risks involved in documenting policies, it's more hazardous not to have an employee handbook. That handbook should be understood by all employees and should cover important policies, rules, and regulations. Management updates policies constantly because of changes in laws, services, and personnel matters.

Policies That Have Received Recent Attention

- modification of salary and benefits programs
- job sharing, flexible scheduling, and work-at-home programs
- smoking and drugs
- exposure to hazardous agents
- precautions regarding care of patients with acquired immunodeficiency syndrome (AIDS)
- sexual harassment
- cultural diversity
- discrimination because of age or disability
- employment of people with disabilities
- requirements of accrediting and regulatory agencies

Policy regarding use and abuse of e-mail provides an impressive example of why policy manuals are in a constant state of flux. When employers fail to develop appropriate e-mail policies and procedures, they run the risk of legal problems. These e-mail problems relate to sexual harassment and interference with the privacy rights of employees.

Many state laws require that written policies be distributed to employees. Therefore it is almost mandatory that each organization provide its employees with policy and procedure manuals. To reduce exposure to legal liability, these handbooks include disclaimer language throughout (eg, advising employees that benefits may change at the employer's discretion).

USES OF POLICIES

Well-formulated policies have several important uses:

- To promote understanding, clarity, and consistency of behavior. Employees who know what is expected of them feel more confident, and they police themselves.
- To eliminate repetitive decision making, to standardize responses, and to save time
- To help in the orientation of new hires
- To provide documented controls as required by licensing and accrediting agencies

ENFORCING UPPER MANAGEMENT POLICIES

To be effective, policies must be explicit, publicized, and enforced without favoritism. The first-line supervisor is the chief activator or enforcer of policies. Supervisors must know, interpret, promulgate, and enforce policies. Often supervisors must carry out policies that they had no hand in developing. They might not comprehend the rationale behind, or agree with, some of these policies, but they still must enforce them. Handing out employee handbooks is not enough. Supervisors must understand the purpose of each policy and know how much freedom they have in modifying or originating policies. For example: Supervisor Sue says to one of her employees: "Sally, you don't look well. Take the rest of the day off. It won't count as sick time." This is good faith and legal, but what is the organization's policy regarding it?

Insecure managers divorce themselves from unpopular policies by saying things such as: "Do not blame me for that stupid policy" or "Management expects you to. . . ." Even worse, they may ignore the policy or depend on others to enforce it. The result is a loss of respect for both the organization and the manager who takes this approach. When supervisors feel that a policy is inappropriate or is causing problems, they should discuss the problem with their superiors. Usually there is a rational explanation for it. If you find that a policy is hurting morale more than helping a situation, discuss the problem with your manager. Perhaps you have a suggestion on how the policy could be modified. In any event, keep your employees posted on your efforts to change the situation.

There are times when supervisors must bend or even ignore a policy; this is a matter of risk taking. For example:

> Hospital A has a strict policy that prohibits employees from bringing young children into the clinical laboratory. A blood bank technologist receives an urgent call late one night to return to the hospital because of an emergency. Having no one to care for her 6-year-old daughter, she brings her daughter with her to the laboratory. Should this technologist be reprimanded or thanked for this behavior?

POLICIES FORMULATED BY SUPERVISORS

Common Situations That Need a Policy or a Policy Change

The following situations may require the creation of a policy or the modification of an existing one:

- Introduction of a new service
- Frequent violations of procedures or rules

- Problems of productivity, quality, schedules, or time
- Frequent complaints from customers or employees
- Legal, ethical, or moral problems
- Behavioral inconsistencies
- Repetitive questions being asked about procedures or rules

Your policies must harmonize with those mandated from higher management. They must not exceed your authority. Use plain language. Avoid legalistic phraseology or jargon to impress people or to make the policy sound more authoritative. See Exhibit 6–1 for more information on how to formulate a policy.

Publish the finished document. Make certain that every employee receives a copy and signs a log acknowledging that.

Enforce the policy fairly, firmly, and uniformly. Unenforced policies become meaningless. Supervisors often overlook transgressions by their more valued employees. Unfairness of this type often translates to the filing of grievances. Fur-

---

Exhibit 6–1 A Procedure for Formulating a Policy

1. State the need for, and describe the purpose of, a new policy or a revision of an old one.
2. Decide whether the need is great enough to warrant a new policy or change.
3. Consider alternate solutions (eg, a notice on the bulletin board or a memo).
4. Gather data and input from others, especially the people affected by the policy.
5. Check the rough draft for the following:
   - compliance with institutional philosophy, mission, values, ethics, and established policies, rules, and regulations;
   - completeness, clarity, and understandability;
   - answers to questions of what, when, where, who, how, and why;
   - anticipated acceptance by persons who are impacted; and
   - enforcement problems.
6. Circulate a rough draft or discuss it with others or both. Get approval of superiors. Have a legal expert check whether there are liability aspects.
7. Make any necessary modifications. Ask yourself whether the policy meets the following criteria:
   - it is needed;
   - it will be understood;
   - it is achievable;
   - it is flexible and fair;
   - it will be acceptable; and
   - it can be enforced.

thermore, supervisors must make certain that they themselves comply with the letter of the policies. They serve as models for their staffs. The old cliché "Do as I say, not as I do" does not work.

Heavy-handedness in enforcement can be counterproductive. Employees are more skillful in avoiding compliance than managers are in enforcing policies. Sometimes the violating of rules becomes a game, especially when the supervisor is unpopular or autocratic.

Be willing to admit when one of your policies turns out to be a dud. Modify or eliminate such policies when appropriate. Do not regard the policy as written in stone. Give your policy manual an annual checkup.

POTENTIAL PROBLEMS WITH POLICIES

Selection of Job Candidates

Usually the personnel department screens candidates, but the actual selection is left to supervisors. Hazards for inexperienced interviewers include questions of illegality and the absence of a basis for excluding candidates.

When job descriptions or performance standards are inadequate or obsolete, even experienced interviewers may select the wrong candidates.

Orientation of New Hires

Personnel departments may be responsible for orientation and training, but much of this task still is left to supervisors. Supervisors may provide incorrect answers to questions about payroll deductions and benefits packages.

Faulty indoctrination policies or negligent implementation of guidelines result in poor work performance and the overrating of poor performers at the completion of their probationary periods.

Schedules

Vague or unwritten policies about schedules can destroy morale and lead to the filing of grievances, especially in unionized organizations. Hazards include discrimination in assigning work, vacation, overtime, or call-back schedules.

Safety and Health

With the explosive increase in workers' compensation claims, supervisors must be emphatic about reporting, correcting, and following up on suspected safety or health hazards. Failure to follow established policy, including the careful documentation and the prompt handling of injuries, can be costly to organizations. It can also damage the careers of supervisors who have failed in this responsibility.

A touchy situation is that of AIDS. First there is consideration for the employee who has the disease, and then there is consideration for the coworkers who are concerned about being infected. This is particularly acute in health care, where there is an increased risk of workers contracting AIDS from patients and where problems of confidentiality are involved.

The policy should state that employees who have AIDS are treated as other persons with disabilities. It must explain the rights of both the employees with AIDS and their coworkers. This must be known and understood by all employees.

Supervisors should be ready to cope with workers who object to working with an employee who has AIDS. Training programs for managers and workers are essential. The inadvertent mishandling of an employee with AIDS can leave an organization liable for discrimination, invasion of privacy, or unauthorized disclosure.

Handling Problems or Special Employees

Grievances usually are filed after disciplinary measures have been taken. Poor leadership leads to poor followership, which leads to reprimands or other disciplinary actions, which then leads to grievances.

Mishandled severance procedures can be costly in both dollars and feelings. Supervisory botching of charges of sexual harassment or discrimination can be embarrassing and expensive for employers.

Effective resolution of personnel problems starts with good policies and ends with skillful enforcement of these policies. In sexual harassment, the blanket grievance procedure usually calls for the immediate supervisor to be the first person contacted. But in sexual harassment, the immediate supervisor is often the perpetrator. A separate policy for sexual harassment is mandatory.

Policy must spell out limits on drug testing. Is it routine or random? Who will be tested? How about the invasion of privacy issue?

Special Case: Americans with Disabilities Act

Policies must address the new federal regulations regarding hiring, assigning, promoting, and accommodating people who have physical or mental disabilities, as specified by the Americans with Disabilities Act (ADA). This translates into making changes in position descriptions, performance standards, and recruiting, testing, and interviewing of candidates.

A particularly sensitive area of concern to supervisors is accommodating. Reasonable accommodations under the ADA include making existing facilities accessible to individuals with disabilities, job restructuring, or job reassignment. Managers may offer part-time employment or modified work schedules or may grant unpaid leave. Often it is necessary to acquire or modify equipment, provide readers or interpreters, and modify examinations, training materials, or policies.[1]

Reasonable accommodation requires employers to modify examinations, training materials, and policies. Jobs must be restructured so that marginal or nonessential duties that exclude people with disabilities are eliminated when possible.

Employers must be able to justify exclusionary qualifications or capabilities. Candidates may not be tested for functions and knowledge that are not essential to the job. Supervisors must know, however, that bumping another employee out of a position to create a vacancy for one of these candidates is not required.

NOTE

1. *EEOC Regulation Pertaining to ADA under Title I Employment* (Title VII, Civil Rights Act of 1964), *Federal Register* 35 (July 26, 1991): 736.

Chapter 7

Personnel Recruitment and Selection

- the imperatives of the selection process
- the kinds of candidates employers are looking for
- legal constraints to the hiring process
- recruitment sources
- how supervisors can help in the recruiting process
- personnel selection instruments
- the employment interview
- questions by the interviewers
- recommended questions
- candidates who had no previous employment
- questions by the candidates
- sensitive issues
- how to get candidates to accept the job offer
- closing the interview
- after the interview
- getting references

*"It's a heck of a lot easier to hire the right people
to begin with than to try to fix them later."*[1]

Brad Smart

Finding the right employees in today's fast-changing health care environment is becoming an increasingly important activity for supervisors. Of all their responsibilities, the selection of new employees ranks near the top in importance. Motivational problems, personnel turnover, difficult people, propensity to turnover, and susceptibility to unionization are all reduced by hiring the right people.

Better selection of new employees is an integral part of improved customer service, team building, successful quality management strategies, and cost control. Poor recruitment and selection are expensive. The eventual cost of one bad hire may be several times that employee's annual salary.

Expenses Associated with a Bad Hiring Choice

- training a replacement
- advertising
- time
- potential customer loss
- lower productivity
- possible unemployment compensation claim
- potential lawsuit

IMPERATIVES OF THE SELECTION PROCESS

"Cast a very wide net and carefully sift through what you catch in it."[2]

Linda S. Goldzimer

Institutions that are known for excellent customer service take pains to hire people who have displayed commendable customer-service attitude in their previous work and social conduct. Once a person has been hired, you find it easier to reinforce good attitudes than to change bad ones.

To get the kind of employees we want, there are three imperatives:

1. A recruiting program that provides many good candidates to choose from.
2. A selection process that can pick the best candidate with a high degree of confidence.
3. The ability to persuade candidates of our choice to accept our offers.

If job competencies can be lowered safely, there will be more candidates to choose from. Separate the must-haves from the nice-to-haves. Does the person really need a college degree and three years of experience? Be careful about your mandatory qualifications. If your standard is challenged by a candidate from a protected group, can you justify the requirement in court? This risk can be reduced by stating that a competency is highly desirable, not mandatory.

DESIRABLE CANDIDATES

Health care institutions are looking for more people who can contribute to the continuous improvement of customer service, productivity, and creativity. Finding candidates with the technical or professional skills needed is easier than finding people who exhibit the types of behaviors that fit into your organization's culture.

Besides job expertise, there are other factors that make for success in dealing with customers. These factors include social skills. By social skills we mean being articulate and able to say and do what is necessary to maintain rapport with customers. Other positive attributes include teamwork, cooperation, and collaboration. Unfortunately, the most frequent questions put to job candidates—and the chief factor in picking a new employee—relate only to experience and professional or technical skill.

The best candidates for most positions are those who:

- have a broad technical or professional background,
- are good communicators and rapid learners,
- can deal effectively with people, and
- are flexible (eg, can easily move among disparate competencies as needed).

When we hire only highly specialized people, we run the risk of falling into the talent obsolescence trap. Due to the rapid changes in technologies and services offered by organizations, the needed qualifications of personnel also change rapidly. Job descriptions that are too finely tuned can result in hiring employees who are qualified for today's job, but not for tomorrow's.

LEGAL CONSTRAINTS TO HIRING

The thrust of federal and state legislation is to ensure that hiring, retention, and promotion decisions are made only on the basis of an employee's ability to do the job.

Affirmative Action

The Civil Rights Act of 1964 and the Executive Order 11246 (Amended by Executive Order 11375) require that employers identify areas of minority and female underutilization, numerical hiring, promotion goals, and other actions that increase minority and female employment in job classifications where they are currently underutilized.

Supervisors must be aware of the legal requirements of Equal Employment Opportunity Commission (EEOC) regulations and of their organization's policies and practices related to EEOC and the Americans with Disabilities Act (ADA). They must recognize and eliminate stereotyping and preconceptions and provide clear and achievable expectations for all their employees.

Unlawful Inquiries

Each state also has its own requirements regarding Title VI of the Civil Rights Act of 1964. Ask your human resources department for a copy. Here is a partial list of questions interdicted by the EEOC:

- age, nationality, and marital status
- spouse's occupation or place of employment
- pregnancy or plans for pregnancy
- child or baby-sitting arrangements (You may ask whether there are problems in getting to work, such as call-backs.)
- military record, except as related to work performance
- arrest record (You may ask whether the person has been *convicted* of a crime but not whether he or she has been arrested.)
- membership in organizations other than work-related ones
- religious affiliation
- nature, severity, or existence of physical or mental impairments. Avoid questions about use of sick leave. (You may ask how often the person was absent from work as long as the question is not limited to absences resulting from illness or injury.)
- workers' compensation history (This may be obtained after hiring.)
- questions asked only of members of a protected group (If you want to ask women whether they can lift a 50-pound child, you must ask male candidates that same question.)

Age Discrimination in Employment Act of 1967

As amended in 1986, this act prohibits employers from placing an age limit on candidates for employment. There are exceptions for those occupations for which age is a bona fide qualification (eg, police officer or fire fighter).

Rehabilitation Act of 1973 and the ADA

The major thrusts of the Rehabilitation Act of 1973 and the ADA of 1992 are (1) those dealing with hiring and promotion practices (2) and those that require reasonable accommodation.

The cardinal rule is that any question asked of candidates should relate to the job in some way. You can ask whether an applicant can perform all job-related functions and meet attendance requirements. You may not ask about an applicant's current or past medical or health conditions. If an applicant reveals that he or she cannot perform an essential function, do not probe into the medical history. Instead, tailor your questions to identify how the disability renders the applicant unable to perform the job's essential functions. Find out what accommodations would enable the applicant to do the job.

Reasonable accommodations refer to measures that an employer may take to enable a person to perform essential functions. These could be physical changes such as wider doors or magnified displays, or they could be the elimination of some nonessential or infrequently performed tasks. For example, if a job requires occasional typing and the candidate lacks the mechanical ability to type, that activity could be assigned to other employees.

Because of the ADA, interviewing job applicants is more hazardous. Here are five questions that are now illegal:

1. Have you ever filed a workers' compensation claim?
2. Do you have any physical problems or injuries?
3. How many days were you sick last year?
4. Are you currently taking any medications?
5. Have you ever been treated for drug abuse?

Under revised guidelines, the EEOC permits employers to ask questions about accommodations at the initial interview stage in a few specific situations. For example, the employer reasonably believes an applicant will need accommodations because of an obvious disability (eg, the applicant uses a wheelchair or has severe visual impairment) or the applicant voluntarily reveals the need for accommodation during the interview (eg, discloses a hidden disability such as diabetes or states the need for breaks to take medication). Except for these circumstances, the law on inquiries remains unchanged. All other disability-related inquiries must wait until after a job offer has been made.

RECRUITMENT SOURCES

Recruitment Sources

Employee referrals
Newspaper job listings
Recruitment firms
College recruitment

Direct mail
Employment agencies
Computerized databases
Job fairs
Walk-in applicants
Unsolicited resumes

One of the best recruitment methods is employee referral. Your workers have friends and acquaintances working for other employers in your area. Employees have their own networks and may bring their friends in for interviews.

The Internet is the hottest new tool in recruiting. In addition to search engines, such as Yahoo!, there are bulletin board systems, news groups, and job banks (eg, http://www.careercenter@AOL.com.). Many organizations have recruitment web sites.

If your organization has a reputation as a great place to work, the best people will find you.

HOW SUPERVISORS CAN HELP IN THE RECRUITING PROCESS

You may think that you have no influence on your organization's recruiting practices, but you can play an important role in this process. Be on the lookout for potential candidates in other departments. That young lady in the housekeeping department who always greets you with a smile might do a great job as a receptionist or could be trained as a phlebotomist or patient care technician. Get your staff to serve as unofficial recruiters.

Provide your recruiters with condensed versions of position descriptions that also comment on the attractive features of the job. Recommend the most appropriate publications in which to place advertisements. Obtain and share a list of technical or professional schools where potential candidates train. Participate actively in career programs.

PERSONNEL SELECTION INSTRUMENTS

Application Forms and Resumes

Resumes are the public relations sheets of candidates' balance sheets without the liabilities. As Dortch states, "Some of the best fiction writing in the world is in the form of resumes."[3] [(p. 46)]

When studying these forms, look for signs of customer service (eg, volunteer work and membership in social organizations), teamwork, and responsibilities that exceeded job requirements.

Frequent job changes call for close questioning of candidates. When moves are to jobs with lower pay, less responsibility, or requiring less competency, watch out. Equally significant are job changes attributed to personal reasons or explanations such as "My boss and I had different chemistries." Other red flags are long time gaps in employment, inconsistencies in salary history, incomplete information on previous employers' addresses or names, and vague reasons for leaving previous jobs.

Having outside interests may be favorable, but some of these interfere with attendance or performance.

Avoid the halo effect. A person's success in one type of job does not ensure his or her success in another.

Pay attention to the clarity, grammar, and spelling in the resume and any correspondence with the applicant, especially if you seek a meticulous worker.

Credentialing

Confirm licenses, certifications, or registrations.

Preemployment Tests

Preemployment tests can be very revealing and are underutilized. Employment managers do not like to take the time to administer these. They worry about violating antidiscrimination laws (employers must be prepared to prove that the tests possess validity and reliability). However, as long as you base a test on a required skill or on knowledge as documented in the job description, such fears are groundless. For example:

- Phlebotomist (or patient care technician) candidates make preparations for collecting a blood specimen.
- Clerk-receptionist candidates take some incoming phone calls.
- Candidates who will have teaching responsibilities give a short lecture or demonstration.
- Candidates serve in temporary jobs before being hired on a permanent basis.

An alternative to the above action tests is to ask candidates to tell you in as much detail as they can how they performed certain tasks. Only people who have actually done what they claim can tell you how.

Special Questionnaires

Some commercial job-applicant questionnaires purport to measure honesty, loyalty, and positive attitudes, but the jury is still out on the validity of these tools.

EMPLOYMENT INTERVIEW

Employment techniques are based on the concept that candidates who have already displayed certain competencies are likely to continue to display those characteristics.

Who Should Conduct the Interviews?

These interviews are so important that the principal interviewer should be someone who is trained in this skill. One trained interviewer can usually achieve more than a battery of untrained or marginally interested interviewers can.

Experienced interviewers can hold unstructured meetings (no prepared questions) and still maintain fair and legally valid interviews. Inexperienced interviewers should prepare lists of questions before the interviews, and use the same questions for each candidate to ensure fairness and validity.

Skilled interviewers ask the right questions, and listen with their eyes as well as their ears. They show enthusiasm about their organization, their staff, and the job being discussed.

When a team approach is used, one or more of the candidate's future peers should serve on the interview team. Employees have self-interest in new associates and can often spot people they would like to have (or not like to have) working with them.

Computer-Assisted Interviews

Corporations that use expert computer systems report improvement in the quality of new employees and claim beneficial effects on turnover, absenteeism, theft, and productivity. Surprisingly, most candidates are more willing to feed information into computers than tell it to interviewers. A typical program consists of about 100 multiple-choice questions and takes about 20 minutes.

Preparations for the Interview

The following are guidelines for interviewers that will help to ensure an effective interview:

- Familiarize yourself with the position description. Concentrate on the duties and required qualifications. Make certain that the document has been updated.
- Study the applications and resumes.
- Draft a list of questions for the candidates, and eliminate those that violate employment laws.
- List the positive features of the job.
- Familiarize yourself with salary and benefits.
- Visualize the tour of your facilities that you will provide, and alert the people you want the candidate to meet.
- Schedule a time and place that ensures privacy and freedom from interruptions.

Two Initial Steps

Ice-Breaking

A nonthreatening introduction can make candidates feel comfortable and relaxed. Be enthusiastic and persuasive, but honest and sincere. You get only one chance to make a good first impression, so start right. Also, your first impression of candidates is important. What you see is what future customers will see when they first meet this person.

Be on time and greet interviewees by name. When you introduce yourself, include your title. Thank them for coming. Offer a rest stop or coffee.

Do not interview them from behind a desk. Seat them next to your desk rather than across from it. Do not remain standing or perch on the edge of your desk.

Make brief small talk to get them into a talking mode and you into a listening one. Attempts at small talk may include questions that violate EEOC restrictions, so beware of those illegal questions. Ask:

- how they learned about the job,
- what their understanding of the job is,
- if they had a parking problem when they arrived,
- if someone is going to pick them up, and
- about an outside interest mentioned in their resume.

Review the interview agenda, assuring interviewees that they will have an opportunity to ask all the questions they wish. Ask whether the allotted time poses any problem—they may be scheduled elsewhere after your interview. Then briefly describe the job being offered.

Chronological Review

Have the candidate start with college (high school, if there was no college). Inquire about academic standing, study habits, jobs held, attendance record, athletic and social activities, and leadership roles.

Move on to the work history (eg, "Tell me about your jobs. For each job you've held, I'd like to know things like starting and final salary, duties, how you handled setbacks, the most and least enjoyable aspects of your job, reason for leaving, and what your supervisor was like"). Some interviewers like to ask candidates to describe a typical workday.

Ask probing questions using the list you prepared.

Finally, market the job, and answer the candidate's questions or concerns.

INTERVIEWERS' QUESTIONS

Kinds of Questions

Closed-ended questions can be answered in one or a few words (eg, "When are you available?"). Use closed-ended questions to get basic data, but not to elicit detailed information. You won't learn much from the question "Did you like your last supervisor?"

Open-ended questions cannot be answered with a few words and are better for getting detailed information. Change the above closed-ended question to "Tell me about your last supervisor" and you will learn much more.

Probing questions address the five w's: why, what, who, when, and where, plus how. These are excellent, but if overused they may create a dialogue that sounds like grilling. Here are a few examples of probing questions:

* How did that situation arise?
* Why was that allowed to happen?
* In retrospect, what would you have done differently?

Hypothetical questions include questions such as "What would you do if . . . ?" These situational queries can be very informative when discussing technical or personal skills.

Illegal questions are those prohibited by federal and state statutes. If you do not have a list of these, get one from your human resources department before you interview your next candidate.

Leading questions reveal to the applicant the answer you want (eg, "You are willing to serve on committees aren't you?"). Leading questions should be avoided.

Knock-out questions address items that automatically eliminate candidates (eg, lack of license or certification).

Questions about general responsibilities can be formulated based on the position description and job qualifications. These questions cover education, training, experience, knowledge, and skill.

Questions to evaluate service attitudes and interactive skills are useful. Novice interviewers ask questions that deal more with technical skills and experience rather than people skills. We want questions that evaluate competence ("Can do") and motivation ("Will do").

RECOMMENDED QUESTIONS

Questions To Determine Professional or Technical Competency

These questions should be criterion referenced. That is, they are related to duties and responsibilities as documented in the job descriptions. Use hypothetical situations or pose questions such as the following:

- How would you . . . ?
- Describe your technique for . . .
- If you encountered . . . what would you do?
- Tell me about your experience with . . .
- Explain your role in . . .
- What aspect of this job would you find most difficult?
- What strengths would you bring to this position?
- What competency would your former boss recommend that you strengthen?

Questions To Measure Motivation

In every department there are clock watchers and other people who could do better if they wanted to. The following questions will help you spot the goof-offs:

- What have you done at work that shows strong initiative?
- What did you do to become more effective in your previous position?
- Tell me about a time when you went the extra mile.

Questions To Evaluate Teamwork

Teamwork demands communication skill, congenial relationships, cooperation, the ability to compromise, and a lot of idea interchange. The following questions evaluate that trait:

- Do you prefer responsibility for your own work or do you like to share responsibility with others?
- What kinds of people do you get along with best? What kinds of people do you find difficult? How do you deal with them?
- What other departments did you have dealings with, and what difficulties did you encounter with any of these?

Questions To Evaluate Followership Skill

Although you're not looking for a clone of yourself and you want people who complement your strong points, you do not want problem followers. Award bonus points to candidates who speak well of previous employers. These questions help you to pick a congenial teammate:

- Describe the best boss you ever had. Describe the worst. Watch the body language.
- What are some things you and your boss disagreed about?
- Give me an example of how you handled unjust criticism.

Questions To Evaluate Stress Resistance

All of us have variable stress thresholds, and different jobs generate different amounts of stress. If the position is a stressful one, include questions such as the following:

- When was the last time you got angry at work? What caused it, and how did you react?
- What was the most difficult situation you faced at work? What feelings did you have and how did you react to them?
- What are some of your pet peeves?

Questions To Determine Retention Potential

Because one goal of personnel selection is to improve employee retention, questions such as the following are worthwhile:

- What do you want to be doing five years from now?
- What do you think you will be doing five years from now?
- What do you think you will be earning five years from now?
- Let's briefly review your career goals and plans.

Questions To Determine Customer Orientation

- What does superior service mean to you?
- Who do you think our external and internal customers are?
- Give me an example of how you made an extra effort to serve a client.
- What do you do when a caller becomes insulting or abusive on the phone?
- How could your previous employer have provided better service?
- Did you ever take care of a chronically ill relative? Tell me about it.
- Did you ever work in a nursing home? What was it like?
- Did you ever baby-sit or work in a restaurant? Describe that experience.

CANDIDATES WITH NO PREVIOUS EMPLOYMENT

Most college graduates have had part-time or summer jobs or were employed before attending college. Inquiries into these employments can be worthwhile. The following questions assume greater importance when the employment history is skimpy:

- Describe a teacher that you had problems with. How did you handle that situation?
- What are some problems you faced at school or at home? If you had it to do all over, what would you do differently?
- What have you done that shows initiative and willingness to work?
- What are your long-range goals and expectations? How do you plan to fulfill these?

SENSITIVE ISSUES

Be tactful when you probe into the soft spots. Start by saying that one way you evaluate maturity is by the ability of people to recognize performance that could be improved. Point out that such people have already taken the first step toward career improvement.

Avoid strong words such as weakness and deficiency. Substitute phrases such as area of concern, need for more experience, and need to enhance full potential. Use the questions "Is it possible that . . .?" or "How did you happen to . . . ?"

Clues to Untruthfulness

- Their resumes and comments seem too good to be true.
- You have difficulty believing what they say they did or earned. They exaggerate or falsify their educational achievements (eg, "attended" becomes "graduated from").

- Their answers to challenging questions lack substance.
- Their body language may give them away. They show signs of discomfort or restlessness when closely questioned, and they avoid eye contact. You note blushing, sudden heavy perspiring, a change in voice (pitch, volume, or rate), squirming or fidgeting, and blinking.
- The information you get from their references does not correlate with what they told you, or their stories lack consistency.

CANDIDATES' QUESTIONS

Some candidates will ask only selfish questions (ie, questions about salary, benefits, vacation policies, and overtime). Others ask only superficial questions such as how many employees are on board. Then there are those who do not ask any questions at all. This tips you off that they are not very sharp or have little interest in the job.

Candidates' questions reveal insights about their values and goals in addition to their professional or technical knowledge. This is especially true of the questions they pose and the interest they show when given a tour of your department. I like candidates who not only ask technical questions, but also ask questions such as: "How would you describe the personality of your organization" or "How long have you worked here, and what attracted you to this organization?" Another great question is "Please describe your mentoring and training programs."

EVALUATION OF CANDIDATES

Interviewers usually have a "gut reaction" to candidates. Some react impulsively and make poor decisions. Others do their best to ignore these instinctive responses. Skilled interviewers pay attention to these feelings and decide whether these intangible factors are truly job related.

Additional Tips for Evaluating Candidates

- Weigh negatives more heavily than positives.
- Evaluate the likelihood of flexibility and the ability to adjust to change.
- Watch for strong feelings and beliefs. They often suggest rigidity and intolerance.
- Note where their emphasis is. Customer-oriented people talk about service and interpersonal relationships; task-oriented individuals focus on duties. Burned-out folks frequently use the word "stress", and they sigh a lot.
- Do not leap to conclusions during the initial phase of the meeting.

HOW TO GET CANDIDATES TO ACCEPT JOB OFFERS

Remember that the better the candidates, the more competition there is for their services. When you interview outstanding candidates, you find that they are interviewing you and your organization. They know that you want them, but do they want you?

Here are some practical tips to help sell the job:

- Send a map and directions for getting to the interview site. Include a copy of the position description. This displays a caring attitude.
- Provide a tour of your facilities. Show off the pleasant environment, efficient arrangements, modern equipment, and access to other departments and facilities. Point out that the personnel smile a lot and do not seem harassed.
- Introduce the candidate to one or two key people (but do not overdo this).
- Create a positive vision in the candidate's mind by matching what the job offers with what you have learned the candidate wants. Focus on any special features that are attractive to the person.
- If the person has shown a special interest (eg, in research or teaching), discuss what you have to offer. Create a positive picture of the daily routine in the candidate's mind.
- Do not forget spouses. Frequently they cast the deciding vote. It's wise to have them sit in on part of the meeting. How do they feel about the community and the job opportunity? Are they, too, looking for new employment? If so, what can you offer or suggest?
- Answer questions completely and honestly. Do not conceal negative aspects of the job. Refer to these aspects as challenges. On the other hand, do not dwell on the bad features or say that it has been difficult to keep people in that slot.
- Avoid salary negotiations until you make an offer. If the person expects more money, keep the door open. Say that you will give more thought to it and report back.
- If you have a mentoring program, mention that to candidates. The availability of such programs is an attractive feature to some candidates.

Special Incentives

In addition to cash bonuses, noncash hiring incentives include relocation packages, tuition reimbursement, paid employee training, flextime, and transportation reimbursement.

CLOSING THE INTERVIEW

Ask for the person's level of interest (eg, "Although neither of us can make a decision at this point, what's your level of interest?"). Explore doubts or reservations. If the person is noncommittal but is a good candidate, set a deadline for an answer.

State when the selection decision will be made and how you will notify the person. Make certain that you have the person's current phone number and address.

Take the candidate to the next interviewer, to another on-site destination, or to the exit closest to their transportation as appropriate. Thank the candidate for coming.

POSTINTERVIEW ACTIVITIES

Writing and Organizing Your Report

Eyeballing rough notes is not the preferred approach. Match your findings with a written list of criteria you had established. Review information from other sources (eg, application form, resume, and references). If you must use subjective words (eg, cocky, pompous, abrasive, personable, ideal, immature, practical, or sarcastic), describe what they said or did that led you to those impressions.

Prepare a brief summary of the candidates' strengths and weaknesses. You may want to use a numerical weighing system to evaluate the candidate's major assets and liabilities.

If multiple interviewers participate, compare notes with them. Subsequent meetings with the more promising candidates are often desirable.

Notification and Medical Testing

Do not wait too long before offering the job (24 hours is usually too short and a month is too long). For jobs for which there are few candidates and many competitors, you must make a decision immediately. Notify your top choice first, and wait for that person's response before notifying the others.

The job offer is usually made in a formal letter from your human resources department. It may be preceded by a phone call. The candidate should be told how much time he or she has to respond.

Under the ADA, once an employer has made a conditional job offer, the organization is free to ask the applicant to undergo medical tests.

GETTING REFERENCES

An employee may fail in one position but star in another, so get references from more than one source. Obviously the job that most resembles the one being offered is the most important.

Previous immediate supervisors are much better sources of information than are senior managers or human resource departments. Because of the fear of litigation, many employers limit responses to dates of employment or confirm data supplied by the applicants. These barriers are not insurmountable. Most reference sources will talk to you if you use the right approach.

Get permission. The application form should contain language whereby applicants grant permission to contact former employers. If not, get written permission at the time of the interview. Most currently employed people won't oblige. Abide by that. However, if that person turns out to be the best candidate, make the job offer contingent upon receiving a satisfactory reference from his or her employer. Another strategy is to ask for a copy of the candidate's last performance appraisal in lieu of the reference.

How To Conduct a Telephone Reference Check

- Make sure you have permission to make the calls.
- Make the calls yourself. Colleagues are more likely to talk to you than to some clerk.
- Ask if this is a good time and place to talk. The person may want to go to another site for more privacy or may want you to call back later.
- Begin by verifying the information provided by the applicant. If the person states that it's against company policy to furnish such information, respond by asking if an exception can be made because the lack of the information probably will exclude the candidate from further consideration. If that does not work, ask to speak to someone at a higher management level.
- Use some of the same questions you asked the candidate. This has the added advantage of evaluating the veracity of the applicant.
- Follow with more sensitive questions after assuring the respondent that the information will not be revealed to the applicant.
- Be sensitive as to HOW respondents talk about the employee. Are they enthusiastic or brief and guarded?

NOTES

1. B. Smart, *The Smart Interviewer* (New York: Wiley, 1989), vii.

2. L.S. Goldzimer, *"I'm First": Your Customer's Message to You* (New York: Rawson, 1989), 109.

3. C.T. Dortch, "Job-Person match," *Personnel Journal 68* (1989): 46.

RECOMMENDED READING

P. Anderson and M.A. Pulich, "Team-Based Participation in the Hiring Process," *Health Care Supervisor 15,* no. 4 (1997): 69–76.

D. Scotto, "Inventive Strategies for Laboratory Recruitment," *Medical Laboratory Observer 29,* no. 7 (1997):50–59.

W.S. Swan, *How To Pick the Right People* (New York: John Wiley & Sons, 1989).

K.J. Yate, *Hiring the Best,* 3d ed. (Holbrook, MA: M.A. Adams Inc., 1987).

"Labor News Briefs," *HRFocus 74,* no. 10 (1997): S1–16.

Chapter 8

Orientation and Training of New Employees

- objectives of an orientation program
- 10 important assumptions
- hospital orientation programs
- needs assessment for departmental programs
- preparations for the arrival of new orientees
- the welcome wagon
- "nuts and bolts" talks
- departmental values
- show and tell
- meeting colleagues
- help from your specialists
- training the new employee

At no other time is there a better opportunity to open lines of communication with new hires. They are free from the distortions of peer groups. They haven't yet formed strong opinions about the job, company, or boss. They are eager to please.[1]

The design of an orientation program has three considerations. The first is to nudge new employees toward better customer service. The second is to regard the orientees as our clients, since we provide them with our training services. The third is to infuse the latest concepts of quality improvement and cost containment. In this chapter we'll concentrate on the first two objectives. Our vision and mission is to help trainees see their jobs as contributions to the organization's total impact on the customer and to start them out on their holy grail.

OBJECTIVES OF AN ORIENTATION PROGRAM

On the first day, make newcomers feel like honored guests. By the second week make them feel like family.

77

We want to get our new employees off on the right foot, and they're most impressionable when they first come on board. The following objectives help you plan your program:

- To create a favorable impression of the organization, the department, and you.
- To fix responsibilities and accountabilities. Your expectations of their performance must be crystal clear.
- To ensure that they learn everything needed to perform their work.
- To provide full information on pay, benefits, working ambiance, and conditions of employment. This includes opportunities for training and advancement.
- To describe policies, rules, and regulations in detail.
- To provide checklists of tasks to ensure that all topics in the orientation process are covered.
- To encourage feedback on the effectiveness of the orientation program.
- To emphasize the importance of teamwork, flexibility, adjusting to change, and innovativeness.
- To satisfy their need to be accepted by coworkers and to establish rapport through collegial communication.
- To provide initial experiences that result in early successes. This creates a sense of self-value, instills confidence, and promotes positive attitudes. Most athletic coaches like to begin their season against weaker teams for that same reason.
- To identify the kinds of customers and to emphasize the importance of satisfying them.
- To initiate the newcomers into the rituals and practices of your work group and your quality improvement program. These rituals and practices may include activities such as team project completion celebrations, customer attendance at staff meetings, group "brag sessions," and ceremonies for things such as special achievements, perfect attendance, and promotions or role changes.

TEN IMPORTANT ASSUMPTIONS

The Corning glass works designed a new orientation system based on the following 10 assumptions[2]:

1. Early impressions last.
2. The first 90 days are crucial.
3. Orientation starts before the trainees arrive (preparations).

4. Day 1 is crucial.
5. The new employee is responsible for learning.
6. Teaching the basics comes first.
7. New employees should understand the total company.
8. Information is timed to employees' needs.
9. Informational overload must be avoided.
10. Orientation doesn't work unless the employee's supervisor is involved.

HOSPITAL ORIENTATION PROGRAMS

New employees are usually enrolled in a hospital orientation program that is directed by the educational or human resources department. Traditionally these programs start with the history, mission, and core values of the organization. Other important topics include information about fires, safety, infection control, and resuscitation procedures.

However, new employees prefer to hear about things that help them adjust to their new roles. These include when they get paid, where they park their cars, when the snack bar opens, and how they request educational support and other benefits. Often, orientees are dozing off by the time the presenter gets to those topics.

NEEDS ASSESSMENT FOR DEPARTMENTAL PROGRAMS

The conceptualization of a departmental program starts with an analysis of what is needed by the new arrivals. The assessments consider future and current requirements. The planning and the implementation phases are often slighted because at the time that the new folks come on board, the department is usually understaffed.

New employees arrive loaded with questions. Planning is helped by addressing the following questions before they are articulated by the new people.

- Where is my workstation, the cafeteria, restrooms, parking area?
- What are my duties?
- How do I answer the phone, get supplies, operate the computer and all those other gadgets?
- How will I know if I'm doing satisfactory work?
- Why do I have to do these things?
- Why do we do it that way?
- When do I come and go? When is payday? When does my probationary period end? When do we get the daily work breaks and how long are they?
- To whom do I report? Who will answer my questions, evaluate my work, or be my friend?

PREPARATIONS FOR THE ARRIVAL OF NEW ORIENTEES

Tips for Preparing for the Arrival of New Employees

- Send a letter of welcome. Include verification of date, time, and place of reporting, the first day's agenda, and any special instructions or suggestions, such as what they should bring or wear.
- Arrange your schedule so you can devote most of the first day to the orientee.
- Review the orientation and training checkoff lists.
- Prepare an agenda for the first week.
- Prepare an orientation packet that includes:
  1. statement of departmental vision, mission, values, and goals
  2. department organization chart
  3. position description and work standards of the job
  4. personnel policy and procedures manual
  5. orientation and training schedules
  6. checklists and program evaluation forms
  7. performance appraisal forms
  8. probationary evaluation form, if it's not the same as the performance appraisal form
  9. safety, infection control, and quality assurance policies, procedures, and rules
  10. names, titles, and locations of trainers
  11. key telephone numbers or condensed telephone directory

THE FIRST DAY—THE WELCOME WAGON

New employees usually report first to the human resources department. Get off to a good start by meeting your new people there. Greet them as you would welcome visiting friends. Have a well-prepared speech and deliver it with enthusiasm. For example:

> One reason we selected each of you is that you have shown the kind of attitude we always look for. As you know, the major goal of this position is to meet our customers' expectations. Our customers include patients, the patient's families and visitors, clinicians and other care providers, third party payers, teammates, students and trainees, and departments served by us.

> I know that you understand the importance of customer service, and you will soon learn how we want you to deliver it. You're obviously not allergic to work or to change, and in your past jobs you showed the flexibility and innovativeness we like.

Finally, review the agenda of the orientation program and give the new employee his or her orientation packet.

"NUTS AND BOLTS" TALKS

On the second day, ask how the first day went. Then establish a dialogue based on the following:

- The mission, corporate values, and goals of the organization (which they probably were not tuned into during the hospital orientation phase).
  Explain how the department's functions focus on supporting the corporate mission, goal, and core value statements.
- The employee's position description and performance standards.
  Refer to these documents as contracts that must be honored. Tell them what behavior is rewarded and what is unacceptable.
- "Survival information"
  Work hours, overtime, compensatory time, vacation and sick leave policies, assigning of lockers, and completion of personnel data.
- How performance is evaluated and reported.
- Explanation of current managerial initiatives
  These may be reengineering, new quality improvement or cost-cutting strategy, employee empowerment, or self-directed team building.
- Description of current educational or marketing programs relating to customer-service
  For example, telephone courtesy, point-of-care testing, cost-cutting, or improvements in quality and/or turnaround time.
- Some things that you personally like and dislike
  These are not all found in formal documents. It's better to prevent what you do not like than to have to correct it after the fact. Here are some items that you may want to cover:
  1. how you like to be addressed (formally or on a first name basis)
  2. that you expect everyone to be innovative
  3. that you welcome suggestions and insist on hearing about any complaints or comments from customers. (Say "In this department we do not kill the messengers of bad tidings, we applaud them.")
  4. things that annoy you (eg, tardiness, abuse of sick leave, people who are chronically late for meetings, untidy clothes, or verbal expressions such as, "That's not in my position description" or "I only work here," or comments that suggest that customers get in the way, such as "I wish those relatives would stop making all those nuisance calls.")

- Explain how each job has a chain-reaction effect on other staffers' ability to do their jobs and therefore eventually affects customers.
- Repeat the list of internal and external customers and the importance of customer satisfaction. Remind them how hard your unit worked to attract customers and how important it is to keep them. Explain how poor service creates stress for both parties and how they'll gain psychological benefits when they treat customers properly. If true, state, "Your pay and advancement will depend on how well customers are served."
- Tell them that you are interested more in the development of their potential than in their immediate output.

Chip Bell[3] offers the following four keys to exceeding customer expectations. Share them now with your new people:

1. Be a risk taker. Be willing to make tough decisions and take action for customers that may be against policies or rules provided they are legal, moral, and ethical and represent your best judgment.
2. Be friendly.
3. Be sincere.
4. Relax and have fun.

MAJOR DEPARTMENTAL VALUES

The following is a list of values that should be shared with all new employees.

- Honesty—not concealing mistakes or blaming others; not calling in sick when you're not
- Integrity—doing what you promise to do
- Pride—demonstrating pride in your appearance and performance, maintaining a tidy workstation
- Loyalty—putting in an honest day's work and not bad mouthing management
- Courtesy—knocking on a patient's door before entering, addressing people by their formal names, not calling them "honey" or "dearie"
- Work ethic—showing up on time, not abusing breaks or calling in sick when you're not ill
- Customer service—going the extra mile, listening patiently, a "can-do" attitude

SHOW AND TELL

Avoid informational overload. Do not try to cover everything during a single tour of the premises—that's too confusing.

- Point out the physical facilities. Do not stop repeatedly to introduce all of the personnel. Do this later when people are less busy. Show them where the supplies are kept, reports are filed, and paper copies are made.
- On a subsequent tour, follow the sequences of various work flows. For example, trace a test request from its point of origin to the physician's receipt of the results. Instruct the indoctrinees to diagram these work flows. Show how customer service is affected by glitches in any step of these work flows.
- Devote one session to a discussion of budgets, charges, and costs. Show orientees how charges appear on patients' bills and how employees can respond to customers' questions about them.
- Direct attention to the communication systems, and demonstrate their use. Stress the importance of proper telephone etiquette. Include the intercom, bulletin boards, mailboxes, and message centers. Point out where schedules for work, off-duty assignments, and vacations are posted. Show them how the different shifts communicate with each other. Demonstrate how photocopying and filing are done.
- Discuss the location and use of safety equipment later.

After the tours have been completed, ask the new people to diagram the topography of the department. This should include the labeling of each room. Later, have them draw more detailed diagrams of the room(s) to which they are assigned and to locate each workstation and major piece of equipment on these drawings.

MEETING COLLEAGUES

We recommend that you limit the number of introductions during tours of the department. Employees do not like to be interrupted in the middle of their tasks, and their reactions (of lack of reactions) may be misinterpreted by the orientees as signs of unfriendliness. Also, the new folks get confused by all the faces, names, and titles when these are encountered in rapid succession. Make the introductions during breaks, when people are relaxed and more inclined to be amiable. Also, present newcomers at a staff meeting. Encourage them to talk about their educational and recreational interests at that time.

When you introduce someone, explain how that employee's responsibilities or interests relate to those of the newcomer. An introduction might go like this: "Joyce, I'd like you to meet Sue Smith. Sue is in charge of our main storeroom. If you can't find something there, see Sue." The new employee should meet with each senior member of the staff, preferably in his or her office.

GET HELP FROM YOUR SPECIALISTS

In medium to large departments, certain staff members have special expertise or responsibilities that make them better qualified to cover certain topics. In the absence of these specialists, you are responsible for this training.

Trainer or Educational Coordinator

If you delegate training, have the new employee meet the trainer early in the orientation program. Pick trainers with care. Prerequisites include teaching ability, professional or technical expertise, sufficient time, willingness, and loads of enthusiasm. Trainers should be aware of the qualifications and experience of the indoctrinees so they can tailor the training to the particular needs of each individual.

Give trainees folders in which to keep their continuing educational records. Most departments have requirements for the number of educational hours required for each job category. Show the trainees how to keep these records, and remind them that it is their responsibility to do so.

Safety Coordinator

Some departments have a safety coordinator who shows new hires the location and proper use of safety equipment and reviews safety policies and regulations. New people often have questions about the dangers of hepatitis, acquired immunodeficiency syndrome (AIDS), and other infectious diseases. The safety expert can allay these fears while explaining the best way to minimize these dangers. When discussing AIDS, the expert also warns against disclosure of confidential information.

Quality Assurance or Quality Improvement Coordinator

This person may be the chair or the recorder for the quality assurance committee. The coordinator may limit the discussion to the global aspects of the program, leaving specific quality control details for the orientee's immediate supervisor to cover.

Mentors and "Buddies"

Mentors are experienced people who willingly share their wisdom or political clout with their proteges. They are unofficial advisors, supporters, and confidants. Encourage new employees to find and to establish alliances with those individuals who go out of their way to please customers. In some departments the "buddy system" is used. Each new arrival is assigned to an experienced employee in the same work section.

> *When new employees complete their orientation, hold a simple celebration.*

TRAINING THE NEW EMPLOYEE

The triple approach to success in customer satisfaction is train—train—train. We certainly believe this because we devote much of this book to that subject. Training is especially important during and immediately following the orientation

---

Exhibit 8–1 Form for Evaluating Orientation Program

Check the items with which you agree:

1. On the first day, I was welcomed with enthusiasm.
2. By the end of the first week, I knew I had been accepted by the team.
3. My immediate supervisor spent a lot of time with me.
4. The entire program was well organized.
5. Everyone was patient and encouraging.
6. I quickly learned what was expected of me and how to do my job.
7. The new employee handbook (packet of information) is very helpful.
8. They made it easy and relatively painless to learn about important policies and rules.
9. My fears of infection and other safety factors were alleviated quickly.
10. I was made to feel important.
11. I received a lot more praise than criticism. When my work had to be corrected, they always explained why.
12. During the first few days, I met not only my colleagues but also important people in other departments.
13. I now understand how my job fits into the big picture of what our organization is all about.
14. I know how the communications systems work and how to make full use of them.
15. I had plenty of opportunities to ask questions and express my opinions.
16. I am familiar with the salary and benefits package and how performance is evaluated.
17. I understand my role in the quality improvement program.

phase because new hires are most open to learning at these times. Initiate good work habits, behavior, ethics, and attitudes before bad ones develop.

Assign your best people to do your training. It's a long-term investment that pays off quickly.

Training during the orientation phase must be tailored to each orientee's need, and that depends on his or her previous education and experience. At this juncture, list all the skills necessary to handle the job, and prepare checkoff lists of tasks to be learned. Divide the individual tasks or responsibilities into those that can be learned on the job, those that must be taught formally, and those that can be self-taught. Prepare a rough timetable for achieving the training goals.

At the completion of the formal orientation/training program, get feedback from each participant on the value of the program. See Exhibit 8–1 for example. Get written or verbal comments from each person who helped with the training.

NOTES

1. W.B. Werther Jr., *Dear Boss* (New York, NY: Meadowbrook, 1989), 189.
2. "Ideas & Trends in Personnel," *Human Resources Management Issue 174* (July 26, 1988).
3. C. Bell, *Customers as Partners: Building Relationships That Last* (San Francisco, CA: Barrett-Koehler, 1994), 86.

RECOMMENDED READING

D. Arthur, *Recruiting, Interviewing, Selecting, & Orienting New Employees* (New York, NY: AMACOM, 1986).

C.M. Cadwell, *New Employee Orientation* (Los Altos, CA: Crisp Publishers, 1988).

A. Haggard, *Hospital Orientation Handbook* (Gaithersburg, MD: Aspen Publishers, Inc. 1984).

Chapter 9

Team Building

- benefits of and disadvantages of teams
- characteristics of effective teams
- why teams fail
- team dynamics
- stages in team maturation
- group norms
- importance of rituals and status symbols
- responsibilities of team leaders
- leadership style
- characteristics of good team leaders
- when you inherit a team
- rewards for teams

As enterprises become more complex, they depend more on the effectiveness of group efforts and cross-functional activities. In health care few individuals work as solo practitioners anymore. For example, in the old days, an emergency department (formerly called emergency room) was staffed by a physician and a few nurses and aides. Now it features dozens of professionals and technicians with diverse skills and experience who work as a team to save lives.

Various health care institutions are setting up satellite facilities, developing new services, implementing changes to comply with legal and other mandated requirements, and establishing comprehensive quality improvement programs. In the new health care paradigm, cross-functional teams regularly span departmental boundaries, and the payers become senior partners of a health care team.

A team is a group of people who are committed to achieving common objectives. An effective team has members who work well together, enjoy doing so, and produce high-quality outcomes. Teams have become the utility vehicles of today's organizations.

BENEFITS OF TEAMS

Health care institutions now use teams to handle virtually any task or problem. They recognize the following benefits of teams:

- Greater total expertise. Although team development is not a panacea, it does refine a group's skills and increase its ability to solve problems. Teams are especially useful when they deal with procedures, relationships, quality, productivity, and problem solving.
- Synergy. Total results are greater through team effort than achieved by members acting independently.
- Higher morale. The motivational needs of affiliation, achievement, and control are satisfied.
- Greater personnel retention. Employees are less prone to leave when they are members of teams.
- Increased flexibility. There is less dependence on individuals. Services do not suffer when one member of a team is missing.

DISADVANTAGES OF TEAMS

Health care institutions should also be aware of the disadvantages of team work:

- Teams are not always needed. There are many situations that can be handled as well or better by individuals. Specialists handle specific situations faster, and without consulting others or getting the approval of other members of a work group. Attempts to introduce work teams in departments where there are no interdependencies are usually a waste of time and effort. However, in most health care units, people do depend on one another.
- Team building requires start-up time.
- Teams may become bureaucratic. When an enthusiastic task force turns into a standing committee, the topics often become repetitious and boring.
- When quick action is needed, someone must take charge and get things rolling. When someone yells "fire," it's not the time to call a meeting.

CHARACTERISTICS OF EFFECTIVE TEAMS

An effective team:

- is not limited to a departmental work group. Its members may include vendors, customers, people from other departments, and key supportive personnel.

- possesses all the necessary knowledge, skill, and experience required to get the job done.
- searches for excellence in quality, productivity, and customer service. It removes factors that inhibit quality performance.
- welcomes innovation, new services, and new techniques.
- is democratic—there's an absence of rank or formal authority. It has a leader who refers to his or her coworkers as associates, colleagues, or teammates, not as subordinates.
- has great multidirectional communication. It displays openness and candor.
- is inspired by a vision of what it is trying to accomplish. Its goals are clear, and all members aim for the same goals.
- actively constructs formal and informal networks that include people who can help it.
- has power based not on formal authority but on the team's credibility.
- has members who trust each other and are sensitive to each other's needs. They understand their roles, responsibilities, and degrees of authority.
- reduces conflict with other teams or non-team employees through collaboration, coordination, and cooperation.
- adheres to ethical and moral considerations.
- is optimistic and has fun.

WHY TEAMS FAIL

There are many reasons why teams can fail. Unrealistic mandates from upper management and the lack of purpose and direction are major factors. Poor leadership is the most common problem. This may be the fault of the person to whom the team reports or the unwillingness of any team member to assume a leadership role. Reviews of failed teams almost always reveal that there was a breakdown in communication.

Here are some other causes:

- Players with higher status, greater knowledge, or more aggressiveness dominate other members of the team. Other problem members are the pessimists, negativists, obstructionists, prima donnas, and goof-offs.
- Lack of support (eg, insufficient resources or time, understaffing, or unpleasant work environments).
- Internal politics, hidden agendas, conformity pressures, favoritism, and excessive paperwork.
- Some teams develop into cliques that attempt to isolate the group from the rest of the organization.

- Competition among team individuals for promotions, merit raises, recognition, and access to superiors can be destructive.
- Unrealistic expectations can result in discouragement when there are setbacks.
- Disapproval or lack of action on suggestions or recommendations of the team to upper management or failure of a team to respond to the ideas of its individual members quickly quenches enthusiasm.
- Lack of progress, failure to meet deadlines, setbacks, and bad results may be disheartening.

TEAM DYNAMICS

Team dynamics refer to interactive forces brought to bear by individuals singly or collectively in a group activity. The success of group dynamics depends largely on how willing team leaders are to share authority, responsibility, information, and resources. Sharing is what participative management is all about.

Stages in Team Maturation

Stage 1: Confusion.

This represents the transition from a group of individuals to a team. Participation is hesitant as members wonder what is expected of them. Team members may show suspicion, fear, anxiety, and low productivity.

Stage 2: Dissatisfaction.

Some members display negativity, hostility, bickering, or outright resistance. Infighting, defensiveness, and competition are common. Low productivity persists.

Stage 3: Resolution.

If the team is to be successful, group norms and roles emerge. Dissatisfaction and conflict diminish, and a sense of cohesiveness develops. Dependence on formal leaders is decreased. This cohesion is achieved when individuals feel responsible for the success of the team. There is now moderate productivity.

Stage 4: Maturation.

Productivity is high and performance smooth. Members have developed insight into personal and collective processes. Team members have learned how to resolve their differences and give each other constructive feedback. All this takes time, and progress is up and down, not in a straight line. Mature teams change membership. Moreover, priorities change, and a host of other variables constantly shift the nature and makeup of the teams.

Group Norms

Group norms may be functional or dysfunctional. A functional form is present when team members defend their team and their organization. A dysfunctional form develops when members feel that their organization is taking advantage of them, and they believe that teams are being assembled only to squeeze more work out of them.

In some dysfunctional forms, members struggle so hard to avoid conflict that team decisions suffer. Some conflict is essential to effective problem solving. Cohesion does not mean the absence of differences of opinion, arguments, or disagreements. Members of great teams can frequently be heard debating heatedly among themselves.

At the Marine Corps boot camp on Parris Island, drill instructors turn undisciplined men and women into confident leaders. Their group norms are very high. The instructors teach a few key lessons and model the behavior they want. Those key lessons are:

- Tell the truth.
- Do your best, no matter how trivial the task.
- Choose the difficult right over the easy wrong.
- Look out for the group before you look out for yourself.
- Don't whine or make excuses.
- Judge others by their actions, not their race.
- Don't use "I" or "me."[1]

IMPORTANCE OF RITUALS AND STATUS SYMBOLS

Rituals are important to team success. Positive rituals include expressions of appreciation (eg, trophies, awards, parties, picnics, and special dinners). A negative ritual is the hazing or taunting of new employees. Even some positive rituals may change their polarity. For example, the employee of the month award is regarded with scorn when undeserving candidates are selected or deserving ones are overlooked.

Team status symbols can also be important. Take uniforms for instance. For years the long, white hospital coat was worn only by attending physicians and senior house staff members. That is no longer the case. In many units the green scrub suit complete with stethoscope has become a uniform of choice of caregivers at all levels. The time-honored nurse's cap has all but disappeared. How sad for us old-timers!

TEAM LEADERSHIP

"A team is like a wheel in which each member is a spoke. It's the team leader's responsibility to have enough spokes and to keep the spokes the same length." [2]

Many health care managers are unwilling or unable to adopt the concept of the self-directed team or even to take measures to encourage team efforts. Health care leaders must develop dual professional and supervisory skills. Team players must be given opportunities to develop their professional or technical skills (task skills) and skills that pull teams together. The five major responsibilities of team leaders are discussed below:

1. Plan. Team leaders must know how to make their team effective and efficient—to work smart. This can't be accomplished without planning. Managers, in concert with their team members, should answer the following questions:
   - What do our customers want or need?
   - What additional information do we need?
   - What past successes have we had in meeting these wants and needs?
   - What are our strengths, and what needs improving?
   - What new objectives and strategies do we need?
   - How can we do it faster or at less cost?
   - What are the barriers, and how can they be eliminated?
   - Should we find out how others are doing it?
2. Develop people. Every work team player, like members of an athletic team, has certain competencies plus the ability to develop more. After structuring position descriptions and performance standards, team leaders select the best people for the team, then orient, educate, train, coach, and motivate them. Each of these responsibilities is covered in more depth in other chapters.
   When a team is getting started, ask each person to share a one-word characteristic they want in a teammate, and to relate a scenario when someone had that trait or lacked that trait. The story fleshes out the characteristic they want. If everyone shares a trait they value and the way it has come up in the past, the group will develop useful ground rules.

> *Building a team is like converting a group
> of musicians into an orchestra.*

3. Build the Team. Team building involves developing relationships, communicating, holding meetings, and interacting on a daily basis. Leaders must create an ambiance that supports and rewards creativity, openness, fairness, trust, mutual respect, and a commitment to safety and health. There must also be opportunities for career growth.

   Evaluate your team-building ability by taking the quiz shown in Exhibit 9–1.

4. Lead the team. With the help of the other team members, the leaders prepare mission statements, set goals, develop strategies and plans, design or improve work processes, facilitate, coordinate, and troubleshoot.

Example of a Simple Departmental Mission Statement

Our department is committed to providing quality care at low cost to inpatients and outpatients. Staff members maintain their expertise through continuing education and development.

Leaders must satisfy the affiliation needs of each team member. All employees want to be accepted by their colleagues. Leaders also encourage team members to train and coach each other.

5. Coordinate. The team or its individual members often participate in cross-functional activities. Team leaders must coordinate these activities with other departments and services. Leaders must also be ready to serve as followers in some interdepartmental task forces, committees, and focus groups. Typical topics relate to new services, safety, quality management, customer satisfaction, and employee morale.

LEADERSHIP STYLE

The ideal leadership style for team building is based on the perception that personal power is having power with, not over, people. Situational leadership fits that perception. When new employees join a team, the leader uses a directive (paternalistic) style. He or she tells the employees what to do, shows how to do it, explains why the work is important, and relates how it fits into the big picture.

Exhibit 9–1 Rate Yourself as a Team Builder

—My teammates help each other and share advice.

—My team functions well when I am not around.

—I hire people who may be able to perform some tasks better than I can.

—I do not try to hire people who are just like me.

—Each member of my team learns at least one new skill every year. Each one is working on a new skill now.

—Each member of my team makes at least one suggestion every month.

—I encourage differences of opinion and suggestions for improvement.

—We resolve rather than avoid conflict and problems.

—Every member of my team can name all our external and internal customers.

—Every member of my team, in his or her own words, can state the mission of our organization.

—Every member of my team can describe how our quality management program has affected our service.

—Every member of my team follows safety procedures.

—We prefer team over individual competition.

—Every member of my team feels valued and accepted.

—Our team has a "can do" attitude. We underpromise and overproduce.

—Our team has a reputation for cooperating with other teams and individuals.

—I would describe our team attitude as one of optimism and enthusiasm. Negativism and complaining are rare.

Knowing that workers at this stage are frightened, insecure, and stressed, team leaders are patient and highly supportive at this time. Blanchard and Tager[3] warn against the "leave alone-zap" style, in which inexperienced workers are not given enough direction and then are zapped when they make mistakes.

As employees develop confidence in their ability, the leaders back off, give them more latitude, and encourage them to solve their own problems. Some supervisors fail to move on from the initial show-and-tell stage to one that expresses confidence in their employees. The result is that employees remain dependent on their leaders or are irritated by the continued spoon feeding. Parents encounter the same difficulty when they continue to treat adolescents as children. Most employees can advance to a self-confidence level or even to a consultative stage in which they participate actively in planning, decision making, and problem solving.

The delegative style, in which team members assume some or many supervisory responsibilities, is appropriate for some team members. In this participative paradigm, the team leader serves as a facilitator and moderator rather than as a manager. Autonomous (self-directed) teams feature a democratic system in which there are no supervisors or first-line managers. The team members select a group leader, or leadership is rotated. Characteristics of good team leaders are listed in Chapter 11.

WHEN YOU INHERIT A TEAM

You may be reassigned to lead a new team, promoted to a leadership role, or come in as an outsider. If you have been a member of a team, you must make the adjustments discussed in Chapter 1. If you worked previously with the group in a cross-functional activity, put aside old prejudices and stereotypes. Overlook previous areas of friction or irritation.

If you are new to the organization, get as much information as you can about the history, reputation, culture, and rituals of your new employer. Check the leadership style of the previous group leader. How had the group members responded? How effective was that style? You can learn about this from the person to whom you report, and from team members. Hold group meetings to discuss mission, strategy, values, plans, your leadership style, and your previous experience.

Study the position descriptions and performance reviews of each employee, and hold individual meetings with team members. Find out as much as you can about their aspirations, complaints, and suggestions and about how you can make better use of their services. Prepare an inventory chart of the team's skills.

TEAM REWARDS

The focus on teams is changing the way organizations reward people. Traditional reward systems encourage individual achievement. When traditional merit pay systems are in place, team cooperation often suffers. Individual rewards may cause competing employees to withhold information, undermine peers, and hamper cooperation. On the other hand, in the absence of individual rewards, there is bound to be some resentment among the high performers, and the slackers have no incentive to improve. This dilemma is resolved by providing both team and individual rewards. The group recognition builds camaraderie and cooperation. Also, when employees know that their performance ratings are impacted by how much they show teamwork, the adverse effect of individual rewards is mitigated.

Include some of the following actions in your team reward strategy:

- Reward employees who participate in group functions such as serving on committees, problem-solving groups, or task forces.
- Recognize the entire team when goals are met.
- Arrange for a team to present its special projects to other departments or to upper management.

- Bring in donuts or pizza for the team.
- Organize a car wash day when managers wash employees' cars.
- Make special equipment or publications available.
- Thank team at a special coffee or lunch.
- Attend some of their committee or problem-solving meetings and comment favorably.
- Display pictures of the group in action.
- Broadcast congratulatory news such as completed projects, new services, favorable customer comments, or successful cost cutting.
- Spruce up the lounge and provide amenities such as a coffee maker and microwave oven.
- Take practical measures to improve communication systems, and make more information available.
- Eliminate unnecessary meetings, and reduce wasted time at all sessions.
- Delegate more authority to the team.

Note: Some of these suggestions were taken from the excellent book by Deeprose.[4]

NOTES

1. T.E. Ricks, "What We Can Learn From Them: Lessons from Parris Island," *Parade Magazine,* November 9, 1997: 4–6.
2. Keye Productivity Center, *How To Build a Better Work Team,* 2d ed. (Kansas City, MO: Keye Productivity, Center, 1991), 3.
3. M. Blanchard and M.A. Tager, *Working Well: Managing for Health and High Performance* (New York, NY: Simon & Schuster, 1985), 50.
4. D. Deeprose, *How To Recognize & Reward Employees* (New York, NY: AMACOM, 1994), 100.

RECOMMENDED READING AND LISTENING

D. Harrington-Mackin, *The Team Building Tool Kit* (New York, NY: AMACOM, 1994).

A.R. Montebello, *Work Teams That Work* (Minneapolis, MN: Best Sellers Publishers, 1994).

M. Sanborn, Team Building: *How To Motivate and Manage People* (Boulder, CO: CareerTrack Publishers, 1989), 2 audiotapes.

W. Umiker, *The Empowered Laboratory Team: A Survival Kit for Supervisors, Team Leaders, and Team Professionals* (Chicago, IL: ASCP Press, 1997).

Chapter 10

Safety and Workplace Violence

- causative factors of violence
- effect of violence on victims
- laws and standards relating to workplace violence
- responsibilities of management
- essentials of a violence control program
- eight supervisory principles for reducing violence
- bomb threats
- breaking up fights

Violence in health care institutions is escalating and is not limited to emergency departments and psychiatric units. For women, violence on the job is the number one cause of death.[1] While violence is more common in facilities located within high-crime areas, it's reported increasingly in suburban settings and rural areas.

Employers and managers share responsibility for providing a work environment that minimizes the danger of injury. Medical costs and litigation charges against medical institutions from injuries caused by or to patients and others are considerable. Expenditures for security, workers' compensation, and legal charges continue to escalate. The goal of management is to decrease the number and damage of assaults and disruptive incidents.

CAUSATIVE FACTORS OF VIOLENCE

In our multiracial, multiethnic society, we face many situations in which violence may emerge. A list of common predisposing factors is seen in Exhibit 10–1. See Exhibit 10–2 for the characteristics of violence-prone individuals.

Violent incidents often involve disgruntled or vengeful employees or former employees. These incidents are frequently the result of real or perceived maltreatment or inept management of work conflicts. The addition of just one more problem, even a minor one, may push a person over the edge.

Exhibit 10–1 Factors Predisposing to Violence

Societal factors
Easy availability of weapons
High crime rate in community
Catastrophic life events (eg, illness, accident, or death of loved ones)
Distraught or vengeful spouses or other family members

Workplace situations
Layoffs, job outplacements, mergers, reengineering, affiliations, and alliances
Series of threats of violence or aggressive incidents
Jobs that involve money, drugs, or valuable property
Working alone, especially late at night
Assignments in emergency departments or psychiatric units
Frequent harassment by coworkers or superiors
Weapons brought to work site
Interpersonal workplace conflicts
Chronic labor/management problems or disputes
Frequent grievances or stress-related worker's compensation claims filed by employees
Poorly lighted or inadequately monitored parking areas

Management deficiencies
Inept handling of work problems
Inconsistent, inequitable, or insensitive supervision
Failure to recognize and intervene early in the cycle of violence
Lack of responsiveness to violence warning signs of a potentially violent situation
Authoritarian management
Lack of staff training in violence prevention

Investigations following a violent event usually reveal that there were clearly visible warning signs that should have raised concern. Awareness of these signals is a key to violence prevention initiatives.

Overt threats of violence may be absent, but warning signs are usually present. Violent prone people often show expressions of bizarre thoughts, fixation with weapons, romantic obsession, depression, or chemical dependence. Offenders may be involved in bitter, repetitive arguments or may issue frequent accusatory memoranda. They often cease to associate with coworkers, even their old friends.

The typical profile of a violence-prone employee is that of a male military veteran who has a quick temper on a short fuse. He suffers from low self-esteem, paranoia, or depression and is a loner who resents authority. He blames cowork-

Exhibit 10–2 Characteristics of Violence-Prone Individuals

Drug or alcohol abuse
Reputation as a loner
Obsession with weapons
Involvement with racist hate groups
Always feels unjustly treated, files many grievances
Does not tolerate criticism
Low frustration tolerance level
Dramatic change in personality, behavior, or performance
History of violence toward animals, women, and others
Pattern of verbal or physical aggression (threats, intimidation, verbal abuse)
"Hair trigger" temper: kicking vending machine, fist through wall, throwing chairs
Frequent disputes with superiors over policy violations
Object of criticism or harassment from coworkers, real or perceived
Mentally disturbed, especially paranoid person who perceives injustice
Projects responsibility for problems onto others
Has made statements suggesting feelings of despair about personal or job-related matters
Is experiencing heightened stress at work or home
Obsessive behavior toward coworkers (eg, holds a grudge or has a romantic obsession)

ers, management, or someone else for any problem that arises. There is often drug or alcohol abuse, a record of criminal assault, or a fascination with weapons. The likelihood of his becoming violent accelerates if there is unresolved conflict and frustration at home or at work.

There are several common events that predispose some individuals to violence. The person may have recently undergone counseling or disciplinary action. He or she may have been passed over for promotion or is very concerned about job security. Perhaps the person encountered a series of stressful events or one major emotional shock. There may be extreme frustration or an assault on self-esteem (eg, a request for time off is denied or a customer is treated shabbily). There may have been harsh criticism, a verbal attack, or a threat of physical harm.

EFFECT OF VIOLENCE ON VICTIMS

Employers and managers must be sensitive to the effect of violence and potential danger on their employees. Victims include internal customers (eg, caregivers and students) and external customers (eg, patients, physicians, visitors, and blood donors).

After a violent event, victims and their associates are generally less productive; some may become severely depressed and seek treatment for conditions such as anxiety, insomnia, or panic attacks. Family relationships may suffer, and some individuals turn to alcohol or drugs. There are often expressions of rage at employers or managers for failing to protect them. Injured employees may seek to recover lost wages and medical expenses through worker's compensation rather than by suing. They're protected by law from being discharged because they sued their employers.[2]

LAWS AND STANDARDS RELATING TO WORKPLACE VIOLENCE

The Occupational Safety and Health Act (OSHA) has long held that well-informed workers are at less risk than those who are unaware of the potential dangers. Unfortunately training is often the most overlooked part of compliance with OSHA standards. The General Duty Clause of the new OSHA regulations includes many guidelines[3]:

When an employee injures another person, his or her employer may be liable under the doctrine of respondent superior. State and federal courts charge employers with the responsibility to ensure a safe, nonviolent work environment. Simultaneously, employers must not violate the individual rights of employees. These rights include the right of privacy and equal opportunities as provided by the Americans with Disabilities Act.[4]

The Joint Commission on Accreditation of Healthcare Organizations required in 1995 that all hospitals conduct security assessments and provide personnel with training in management of workplace violence.[5]

RESPONSIBILITIES OF MANAGEMENT

Employers must make every effort to avoid hiring individuals who pose risks to employees and customers. When an employer becomes aware of a dangerous employee, that employer has a duty to investigate and sometimes to discharge the employee.

While the expense of security measures can be considerable, the lack of such precautions can be much more costly. Besides financial costs, there are many other consequences of frequent violent episodes. These additional consequences include a negative impact on employee attendance, morale, personnel retention, and recruitment.

Employees are told whom to contact—preferably through a hotline—and are provided with a step-by-step protocol in the event of real or perceived violent behavior or threats.

ESSENTIALS OF A VIOLENCE CONTROL PROGRAM

Significant Policies

Employer responsibility requires policies, procedures, and protocols that foster workplace harmony and minimize the potential for violence. There must be vigorous implementation of these measures.

An effective initiative starts with a statement of zero tolerance for violence and harassment. This statement includes descriptions of prohibitive behavior (eg, banning the use of controlled substances on the job and carrying weapons on the premises). The delineation of possible scenarios of workplace violence is highly recommended.

Supervisors must understand the reasons behind any policies relating to violence control and respond effectively to situations that require intervention. Policies should include the following:

- Conduct as part of formal performance evaluation
- Alcohol and drug policy
- Comprehensive disciplinary and employment termination policies
- When and how workplace searches for drugs or weapons are conducted
- Accommodations for employees with mental and other kinds of impairments
- Proper use of restraints of violent patients and others

Improved Screening of Job Candidates

To help eliminate candidates who have histories of workplace violence, the screening process may include:

- pre-employment psychological testing;
- background investigation, especially criminal convictions;
- reference checks (A previous employer has an obligation to inform a prospective employer of any violent tendencies of the employee in question if there is a substantial likelihood of recurrence); and
- drug testing.

Education and Training of Supervisors and Workers

Supervisors and workers should be familiar with safety rules and procedures. Employers must:

- train interviewers on how to recognize potential troublemakers during employment interviews.

- teach communication skills that help prevent aggression.
- teach managers and supervisors how to recognize the victims of domestic violence.
- describe how their employee assistance program (EAP) or alternative employee support programs function, when and how to refer employees, and how to handle employees during and after treatment.
- provide periodic staff training and retraining in:
  1. prevention and control of violence,
  2. how to recognize early warning signs of potential violence,
  3. conflict resolution and deescalation techniques,
  4. behavioral modification,
  5. self-preservation techniques and how to protect bystanders, and
  6. use of telephone number "*57" or alternative system to trace phone calls from harassers or callers who report bomb threats.

Improved Communication

Management is expected to:

- determine the need or effectiveness of safety improvement by getting accurate base-line data, setting precise goals, providing ongoing feedback, and rewarding success.
- establish a hotline and a confidential procedure for reporting threats, intimidation, belligerence, and other inappropriate workplace behavior. The hotline can also be used to allow disgruntled people to complain.
- devise special forms and reporting mechanisms for violent incidents.
- improve collaboration between the institution's security personnel and community law enforcement agencies similar to working arrangements with fire departments.
- hold crisis aftermath sessions.

Modify Environmental Factors That Affect Susceptibility to Violence

To enhance safety, management can:

- install bulletproof glass, metal detectors, alarm systems, surveillance cameras, and escape doors in high-risk areas such as the emergency department.
- improve lighting in parking areas and provide security escorts for departing employees.
- provide security for threatened individuals, especially for victims of domestic violence.

- design identification badges that are easier to read and enforce their usage.
- identify and flag charts of violent and suicidal patients.
- make available a telephone system for alerting police when a bomb threat is received.
- improve availability of EAPs or counseling referral procedures.
- form violence response teams to intervene in cases of violence or threats of violence.
- in the case of battered women, employers can provide photographs of the batterers to security officers, install a panic button at employee workstations, and provide personal escorts. EAPs should include therapists specially trained in the treatment of domestic violence victims.

EIGHT SUPERVISORY PRINCIPLES FOR REDUCING WORKPLACE VIOLENCE

The following rules can help supervisors reduce workplace violence:

1. Avoid hiring problem people. Prior to interviewing job applicants, prepare a list of questions that elicit a tendency toward violence. Here are a few examples:
   - What kinds of people do you find it difficult to get along with? How do you manage to get along with these people?
   - When was the last time you became angry at work? What caused it and how did you react?
   - What was the most difficult situation you faced at work? What feelings did you have and how did you react to them?
   - What kinds of things did your boss or fellow workers do that you disliked?
2. Treat employees with dignity and respect. The administration and management of a health care institution should model behavior that encourages trust, helps open communication, and promotes loyalty.
3. Maintain open communication. Encourage people to say what is on their minds by using open-ended questions such as "Jess, what is it that's troubling you?" Listen and respond with empathy and sensitivity to employee concerns and grievances.
   Take the initiative in pointing out to superiors potential problems and in recommending specific additional security measures. Participate in risk management programs, labor-management discussions, and meetings of safety committees.
4. Educate your staff. Train people to recognize symptoms of potential violence, and encourage them to report threats or acts of violence. Assure them

that their names will be kept confidential to prevent reprisals. Articulate your expectations of self-control on the job, and make certain that employees know what behavior you expect and what you will not tolerate.

5. Be alert for potential situational and behavioral problems. Effective personnel control requires cognizance of violence-prone profiles and alertness for internal or external factors that may be propelling an employee in the direction of inappropriate behavior. Be on the lookout for conflict over equipment, space, or services. Associates are usually the first to recognize that something is wrong, but they often find that management does not respond appropriately or promptly to these concerns. When this occurs, workers become frightened and anxious.

6. Enforce policies that deal with violence and its control. Violent outbursts can often be prevented when aggressive behavior elicits quick and appropriate response when that behavior first emerges. When aggressive individuals note lack of workplace controls or consequences for their erratic behavior, the potential for unacceptable behavior escalates. Lack of controls or consequences include:

   • managerial denial that a problem exists.
   • lack of investigation or follow-up of violent or potentially violent situations.
   • failure to tell aggressive or threatening employees that they will be held responsible for any inappropriate behavior.
   • performance appraisals do not reflect erratic behavior.

7. Sharpen counseling and disciplinary skills. Be consistent and fair in your disciplinary actions. Document counseling sessions, and follow them up. Never meet alone with suspected dangerous employees. Do not try to psychoanalyze employees, but do use common sense, reason, and logic. Persuade people that it is to their benefit to resolve conflicts. Do not argue or get caught up in ping-pong repartee such as, "You will do as I say," "No I won't," "Yes you will," "No I won't."

   Choose your words carefully during counseling sessions. Keep your comments and behavior neutral and nonjudgmental. Be sure the employee knows exactly what behavior you want changed. Avoid referring to yourself (eg, "I think you should . . . " or "I'm going to recommend . . . "). This can trigger an explosion of pent-up rage, especially if you do not get along very well with the person. Instead, quote rules or standards (eg, "Hospital protocol is that you contact our EAP.")

   If the employee begins to lose control, terminate the meeting. If he or she refuses to leave your office, you can leave. Better still, hold such meetings somewhere other than in your office.

8. Have the courage to get rid of troublemakers. If termination of employment is required, do it with empathy and compassion, but do it matter-of-factly.

Do it in private unless violence is likely. This must be done with the greatest of care. Follow mandated procedures to the letter, and thoroughly document each incident that led to the termination. Consult with your superiors or your human resources department at all stages. Firings often require legal advice, especially on possible violations of union contracts and antidiscrimination laws.

Since a person whose employment has been terminated may exhibit aggressive behavior, security and sometimes local law enforcement officers should escort the employee off the premises.

BOMB THREATS

McNerney[6] offers the following sage advice:

- Take the threat seriously. Tune out all distractions and focus on the caller.
- Keep the caller on the phone as long as possible so that the call can be traced. Tracer calls can be activated on most phones by punching " * 57. "
- Collect as much information as possible. Ask where the bomb is, when it will explode, what it looks like, who and where the caller is, and why the bomb was planted.
- Take notes and ask the caller to repeat information.
- Note any unusual phrases used by the caller.
- Listen for background noises such as cars or machinery that may help determine where the caller is calling from.

BREAKING UP FIGHTS

Fights usually arise because of attempts to save face, to defend property or territory, or because of fight-propensity of some individuals. The Crisis Prevention Institute[7] recommends the following:

- Be familiar with your organization's policies and procedures.
- Know your responsibility and authority.
- Consider the safety of everyone in your vicinity.
- Be consistent in setting limits.
- Be alert to warning signs.
- Do not underestimate the strength of the combatants. Children, patients, and women can inflict injuries.
- Get assistance to separate the combatants and to remove noncombatants from the scene.
- Identify the aggressor.

- Report the incident with thorough documentation.
- Often it is appropriate to bring the combatants back together to discuss the cause of the conflict, and to discuss the consequences of fighting.

NOTES

1. "A Census of Fatal Occupational Injuries, 1994," *News Bulletin* 95–288. U.S. Department of Labor, Bureau of Labor Statistics.
2. K. McCormick and J.D. Stewart, "Employers Confront Violence in the Workplace of the '90s," *Medical Laboratory Observer 28* (1996): 34–38.
3. D.A. Daugherty, *The New OSHA: Blueprints for Effective Training and Written Programs* (New York, NY: American Management Association, 1996), 9–12.
4. K. McCormick and J.D. Stewart, "Employers confront violence."
5. *Quality Improvement Standards* (Chicago, IL: Joint Commission on Accreditation of Healthcare Organizations, 1995).
6. J.D. McNerney, "Front-Desk Security," *HRFocus* 72 (1995): 18.
7. *Nonviolent Crisis Intervention* (Brookfield, WI: National Crisis Prevention Institute, 1991). Audiotapes.

RECOMMENDED READING AND LISTENING

M. Minor, *Preventing Workplace Violence* (Menlo Park, CA: Crisp Publishers, 1995).

C. Tavris, *Controlling Anger: How To Turn Anger into Positive Action* (Boulder, CO: CareerTrack Publishers, 1989), 4 audiotapes.

M.H. Yarborough, "Responding to a Crisis," *HRFocus 73,* no. 2 (1996): 14.

PART II

Controlling People

Chapter 11

Leaders and Managers

- organizational culture
- leading versus managing
- basic leadership styles
- special leadership strategies
- contemporary leadership activities
- the foundation of leadership
- characteristics of effective leaders
- common mistakes made by supervisors

Leadership is not learned in seminars. It is either intuitive or gained through experience. The best leaders strive to develop the leadership skills of their teammates so that the team's success does not depend on one person. Many organizations have failed because charismatic leaders failed to do this, and when they were no longer around, their backups were unable to cope.

True leaders can influence people over whom they have no authority. This is called horizontal management and is the mark of a true leader. To meet today's interdepartmental needs for coordination and cooperation, health care managers must possess leadership ability.

The best leaders understand how their own prejudices influence the way they lead. Because they can confront their own prejudices, they can deal with those of others. They censure intolerance and ensure equality of opportunity. They pay special attention to people outside the mainstream culture, knowing that these people can easily feel isolated. They learn about the others' values and cultural heritage and become aware of the differences in communication styles and interpersonal relationships.[1]

> *If you are a full-time manager, you are rewarded for what your employees do, not for the tasks that you perform.*

ORGANIZATIONAL CULTURE

Management Provides

- mission statements (why we are doing this)
- visions (what it will look like when we are there)
- goals (when we know we have arrived)
- strategies (the journey of getting there)
- set of values (how we behave on the way)

Leaders shape the culture of their organizations. Organizational culture can be defined as a "pattern of basic assumptions that has worked well enough to be considered valid and to be taught to new members as the correct way to perceive, think and feel in relation to coping with problems."[2] A culture in which the manager's leadership style features coercion and other direct power plays is less effective than those characterized by collaboration and participation."[3] In other words, culture is simply the perception of the way things are done at work.

Today's health care culture demands pervasive and honest communication—openness and authentic interaction in all operations. This translates into the sharing of knowledge, skills, news, experiences, problems, and setbacks. The result is learning at all levels.

To foster a service-oriented culture, supervisors express the values that represent spinoffs from the mission statement. They put values into action by treating employees as they want customers to be treated. They get personally involved in service activities, and they use periodic meetings of their work groups to inspire and to solve problems.

LEADING VERSUS MANAGING

We have many good managers, but there is a shortage of good leaders. Business schools develop managers, not leaders. Here are some differences between leading and managing:

- People obey managers because they must; people follow leaders because they want to.
- Leaders envision (Martin Luther King's "I Have a Dream"); managers marshal resources to achieve other people's visions.
- Leaders often rely on their intuition; managers rely on computer printouts, objectivity, and rationality.
- Leaders have more self-confidence and are more willing to take risks than managers.

- Leaders stress creativity; managers stress conformity.
- Managers project power over people; leaders project power with people.
- Managers strive to satisfy the needs and wants of their customers; leaders astonish customers with new products or services.
- Managers' goals usually arise from necessity; leaders arise from desire.
- Managers are more like scientists; leaders are more like artists.
- Managers say, "I will support you"; leaders say, "Follow me."
- Managers are concerned with the *how*; leaders are concerned with the *what.*
- Managers seek obedience; leaders seek commitment.
- Managers control; leaders empower.
- Managers correct problems; leaders prevent them.
- Managers like big offices and desks; leaders like new challenges.
- Managers find out how successful people do things; leaders explore new paths.
- Managers investigate better computer systems; leaders are more interested in team building.

Can managers be leaders. Of course, they can. The best managers are also excellent leaders.

BASIC LEADERSHIP STYLES

Clusters of leadership characteristics have been identified as leadership styles. Like clothing styles, leadership styles come and they go.

Authoritarian Style

Synonyms for this style are task oriented, telling, tight ship, theory X, top-down, paternalistic, autocratic, directive, and "I" management.

Authoritarian leaders think people must be controlled closely and given external motivation (eg, pay, benefits, and working conditions). They are task oriented rather than employee oriented. They tell their employees what they want, but not why. They do not invite input from their people. Autocratic leaders encourage dependency. Employees of these leaders often exhibit apathy or hostility.

A subset of the authoritarian style is the paternalistic approach. Paternalistic managers exhibit either the features of a kind, nurturing parent (benevolent dictator) or those of a critical, oppressive parent (tyrant). A paternalistic approach is appropriate when one is dealing with emergencies (eg, fire or disaster), inexperienced or insecure employees, hostile people who challenge their authority.

Micromanaging is a form of authoritarian leadership. Despite universal condemnation, many supervisors micromanage because they think that their employees can't function without them. They feel that they have to stay on top of things to prevent mistakes or to make sure that the work gets done. They are certain that their staffers are incapable of making decisions. Some simply think that this is what managers are supposed to do. To be successful in the end, these managers must learn to delegate responsibility and to trust their employees.

Participative Style

Synonyms for this style are people oriented, theory Y, bottom-up, happy ship, and "We" management.

Participative leaders believe that people want to work and are willing to assume responsibility. They believe that, if treated properly, people can be trusted and will put forth their best efforts. Participative leaders motivate by means of internal factors (eg, task satisfaction, self-esteem, recognition, and praise). They explain why things must be done, listen to what employees have to say, and respect their opinions. They're good delegators.

There are several subsets of this style. When in a consultative mode, leaders seek input from their followers before making important decisions. When in a delegative mode, leaders share responsibility with their colleagues.

One simple way to find out if participative management is in place is to determine the number of suggestions each employee makes annually. In many Japanese companies, where participative management flourishes, each employee submits dozens of ideas each year. Equally important is the percentage of suggestions that are acted on by management.

Participative managers articulate two magic phrases: "What do you think?" and "I need your help."

Theory Z Style

Unrelated to theory X and theory Y, theory Z was named Z to distinguish it from A (authoritarian). Adapted by the Japanese, theory Z is characterized by employee participation and egalitarianism. It features guaranteed employment, maximum employee input, and quality circles.

Bureaucratic Style

Synonyms for this style are rules oriented, by the book, and "They" management.

These managers act as monitors or police, enforcing policies, rules, procedures, and orders from upper management. They tend to be buck-passers who take little or no responsibility for directives.

Bureaucrats play negative, self-serving political games. They advance in stable or static organizations by not making mistakes, reducing risk taking, and blaming others. Government agencies and military services are loaded with these people.

Real leadership is incompatible with bureaucracy. However, a bureaucratic style may be suitable for operations in which tasks must always be performed in the same way (eg, sorting mail or typing reports).

Situational Leadership

Synonyms for this style include contingency based, flexible, adaptive, and "different strokes for different folks" leadership.

Flexible leaders adapt their style to specific situations and to the specific needs of different members of their team. As employees gain experience and confidence, the leadership style changes from highly directive to supportive (task related to people related). For example, two new employees may start work on the same date. If one has had previous experience and the other has had none, different directive styles are needed. A show-and-tell approach is needed by the novice, but may not be appropriate for the experienced person.

A practical guideline is to use a consultative or delegative style in areas of expertise and to provide direction in areas of weakness. Some managers, in an effort always to be participative, fail to be directive when direction is needed.

Laissez Faire Style

Synonyms include hands off, catch 22, fence rider, absent, and "not me" management.

These managers avoid giving orders, solving problems, or making decisions. They are evasive physically and verbally, often being masters of double talk.

A positive form of laissez faire leadership is the democratic style. Now very popular, it features self-directed (autonomous) teams in which leadership is delegated to highly trained work groups. The members of these teams know more about the organization and are better trained, more motivated, and more productive than their counterparts in traditional settings. They solve problems, redesign work processes, set standards and goals, select and monitor new employees, and evaluate team and individual performance.

SPECIAL LEADERSHIP STRATEGIES

Manipulation

Manipulators get people to do their bidding by:

- intimidating,
- engaging in emotional scenes (anger, tears, yelling, or seeking sympathy),

- making people feel guilty,
- implying that they are owed something for favors rendered, and
- name-dropping.

Management by Crisis

You can always spot the people who use this approach. They are surrounded by noise, confusion, and emotional upheavals. Every day is characterized by a series of crises for them. They complain that they cannot get things done because they are too busy putting out fires. They react rather than anticipate. They solve problems instead of preventing them.

Management by Exception

Managers who have adopted the technique of managing by exception act as facilitators, supporters, and resource people. Their message is, "I do not interfere. Come to me with problems you can't solve or when you need something I can get you." Management by exception is appropriate when leading certain categories of professionals or specialists.

Management by Objectives

Although management by objectives has lost its popularity, some of its basic features remain useful. For example, when you are reviewing an employee's performance, one way to focus on the future is in terms of future performance objectives.

Management by Wandering Around

This is discussed in Chapter 12.

CONTEMPORARY LEADERSHIP ACTIVITIES

Contemporary leaders are deeply involved in the following activities:

- team building and group problem solving,
- cross-training,
- empowering,
- improved quality and customer service,
- cost cutting,
- managing change (new services, products, or facilities),

- staff reductions or shuffling,
- decentralizing or establishing satellite activities,
- worker safety and health,
- environmental preservation,
- patient home care, and
- point of care (eg, expanded bedside services).

FOUNDATION OF LEADERSHIP

A feature of a well-led work force is the lack of cynicism. Cynicism disappears when employees respect their leaders. They respect their leaders because they perceive them as competent, caring, truthful, and ethical. Those leaders "walk the talk." Their behavior matches their words, and it features integrity and trust. Trust has two parts: being trusting (the ability to believe in others) and being trustworthy (being worthy of others' belief in them). Leading is not only walking the talk, it is also talking the walk. Talking the walk is explaining to your employees why you are taking or rejecting certain actions.

CHARACTERISTICS OF EFFECTIVE LEADERS

Leaders must be walking mission statements who make their visions come alive by talking about them with enthusiasm and conviction. They must express them in attitudes and action more than in words. Enthusiasm is almost magic. It is a positive and optimistic mindset that generates energy, enhances creativity, builds networks, and attracts other winners. It is especially necessary for the supervisory functions of motivation, communication, delegation, and problem solving.

No matter how you feel, start the day with a burst of enthusiasm. ("Fake it 'til you make it.") Throughout the day, feed positive thoughts into your subconscious mind by saying positive things about your performance.

Surround yourself with other optimistic doers. Shun the complaining observers. If you hang around with turkeys, you will never soar with the eagles. Use success imagery, that is, visualize good outcomes in whatever you do. Recharge your energy by relaxing or meditating, especially after setbacks.

Good team leaders use both the helicopter approach and the management-by-wandering-around (MBWA) approach. Like helicopters, they hover over the work area, where they can view the total operation. When they spot trouble, they descend for a closer look or to get involved. In the proactive MBWA process, leaders do not wait for people to bring problems into their offices. Instead they make frequent visits to each workstation. Here they spot potential problems and ask for suggestions. They also seek ideas from vendors and customers.

Important Characteristics of Effective Team Leaders

Effective team leaders are competent:

- They have both professional and team leadership skills.
- People look up to them and respect their expertise.
- Their opinions and advice are sought after by associates within and outside their departments.
- They are asked to serve on important committees.
- They constantly improve their professional and leadership capabilities.
- They can answer most questions. When they cannot, they know where to get the answers.
- They cooperate with their counterparts in other departments.

They are emotionally stable:

- They have a relaxed leadership style.
- They are cool and calm most of the time.
- They handle stress well.
- When they get upset with people, they focus on behavior, not on personalities or traits.

They get the job done:

- They provide a sense of direction and set high expectations and standards.
- They expect and demand good performance.
- They are well organized and always seem prepared.
- They are proactive. They anticipate and prepare for change.
- They focus on important things. They do not nitpick.
- They match people with the right jobs.
- They do not waste their time or that of their followers.
- They stimulate innovativeness and invite ideas.
- They provide all the resources their team needs.
- They get rid of the deadwood.

They are good communicators:

- They use memos, meetings, and other communication channels effectively.
- They give clear instructions and get feedback to make sure that their directions are understood.
- They are articulate and persuasive, but they do not manipulate people.
- They are excellent listeners and are easy to talk to.

- They share information, but not gossip.
- They do not withhold bad news.
- They are good teachers.
- They provide feedback, both positive and negative.
- They criticize behavior, not people or personalities.
- They are quick to praise and to give credit. They praise in public and criticize in private.
- They acknowledge their own mistakes.
- They always seem to know what is going on.

They are unafraid:

- They thrive on responsibility.
- They take risks and bend rules.
- They are innovative and flexible.
- They chalk up failures to experience.
- They keep their fears to themselves.
- They encourage creativity and risk taking.
- They accept responsibility for failures.

They are credible:

- They almost always tell the truth.
- They carry out their promises and commitments.
- They admit their mistakes.
- They do not take credit for the ideas of others.
- They do not play favorites, and their credibility is above reproach.

They develop committed followers:

- They care about their followers and show it.
- They are willing to roll up their sleeves and help out when necessary.
- They go to bat for their people.
- They empower and encourage autonomy and self-reliance.
- They get their people whatever those people need to get their work done.
- They allow much freedom in how people do their work, but they insist on good results.
- They do not play favorites.
- They are just as attentive to people below them as to those above them in the organization.
- They invite and respect the opinions and suggestions of all their employees.

- They provide opportunities for employees to use newly learned skills or previously untapped skills.
- They encourage and support suggestions, comments, and proposals from all management levels.
- They articulate what they value and back this up by their everyday activities.
- They reward cooperation as highly as they reward individual achievement.
- They are helpful and anticipate the needs and problems of their team members.
- They defend their people from outside harassment.

They exhibit charisma:

- They maintain a childlike fascination for things and people.
- They catch people doing something right . . . and tell them.
- They have a warm handshake and smile for a few seconds longer than the other person does.
- They use the other person's name often during their conversation.
- They project energy and enthusiasm.
- They are good role models.

COMMON MISTAKES MADE BY SUPERVISORS

- They pass the buck and try not to accept accountability.
- They fail to delegate and empower their employees.
- They ignore their internal customers and fail to control costs.
- They associate with losers.
- They use a cookie-cutter approach to managing.
- They try to get everyone to like them instead of seeking respect.
- They tolerate incompetence and fail to set performance standards.
- They neglect the training and career development of themselves and their staff.
- They recognize and reward only their top performers.

The Twelve Commandments of Leadership

1. Know what you want.
2. Take control of your career
3. Believe in yourself.
4. Go for the goal.
5. Enjoy the game.
6. Be capable.
7. Let your expertise show.
8. Rely on others.
9. Look for opportunities.
10. Learn the ropes.
11. Never stop networking.
12. Get a mentor.

NOTES

1. R.H. Rosen, *Leading People* (New York, NY: Viking Press, 1996), 207, 213.
2. E. Schein, "Organizational Culture," *American Psychologist 45* (1990): 109.
3. J.A. Young and B. Smith, "Organizational Change and the HR Professional," *Personnel 65* (1988): 44.

RECOMMENDED READING

K. Blanchard and S. Johnson, *The One-Minute Manager* (New York, NY: Berkeley Publishers, 1982).

T. Kent et al. "Leadership in the Formation of New Health Care Environment," *Health Care Supervisor 15,* no. 2 (1996): 27–34.

R.S. Kindler, *Managing the Technical Professional* (Menlo Park, CA: Crisp Publishers, 1993).

R.H. Rosen, *Leading People* (New York, NY: Viking Press, 1996).

S.A. Stumpf, "Strategic Management Skills: What They Are and Why They Are Needed," *Clinical Laboratory Management Review 10,* no. 3 (1996): 231–244.

Chapter 12

Coaching

- characteristics of good coaches
- when should coaching take place?
- managing by wandering around
- enhancing employee self-sufficiency
- defending, facilitating, empowering, and supporting employees
- coaching feedback
- coaching pitfalls

Coaching is an ongoing process of helping people to achieve results. It is an integral part of face-to-face leadership. Zemke, a keen observer and prolific author, crystallizes coaching wisdom as follows: "Select the right players, inspire them to win, and show them you care. Tell them where they stand, how much they are improving, and what they could do to improve more."[1]

Coaching goes beyond the activities of instruction. Coaches deal not only with task outcomes, but also with attitudes, morale, discipline, ethics, and career development. The effective coach is instructor, cheerleader, counselor, disciplinarian, evaluator, resource person, and trouble-shooter.

Coaches are expected to clarify management's expectations of employee performance, modify inappropriate attitudes, instill self-sufficiency, and enhance competencies. Coaches shape values, remove obstacles, build on employees' strengths, stretch worker skills, and build interpersonal relationships.

CHARACTERISTICS OF GOOD COACHES

Good coaches are dedicated, enthusiastic leaders who are technically or professionally competent. They push or pull people to their level of capability, but not to a level of discouragement.

The hierarchical goal of coaches is to get work completed on schedule, ensure quality of service outcomes, and satisfy customers. Personnel goals are to get substandard performers up to speed and help the other employees achieve self-fulfillment. Skilled coaches display the following characteristics:

- They practice the leadership traits featured in the previous chapter.
- They let workers know what is going on.
- They show workers how to get the job done.
- They help workers who have problems.
- They really listen to the workers.
- Their negative feedback is directed at performance, not people.
- They are quick to praise and do it in public.
- They set a good example.
- They provide psychological support.
- They pitch in and help with routine work during emergencies.
- They are technically or professionally competent in their field.

The Principal Reasons for Poor Performance

Employees do not know what is expected of them (coaches tell them).
Employees do not know how to do what is expected (coaches show them).
Employees do not know that their performance is poor (coaches inform them).
Employees could do better if they tried harder (coaches motivate them).
Employees face obstacles that prevent good performance (coaches remove the obstacles).
Employees get discouraged (coaches support and encourage them).
Employees feel that their work goes unnoticed or unappreciated (coaches lead the cheers).

WHEN DO SUPERVISORS COACH?

Coaching starts when a new employee reports on board. It begins with orienting and training. From then on, supervisors coach when someone asks for advice or help or needs assistance, or steps out of line. The more time coaches spend listening to their people and observing what those people are doing, the more often supervisors find opportunities to coach. This gets us into management by wandering around (MBWA).

MANAGEMENT BY WANDERING AROUND

One of Tom Peters' major contributions is his concept of MBWA. The wandering he espouses includes frequent contacts with people outside one's department, such as customers and suppliers, but we will limit our discussion to work-site wandering. Here are some principles of MBWA offered by Peters and Austin.[2]

- MBWA is meeting people in their offices or work areas rather than in yours.
- MBWA is listening more than telling.
- MBWA is asking whether employees have any problems and how you can help.
- MBWA is asking for advice and opinions.
- MBWA is catching people doing something right, *not* catching them doing something wrong.
- MBWA is carrying a little black book to write down employees' suggestions for improving customer service and to note meritorious performance. It is spotting actions and facilities that need fixing.
- MBWA is calling employees by their names and asking about their families or special interests.
- MBWA, when successful, results in fewer memos and unnecessary meetings.

> *Like any management strategy,*
> *MBWA must be done right to be effective.*

- MBWA can backfire if the wanderers are perceived by their staffs as inspectors, critics, or interrupters.
- MBWA is *not* rambling around smiling and waving or saying "How are you doing?"
- MBWA is *not* being a nitpicker, work interrupter, or gossip monger.

When you supervise people who need lots of support, make your visits at the same time each day so they know when to expect you. If you have people who often are not where they should be, vary the time of your rounds.

ENHANCING EMPLOYEE SELF-SUFFICIENCY

Do not overdo the helping-hand bit. For example, a nurse has a problem hooking up an orthopaedic traction setup. The nurse calls for help, but instead of staying to watch how the specialist arranges all the ropes and pulleys, the nurse slips off for coffee.

Do not let employees transfer all their little problems to you. New supervisors must learn when and when not to solve other people's problems. You do not want to be a Teflon manager who ignores all the cries for help. You do not want to be a Velcro manager and let all the problems of other people stick to you.

Insist on completed staff work. This military term simply means that when employees come to a superior with a problem, they must also bring ideas for solving the problem. Once people become aware of this expectation, they will bring you fewer problems, and when they do bring in the problems and their proposed solutions, you may find that their ideas are better than yours.

Do not overdo advising. Try asking first. When someone wants an opinion, respond with "What do you think?" instead of an immediate "Here's what you should do." It takes longer, but pays off in the long haul.[3]

Encourage people to take small career risks. When they make bad decisions (we all do!) or fail to pick the best solution, do not punish their mistakes. Regard them as learning experiences. Do not tolerate repeats of the same mistake.

Insist that they do what they say they will. Ask for definite commitments, set deadlines, and, when appropriate, get them in writing.

DEFENDING, FACILITATING, EMPOWERING, AND SUPPORTING

Employees of effective leaders see their coaches as defenders who protect them from outside harassment. A major source of frustration is to be attacked by people against whom one is powerless. Coaches are the defenders against such hostility. Baseball managers know the importance of this. To prevent their players from getting thrown out of a game, they rush out on the field to protest an umpire's call, sometimes when they know that the call was correct.

Coaches are facilitators who get their team the personnel, time, and other resources needed to function effectively. At times, supervisors must go on the mat with suppliers or people in other departments to demand that some action be taken.

Coaches empower their staffs and strip away red tape to enable the workers to make decisions and solve customer or operational problems. Just being able and authorized to answer customers' questions is appreciated by frontline employees.

Coaches should not be averse to rolling up their sleeves and pitching in to help occasionally. Support also involves providing user-friendly policies, instruments, and procedures and showing respect, fairness, and trust. It is giving a lot as well as expecting a lot. It is being available and visible. It is ensuring employee safety and wellness, and fighting for their rights, benefits, and rewards.

COACHING FEEDBACK

According to the contingency theory of reinforcement, behavior reinforced by positive consequences improves. That which begets negative consequences or is ignored decreases. We violate this every time we overload our reliable performers and reduce the workload of our goof-offs. We neglect this theory when we fail to give positive and negative feedback.

Not to give deserved praise is to overlook one of our most powerful motivators. A simple comment such as "I knew you could do a bang-up job on that important project. I was right" makes even an experienced veteran happy and proud.

Giving undeserved praise consistently reduces the power of positive feedback and makes recipients feel they are being manipulated.

What To Praise

- performance that is beyond the call of duty. The person:
  1. works extra long hours
  2. substitutes for an absent colleague
  3. returns to work after hours
  4. submits a report ahead of schedule or a rush report on time
  5. reports a problem and suggests several good solutions
  6. handles a ticklish situation diplomatically
  7. earns accolades for his or her work unit
  8. receives special awards, achieves an outstanding educational record, or earns an advanced degree
- performance that is not outstanding but is consistently good. The person:
  1. can always be relied on
  2. has a good attendance record and is rarely tardy
  3. is flexible and willing to adjust to changes
  4. consistently meets job standards and work objectives
- substandard performance that improves, even though it is not yet up to your expectations
- an innovative idea is suggested

> *What always amazes me are supervisors who say that they seldom praise because their people only do what they are supposed to do. These are the supervisors who have the highest turnover rate and the poorest productivity.*

When Not To Praise

- When the praise is insincere or only represents flattery
- When it is not earned
- When it would embarrass you, the recipient, or others
- Before you are certain who really earned the praise

Why Praise Should Not Be Delayed

- You may forget to deliver it.
- The recipient is more likely to think that it is not important.
- The recipient may be confused about what behavior is being rewarded.

Why Praise Should Be Specific

- Recipients should know exactly what it was they did that was appreciated. Misunderstandings are prevented.
- The praise is more believable.
- You avoid giving the impression that you like everything they do.
- They know that you know what is going on.

> Example: Nonspecific—"You did a great job last night."
>
> Specific—"You did a great job of getting that emotional parent calmed down last night."

How To Praise

We have already mentioned that praise should be delivered as soon as possible after the deed, that it should be specific, and that the right person or persons should get it. The famous one-minute praisings of Blanchard and Johnson[4] enhance praise by including comments about how the praiseworthy event made you, the coach, feel. These authors also recommend that you pause for a moment after delivering the praise (to emphasize its importance). Then shake hands or touch the person to show your support.

Phraseology such as "great job" or "wow" is important, but voice tone, facial expression, and body language are even more important.

There are exceptions to the old rule "praise in public." Some people are embarrassed when praised in front of their peers. They may be subjected to harassment from some coworkers, and you may be deemed guilty of showing favoritism. Praise these people privately or in writing.

Some supervisors write brief thank-you notes on Post-its® and stick them on the outside of people's doors. Do not be surprised when the recipients of these notes leave them on their door for several days.

A thank-you note or memo with copies to the personnel department or to upper management amplifies the effects of a verbal compliment. In selected instances, get your boss to send a congratulatory note to the person or to make a special visit to your unit to thank that person personally.

Consider submitting a report to the editor of your organization's newsletter or a local newspaper. Put a notice on the bulletin board.

There are also exceptions to the second part of that old rule "criticize in private." At times it's appropriate to criticize in front of others. For example, a glib chronic offender leaves your office after receiving a reprimand. He boasts to coworkers that he was in your office helping to get you out of a jam. Next time chew out that person in public. That will put a quick stop to that practice.

There are also times when witnesses are needed. If you are being subjected to sexual harassment, for example, voicing your objections in public is the intelligent thing to do.

How People React to Negative Feedback

None of us likes to receive criticism—constructive or not—because it attacks our self-esteem. How we react depends on:

- who is delivering it,
- how legitimate it is,
- who else hears it,
- how fragile our sense of self-worth is, and
- how high our stress level is at that moment.

People may react defensively, counterattack, flee, or become emotional. They may look for shortcomings in the critic or weakness in the charge, or they may reluctantly accept the reprimand and promise to improve. They may try to blame others or strive to change the subject.

How To Criticize While Preserving a Person's Self-Esteem

When supervisors find mistakes, they usually respond in one of four ways:

1. They ignore the situation and hope that someone else will correct it or that the subordinate will do it on his or her own.
2. They point out the mistake and ask the person to correct it.
3. They use an indirect approach by asking how things are going, hoping the employee will admit to making the error. If not, they then call attention to it.
4. They use the enhancing value technique. This technique starts with saying something nice about what the person does and then making specific suggestions for improvement. The basis for this approach is to make the person feel that you are there to help, not to judge or demean. The following is a good example: "Ruth, your report is always on time. I appreciate that. Now, let's try to eliminate those typos, OK?"

If you follow the above statement with another positive statement, such as "I know that I can rely on you to take care of this" or "You're too good an employee to make mistakes like this," you have just used the "sandwich technique." The sandwich technique consists of two slices of praise with a reprimand in between.

Tips for Giving Better Constructive Feedback

- Remember that your goal is to alter behavior, not to castigate.
- Maintain a high ratio of praise to criticism. Aim for a four-to-one ratio because it takes at least four positive strokes to neutralize one negative one.
- Attack behavior, not personality or traits. Instead of saying "You are too careless," describe what the person is doing or not doing that provoked your remark.
- Give feedback as soon as possible after the act, but not before you have all the necessary information.
- Avoid critical comments when either you or your report is emotionally upset.
- Use "I," not "you," language. Instead of saying "You have a bad habit of . . . ," say "I get upset when people . . . ." This is less traumatic to one's ego and evokes less defensiveness.
- Avoid subjective terms such as attitude, work ethic, and professionalism. If you feel that you must use such words, make certain that you follow with specific behavioral descriptions or examples.
- Avoid absolute terms such as always or never (eg, "You are always late for my meetings").
- Do not try to diagnose or read minds. When you say, "The trouble with you is . . . ," you're diagnosing. When you say, "You think what you do is clever," you are trying to get into their heads.
- Do not ask "why?" when you do not expect an answer (eg, Instead of "*Why* did you do such a stupid thing?" say, "That was not a very smart thing to do").
- Know when to be tentative (usually when you are not sure what happened or who the guilty party is). For example: "I've been told that someone in our unit has been making very critical remarks in the dining room about upper management. Can you shed some light on this?" Other helpful phraseology includes, "What concerns me," "I'm worried about," or "Perhaps we have a problem with. . . ."
- Always give the person a chance to respond without interruption.
- Avoid being too critical or coming down too hard on your people. If you are, they will react by devising ways to keep their mistakes hidden from you rather than trying not to make the mistakes.

COACHING PITFALLS

- Use a "cookie-cutter" approach to coach all employees. Inexperienced or insecure people need more of your time and support. Situational leadership is flexible and more appropriate.
- Thinking that you have all the right answers.

- Neglecting the coaching process because you do not think you have the time.
- Labeling workers as above or below average.
- Addressing attitude, personality, or character rather than outcomes or behavior.
- Not allowing some leeway in how things get done.
- Overuse of criticism or undeserved praise.
- Offering too much unsolicited advice.

NOTES

1. R. Zemke, "The Corporate Coach," *Training 33,* no.12 (1996): 24–28.
2. T. Peters and N. Austin, *A Passion for Excellence* (New York, NY: Random House, 1985), 9.
3. Zemke, "The Corporate Coach."
4. K. Blanchard and S. Johnson, *The One-Minute Manager* (New York, NY: Berkeley Publishers, 1982), 44.

RECOMMENDED READING

J. Olalla and R. Echeverria, "Management by Coaching," *HRFocus 73,* no. 1 (1996): 16, 17.

M.L. Schack, "Coaching: The Art of Creating Exceptional Results," *Clinical Laboratory Management Review 11,* no. 1 (1997): 28–34.

Chapter 13

Morale and Motivation

- morale versus motivation
- major factors that affect morale
- signs of a morale problem
- obtaining information about morale
- how employers improve morale
- how supervisors improve morale
- proactive and reactive motivational strategies
- how to motivate the unspectacular performer

Employee surveys showed a steady decline in job satisfaction over the last three decades.[1] In the health care industry this decline has accelerated. New technologies and services require a degree of autonomy for professionals that conflicts with the bureaucratic hierarchy. Long-established boundaries between functional departments and workstations are rapidly being erased as procedural flowcharts stream across these previously sacrosanct borders. The result is stress and morale challenges.

MORALE VERSUS MOTIVATION

Morale is a state of mind based largely on the perceptions of workers toward their work, their employer, their colleagues, and their supervisors. Morale must be differentiated from motivation. Morale concerns job satisfaction. If it is high, people are less likely to quit, complain, or give supervisors a bad time. Morale factors are the things that unions fight for: pay, benefits, job security, and work environment (quality of work life).

Morale factors represent the lower three levels of Maslow's hierarchy of needs: survival needs (food, clothing, shelter), safety needs (insurance, permanent job, pension), and social needs (acceptance by fellow workers).[2]

Motivation is a cognitive drive that occurs when Maslow's two higher needs are met. These needs are ego or self-esteem needs, and self-actualization (achieving one's full potential).

Unfortunately, high morale does not necessarily increase motivation. Contented employees may lack the motivation needed to maximize performance. However, motivation dissipates when morale is low.

MAJOR FACTORS THAT IMPACT MORALE

Employee Factors

- Basic personality type, especially optimism or pessimism
- Family and other outside situations
- Ability to adjust to job and fellow workers
- Ease and safety in getting to work and finding a parking space
- Employee-job match

Nature of Job and Job Ambiance

- Work that is stimulating or monotonous, fulfilling or unrewarding
- Prestige
- Opportunity for promotion or growth
- Job security
- Financial status of organization, economic conditions, and threats of competitors
- Amount of stress
- Quality and ease of communication

Attitude and Behavior of Employer and Management

- How rewards are shared (eg, executives get huge raises or bonuses while employees are laid off or are asked to take salary cuts)
- Frequency of promotions from within
- How management adjusts to financial crunches

Quality of Supervision

See previous chapters.

SIGNS OF A MORALE PROBLEM

Productivity plummets. Employees work at the minimum level required to keep their jobs. They complain about parking, safety, pay and benefits, their employer and managers, and their assignments. As they become apathetic or rebellious, they voice these complaints in the presence of patients and other customers.

Employees become resistant to change, rarely volunteer, and seldom pitch in to help. Absenteeism, tardiness, grievances, and turnover skyrocket. Employees do not participate at meetings, except to voice complaints as they sit in the back of the room scowling with folded arms. They eschew making suggestions or approving the ideas of others. They fall silent or walk away when managers approach. Cynicism, sarcasm, and belittling flourish.

Conversations and energy are directed away from productive work. Supervisors hear things like, "Thank God it's Friday," "Do not ask me, I only work here," "We need a union," or "There's no point in knocking yourself out."

Workers talk about retiring, changing employers, or leaving their field. They relate how their friends have better employers. The more qualified employees resign while the deadwood remains on board.

Morale improvement begins with the detection of morale problems. Severe morale problems are easy to spot; milder forms are more subtle. Discovery of discontent at an early stage is as important as the early detection of cancer. As with cancer, the longer poor morale is allowed to continue unabated, the more difficult it is to reverse.

METHODS FOR OBTAINING INFORMATION ABOUT MORALE

- *Attitude surveys.* Whenever a morale slippage is suspected, an alert management circulates an attitude survey and shares the findings with all managers.
- *Exit interviews.* These should be conducted by specially trained personnel rather than by the employee's supervisor. Ideally the function is assigned to outside agencies. The sample size should be enough to reflect the entire staff.
- *Anonymous employee focus groups.* When conducted by outside facilitators, employees' names are not known. Quotes are not attributed to any individual. These are especially effective for evaluating morale during or after a major organizational change.
- *Hotline and suggestion boxes.* These are effective only when they result in quick follow-up.
- *Ombudsman programs.* Ombudsmen mediate employee concerns and report them to management. They can prevent a problem from getting larger or happening again. To be effective, management must have credibility. If people lack trust in their leaders, they will withhold all information from senior people.

HOW EMPLOYERS IMPROVE MORALE

- They use and react quickly to employee attitude surveys.
- They establish a problem-solving culture.

- They control false rumors.
- They share more financial information about their organizations with employees.
- They insist on fair and equitable treatment of all employees.
- They vigorously control harassment and discrimination.
- They spend more time where the work is taking place.
- They make certain that their managers screen job candidates carefully.
- They provide extensive and timely supervisory training.

Salaries and Benefit Systems

Employers upgrade their reward and recognition systems. They know what salaries and benefits their competitors offer, and respond appropriately. They introduce more flexibility into rules and regulations. They reward team and individual efforts and outcomes. They establish alternative promotional ladders to allow professionals to remain in their specialties with parity.

More organizations promote the well-being of their employees. The purpose is not entirely altruistic. In addition to providing a valuable service, they reduce costs by prescribing special programs that increase wellness and prevent illness. Health promotion initiatives include health education, risk assessments and screening, and special programs such as infertility care. Incentives include changes that focus on the family and lifestyles—casual dress, flextime, earlier quitting times on Fridays during summer months.

HOW SUPERVISORS IMPROVE MORALE

Alert supervisors who enjoy good rapport with their employees become aware of morale problems long before upper management does. They respond in a number of ways. Still better, they prevent the slippage in the first place by taking some of the following actions:

- Treat people as winners or potential winners.
- Reward and recognize appropriately.
- Ensure social acceptance of all employees.
- Instill pride through better orientation of new employees.
- Make certain that their employees know the why and how of their tasks.
- Maintain a mindset of optimism and success.
- Assign discouraged workers to teams of go-getters.
- Get rid of troublemakers and morale destroyers.
- Introduce more flexible work schedules.
- Keep all people informed.

- Become a change master.
- Involve people in decision making and planning.
- Help them get raises.

Four Techniques for Getting Raises for Your Employees

1. Rewrite position descriptions. Document the degree of difficulty of their functions and the consequences of errors they may make. Highlight administrative and teaching assignments or anything else that justifies raising their salaries.
2. Train and mentor them to enhance their value to the organization.
3. If possible, give them more prestigious titles.
4. Never try to keep key people by denigrating their performance or qualifications to others.

MOTIVATION

All motivation is self-motivation. Managers can't motivate. What they can do is change the work ambiance in ways that improve motivation.

All employees are motivated. Unfortunately, their motivational energy does not always flow into their work. For example, Steve, who shows little interest in his job or promotion, is a talented musician and an effective leader of a local orchestra. Steve has lots of motivation.

Efforts to effect motivation are either proactive or reactive. Proactive or anticipative measures precede performance; reactive activities follow performance and serve to reinforce desired behavior or outcomes.

The acronym RAGWAR helps you to remember Herzberg's famous list of motivating factors[3]:

R = Recognition
A = Achievement
G = Growth (career)
W = Work itself
A = Advancement
R = Responsibility

We have already noted that while high morale does not motivate, motivation cannot be achieved until morale deficiencies (Herzberg called these factors dissatisfiers or hygienes[4]) have been eliminated.

PROACTIVE STRATEGIES

- Remember that what motivates you may not motivate your employees. Try to see their perspectives.
- Define expectations, set goals, delegate, train, coach, counsel, and provide performance feedback.
- Provide for the maintenance and growth of professional skills to avoid obsolescence.
- Relax "tight" supervisory controls, and delegate decision-making authority.
- Change job titles and rewrite position descriptions to make jobs more important or to appear so.
- Recruit and select motivated people.
- Improve the job itself. The most lasting motivation comes from the job itself, or more correctly from one's perception of the job and its importance. When people like their work but hate their job, watch out!
- Learn as much as you can about your people and their different personalities.
- Do not rely on salary administration for rewards and recognition.
- Take your workers into your confidence, seek their advice, share information, and be fair and consistent.
- Provide the resources and support, and do not stand in their way.
- Be a respected role model.
- Smile. The presence of smiles and a little good humor goes a long way to creating a pleasant work ambiance.
- Increase your employees' opportunities for education and training (see Exhibit 13–1).

> *When the going gets tough, the tough lighten up.*

The meaningfulness of work is based on how much it affects the worker, other people, and the organization. Jobs that require multiple skills and a variety of activities or skills are usually more satisfying.

Most employees also prefer an assignment that allows the person to complete a whole piece of work. For example, most hematology technologists prefer to investigate a bleeding problem by performing a battery of tests rather than doing only one or two tests of the battery. Most patient care technicians prefer to provide a range of services for one patient rather than taking the vital signs of all the patients in a unit.

Interesting work and opportunities to develop skills and abilities, to be creative, and to be challenged are powerful motivators.

Exhibit 13–1 How Many of These Questions about Your Educational Program Can You Answer in the Affirmative?

1. Do you have a formal in-house education program?
2. Is this program available to each and every member of your staff?
3. Do you provide sufficient uninterrupted time for your employees to attend the in-house programs?
4. Does each employee have individualized career goals and plans? Are these discussed at annual performance review meetings?
5. Is there financial support for outside education courses? Do you modify work schedules or numbers of work hours to accommodate employees who enroll in these programs?
6. Do employees have the opportunity to cross-train or to learn new skills on the job?
7. Does each of your employees learn at least one new skill each year?
8. Are there real incentives for learning new skills?
9. When your employees attend seminars or workshops, do you discuss the practical value to your unit and to the employee before the meeting?
10. When your employees return from seminars and workshops, do you discuss what they learned and help them put that new knowledge and skill to use?
11. When you attend professional or technical meetings, do you share what you learned with others? Do you encourage your staff to do likewise?
12. Do you include educational topics in your routine staff meetings?
13. Do all your educational efforts focus on improved customer service?

A high degree of control over one's work provides a healthy mindset. Lack of autonomy leads to frustration and stress. Having control translates into discretionary freedom of scheduling, prioritizing, and selecting methods.

Practical Tips for Increasing the Motivational Value of the Work Itself

- Provide a diversity of experience by giving new assignments, cross-training, or rotating workstations.
- Let people swap assignments. Here you must know the likes and dislikes of each person.
- Assign monotonous tasks or those requiring less expertise to less-qualified employees. It makes two people happy.

> - Allow a little time for practical research, special projects, or service on committees, quality circles, or problem-solving groups.
> - Permit a few fun tasks.
> - Stimulate creativity by talking about new services, products, equipment, or procedures, sharing publications and handouts from seminars, and assigning problems.
> - Provide holistic tasks where employees can see the results of their efforts.

To move up a motivational notch, switch from a directive style to a participative style. To help with this, Leeds[5] recommends asking your employees the following questions:

- What do you like about what you do?
- How can I help you use more of your skills?
- What do you think you (or we) should do differently?
- How can we carry out your ideas?
- What help do you need from me or from others?

Get them involved in decisions about their assignments. Consider differences in their motivational needs. Some people have a strong need for control or leadership, others for task achievement, and still others for socializing. For example, Sue gets her kicks when she chairs a committee, Joe is energized when presented with a balky instrument, and Jan is happiest when she can meet new people or work with a group of her friends.

Delegate and empower. Giving ambitious people more responsibility plus the authority they need to discharge that responsibility is empowering. It is a strong motivator. Most people like to be in charge of something, even when that something is a minor activity.

REACTIVE STRATEGIES

Provide Recognition

When money is scarce for rewarding good service or is no longer the motivator it used to be, recognition and praise become more important. These factors elevate self-esteem, improve morale, and really motivate if applied skillfully.

A frequent complaint of health care workers is that they do not get the recognition and respect that they are due. Supervisors often misinterpret this to mean that upper management is at fault. Recognition, however, is a lot more than formal ceremonies where accolades, plaques, and certificates are handed out. Such events are too infrequent and too impersonal to have a major impact. Of much greater significance is the day-to-day, person-to-person dialogue in which supervisors express their appreciation in ways that convince employees that they are important. This is what really satisfies the employee's ego needs.

Your messages, verbal or written, tell employees whether you truly believe in the value of their efforts and their worth. What gets rewarded informs people of what kind of performance is valued most. Make sure that the recognition is perceived as fair.

In the next chapter we will discuss rewards and recognition in more detail.

How To Motivate the Steady but Unspectacular Worker

Managers spend much time devising gimmicks for rewarding their star performers or coping with their problem people. Meanwhile, they neglect those loyal supporters who show up every day, do not make waves, and who live up to all the specifications of their position descriptions. Most employees fall into this category.

Besides providing the motivators already described, meet periodically with each of these employees to tell them how much you appreciate their efforts.[6] Before the meeting, review their records and your personal observations. Look for noteworthy behavior, such as excellent attendance or frequent volunteering to substitute for absent coworkers. At the meeting, apologize for not spending more time with the person, and congratulate him or her for whatever it is you picked out. Use the opportunity to ask for suggestions for improving your service or the teamwork. Ask whether there is anything you can do to make his or her job more pleasant. Most employees are more relaxed and willing to talk frankly at these informal sessions than they are at formal performance appraisal interviews.

NOTES

1. R.J. Doyle and P.I. Doyle, *Gain Management* (New York, NY: AMACOM, 1992), 9.

2. A.H. Maslow, *Motivation and Personality* (New York, NY: Harper & Row, 1954).

3. F. Herzberg, *Work and the Nature of Man* (Cleveland, OH: World, 1966).

4. Herzberg, *Work and the Nature of Man.*

5. D. Leeds, *Smart Questions* (New York, NY: McGraw-Hill, 1987).

6. F.C. Nail and E.K. Singleton, "Common Sense Survival Strategy for Nursing Supervisors," *Health Care Supervisor 4* (1986): 50–58.

RECOMMENDED READING

D.J. McNerney, "Creating a Motivated Workforce," *HRFocus 73,* no. 8 (1996): 1–6.

J.A. Morris, "How To Motivate High-Achievers," *Training* 33, no. 2 (1996): 74.

A. Vance and R. Davidhizar, "Motivating the Paraprofessional in Long-Term Care," *Health Care Supervisor 15,* no. 4 (1997): 57–64.

Chapter 14

Rewards and Recognition

- four major principles of an effective reward system
- the three steps in designing an incentive strategy
- behavior or results that should be rewarded
- seven guidelines for a reward strategy
- salaries
- benefits and other financial rewards
- nonfinancial rewards
- setting up a reward system
- recognition systems

"Reward people for the right behavior and you get the right results. That's the simple message of the greatest management principle in the world."[1]

Michael LeBoeuf

Most employers feel that they have effective reward and recognition systems in place. Employees disagree. In a national poll, workers were asked, "If you were to improve service quality and productivity, do you believe you would be rewarded accordingly?" The vast majority responded with a resounding "No!"[2] In addition, many of these people feel that policies and promotions are not administered fairly.

To make matters worse, many health care organizations are cutting costs by scaling down their awards. To compensate for these losses, it's imperative for supervisors to fine-tune their recognition and reward skills.

FOUR MAJOR PRINCIPLES OF AN EFFECTIVE REWARD SYSTEM

1. Rewards are awarded principally on the basis of performance outcome: quality of work, cost control, and customer satisfaction.

2. Rewards are also based on special behavior such as acquisition of new skills or knowledge, willingness and the ability to adjust to changes, cross-training, and teamwork.
3. Rewards go to teams as well as to individuals.
4. Rewards are sufficient to retain personnel.

THREE STEPS IN DESIGNING AN INCENTIVE STRATEGY

1. Ascertain customers' needs and wants.
2. Set performance standards.
3. Measure performance against these standards or results.

BEHAVIOR OR RESULTS THAT SHOULD BE REWARDED

- They delight customers.
- They report problems and customer feedback, and offer suggestions for correcting problems and improving customer service.
- They display creativity and assertiveness more than they show conformity.
- They are willing to stick their necks out, make difficult decisions, express unpopular opinions, and take action that may risk their status.
- They do things that are beyond the call of duty, such as:
  1. work extra long hours,
  2. substitute for others willingly,
  3. return to work after hours or are available for advice by telephone,
  4. submit reports ahead of schedule,
  5. volunteer for unpleasant assignments, or
  6. render performance you can always rely on. (They show up during snowstorms, back you up when you need support, and are always ready to help.)

SEVEN GUIDELINES FOR A REWARD STRATEGY

1. Support and justify pay raises for your team and your star performers.
2. When you select a reward for an individual, consider that person's distinctive wants and needs. Ask people what rewards they value.
3. Be consistent and fair in what and how you reward.
4. With marginal performers, express your appreciation for small improvements even though outcomes are not yet up to your expectations.
5. Reward wanted behavior and outcomes. When people struggle against odds with less than desired results, they still deserve some credit for their efforts.

6. Reward your entire team for a team success, and single out individuals who made special efforts that were recognized by the rest of the team.
7. Reward what supports the values of your organization. Most organizational value statements include words such as customer satisfaction, innovation, teamwork, career development, and cost control.[3]

SALARIES

Mention has already been made that low compensation is a dissatisfier, but generous compensation is not a strong or lasting motivator. While it may be true that the motivational effect of a salary increase is transient and that people are motivated more by their work than by the rewards they earn, the importance of compensation should not be undervalued. Managers can keep telling their employees what great performers they are, but if management fails to back these statements with fatter paychecks, those employees soon realize that they are being manipulated.

While base pay still reflects the economics of the marketplace, there have been major changes in compensation strategies in recent years. The old practice of trying to create internal job equity is becoming passé except in unionized organization.

Merit increases have lost much of their luster, largely because of their negative impacts on those who are not selected and feel cheated. Strident charges of favoritism and unfairness are commonplace. Even the folks who get the larger slices of the pie feel uncomfortable and alienated. A more acceptable option is to reward higher performing groups as well as individuals. Whatever system is selected, merit pay must be based on objective data using agreed-upon and observable criteria.

Broadbanding, which collapses many traditional salary grades into a few wide bands, also may be losing its popularity in favor of competency-based systems. The latter systems reward skills, knowledge, and behavior. Competencies that earn the rewards may include teamwork, technical expertise, and innovation. The centerpiece of many skill-based pay systems is the ability and willingness of employees to perform a wide range of tasks.[4]

For a few years, compensation was based almost entirely on meeting predetermined objectives—the product of the management-by-objectives paradigm. This has given way to a different kind of outcome-based compensation system in which customer satisfaction is a principle aspect. By incorporating customer satisfaction measures into their reward systems, employers have a better chance of pleasing their customers. Employees who fail in this effort not only miss out on the rewards, but they also put their jobs in jeopardy.

Whatever compensation system is in effect, supervisors play a pivotal role in explaining and implementing the system.

BENEFITS

The cost and importance of benefits have expanded markedly, and new features such as maternity plans and day care for children and parents keep appearing. A major problem with benefit packages is that they have become so expensive, often exceeding 30% of salaries. To control these costs, employers eliminate some of the more costly offerings, or make employees share some of the expenses. Many large organizations have reduced the numbers of their full-time employees and increased their part-time staff because the latter get fewer benefits.

Another strategy is to outsource some operations or departments. This eliminates not only the benefits, but also the jobs.

A 1995 survey of hospital laboratory supervisors revealed what they perceived as inadequate benefits. Here are some of the highlights of that study.[5]

Top 5 Benefits Not Received	*Top 5 Benefits Deemed Inadequate*
Child care	Pension plan
Eye care	Paid seminar/workshop expenses
Paid professional member-	Paid continuing education
ship dues	Eye care plan
Dental care	Day care reimbursement
Continuing education	

Many organizations have been creative in tying their benefits to their employees' specific physical, psychological, and spiritual needs. Examples include flextime, recreational facilities, wellness programs, telecommuting, and even weekly free massages. Cafeteria plans in which employees choose from a variety of options are very popular.

Providing such benefits improves morale, reduces absenteeism and turnover, and increases productivity and customer satisfaction. Caring employers are always open to suggestions for new benefits—at least those that do not carry large price tags.

Supervisors may propose new ideas for rewarding their employees. They often pick up these ideas at their professional meetings, and from mentors and personal networks—an example of supervisory benchmarking skill.

OTHER FINANCIAL REWARDS

• Promotion or alternative types of advancement that increase salary.

- Bonuses and cash awards. The Japanese get the maximum mileage out of their bonus systems. Many Japanese workers receive 25% of their pay as flexible bonuses; in the United States the average is less than 1%.
- Increased compensation for superior customer service, special competencies, and participation in special activities (eg, process reengineering, teaching, mentoring, or handling tough delegated tasks).
- Financial support for education, training, or personal library.
- Tickets for entertainment events.
- Awards such as pins, jewelry, mugs. While bonuses and salary increases possess an element of recognition, they do not have the same symbolic significance as permanent things.
- Personal offices or expanded work space, services of typists or other assistants, and support for educational or professional advancement.
- Professional or technical publications or a small group library.
- Payment for employees' membership in professional societies.
- Establishment of funds for research or investigation projects.
- Reimbursement to employees for attendance at professional meetings, workshops, or seminars.

NONFINANCIAL REWARDS

"It's harder to satisfy employees with money alone. What were once regarded as rewards are now considered entitlements."[6]

Graham and Unruh

There are many rewards that, with little or no cost, have powerful motivational impacts. Some of the following may be appropriate in your situation:

- Enable your employees to attend in-house educational offerings.
- Delegate things that individuals perceive as benefiting their careers or giving them pleasure.
- Ask them if they would like to serve on a committee, focus group, task force, or cross-functional team.
- Ask them for their opinions and give them credit for any advice that you use.
- Rotate workstations but try not to rotate a person from one boring job to an equally boring one.
- Create training opportunities if these are valued by the employees.
- Provide career counseling.
- Let them represent you at upper-level or professional meetings.

- Grant additional time off for special events.
- Offer meaningful assignments, diversity of experience, or choice of responsibilities.
- Grant opportunities to be innovative.
- Provide more opportunities for challenging work, or to develop new skills.
- Let them handle projects or complex tasks from beginning to end, not in bits and pieces.
- Bring in a treat or have lunch with your group.
- Make more information available—not just information they need to get their work done, but also what they would like to learn about.
- Ask if they would like to serve as a mentor or trainer for new employees.
- Assign them more or less responsibility and authority according to their individual wishes.
- Give them more prestigious titles, if allowed. For example, the title of technical specialist may be preferred over that of technologist.
- Use generous doses of recognition (more on this later).
- Encourage each person to become a specialist in some aspect of your unit's activities.
- Help employees develop goals, objectives, and plans.
- Provide assignments that promote career development.

IMPLEMENTING A REWARD SYSTEM

Establish the goals of your reward system. After reviewing your organization's statements regarding vision, mission, values, and goals, decide what kind of performance outputs and behavior support these statements. Consider criteria such as customer satisfaction, work quality and quantity, problem solving, achieving objectives, improving work procedures, attendance, and new skills. Benchmark by noting the systems and techniques used by other leaders who have reputations for high morale and productivity.

Determine what the team and the individual team members regard as rewards. What makes them smile or frown? What kinds of things do they seem to like doing? What do they talk about during their free time? To avoid making poor choices, try asking people how they feel about a reward before you give it. Give them options. Avoid anything that might embarrass them. Ask their colleagues, friends, or family members for suggestions. Reward everyone who meets the established criteria. Be certain that you reward the right outcomes and behavior, not what you do not want.

RECOGNITION

"The deepest principle of human nature is the craving to be appreciated." [6]

William James, as quoted in Bell

Recognition is our least expensive and most powerful motivational tool. To be effective, it must be earned, specific, sincere, and offered as soon as possible after what the person did or said.

The weakness of the customary institutional award ceremonies is that they are too impersonal and are delivered long after the commendatory service. Also, they usually focus on things such as attendance or length of employment rather than on customer service. Some rituals make employees feel so demeaned that they do not show up at the ceremony.

The philosophical core of recognition is developing self-esteem. Employees who get the recognition they deserve have higher self-esteem, more confidence, more willingness to take on new challenges, and more eagerness to contribute new ideas and improve productivity.

We all need day-to-day recognition if we are to perform at consistently high levels. Recognition can be as simple as a smile and a sincere "good morning." When provided grudgingly or inexpertly, it is ineffective. Some people find it difficult to deliver praise while others are uncomfortable receiving it. Do not confuse praise with flattery. The latter is insincere, unearned, and usually manipulative.

Recognition Must Be Valued

Recognition is powerful, but the same type of recognition does not work for everyone. Different people require different approaches—"different strokes for different folks." Whatever you use must pass the "snicker test." If employees regard an award as having little value, or if they have little respect for its donor, that award will have little impact on the employees' self-esteem or morale. Salary increases represent a powerful form of recognition even if their motivational value may be brief.

Features of Effective Recognition

- It must be earned. Otherwise, it is easily recognized as flattery or manipulation. Meaningful day-to-day recognition comes from the supervisors who really know what's going on in their sections. Undeserved praise, praising the wrong person, and forgetting to praise other deserving individuals are counterproductive.

- It is consistent. Everyone should know what merits compliments. Inconsistent recognition confuses recipients, and unequal recognition smacks of favoritism.
- It is timely. There is little time between the meritorious deeds and the recognition. The high value of day-to-day recognition is its immediacy. The type of reward most preferred by employees is personalized, "spur-of-the-moment" recognition.[8]
- It is frequent. It takes many positive strokes to neutralize the effects of one criticism.
- It is ubiquitous. Most employees can be recognized for something they do well. It may be something they do not do (eg, avoid controversy or tolerate the idiosyncrasies of fellow workers). In the case of marginal workers, little steps in the right direction can lead to still more improvement when they receive some positive feedback.
- It is valued by the recipients.
- It is sincere and specific. Telling someone that they're doing a good job is not specific. Telling someone that you appreciate how they handled an irate physician a short time before is both specific and timely.
- It does not embarrass. Never praise in public when it would fluster the recipient.

To enhance the impact of praising, try the following tactics:

- Praise in public and ask one of your superiors to be present.
- Address the person by name, maintain eye contact, and smile.
- State how the action or statement benefited you, the team, the department, or the organization.
- Follow up with a memo. Include a copy in the employee's personal file and send one to your superiors.
- Submit the commendation to the institution's newsletter and to the marketing department.

Other recognition modalities include the following:

- Write a thank-you note and post it on the recipient's office door or workstation.
- Brag about it to colleagues—it will get back to the person.

- Display commendations and pictures on bulletin boards. Place trophies and plaques at the recipient's workstation.
- Attend meetings of committees and other special work groups to thank the members.
- Select an employee of the month.

Five Cautions

1. Avoid saying what behavior or outcomes you want, but rewarding something else. For example, your value statement may proclaim quality, but you reward people who cut corners.
2. Avoid sending mixed messages (eg, a message containing elements of both praise and criticism). The recipients are likely to be confused or angry.
3. Do not give praise that is not merited or is grossly exaggerated. This is not recognition; it's flattery or manipulation. When praising a problem employee, praise only what he or she has done well.
4. Do not overlook anyone. Many employees feel that the only time anyone notices their work is when they do something wrong. Too often recognition is reserved for an elite few.
5. If you have an employee-of-the month program, skip those months during which no person earned the recognition. Do not restrict the award to one person/month. Make certain that the behavior that is being rewarded is either described in the announcement or is something that everyone in the unit knows. Without such descriptions, the award embarrasses the recipient and gives rise to charges of favoritism. Ask yourself "Do my selections pass the snicker test?"

NOTES

1. M. LeBoeuf, *The Greatest Management Principle in the World* (New York, NY: Berkeley Books, 1985), 11.
2. C. Barbee and V. Bott, "Customer Treatment as a Mirror of Employee Treatment," *SAM Advanced Management Journal 56* (1991): 27–32.
3. D. Deeprose, *How To Recognize & Reward Employees* (New York, NY: AMACOM, 1994), 19.
4. Deeprose, *How To Recognize & Reward Employees.*
5. M. Jahn, "Laboratorians Speak Out on Benefits, Managed Care, and the Bottom Line," *Medical Laboratory Observer 27,* no. 5 (1995): 29–33.
6. G.H. Graham and J. Unruh, "The Motivational Impact of Nonfinancial Employee Appreciation Practices on Medical Technologists," *The Health Care Supervisor 8* (1990): 9–17.

7. C. Bell, *Customers as Partners: Building Relationships That Last* (San Francisco, CA: Berrett-Koehler, 1994), 178.

8. Deeprose, *How To Recognize & Reward Employees,* 125.

RECOMMENDED READING

D. Deeprose, *How To Recognize & Reward Employees* (New York, NY: AMACOM, 1994).

G. Dutton, "Nurturing Employees and the Bottom Line," *HRFocus 74,* no. 9 (1997): 1–4.

Editorial, "Rethinking Rewards," *Harvard Business Review 71,* no. 6 (1993): 37–49.

Chapter 15

Performance Feedback

- day-to-day feedback
- formal performance reviews
- multisource feedback
- preparation for performance reviews of individuals
- the four-step interview
- evaluation of work teams
- common pitfalls

Performance feedback has always been a important responsibility of managers. The rapid and tumultuous changes now unfolding in medical care have resulted in employees taking more responsibility and learning new skills. They try to keep up with new organizational initiatives such as managed care, mergers, alliances, reengineering, customer satisfaction, employee empowerment, and team building. These fast-developing changes mandate more daily feedback to employees, and more comprehensive appraisals.

Today's performance appraisals include new duties and standards because health maintenance organizations and other forms of managed care demand greater customer satisfaction at a lower cost.

Appraisal and reward systems have in the past highlighted individuals. Now we must also evaluate and reward the performance and competencies of teams.

DAY-TO-DAY FEEDBACK

New employees learn on a daily basis how well performance expectations are being met, and they receive help in fine-tuning their skills. This coaching is our most powerful form of feedback. We seek to deliver candid and constructive feedback that is both helpful and enabling. Candid feedback is saying what we really think. Lacking these features, feedback does little to help people improve.

All employees should get more feedback than that provided in the annual or semiannual appraisals. For more on this feedback, see Chapter 12 on coaching.

FORMAL PERFORMANCE REVIEWS

A performance review should be an exchange of information and ideas, not a report card. Effective interviewers help employees recognize what needs improvement, and explore ways to capitalize on their strengths. To inculcate job satisfaction and motivation, supervisors serve more as resources and enablers than as appraisers. In other words, while performance reviews are valuative (matching performance with established standards), they are also developmental (enhancing careers). The valuative aspect depends on documented standards and verbal reinforcement, while the developmental aspect requires mentoring.

Effective reviews combine the features of recognition, self-appraisal, dual problem solving, and management by objectives. Emphasis is on the future rather than on the past. The past is only a prelude to a discussion of how the employee can do better in the future.

These meetings can have a positive or a negative impact on self-esteem. To boost morale and confidence we strive to make our associates perceive themselves as winners. A good performance review and planning session results in both parties leaving the room feeling that they have accomplished something.

Purposes of Performance Reviews

- To ensure understanding of performance expectations by both management and workers.
- To identify training and development needs.
- To ensure fair administration of reward systems.
- To provide recognition for past service.
- To help employees in enhancing their careers.

Four Essentials of Performance Reviews

1. Review and clarify performance expectations based on job descriptions, work standards, rules and policies, and previously formulated objectives. These are often omitted in traditional appraisals. Standards and goals should be clear and agreed upon.
2. Evaluate past performance. The appraisal concerns what was accomplished (eg, objectives met, outcomes realized) and how the employee functioned (eg, ethics, teamwork, attendance). Past performance gets the most attention because the rating process usually deals with prior outcomes and behavior.

   Competency assessments are needed for objective evaluations, but many positions are so complex that lists of these assessments would be impracti-

cal. In these situations competency assessment may be done by exception (ie, finding and documenting what is not done correctly rather than what is done).
3. Express appreciation for what the person has accomplished. This impacts self-confidence, confidence, job satisfaction, and motivation—things often lacking in traditional performance appraisal interviews.
4. Develop a plan. Planning moves from the past into the future and directly impacts work performance. Participative management demands collaboration and promises of support. It should involve much more than attempts to correct the deficiencies revealed on the rating sheets.

Rating Systems

Despite the poor results of most rating systems, employers have been reluctant to discard them because they need them for their merit-pay systems. Once they let the market decide how much people should be paid, they often find that ratings can be eliminated. The absence of a ranking process eliminates most of the negative impact of the performance review on morale and motivation.

The use of "forced-rating" systems in which the number of people who receive high ratings and the number receiving low ratings must be equal have all but disappeared—and good riddance!

MULTISOURCE FEEDBACK SYSTEMS

There are many weaknesses in the traditional top-down feedback systems. Some of these we have already mentioned. Employees benefit from feedback from their peers. Peer reviews are usually more accurate and acceptable and can help to reinforce the emphasis on collective responsibility. Such feedback is especially valuable because the person being evaluated learns how his or her behavior affects the other members.

Evaluating Leaders

In traditional organizations, all the appraising is vertically downwards. Employees are the recipients of the leadership provided by their superiors. Therefore they are customers of the leaders and entitled to evaluate the leadership performance. While in some organizations employees provide such feedback via formal appraisal systems, most employers obtain this information indirectly via employee attitude surveys.

Multisource Feedback

In the 360°multisource feedback system, managers flesh out the evaluation process by obtaining input from colleagues, subordinates, and sometimes customers. This provides a 360° view of how people perceive others on the job. Managers may use this system as a developmental tool or as a formal appraisal instrument.

Use of 360° Feedback Systems as Developmental Tools

People are more likely to modify their self-perceptions in the face of multisource feedback. There is less likelihood that important elements of performance are overlooked.

In development-only systems, the recipients of the feedback are asked whom they would like included in the battery of raters. The data become the sole property of the recipients and are not used in the formal appraisal process. These systems have been getting favorable comments from many employers. Most of the employees being evaluated find the reports helpful and sometimes surprising.

Use of 360° Feedback Systems in Formal Appraisals

Multisource feedback can make an appraisal system more comprehensive, but the employees need to believe that the data is unbiased and objective. They must have confidence in the intentions and credibility of the raters. The anonymity of the raters is usually protected.

Unlike in its purely developmental approach, these ratings become the property of management. Raters may or may not discuss their ratings with each other prior to releasing them to the person being rated, and to his or her superiors.

There are severe drawbacks to the use of these systems in the formal appraisal process. Lepsinger and Lucia[1] urge a cautious approach. They suggest that management first introduce the 360° system into their career development program. Then, if that is successful, a pilot study can be undertaken using the system for formal appraisal.

Drawbacks to 360° Feedback in Formal Appraisals

- Recipients may resist feedback that affects their salary and chances for promotion.
- When raters think they may hurt others by what they report, they're less likely to be honest.
- The raters may be competitors for rewards or promotions.

- The organizational culture may not support open, honest feedback.
- It makes an already time-consuming process still more demanding of time.

PREPARATION FOR PERFORMANCE REVIEWS OF INDIVIDUALS

The meeting has two components, process and content. The process consists of the format and the interviewer's skill. The content is what occurs during the meeting. As for any meeting, advance planning is the key to success. Too often the preparation by the interviewer consists of summarizing the employee's deficiencies and neglecting to look for the person's accomplishments and special efforts.

Review the Rating Form

Most organizations design their own evaluation forms, and supervisors have little input into the format. However, this should not prevent the interviewer from introducing additional items, including those that relate to teamwork and customer service. Such items may include:

- participating in team efforts,
- willingness to express opinions or assume responsibility,
- helping to solve problems,
- adjusting to major changes, and
- taking special actions to "delight" customers.

Highlight the items that are to receive special attention. Many all-purpose rating forms are deficient in listing competencies of people in leadership roles. The list in Exhibit 15–1 may be helpful.

Get Employee Input

Employees should have the following documents before the meeting:

- a copy of the position description, including performance standards;
- a copy of the evaluation form used to report the review (If employees hand in a completed form to the interviewer, two copies are provided, and one is retained by the employee.);
- a copy of the report of their previous formal review;
- departmental objectives for the current and subsequent year; and
- instructions on how to prepare for the meeting (see Exhibit 15–2).

Exhibit 15–1 Managerial Competencies

Maintains contemporary professional knowledge and skills
- Keeps up to date in both professional and managerial fields.
- Regularly attends seminars and other meetings.
- Meets all continuing education standards.

Demonstrates initiative and flexibility
- Identifies needs for innovation and change, and effectively implements changes.
- Solves problems quickly and skillfully.

Maximizes the use of personnel and material resources
- Keeps within budgetary limits.
- Manages time of self and subordinates effectively.
- Evaluates, selects, and maintains equipment and supplies skillfully.

Communicates effectively
- Keeps vertical and horizontal channels of communication open and active.
- Enjoys good rapport with other team members.
- Makes efficient use of meetings and other information systems; has mastered our computer system.
- Is skilled in interviewing techniques.
- Possesses good writing ability.

Shows other leadership abilities
- Coaches, counsels, and evaluates performance well.
- Maintains high morale, enthusiasm, and motivation.
- Is skilled in selecting, orienting, and training new hires.
- Deals promptly and effectively with personnel problems.
- Coordinates and cooperates well with other work units.
- Delegates and empowers effectively.
- Organizes, assigns, and schedules skillfully.
- Recognized as a good team builder.
- Accomplishes assignments and challenges on time and to the satisfaction of superiors.

You may choose to have employees fill out the evaluation form and give it to you before the meeting. There are two advantages to this practice. First, it introduces a spirit of collaboration. Second, it enables the interviewer to note the areas of disagreement or sensitivity.

Employees prepare a list of objectives and plans relating to personal improvement needs and career development, including specific requests for assistance needed to achieve the new objectives. Encourage them to prepare a list of what they regard as their significant contributions to the organization, and to include those activities that gave them the most satisfaction.

Exhibit 15–2 Employee Preparation Instructions

1. Review your position description. List any changes since your last review. Pencil in any changes you would like.
2. Scan your last review. Be prepared to discuss the objectives you achieved and those that were not achieved.
3. Prepare a new list of objectives.
4. Review your current continuing education record.
5. Jot down or be prepared to discuss:
   - how you feel about your performance since the last meeting
   - what you consider your most valuable contribution to the organization since your last review and what gave you the most satisfaction
   - what changes in systems, procedures, equipment, service, cost containment, or quality improvement you suggest we consider
   - anything that is preventing you from reaching your full potential
   - what frustrates you most at present
   - what we can do to help

Review Employee's Personnel File

Personnel records should include:

- the position description and performance standards;
- continuing education and attendance records;
- commendations, special recognitions, or awards;
- incident reports;
- records of counseling or disciplinary actions; and
- a copy of the previous appraisal.

Prepare an Agenda

Set a date, time, and place. Give the employee sufficient time to prepare for the meeting. Set aside at least one hour for the interview.

Formulate Key Remarks

Select the exact words to use for introductory statements, to criticize, and to confront defensiveness. Anticipate problems. Be ready to cite specific anecdotes to support any negative feedback or low ratings.

FOUR SEGMENTS OF THE INTERVIEW

1. Review and upgrade the position description and performance standards. This may be a good time to document changes relating to quality improvement, customer service, and empowerment strategies.

2. Discuss the performance ratings using the prescribed form. Begin on a positive note by focusing on items that were rated highest by both you and the employee. Do not gloss over these with something like "we agree on that." Compliment the person and relate instances of outstanding work that led to the high rating.

   Review the items that you rated higher than your report did. They will appreciate your discussing why you thought that they deserved a higher grade. Save the items that you rated low and the other person rated high for last. Here is where the defensiveness or emotional outbursts may occur. In Exhibit 15–3 we provide suggestions for discussing performance deficiencies.

> *A caveat:* Most experienced managers will confess that the biggest mistake they made in the past was to overrate marginal performers. This tendency all too often ends with an embarrassed manager trying to explain to a superior why he wants to fire a problem employee.

3. Critique accomplishments related to performance objectives formulated at the last review. Congratulate person for success in these areas. Decide which of the objectives that were not reached should be retained and which should be abandoned.

   End this segment by thanking the person for his or her accomplishments since the previous review.

4. Discuss future performance. Past performance only provides the database for planning. Most of the interview time should deal with expectations for the future. The first goal targets activities needed to improve performance. The second deals with career development—reaching one's full potential.

   Goals are meaningless—like most New Year's resolutions—if there is no commitment. Do not accept "I'll try." This is just a noisy way of doing nothing (eg, when people say that, they're building excuses for failure). If they fail, they claim that they did what they said they would—try.

   In this step you jointly develop a list of objectives that jibe with departmental goals and objectives. When interviewees have difficulty formulating objectives, help them. Ask them what they think should be done differently in

Exhibit 15–3 Suggestions for Discussing Performance Deficiencies

---

- Limit criticism to one or two major problems. If there are others, discuss them at another meeting.
- Offer your support.
- Save critical remarks for last.
- Before you criticize, encourage self-criticism.
- Use all your listening skills.
- Respond supportively:
  —Reinforce points of agreement
  —Handle disagreement diplomatically
  —Use joint problem-solving approaches
  —Avoid being defensive
- Avoid terms such as *attitude, work ethic, professionalism, weakness,* and *deficiency.*
- Do not use the global comment "needs more experience" when documenting improvement needs. Spell out the exact experience that is needed.

---

their unit and what role they would like to play in any such change. Do not give up on this too quickly. If the person still comes up empty, suggest a few things you would like the person to do. Then ask them what you could do to make their jobs more satisfying.

Use the Acronym SCRAM to Recall the Characteristics of Good Objectives

Specific. Specific feedback focuses on concrete and observable behavior, not inferences about traits or personality characteristics.

Challenging. If it is not challenging, it probably is not worth very much.

Relevant. It must be related to the person's responsibilities.

Achievable. It should be challenging but doable. Failures lead to frustration and loss of self-confidence.

Measurable. Statistics and charts are good (hard data), but sometimes behavior is not easy to quantify. While some words such as caring, respect, and courtesy can't be meaningfully measured with digits, the key is verifiability.

Conclude the Interview

End the session with an affirmation—an expression of confidence in the ability of the interviewee to achieve the new objectives. Thank the person not only for what they have accomplished, but also for their cooperation during the interview.

Postinterview Actions

Make certain that you have filled out the appraisal form completely and documented the new objectives and action plans. Employees must be given an opportunity to respond verbally and in writing to adverse comments and/or unfavorable performance ratings. Do not neglect to:

- Keep tabs on the person's progress. Remind them about their plans and objectives if necessary.
- Congratulate them when they have reached each objective or show areas of improvement.
- Confirm promised support or offer more when obstacles are perceived by the employee.
- Modify, replace, or cancel objectives as appropriate.
- Document their achievements.

PERFORMANCE EVALUATION OF WORK TEAMS

Different teams require different approaches to measurement. Teams of floor nurses and their ancillary care providers are evaluated largely by patient satisfaction. The performance of a laboratory team is usually judged by turnaround time, accuracy, and reliability of test results.

Appraising teams involves the *what* and the *how* of team efforts. The *what* refers to the goals, objectives, and key results that the team and each individual achieve. The *how* refers to the performance behavior important in promoting teamwork and achieving the team goals collaboratively.

Teams may be evaluated by team facilitators, with or without participation of team players. Both individual and team performance is evaluated by members of self-directed teams, except in the early phases of team building when the supervisor still does it.

COMMON PITFALLS

- The process is not taken seriously by either party. This is manifested when there is inadequate preparation by the participants, the meeting is repeatedly postponed—or left until the last minute—and then done hurriedly. Or, the interviewer tolerates frequent interruptions during the meeting.

- The manager has only superficial knowledge of the employee's performance. It has been truly said that the less a manager knows about what a subordinate does, the better chance the subordinate has to do whatever he or she wants— or how much. This pitfall is eliminated when self-directed teams are in place.
- There are no documented, updated, specific work standards or objectives.
- The evaluation is highly subjective or lacks honesty. Failure to honestly critique an employee's performance hurts the organization and the employee.
- There is too much judging and too little listening by the interviewer.
- There is insufficient positive feedback or respect for the employee's self-esteem.
- The interview consists of little more than "You're doing just fine," handing out reports without comment, or only inviting questions about the report.
- The rating forms are inappropriate—and most are!
- The review is used to allocate salaries instead of to improve performance.
- Emphasis is on the past rather than on the future.
- New objectives are missing, nonspecific, inappropriate or lack challenge.
- The employee has little participation in formulating objectives or resetting standards for future performance.
- Reprimands or criticism had never been discussed prior to the meeting, catching the interviewee by surprise.
- The manager saves up all the deficiencies and hits the report with the entire list during the interview. When the employee also gunnysacks complaints and strikes back at the interviewer with the whole sack, the fur can really fly or the tears roll.

NOTE

1. R. Lepsinger and A.D. Lucia, "360° Feedback and Performance Appraisal," *Training 34,* no. 9 (1997): 62–70.

RECOMMENDED READING

C.M. Chesser et al. "Job Descriptions and Performance Appraisals," *Health Care Supervisor 15,* no. 4 (1997): 1–34.

S.H. Gebelein, "Multi-Rater Feedback Goes Strategic," *HRFocus 73,* no. 1 (1996): 1, 6.

J. Ghorpade and M.M. Chen, "Appraising the Performance of Medical Technologists in a Clinical Laboratory," *Clinical Laboratory Management Review 11,* no. 2 (1997): 132–141.

Chapter 16

Counseling

There are two kinds of counseling: career counseling, when the supervisor serves as an advisor or mentor, and remedial counseling. Remedial counseling addresses employee performance that has strayed from established norms. This chapter focuses on the latter.

The goal of counseling is to correct deviant performance while preserving the self-esteem of the individual. A confrontation provides the employee with an opportunity to look at his or her behavior and to decide whether or not to change. Our objective should never be to release anger or frustration or to punish.

Unsuccessful counseling usually culminates in disciplinary measures.

FIVE MOST COMMON REASONS FOR COUNSELING

1. Unsatisfactory productivity or work quality
2. Poor work habits or violation of policies, rules, procedures, or ethics
3. Inability to get along with others
4. Chronic complaining
5. Complaints from customers

IS THERE REALLY A PROBLEM?

When performance or behavior is borderline, you must decide whether action is needed and, if action is needed, what it should be. In marginal instances, ask yourself "What if everyone did that?" or "If I do not do anything, what adverse effects are likely to result?"

If you have a team of overachievers, you may regard the performance of marginal performers as unsatisfactory because it compares unfavorably with that of the overachievers. This trap can be avoided if you match performance with established standards, not with other employees.

IS COUNSELING THE SOLUTION?

Counseling is not the remedy for all personnel problems. It is preventive medicine. It can solve small problems before they become big ones that require formal disciplinary measures. Figure 16–1 shows a flowchart that you can use for this purpose. Note that counseling is usually not the best remedy.

WHY EMPLOYEES VIOLATE RULES

- They never learned the rules or they forgot them.
- They see the rules as meaningless, too restrictive, or unfair.
- They know that the rules are rarely enforced.
- They are influenced by other workers.
- They find that the rewards of misbehavior are higher than the risks or the penalties.
- They are misfits or malcontents.

WHERE MANAGERS GO WRONG

- They do not take action because:
  1. they are not aware of the problem.
  2. they ignore the problem.
  3. they postpone action until the next performance review.
- They assume that the problem is one of poor attitude.
- They fail to monitor postmeeting behavior.
- They fail to escalate from counseling to disciplining when no improvement occurs or frequent relapses occur.

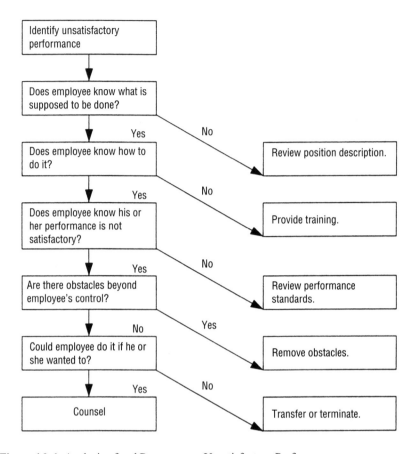

Figure 16–1 Analysis of and Responses to Unsatisfactory Performance

PREPARING FOR THE COUNSELING INTERVIEW

Get the facts:

- What have you or others observed?
- What have you documented?
- Is this a relapse? If so, what was agreed upon at previous confrontations?
- Review the employee's record, especially any written reprimands, customer complaints, and the last formal performance appraisal report.
- Be certain of the content and context of any violated policy or rule. Study the document yourself, word for word.

- Look for patterns. For example, with absenteeism, individuals may call in sick only on Mondays, Fridays, or on days when they're scheduled for unpleasant assignments.

Explore the perceived benefit-risk ratio of the behavior from the employee's viewpoint. For example, when an employee goes shopping on sick days or takes long breaks and is never called on it, the benefit-risk ratio is high. There is no incentive to reform.

Do not procrastinate. Think of the damage that is taking place while you hesitate. Also, the more you delay, the harder it will be to convince the person that the matter is important.

If you are inexperienced in these matters and the problem is a serious one, consult with your manager or a member of the human resources department.

Schedule a place, date, and time. The location should be one where there will be no interruptions (your office may not be the best location). Hold the meeting in the morning. Then you have the rest of the day to show by words and behavior that you do not bear a grudge toward them, only toward their behavior. Smile and chat just as you would if you had not held a counseling session.

Mentally rehearse the most important or sensitive aspects of the upcoming meeting. Appropriate items include:

- your exact opening remarks,
- statements to boost the employee's confidence,
- the solution you hope to lead to, and
- how you will respond to rebuttals, defensive reactions, anger, tears, or threats.

EIGHT-STEP COUNSELING INTERVIEW

Let's review your counseling interview with Joyce, who has a behavioral problem.

Step 1. The theme of the initial session should be one of helpfulness and caring. Greet Joyce with a smile. You're going to help, not punish, her. Thank her for coming.

Never apologize for calling the meeting. You weaken your position when you start with something such as "Joyce, I hate to bring this up, but . . . ."

Equally bad is socking her with an intimidating statement such as "Joyce, we've got to talk about your poor performance."

Assume that she wants to do a good job, and say so. Affirm that assumption by articulating some specific attribute (eg, "Joyce, I receive many compliments from our medical staff about your gentleness toward patients." Continue with, "Joyce, I have a problem that I need your help with." [This is true. It really is your problem!])

Step 2. Find out whether Joyce is aware of the problem, especially if a policy or rule is being violated. Describe the situation in specific, nonjudgmental terms. Be tentative if there is some question as to the validity of the charge.

Use the words you selected carefully in your preparation. Attack the behavior, not Joyce. Your hope is that Joyce joins you in that attack. The more able you are to move into a problem-solving mode, the more successful the outcome will be.

Step 3. Explain how the behavior affects your department and other people. To convince her that this is important, emphasize how the behavior affects you (eg, "When I see . . ., I get very upset"). Avoid absolute words such as always and never. These words are usually inaccurate and invite contradiction. For example, "You're never on time" is countered with "I'm on time most of the time." Avoid sarcasm, kidding, or other put-downs. These elicit resentment and serve no useful purpose.

Do not quote from policy manuals unless the employee challenges the authenticity of your charge. Taking refuge in a handbook makes you appear weak. For the same reason, do not say, "Management expects. . . ." Do say, "I expect . . . ."

Step 4. Give her time to respond. Listen until she runs out of gas. Do not interrupt, even if she utters untruths or makes countercharges. Do not become defensive or lose your cool.

Respond appropriately. Instead of judgmental responses ("You do not try hard enough") or defensive responses ("That's not true and you know it"), use empathetic responses ("I can understand why you . . . ") and probing responses (when, where, who, why, and how). Paraphrase ("What I hear you saying is . . . ") and summarize ("Then we agree that . . . ?").

Jot down key points Joyce makes. You may need to refer to these later.

Step 5. Get Joyce to admit that there is a problem and that she is part of it. This is often difficult, especially if the behavior has been tolerated for some time. She may respond sarcastically with "Big deal" or some similar remark.

Ask her what she thinks the effects of this continued behavior could be on her employment or relationships (eg, impact on her next performance appraisal). This forces her to reflect on the consequences that are not in her best interest.

Empathize with any aired frustration (eg, "You say that you feel like a victim of the system. I can appreciate that").

Step 6. Emphasize that the problem must be solved and that it's up to her to solve it. Add that you're always there to help. Reiterate the point that she should solve her problem.

Why You Should Avoid Prescribing Solutions

- Quick solutions by you make the person feel stupid.
- When your solution doesn't work, you look stupid.
- Employees feel obliged to take your advice even when they know that they have a better solution.
- An employee tries harder when it is her solution.
- Employees become dependent on you for all their solutions.

If you cannot accept her first offering, keep asking for alternatives until she comes up with one that you can live with. Discuss the pros and cons of each suggestion. Avoid directive phrases such as "If I were you . . . " or "Here's what you should do." Compliment her for coming up with solutions.

If the discussion stalls, ask some leading questions to guide her to more options. Do not impose your solution unless absolutely necessary.

Offer to help (eg, "Joyce, it's up to you to take care of this. However, I will cooperate. When I notice . . ., I'll remind you").

Step 7. Summarize what is agreed upon. Repeat your expectations clearly and insist on her commitment to the solution. Include a deadline for the problem to be solved.

End on a positive note and with an affirmation. Thank her for cooperating, and express confidence in her ability to solve the problem. For example, "Joyce, I appreciate your cooperation. I knew that I could depend on you to take care of this. This past performance is way below what I know you are capable of."

If it's obvious that despite your best efforts you're not getting near a solution, do not make it a matter of wills. Simply state your position and what you expect. Then end the meeting. It's sometimes a good idea to set a date for a follow-up meeting.

Step 8. Document. A common and serious deficiency is the lack of documentation. All too often, counseling is not successful and must be repeated or ratcheted up to disciplinary level. In either instance, you'll be grateful for having the record.

The record should include:

- the date,
- a description of the problem,
- the employee's comments (exact words are best),
- the agreed-upon resolution,
- any warning given by you,
- the deadline for the problem to be solved.

I recommend that these notes not be placed in the employee's file. If you do that, you have given a written reprimand—the second step in disciplining. You have not held a counseling session. You must also give the employee a copy. More significantly, your role changes from counselor to disciplinarian—a change that erodes your relationship with that employee.

Maintain confidentiality. Keep your notes locked up, secure from prying eyes. Do not discuss the meeting with anyone other than your immediate superior.

FIVE COMMON DEFENSIVE RESPONSES BY EMPLOYEES

Keep in mind that any behavior displayed or comments made by the employee during the interview represents behavior that the individual has found effective in the past.

1. They balk at any discussion.
   - They say they do not want to discuss the matter right now.
   - They deny everything you say.
   - They refuse to listen or keep interrupting.
   - They talk louder and faster.
   - They weep.
   - They storm out of your office.
   - They clam up and will not say anything.
   Solution: Insist on a dialogue. Respond to loud, angry outcries with something such as "You're starting to yell, Joyce."
   If Joyce runs out of your office, do not chase after her. Simply wait until later in the day, or the next day, and then send for her again. Start all over.
   If she cries, hand her a box of tissues and wait for the tears to stop.
   A person who suddenly clams up may be trying to decide whether to say something of a sensitive nature. If you break the silence too soon, you may never know what that was. If the silence persists, say, "Joyce, I thought we were having a conversation." Lean forward and look like you expect a response. If you repeat this without success, sigh or frown and say you will

try to establish a dialogue at another time. If a second meeting also ends in failure, you must move on to take disciplinary action.

2. They try to minimize the problem.

They retort sarcastically, "OK, I haven't been the employee of the month. I'll try to do better if that'll make you happy."

Solution: Never accept this. Say you're glad they recognize there is a problem. Emphasize that this is an important issue and that something definite must be done about it.

3. They challenge you.

Joyce may say, "The old boss never said anything about that."

Solution: Respond with, "I'm not your old boss."

She may say, "If this is so important, how is it that you never said anything about it before?"

Solution: Respond with, "I thought that you would take care of it without my direction." Or admit that you should have acted sooner.

She claims that work is not affected (eg, "I get my work done, don't I?").

Solution: Respond with, "Yes, but you interfere with the work of others and set a bad example for the new employees."

4. They counterattack.

She threatens to quit or to go over your head. She may accuse you of the same behavior (eg, "You have gall, accusing me of that. I have seen you doing the very same thing.")

Solutions: If she threatens to quit, to go over your head, or to expose something damaging about you, reply that she may do whatever she chooses, but that you recommend that she first give serious thought to the possible consequences of that act.

5. They try to sidetrack the discussion.

She accuses others (eg, "Helen does the same thing. How is it that you never say anything to her?"). Or she blames a myriad of personal problems at home.

Solutions: If she tries to sidetrack the discussion, respond that nothing will be accomplished by accusing others. If she blames problems at home, channel the discussion back to the work situation. If signs and symptoms suggest a serious personal problem, however, recommend professional help. Usually an appropriate comment is "Joyce, I'm not qualified to help you with those kinds of problems. I can recommend a professional counselor if you like, but for now let's get back to the problem at hand."

FOLLOW-UP

The counseling process does not end with the interview. Managers often dismiss the subject from their minds because they are so relieved that the confrontation is over and that the employees have promised to solve the problems.

The follow-up consists of monitoring performance and reinforcing desired behavior. Positive strokes motivate; negative strokes or the absence of feedback demotivate. Support improvements with smiles and pats on the back. Do not wait until perfection has been achieved. Reinforce each small step with something such as "I know that you are making a special effort, Joyce, and I appreciate that."

Identify and address specific concerns that call for exploration or reassurance.

When the problem appears to have been solved, hold a commendatory meeting. At that meeting, describe the improvement you've noted and encourage the person to relate how he or she achieved it. At this time you can offer to help with any unanticipated roadblocks. Close the meeting with expressions of appreciation and an affirmation.

If the undesired behaviors or results persist, you're faced with several choices. You can extend the deadline if there has been some progress, you can begin disciplinary actions, or you can counsel again. Most often you will choose to repeat the counseling session. Now you have the initial problem plus a new one—the employee failing to deliver on his or her commitment.

Your objectives in the repeat session are to:

- let the employee know that you are aware of the continued problem,
- inform the employee of the risk he or she is taking, and
- offer one more chance before you take disciplinary action.

To emphasize the importance of the meeting to the wayward employee, ask your manager or a representative of the human resources department to sit in.

At this session, manifest less patience, and skip the smiles and affirmations. On the other hand, avoid accusatory expressions (which are usually the ones that start with "You didn't try very hard" or "Why did you . . .?").

Probe for possible roadblocks beyond the employee's control. Most important, insist that the employee come up with a new solution (or resolution), and state what the consequences of another failure will be.

Make certain that you set a target date.

Seven Key Points to Be Covered in the Repeat Session

1. Review the agreements reached at the previous session.
2. State what you have observed or learned that shows that the agreement has been broached.
3. Ask for an explanation.

---

4. Insist on a new solution or effort.
5. State the consequences of continued noncompliance. Avoid making a threat that you do not intend to carry out.
6. Agree on the new action to be taken and a new follow-up date.
7. State your reluctance to give up on the employee and your belief that he or she can correct the situation.

COMMON BARRIERS TO SUCCESSFUL COUNSELING

The excuse often given by supervisors is that there were so many other more important things to do that they never got around to it. Often the supervisor is intimidated by the person or fears legal repercussions. They may not be trained in interviewing techniques. Perhaps they are hazy about policies or procedures. Often they're dealing with someone who is influential because of seniority, special expertise, or powerful friends. Sometimes they fear loss of friendship, particularly when there had been a peer relationship before the promotion to supervisor. At other times, a supervisor has sympathy for a troubled person and fears making matters worse for that person.

PRINCIPLES OF SUCCESSFUL INTERVENTIONS

- Initially confront as a friend, not as an antagonist.
- Be direct and honest.
- Listen more than you talk.
- Say how you feel. Ask them how they feel.
- Select the best time and place for confrontations.
- Do not nitpick.
- Make them come up with solutions.
- Strive for win-win solutions.
- Be willing to compromise.
- Work with facts, not assumptions.
- Be optimistic. Expect positive results.
- Preserve their self-esteem.
- Do not pontificate or be condescending.
- Do not expect the impossible.
- Look for the good in the person.
- Monitor and reinforce.
- Be specific and consistent.
- Avoid arousing defensiveness.

RECOMMENDED READING

C.R. McConnell, "Effective Employee Counseling for the First-Line Supervisor," *Health Care Supervisor 16,* no. 1 (1997): 77–86.

Chapter 17

Disciplining

- the nature of discipline
- counseling versus disciplining
- the reward/risk ratio
- progressive discipline
- reactions to being disciplined
- other punitive measures
- nonpunitive discipline
- eight sound disciplinary principles
- getting rid of the deadwood

NATURE OF DISCIPLINE

Disciplining is not punishing, at least not at first. Disciplining is an educational effort to nudge unsatisfactory performance up to an acceptable level. The initial goal is not greasing the slide to separation. Au contraire, it is providing traction for employees to correct deviant behavior. When done skillfully, employee self-esteem is preserved.

Discipline should be fair, firm, and fast. Delay only increases tension. If all you do is complain to others about an employee, you deserve what you get—continued problem and loss of respect of your superiors and the people who report to you. Proper discipline has been likened to a red-hot stove. It provides a warning (red or sizzling), does not discriminate (everyone who touches gets burned), and is immediate, consistent, and effective.

When managers treat their employees as they would like to be treated, they have fewer disciplinary problems. They spot potential trouble areas and avoid the need for discipline by utilizing their coaching and counseling expertise. The best discipline is self discipline and is achieved when employees are treated as responsible adults. Some managers treat their employees as children and then are surprised when these employees behave like children.

Supervisors who practice management by intimidation spend much of their time trying to catch people doing something wrong. The employees respond not so much by cleaning up their act as by avoiding being caught. Many grievances are the aftermaths of disciplinary actions.

COUNSELING VERSUS DISCIPLINING

Disciplining interlocks with counseling. Counseling may be regarded as an informal first step in the disciplinary process. It becomes a formal disciplinary step—the oral reprimand—when the employee is warned of the consequences of failure to perform up to expectations. Most organizations require one or more oral reprimands for most offenses before punitive measures are administered.

Counseling or reprimands are not appropriate for some serious forms of misbehavior where immediate suspensions or dismissals are indicated. Your organization probably provides written guidelines and appropriate penalties for various disciplinary infractions. See Exhibit 17–1.

REWARD/RISK RATIO

Most employees do not misbehave because they are bad or want to harass their superiors. It is usually a matter of deriving some benefit—sometimes an unconscious one—from misbehaving.

When supervisors fail to detect violations of rules, policies, or procedures, or they fail to take corrective measures, employees have no incentive to change. Consider the ratio of reward to risk. We all play this game on the road every day. We drive a little over the speed limit because we are in a hurry. The reward is getting to our destination quicker. Most of us do not drive at breakneck speed because we know that this increases the risk of being killed or arrested. Once you recognize what reward an employee derives from his inappropriate behavior and what he fears, you can more easily modify that behavior by decreasing the reward or increasing the risk.

For example, Ken frequently arrives late for work on the evening shift because he knows that the day crew will take care of some of his duties. His previous supervisor never said anything to him. The new supervisor quickly becomes aware of the situation and tells the day crew to stop doing Ken's work (less reward). The supervisor also warns Ken and tells him to check in with her when he arrives (increased risk).

Exhibit 17–1 Guidelines for Disciplinary Action

Class I: Minor Infractions

Discipline

First offense—Oral warning
Second offense—Written warning
Third offense—1-Day suspension
Fourth offense—3-Day suspension

Typical Subjects

- Unsatisfactory quality or quantity of work
- Discourtesy to patient, staff member, or coworker
- Lateness
- Absenteeism

Class II: More Serious Infractions

Discipline

First offense—Written warning
Second offense—3-Day suspension
Third offense—Discharge

Typical Subjects

- Unavailability when scheduled for work
- Performance of personal work on hospital time
- Violation of smoking, safety, fire, or emergency regulations
- Unauthorized absence

Class III: Still More Serious Infractions

Discipline

First offense—Written warning
Second offense—Discharge

Typical Subjects

- Insubordination
- Negligence
- Falsification of records, reports, or information
- Improper release of confidential or privileged information
- Sexual harassment

continues

Exhibit 17–1 continued

Class IV: Most Serious Infractions

Discipline

First offense—Discharge

Typical Subjects

- Absence without notice for three consecutive days
- Fighting on the job
- Theft or dishonesty
- Intoxication or use of alcohol or drugs on premises
- Willful damage to hospital property

PROGRESSIVE DISCIPLINE

This discipline is called progressive because the disciplinary measures will become increasingly severe until there is a resolution of the problem. In its traditional form, progressive discipline consists of four steps:

1. oral reprimand,
2. written reprimand,
3. suspension or probation, and
4. discharge.

Oral Reprimand

Avoid gunnysacking. Gunnysacking is saving up all your complaints and then, one frustrating day, dumping the entire load on someone. Deliver reprimands as soon as possible after the misbehavior, but not until you have control of your emotions. Keep it confidential. Do it in private. Your office may not be the best location.

Do not be apologetic. Describe what is wrong and how you feel about it. Do not exaggerate. Attack the problem, not the person. Avoid starting sentences with an accusatory "you," or using subjective words such as attitude, work ethic, professionalism, and the absolute words "always" and "never."

Let the person respond, but cut short a litany of lame excuses. Anticipate remarks such as "You're not being fair" or "You can't say things like that to me." Say exactly what you expect the person to do or to stop doing.

If this is a repeat reprimand or has previously been addressed by counseling, use the counseling technique you learned in Chapter 16. Be less empathic and more formal, however. Show that your patience is running out. Warn of future action.

For example, "If this is not corrected immediately, it will be necessary for me to. . . ."

If the wayward employee was hired by a superior or was highly recruited, make certain that you discuss this problem with your manager. When you discipline employees who are popular with their coworkers, you must rely on the support you have built up with your team. If they trust you and know that you are fair, they will support your decision.

Written Reprimand

The written reprimand often leads to a discharge with all its legal ramifications, so proceed with caution. Your human resources department may have a special form that you must use for this purpose. Find out whether you have the authority to issue written reprimands. In well-run organizations and with competent leadership, these should seldom be necessary.

Discuss the problem with your manager before you write up the report.

Craft the warning carefully. It is a legal document and may end up in court. Avoid statements that you cannot prove. Provide observations and facts, not opinions or hearsay. A list of essentials is presented in Exhibit 17–2.

When you meet, explain that a written reprimand is a formal warning and will be documented in the employee's personnel file. Review and document any previous counseling sessions or oral reprimands for the same problem.

Be specific as to your expectations and the final date for compliance. For example: "If within the next 60 days you're late for work another time without an acceptable excuse, I will send you home on a one-day suspension without pay." This sounds juvenile, but sometimes people who fail to act maturely must be treated that way.

Tell the person that after a specified time (eg, six months) and without further similar kind of incident, the record of the disciplinary action will be expunged from the personnel file.

Insist that the employees read and sign the report. Inform them of their right to attach a rebuttal or to confer with your superior.

Suspensions

Some offenses call for immediate suspension or discharge without any antecedent counseling or reprimands. In many organizations, supervisors may only recommend such action; the actual order must come from the personnel department or a senior executive.

If the employee has received oral and written warnings in the past, a formal meeting may not be needed. Your human resources department will provide the necessary form or instruct you on how to prepare the report.

Exhibit 17–2 Essentials of a Written Disciplinary Report

Description of the problem
- State facts, not assumptions, hearsay, or opinions.
- Give dates when possible. Provide examples.
- Record names of witnesses and/or involved persons.

Record of previous warnings
- Give dates.
- Indicate what was said by you and by the employee.
- State what changes in conduct, if any, resulted.

Record of previous written reprimands or punitive actions
- Attach copies.
- Indicate what punitive measures were taken.
- State what changes in conduct, if any, resulted.

The employee's document of explanation, denial, or rebuttal
- If the employee chooses to do this, include a copy.
- If the employee chooses not to do this, describe what the employee stated as accurately as possible. Include the statement that the employee chose not to prepare such a document.

Record of punitive action now being decreed
- Include a statement that the punishment was explained to the employee.
- Include a statement that the employee understood what was to happen.

Description of expected performance
- Include the target date for achieving satisfactory performance.
- Describe what will or will not be tolerated.
- Provide your signature and that of the employee. If the employee refuses to sign, call in a witness and repeat the question; if the employee still refuses to sign, have the witness verify that.

When individuals return to work after suspensions, treat them like any other employee. Be businesslike, neither clubby nor aloof. You have already chastised them.

Discharges

Today's managers are reluctant to fire people. They feel that it is all but impossible to fire anyone. They cite all the roadblocks and potential legal backlashes that may result from such action. However, if specific work standards are in place and mandated procedures are followed, terminations are not that difficult.

Too often supervisors create the problem by accepting unsatisfactory performance or behavior for a long time, and by rating performance as satisfactory when it is not. Townsend[1] claims that purging bad performers is as good a tonic for an organization as rewarding its star performers.

One surprising observation is that years after being fired, people often admit that the firing was not only justified, but was the turning point in their careers.

Follow your organization's prescribed procedure for discharging people. Usually your human resources department has the responsibility for carrying out the procedure.

Employers protect themselves by providing employee handbooks that state the organization's disciplinary policies. They avoid any mention of permanent employment or statements that employees can be terminated only for cause. They warn their managers about the danger of rating people higher than they deserve.

Some cautious employers insist that employment lawyers approve discharges before the employees are notified. This is for good reason. Many fired employees file wrongful dismissal suits, and these can be expensive and time consuming. Those who sue usually charge that they were fired without cause or for insufficient reasons. Others claim that the termination violated a written or verbal agreement they or their union had with the employer.

To sustain a discharge against legal challenges, an employer must prove:

- that there are specific and documented work standards and policies and that employees are repeatedly reminded about these;
- that what was alleged did take place, involved the employee, and warranted the discharge;
- that such behavior had not been condoned in the past and/or that other workers had been discharged for similar offenses;
- that the sequence of discipline followed prescribed policies and procedures;
- that the employee made no genuine effort to heed the previous warnings even though he or she had been informed as to the consequences;
- that the firing was based on behavior or results, not on any of the following (wrongful discharge):
  1. discrimination (gender, race, religion, age, or disability)
  2. whistle blowing related to safety practices, illegal acts, sexual harassment, military or jury duty, or workers' compensation claims
  3. violation of implied contract (the employee was promised a permanent job).

Termination Meeting

You may choose not to hold a termination meeting. Let your human resources department handle it. A good time to hold the meeting is Friday afternoon after other employees have departed and shortly after the employee has received written notice from the human resources department. Never discuss the possibility of reconsideration. All such possibilities should have been exhausted before the final meeting.

Say that you're sorry things did not work out, and wish the person well. If the person gets angry or breaks into tears, stay calm. Do not get drawn into a debate, or agree with any charges the person makes. Say that the human resources department will discuss any additional administrative matters such as terminal pay and benefits, and will have the person's final check.

Tell the person exactly what information will be released to potential employers who request the data and that it will be released only by the personnel department. Your responsibility may include ensuring that the employee has returned keys, identification tags, and other items that belong to the organization. Security codes in computers and keys to secured areas may have to be changed.

EMPLOYEE REACTIONS TO BEING DISCIPLINED

Some disciplined employees quit and leave. Others quit psychologically but remain on the job because of vested time, unwillingness to look for new jobs, or lack of opportunities elsewhere. Those who stay often become marginal performers at best. Many employees file grievances. They seek redress via unions, courts, the Equal Employment Opportunity Commission, the Occupational Safety and Health Administration, or some other governmental agency.

OTHER PUNITIVE MEASURES

There are other disciplinary actions. Innovative supervisors can come up with almost as many punitive measures as their employees can find ways to avoid them. Some of these measures include:

- withholding, or delaying, salary increases;
- denying promotions;
- lowering performance ratings;
- placing on probation;
- demoting or transferring;
- denying requests for educational support or time off;
- withdrawing special privileges or authority;
- giving unpleasant assignments;
- canceling special projects; and
- removing from teams, committees, or other work groups.

NONPUNITIVE DISCIPLINE

Punishment breeds resistance, encourages subterfuge, and undermines employee willingness to make future contributions to the organization. The nonpunitive or positive disciplinary approach has been successful in overcoming many of these adverse effects.[2]

The nonpunitive approach usually works better than the traditional method because it places more responsibility on the employee. It makes it difficult for that person to be hostile toward the organization if he or she is eventually terminated.

This strategy has reduced the filing of grievances over terminations, decreased involuntary turnover, and improved morale. The only objections have been from employees' coworkers. They resent someone getting a day off with pay while they must do that employee's work.

The theme of the nonpunitive approach is building commitment instead of enforcing compliance. It is congruent with the principle of participative management in that it, too, is treating employees as adults, not children.

Encouragement replaces threats. Rules are called employee responsibilities; verbal and written warnings are expressed as suggestions. Discussions are low key with emphasis on problem solving. For example, you tell a person that her performance threatens your unit's success and her future.

When these discussions fail, the suggestion is made that there may be a poor employee-job fit and that a change in employment may be beneficial for all parties.

The most radical departure from the traditional disciplinary approach is the one-day suspension with pay. The employee is given a day of decision.

Typical Steps in Nonpunitive Discipline

Step 1. Offer the employee an informal, friendly reminder that a work rule has been broken and explain the reasoning behind the rule. Get the employee to agree that his or her behavior is inappropriate and should not be repeated.

Step 2. After a second violation, hold a repeat session, but this time have your manager or a representative of the personnel department sit in on the meeting.

Step 3. If there is still another violation, tell the employee that if the rule seems distasteful, perhaps he should find another employer. Confirm this conversation in a letter sent to the employee's home. For example:

Our solutions have not worked. I have serious concerns about whether you want to continue here. I do not want a final commitment right now. Take the rest of the day (or tomorrow) to think over what you want to do, then let me know what you've decided. As a token of our faith in you, and as a sign that we want you to stay with us, you'll receive full pay for the day of decision.

If you want to continue on our team, fine. However, you'll have to give me a signed, firm commitment that you will fulfill all your responsibilities. If you do not, then we both have failed and your employment will end. If I do not hear from you, your services will be automatically terminated.

If the employee returns to work and agrees to abide by the rules but violates that agreement within a few months, terminate him.

EIGHT SOUND DISCIPLINARY PRACTICES

1. Inform your employees of the rules of employment. Repeat this periodically and to each new employee.
2. Do not let misbehavior develop into habits.
3. Do not act before you get the facts.
4. Reprimand in private.
5. Do not play "Do as I say, not as I do."
6. Use punishment only as a last resort.
7. Use either progressive or nonpunitive discipline according to the policies of your organization.
8. Remain aware of your goal.

SOUND DISCIPLINARY PRINCIPLES

- Know:
  1. exactly what the unacceptable behavior is and what policy or rule has been violated,
  2. any mitigating circumstances,
  3. the scope of your authority, and
  4. how similar offenses have been handled in the past.
- Assume that:
  1. employees want to do good work,
  2. employees must perceive some benefit from their unacceptable behavior,

3. you or others may be partly to blame, and
4. you have many punitive options.
- Act:
  1. quickly once you have the information you need;
  2. appropriately by consulting with your superior or the human resources department;
  3. consistently and fairly;
  4. by using punishment only as a last resort;
  5. by selecting penalties that are appropriate for the offenses;
  6. by documenting, documenting, documenting; and
  7. by having the terminated employee leave the premises as soon as possible.
- Do not:
  1. let misbehavior develop into habits;
  2. act before you get the facts;
  3. be apologetic;
  4. use words such as loyalty, attitude, work ethic, professionalism, or maturity;
  5. say "Management expects . . ."; say "I expect . . ."; or
  6. trap yourself into a series of verbal warnings for the same problem with the same employee.

GETTING RID OF DEADWOOD

Termination may be necessary because of inability to meet minimum work standards and failure of retraining attempts. Every once in a while you find that you have someone who makes the same mistakes over and over. He or she feels bad about it, but can't shake the jinx. Bad luck seems to follow these poor souls. They admit that they had similar problems at other jobs. Since in health care these mistakes can jeopardize lives, you must get rid of these people.

Before discharging the employee, make certain that the employee has been given ample warnings during performance reviews and had abundant opportunities to shore up his or her performance. The unsatisfactory work record must be adequately documented. Even one laudatory performance appraisal may get you into a legal mess.

NOTES

1. R. Townsend, *Up the Organization* (New York, NY: Fawcett World Library, 1971), 45.
2. J.R. Redeker, "Discipline, Part 2: the Nonpunitive Approach Works by Design," *Personnel 62* (1985): 7–10.

RECOMMENDED READING

D. Grote, "Discipline Without Punishment," *Training 33,* no. 1 (1996): 129.

J.L. Raper and S.N. Myaya, "Employee Discipline: A Changing Paradigm," *Health Care Supervisor 12,* no. 2 (1993): 67–77.

Chapter 18

Cultural Diversity

- ethnically, socially, and economically diverse work forces
- cultural core values
- corporate values
- personal values
- diversity management programs
- responsibilities of supervisors
- tips for supervisors
- promotions for women

ETHNICALLY, SOCIALLY, AND ECONOMICALLY DIVERSE WORK FORCES

"Diversity Management" is a hot item in this decade. It refers to how managers hire, supervise, use the skills of, and promote employees of varied backgrounds. These backgrounds are multiracial, multicultural, multiethnic, and gender oriented. They also include differences in age, education, economic level, and tenure and in the presence or absence of disabilities. Service workers (food preparers, aides, orderlies, attendants, housekeepers, and maintenance people) usually represent the most multiracial and culturally diverse component of a health care institution.

Each work group values their "in-group" more positively than they do any "out-groups." Management and workers have different values and attitudes and often have different political affiliations. Managers and professionals look at the same thing with different colored glasses. Professionals bond stronger to members of their specialty or profession than they do to other people in the same organization. Their personal networks may show little overlapping.

Appreciation of cultural differences and appropriate bonding with employees who have these differences can increase the number of customers and job applicants. Failure to make these adjustments creates resentment, low morale and performance, and increased turnover. Recruitment can suffer severely. Employees may file grievances or create other legal problems.

CULTURAL CORE VALUES

Core values are the things that we believe in so strongly that they affect our goals, ethical decisions, and daily behavior. Cultural core beliefs and values impact on-the-job goals and behavior.

Different cultures place different values on privacy, courtesy, respect for elders, and work ethic. These values provide the basis for attitudes and behavior. Here are some examples:

- In the Philippines and Arab countries, unequal power distribution in institutions is highly valued. Status symbols are regarded as deserved and expected. However, in Austria and Sweden, power disparities are anathemas.
- In many corporations in the United States and Canada, there are policies that limit the hiring of one's relatives, labeling it favoritism. In contrast, the cultures of Korea, Pakistan, and Taiwan view the hiring of a relative as desirable, even obligatory.
- Japan, Austria, Italy, and the United States emphasize assertiveness, competitiveness, and the acquisition of money and material things. In the Netherlands and Sweden, the opposite holds. Nurturing and quality of life are valued more. Even among American workers, there are great differences in the relative importance of money. Some people never have enough while others are satisfied with just getting by.
- The Greeks and Japanese minimize the discomfort of risk by adhering to strict laws and rituals, while Jamaicans and Swedes have little risk aversion.

CORPORATE VALUES

Corporate values serve as guidelines for employee behavior. Key values are often expressed as slogans (eg, "The customer is always right," "Quality is Number One," or "We aim to please"). Some slogans, such as "Our employees are our greatest asset," fail to pass the snicker test.

Most corporate values and ethical considerations deal with honesty, integrity, and loyalty—the foundation of a moral organizational culture. However, what each person considers ethical and unethical depends on his or her individual value system. That is one reason that ethics can be so murky.

The impact of corporate values quickly dissipates when the behavior people see around them is contrary to the expressed values. This is especially true when it is their leaders who show the inappropriate behavior. The effect of corporate values also plummets when employees who violate those values are not chastised.

Employees are most impressionable when they are first hired. Most orientation programs emphasize the values that reflect the philosophy of the organization. Corporate decisions are often based on those values.

Providing a list of corporate values to new employees has little meaning unless the behavioral aspects of each value are described. Trainees understand what you mean by integrity if you tell them that when they make a mistake they must admit it and not blame someone else. They know better what you mean by honesty if you point out that falsifying time and patient records are grounds for dismissal.

A culture takes its tone and values from its leaders. Effective leaders have strong values and the courage to accomplish good works despite great obstacles. They know that improper employee behavior based on faulty value systems can be modified by using the old carrot and stick approach. Nevertheless, they prefer to rely on modeling the kind of behavior they want their followers to copy. Poor models destroy corporate and personal values. A manager can articulate the importance of integrity and honesty, but her employees recall the many times when she broke her promise. Another manager claims that quality is king. However, when the work piles up, he forces his staff to hurry, knowing full well that they must cut corners to do so.

PERSONAL CORE VALUES

When corporate and personal values are in sync, a team spirit is fostered and conflicts become less frequent and are easier to resolve. Productivity increases. Teamwork demands a set of values that encourage listening and responding constructively and patiently to views expressed by others. It requires team members to provide support, share knowledge, and maintain high ethical standards.

Our primary personal values are family, career, health, and social or recreational activities. Secondary values include recognition, quality, political affiliation, and ethical considerations. Stress occurs when our behavior does not support our values. For example, when we value our family relationships and activities but spend most of our waking hours tending to our career, stress results.

Some employees value friendships. Other employees are loners. The relative importance of family and career also differs widely. Many people are passed over for promotion because they refuse to give up time with their families. Others destroy their marriages because their career takes precedence over family life.

Americans are increasingly reluctant to take jobs or promotions that involve moving their families. Heier[1] reports that 75% of the employees he interviewed claimed they would not relocate for their employer.

Some managers can't understand why many professional and technical people show no interest in becoming managers—again, a matter of values.

Value Modification

Employees who have values that conflict with corporate values must modify their personal values to some extent. Failure to make that adjustment leads to confrontations, isolation or rejection, and ultimately to dismissal. Employees whose core values are markedly different from those of other members of their work and social groups find it difficult to develop personal networks.

Values, like attitudes, are hard to alter. Behavioral modeling by managers and coworkers can gradually influence individual values. Employees are most susceptible to change when they are first hired. Trainers and managers who earn the respect and trust of trainees have a powerful impact on value modification. The best of these leaders reinforce corporate values by sharing anecdotes of successes and failures and by providing positive feedback.

DIVERSITY MANAGEMENT PROGRAMS

In an ideal workplace social acceptance is based on merit. Yet even among the most open-minded individuals, stereotypes and subtle prejudices can create difficulties. Managers can seldom change opinions, but they can see to it that all workers are treated fairly. An effective diversity program voids charges of discrimination and enhances creativity.

The goal of a diversity program is to create an environment that allows employees of all backgrounds to reach their full potential and to work well together. The people do not all have to be friends, but they must be respectful of each other. Ideally employees go beyond tolerance to a true appreciation of differences. In this mutual adaptation paradigm, the parties accept and understand differences and fully adapt to the entire diversity mixture.

The basic strategy is simple. Change what is not working but leave other areas alone. Be sure that you abide by all laws, rules, policies, and procedures. Value modification starts with a review of current practices. This review can be accomplished by focus groups or surveys. Allstate Insurance Company surveys all of its employees quarterly on how well it is meeting its commitments. It probes how well employees feel their managers are carrying out their program. Its "diversity index" determines 25% of a manager's merit bonus.[2]

There is widespread dissatisfaction with affirmative action. White males perceive it as reverse discrimination. Highly qualified members of minority groups are also unhappy with affirmative action. They point out that they are stigmatized as people who could not have made it on their own.

The assimilation approach, in which management attempts to force minorities to become similar to the majority, seldom achieves its goal. Another unsatisfactory technique is the suppression approach. Here, managers admit to minorities that there is a problem but that the minorities have to put up with it.

Elements of a Diversity Program

The following are elements that can ensure an effective diversity program:

- Training programs that provide employees with the skills needed to deal with a diverse work force.
- Monitoring using periodic attitude surveys and audits of production and attendance records.
- Holding managers accountable for reaching the organization's diversity goals within their units.
- Helping employees establish networks or support groups to which minority members can turn in times of stress.
- Equal assistance to workers who have family problems (eg, child and elder-care needs).
- Ongoing communication to reinforce the organization's commitment to diversity and to keep the work force aware of the need to cooperate.
- Mentors available for any worker who needs support and advice.

Diversity Awareness Training

Health maintenance organizations and malpractice insurers recognize the importance of diversity training. One medical malpractice insurer offers premium discounts to doctors who attend a workshop about cultural differences.[3]

Diversity awareness training is adapted to the culture of the organization. It can vary from a one-time session to a series of training exercises. If people have had limited contact with these cultural differences in the past, they feel uncomfortable when faced with them. It is up to each employee to appreciate and value these differences and not to expect that minority customers and employees want to "blend in" with the mainstream culture. Most employees prefer to maintain their cultural identity.

In these programs workers learn about antidiscrimination laws, cross-cultural communication, respect, and bias. Useful techniques include role playing, videotapes, and discussions. The training emphasizes the importance of language or dialect, a very important cultural variable. A Filipino patient is likely to view caregivers as authority figures and thus be quiet and subdued in their presence. Asians and others are reluctant to admit that they do not understand instructions.

They are concerned that saying that they do not understand might be an insult to your teaching ability. You must ask them questions to ensure that they comprehend what you have said.

Body language is equally important. For example, Native Americans and some Asians avoid eye contact when conversing. In the United States when you hold up your hand with thumb and forefinger together, you mean "OK." In France it means that you are a zero. In Japan it is a request for some change. In some countries it's an obscene gesture. The "V" gesture in the United States means Victory, but in Australia it is the "middle-finger" salute.

Diversity training without follow-up and institutional support is incomplete. Trainers have little or no authority for follow-up or backup outside the training room.

RESPONSIBILITIES OF SUPERVISORS

Upper management can use surveys to detect cultural problems, but it is up to supervisors to make diversity programs work. They check for tensions that may be disrupting harmony or interfering with productivity. They implement the provisions of any diversity program.

Experienced supervisors know that corporate values mean little to employees unless they are explained in behavioral terms. New supervisors quickly learn that what they value is not what many of their employees value. Supervisors usually like challenges, interesting work, recognition, and the sense of having control. Their employees may only want to do their routine work and go home.

Karp[4] warns against reinforcing the role of victim of prejudice or discrimination. Victims focus on their pain and weakness. When this occurs during a training program, "suffering contests" may emerge among subgroups. Each group tries to prove that it has suffered the most. People leave these meetings feeling more vulnerable and abused than when they came in.

Develop programs that reinforce the role of survivor of discrimination. This strengthens the individual. Ask them how it felt and what they did to overcome it. This reinforces individual responsibility for taking care of themselves.

Tips for Supervisors

- Be alert to catch your own assumptions and those of others.
- Do not allow unfair assumptions to go unchallenged.
- Help new arrivals feel more comfortable by discussing the unwritten rules and practices. These may include appearance, acceptable language, how to disagree or complain, and how to ask for help from others.

- Discuss the importance of cultural diversity at orientation sessions and at staff meetings.
- Do not tell people that they shouldn't feel the way they do when they feel mistreated. Do make it safe for them to have and to express those feelings.
- Challenge stereotypes and assumptions about minority groups. Avoid terms like "YUPPIE" (Young, Upwardly Mobile Professional), "DINK" (Dual Income No Kids), "old," "white male," "subordinate," "honey," and "girl."
- Show interest in people's differences without prying into their personal lives. Seek information regarding various special ethnic observances and events (eg, Chinese New Year, Black History Month, Martin Luther King Jr's birthday, Asian Pacific Heritage Week, National Hispanic Heritage Week, and Yom Kippur).
- Become more knowledgeable about the religious, family, and food customs of the people you work with.
  Tactfully ask someone from that national culture after establishing appropriate rapport.
- Use humor carefully and avoid ethnic, sexist, or stereotypic jokes.
- Be familiar with your organization's policy on sexual harassment, and live up to this policy to the letter.
- Involve representatives of all minority groups in the decision-making process.
- Let minorities wear their ethnic clothes or hairstyle unless these interfere with their work or offend customers.
- Encourage all employees to get to know the people around them who are different.

> *By embracing differences, we can all make a difference.*

PROMOTIONS FOR WOMEN

We still hear much about the glass ceiling and the "old boys" network. While it is still true that women have fewer offices in the executive suites, they now fill many middle, hierarchical slots and most of the supervisory positions in hospitals. Have you noticed the number of women in charge of nursing homes and home care programs? Women are very active in professional societies and increasingly serve as officers in these organizations. For the most part, doors of opportunity for women in health care institutions are wide open. Women who sincerely want leadership roles find the glass ceiling to be illusory.

Now men complain that they're excluded from some informal networks in health care institutions. Others feel that female managers show favoritism toward female employees.

NOTES

1. W.D. Heier, "Company Loyalty: a Zero-Based Asset?" *Management Review 69,* no. 4 (1980): 57–61.
2. L.E. Wynter, "Allstate Rates Managers on Handling Diversity," *Wall Street Journal,* Wednesday, 10/1/97, B1.
3. G. Anders, "Doctors Learn to Bridge Cultural Gaps," *Wall Street Journal,* Thursday, 9/4/97, B1.
4. B.B. Karp, "Choices in Diversity Training," *Training 31,* no. 8 (1994): 73, 74.

RECOMMENDED READING

J.G. Bruhn, "Creating an Organizational Climate for Multiculturism," *Healthcare Supervisor 14,* no. 4 (1996): 11–18.

J. Notwani et al. "Managing Diversity in the Health Care Industry," *Health Care Supervisor 13,* no. 3 (1995): 16–23.

S.M. Paskoff, "Ending the Workplace Diversity Wars," *Training 33,* no. 8 (1996): 42–47.

S.M. Sack, *The Employee Rights Handbook* (New York, NY: Facts On File, Inc., 1990).

R.R. Thomas, Jr. *Redefining Diversity* (New York, NY: AMACOM, 1996).

Chapter 19

Conflict and Confrontation

- the major causes of conflict
- the dangers of escalating or suppressed conflict
- the five basic strategies for coping with conflict
- preparations for a confrontation
- the confrontation
- suggestions for more effective confrontations
- how to confront an angry person

The workplaces of health providers in the 1990s are filled with tension and strife, and there are no signs of abatement. Conflicts arise under pressure-cooker deadlines, increased workloads, fear of layoffs, and the relentless demand for higher productivity.

Disagreements are healthy as long as they culminate in win-win solutions. They prevent serious mistakes or inappropriate actions, force second looks, and lead to service improvement. If resolved, disputes lead to better relationships.

Some dysfunctional work groups suppress conflicts. These suppressed conflicts fester and eventually disrupt working relationships. Other groups get involved in relationships in which the employees compete with each other and with management instead of cooperating. Adversarial conflicts feature anger, hostility, humiliation, or rancor.

MAJOR CAUSES OF CONFLICT

The etiology of a conflict is not always apparent. Often there is a covert issue camouflaged by a less important overt factor. Other situations are murky because the cause is multifactorial.

Unclear Expectations or Guidelines

Employees do not know what they are to do, how to do it, or what the outcomes must be. Policies and rules can be ambiguous. For example, a policy con-

191

cerning sexual harassment may not explain exactly what constitutes sexual harassment.

Poor Communication

Conflicts attributed to ill will are frequently the result of communication short circuits, especially poor listening; hastily scribbled memos; or garbled e-mail messages. Faulty perceptions or assumptions cause misunderstandings. We all can cite personal examples of hurt feelings and broken friendships that resulted from distortions or half-truths.

Lack of Clear Jurisdiction

When limits of power are not spelled out, disputes erupt. Conflicts may arise over funds, space, time, personnel, or equipment. Squabbles over work and vacation schedules are common.

Incompatibilities or Disagreements Based on Differences of Temperaments or Attitudes

These are often complex, with overlays of race, religion, nationality, age, politics, ethics, and values. For example, nurses and physicians may disagree about how dying patients should be dealt with.

Individual or Group Conflicts of Interest

There may be chronic friction between departments or between shifts. For example, disagreements arise between the purchasing department and a unit manager.

Operational or Staffing Changes

Whenever there are organizational or functional changes, conflicts are bound to arise.

DANGERS OF ESCALATING OR SUPPRESSED CONFLICT

When conflict is allowed to escalate, the parties become impatient, angry, or frustrated. They turn their attention from problem solving to attacking the other persons. Blame and threats spew forth, and issues proliferate from one to many. Old grievances emerge to compound the situation. Relationships are damaged.

Bitterness leads to thoughts of how to get even rather than how to solve the initial problem. Eventually the parties may enlist supporters from among the bystanders, resulting in the formation of opposing cliques.

When an organization attempts to suppress conflict, the consequences are chronic complaining; decline in productivity, attendance, morale, and loyalty; increased stress; and, possibly, sabotage or violence.

FIVE BASIC STRATEGIES FOR COPING WITH CONFLICT

Each of the following strategies is appropriate for certain situations. Face your next conflict by picking the right strategy.

1. Avoidance. This may be to deny that there is a problem, to physically escape, to pass the buck, or to procrastinate. The problem remains unresolved. This "gunnysacking" results in the buildup of anger that eventually explodes.

When Avoidance Is Appropriate

- It is not your problem.
- There is nothing you can do about it.
- It's not worth the effort to face.
- You need additional information.
- You or the other individual is emotionally upset.
- Potential disruption outweighs the benefits of resolution.
- The situation will ameliorate if you can wait it out.

Avoidance can be an escape mechanism. For example, when you're challenged by someone in the presence of your manager, you turn to your manager and say emphatically, "I want to respond to that, but not here and now. I'll do that at the next staff meeting."

2. Fight. There are several booby traps in this aggressive approach. You can lose! Even if you win a skirmish, your opponents may regroup and return to the fray or wait for another opportunity to retaliate. They may become saboteurs. Use this tactic when quick action is necessary (eg, when someone is violating an important safety regulation). It is also appropriate when you observe severe ethical or legal violations.

3. Surrender. Nonassertive people often succumb to this response, thus building up internal frustration as self-esteem erodes.

In addition, these passive people draw conflict. They wear "Kick Me!" signs.

When Surrender is Appropriate

- The other party is right.
- It does not matter to you.
- You have little chance to win.
- Harmony and stability are especially important.
- Giving in on a minor item means winning a more important one later.

---

4. Compromise. This partial-win strategy is often what you must settle for. Compromise permits each party to get part of what they want, so there is some satisfaction for both parties. Most union-management or international disputes are settled in this manner.

On the negative side, neither party gets everything it wants. In addition, compromise may involve game playing, with each side pumping up its demands or disguising them. The most frequent mistake is to adopt this alternative prematurely, without making a greater effort at collaboration.

When Compromise Is Appropriate

- Opposing goals are incompatible.
- A temporary settlement to complex issues is needed.
- Time constraints call for an expedient solution.
- Discussions have stalled.

---

5. Collaborate. Collaboration is when disputing parties attack problems rather than each other. Problems are resolved through honest and open discussion. Collaboration builds healthy relationships. It uncovers more information, challenges false assumptions or perceptions, and promotes understanding. It leads to better decisions. This win-win approach is usually the best alternative, but usually requires more creative solutions. The best answer is one that neither side had originally considered. An added benefit of this approach is that it builds positive relationships.

This strategy is usually the best one, especially when the issue is too important to be settled any other way or when you must have a consensus. There are negative aspects to this approach. More time may be required. Decisions may have to be delayed. The parties may become frustrated when no consensus is reached. While more time is spent seeking solutions, the overall time may be much less because there is less haggling or involvement in side issues. Two angry participants prolong arguments. Sometimes you have to call additional meetings to permit tempers to cool.

PREPARATIONS FOR A CONFRONTATION

Analyze the situation by answering these questions:

- What do I want to accomplish?
- What's the most I will give up?
- What do I think the other person wants? What covert goals might she have?
- What false assumptions or incorrect perceptions might she have?
- Which strategy should I use?
- What are my "hot buttons," and what should I do if they're pushed?
- If I plan to use a collaborative approach, what special precautions should be taken?

Get psyched up using these three techniques:

1. Practice success imagery. Visualize a successful confrontation. Picture your body language, hear your words and voice tone, and envisage a successful outcome. Athletes and professional speakers have used this technique with great success.
2. Adjust your self-talk. This is converting negative thoughts to positive ones when talking to yourself. All of us carry on a constant inner dialogue with ourselves. When we are in a passive mode, these internal conversations are negative and pessimistic: our subconscious mind conjures up statements like, "I could never say that" or "She'll just blow me away." Let your positive affirmations take control. Say to yourself, "I'll be in control." Avoid weak statements like, "I'm going to try to stand up to her next time."
3. Rehearse. After you have selected your dialogue and its appropriate body language, rehearse the anticipated encounter. Do this over and over. Do it in front of a mirror and out loud. Still better, get someone to role play with you. Do not be satisfied until your performance is down pat.

CONFRONTATION

Confrontations are seldom as bad as anticipated, especially when you're prepared. Here are some practical tips for holding a collaborative confrontation:

- Avoid sitting across from the person. This invites opposition. Sit next to each other. Still better, take a stroll side by side.
- Open discussions by saying something like, "Let's see how we can solve this in a way that satisfies both of us."
- After outlining the problem, move on to areas of agreement. To do this, start with questions you are certain will be answered affirmatively. It is then easier to get a yes to more controversial questions. For example, "Lou, don't you agree that we must put team goals before our individual agendas?"
- Be an attentive listener, asking lots of questions and keying in on what the other person is saying. Be empathic. Respect the other person's feelings, but still feel free to respond forcibly.
- Often it pays to ask the person what he or she wants. You may be pleasantly surprised to find that what he or she wants is less than you were prepared to offer. On the other hand, do not neglect to say what it is that you want.
- Let the person know that you hear and understand—both content and feelings. Validate feelings with something like, "As I understand it, Joan, you're angry because I asked one of your assistants to give me a hand with my project. Is that right?" Validating has two benefits. It clarifies the problem and lets the person know that what he or she is saying is important.
- Use the person's name frequently. Our name is the sweetest sound we humans hear.
- Seek a bigger pie instead of dividing up the pie. This means finding something more for both of you—a win-win solution.
- Emphasize that you can't change the past and want to concentrate on the present and future.
- Stay cool and avoid rhetorical or emotional escalation. When upset, people exaggerate. This increases anxiety and makes it more difficult to solve the problem. When forced into a corner, say, "I find myself getting upset, Lou. Let's take a 10-minute break, OK?"
- Let him save face. He should come away with something.

SUGGESTIONS FOR MORE EFFECTIVE CONFRONTATION

- Be prepared, just as you would be for a debate.
- Pick the best time and place. Do not meet when your self-esteem is low or when either of you is upset.

- Regard the other person not as an enemy but as a partner in problem solving.
- Clarify the other person's viewpoint and your own. Do not go on until these viewpoints and the desired outcomes are clear.
- Focus first on a point of agreement, and work from there.
- Be assertive, not aggressive. Use "I" statements (eg, "I get concerned when people approach me like this"). Use nonconfrontational phrases such as "help me understand why."
- Attack the problem or behavior, not the other person. Disagree without being disagreeable or trying to prove that the person is wrong.
- Don't cause your opponent to lose face. Don't threaten or issue ultimatums.
- Don't be sarcastic or critical.
- Avoid using the word "you." It almost always is followed by an attack on the person's ego.
- To avoid retaliation, use the strawman technique.
- Watch your body language. Maintain eye contact, sit or stand up straight, and appear relaxed. Do not fidget or squirm. Avoid threatening gestures such as finger pointing, fist making, crossed arms, hands on hips, or scowling. Smile when you agree; remain expressionless when you disagree.
- Control your voice. Keep its volume, pitch, and rate under control. Stop if you find it growing louder, faster, or high pitched.
- Be diplomatic and tentative when facing firm resistance. Use words such as maybe, perhaps, or you may be right.
- When cornered or upset, escape by pleading stress.
- Do not get stuck believing that your solution is the only good one. Focus on the benefits of your argument to the other person.
- Promise rewards ("If you will. . ., then I will. . . ").
- End on a positive note.

CONFRONTING AN ANGRY PERSON

We may provoke anger in others when we criticize, pressure, threaten, deny, irritate, or deride—anything that attacks self-esteem. Almost anyone can be provoked into anger if the stimulus is intense enough, but each of us has a different threshold. Some associates are too sensitive. They may have explosive tempers on short fuses. Some people use anger because they have learned through personal experience that it enables them to avoid unpleasant assignments. These individuals take everything personally. They quickly and angrily charge favoritism or discrimination. Your children are probably already expert at this.

Tips for Coping with an Angry Person

- Don't lose your cool. Never shout—or even raise your voice. Avoid any threatening gestures or aggressive body language. Never touch. When you're angry, don't say a word until your emotions are under control.
- Don't make comments about the other person's anger or tell him or her not to be angry (eg, "Why don't you calm down?").
- Don't patronize or lecture.
- If a person walks into your office and you sense that he or she is angry, greet the person like a friend. *The person who speaks first sets the mood.*
- Ask questions. *The person who asks the most questions controls the agenda and the direction of the exchange.*
  The key question is, "What do you want me to do?" Find out exactly what he or she wants and satisfy that want if possible. If you can't, offer your solution.
- Listen to the person's outbursts without interrupting. This has a powerful, calming effect. *The person who listens best usually comes out a winner.*
- Make certain that you understand the problem.
- Don't become defensive or argumentative.
- Empathize by paraphrasing what you think the person is angry about and why he or she feels that way.
- Assure the person that something will be done.

Note: Negotiation, mediation, and arbitration are special forms of conflict handling and will be discussed in Chapter 36.

RECOMMENDED READING

R.W. Lucas, *Effective Interpersonal Relationships* (New York, NY: Irwin Publishers, 1994).

D. Tjosvold, *Learning To Manage Conflict* (New York, NY: Lexington Books, 1993).

W. Umiker, "Collaborative Conflict Resolution," *Health Care Supervisor 15,* no. 3 (1997): 70–75.

Chapter 20

Employees with Problems

- the marginal performer
- the absent employee
- the employee with a personal problem
- company policies
- handling employees with personal problems
- employee assistance programs
- special precautions
- two employees are feuding
- unethical behavior

THE MARGINAL PERFORMER

Among the marginal performers who could do better if they so wished are employees who are just putting in time until their retirement, those who regard their job as interim employment, and those who lack motivation for a variety of reasons. The first step in dealing with these people is to get to know them better and to find their motivational buttons.

Ask yourself these questions:

- Are they bored with their jobs?
  Consider job enrichment, cross-training, special projects, committee assignments, teaching responsibilities, job rotation, or participation in research.
- Are their social needs being met? Do they prefer solo or group work? How do they get along with their peers?
- Consider transferring them to fast-moving, energetic groups or assigning them individual work according to their preferences.
- Are their ego needs being met? Do they get the attention and respect that they think they deserve? Are you making a special effort to give it?
  Maybe they need a status symbol, such as a change in title, a bigger desk, or a nameplate. Give them more recognition, as we discussed in a previous chapter.

Do not accept unsatisfactory performance. Do not reward poor productivity by transferring some of their work to the high performers. Do not give satisfactory performance ratings to undeserving employees. Every experienced supervisor has made that mistake and has ultimately regretted it, especially when they wanted to fire the employee.

Be careful about using marginal employees for orienting and training new employees—a bad attitude can be contagious.

The Older Employee

Most older employees are excellent workers. They often run rings around their younger coworkers. However, some of them lose their spark, allow their expertise to become obsolete, and are unwilling to learn new skills. They may adjust poorly to organizational and procedural changes. The following may be helpful:

- Acknowledge their experience by seeking their advice.
- Get them an understudy or involve them in orienting new employees or in providing on-the-job training (select who and what carefully).
- Explain the need for change, get them involved, and give them training if needed.
- Encourage them to attend professional meetings.
- If they are nearing retirement, approve their requests for time off without pay. Hire part-timers to fill the gaps, if necessary, rather than overload their co-workers while they are away.
- Listen to their plans for retirement. Be sympathetic.

The Goof-Offs

These folks have lousy attendance records. They are all great excuse makers. They always have rational excuses that invite sympathy (eg, "My wife is sick again," "My son is in trouble with the law," or "My car keeps breaking down.") They waste their time and often the time of others.

Do not allow them to trap you into supporting their self-pity or debating the merits of the excuses. Focus on job standards and performance objectives.

Parents of Latchkey Children

Parents of children who go home from school to an empty house are understandably concerned about the welfare of their children. This concern can result in frequent telephone calls and mental distractions that interfere with job performance. The following may be helpful:

- Talk to the parent about after-school child care. Contact the human resources department to see if assistance is available in the community.
- Explain to the parent that this concern is affecting job performance. Express your desire to help.
- Consider other solutions:
  1. Rearrange the parent's work schedule, if possible. For example, coffee breaks may coincide with telephone calls to the child.
  2. Assign low-priority tasks at the time their children are getting home from school.
  3. Ask the parent to limit the length of calls and to limit calls to important messages.
  4. Be tolerant about allowing the parent to take time off when crises develop, but know where to draw the line.

THE ABSENT EMPLOYEE

It has been estimated that the average American employee takes from 7 to 12 days of unscheduled absences every year. Absenteeism costs American businesses more than $26 billion annually.[1]

Absenteeism may be external (eg, failure to show up for work, tardiness, or early departures). It may be internal (eg, extended coffee or meal breaks, absence from the work area, socializing, and daydreaming).

Calculation of absentee rate: Total hours absent/total hours paid for × 100

A rate of 3% is considered a reasonable level by the U.S. Department of Labor. The average absenteeism rate for a group of American hospitals was 2.68% in 1982.[2] It has probably not changed much since that date.

The two most frequent causes of absenteeism are job dissatisfaction and the availability of paid sick leave. The number of days lost because of alleged illness seems to equal the number of paid sick days allowed. Although supervisors have little control over sick leave policy, there are measures at their disposal that can minimize sick leave abuse. They can:

- stress to their employees that sick leave is a benefit, not a right;
- eliminate causes of job dissatisfaction;
- set a good example;
- keep good attendance records; and
- look for patterns of absenteeism (eg, Mondays, Fridays, hunting seasons, or paydays).

When an employee calls in sick, take the call personally. If a spouse makes the call and the employee is not seriously ill, ask to speak to the employee. Ask if the person has seen a physician, whether he or she is receiving adequate treatment, and if there is something you can do (makes them feel guilty if they are not really sick), and when they think they can return to work.

When they return, welcome them back. Ask if they are up to putting in a full day.

When absence is excessive, follow your counseling procedure that we discussed in Chapter 16.

EMPLOYEE WITH A PERSONAL PROBLEM

A personal problem is any emotional or behavioral condition that limits an employee's ability to perform his or her job. Such problems include family stress, alcohol abuse, misuse of drugs, emotional disorders, and legal or financial difficulties. Supervisors are responsible for detecting and attempting to correct a deteriorating job performance, but they are not expected to diagnose or treat personal problems.

When supervisory efforts do not improve behavior or performance and a personal problem may be the cause of the difficulty, refer the employee to your employee assistance program or to a professional counselor.

Suspect that an employee has a personal problem when you observe any of the following:

- increased absenteeism,
- frequent absence from the workstation,
- confusion or difficulty in concentrating,
- decreased productivity or work quality,
- friction with other employees,
- unusual behavior (eg, temper tantrums or emotional outbursts),
- accident proneness, or
- alcoholic breath.

Suspect drug involvement when, in addition, an employee:

- is visited by strangers or employees from other areas or meets them in the parking lot,
- is suspected of theft,
- makes secretive telephone calls,
- visits the washroom for long periods,
- wears dark glasses indoors,
- wears long-sleeved shirts in hot weather,

- has blood stains on the shirt sleeves, or
- perspires excessively.

Company Policy on Personal Problems

All organizations should have a well-documented policy and an established procedure (see Figure 20–1) for handling employees who have personal problems. Some type of employee assistance program is usually available without charge to the worker. Employees who use the services of the program are guaranteed confi-

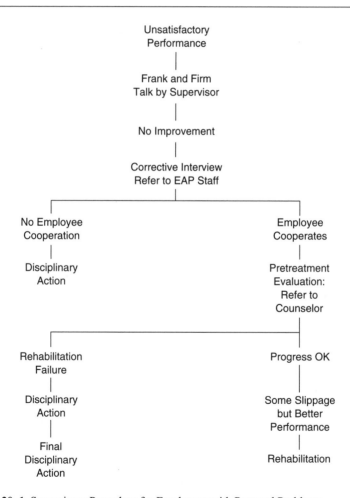

Figure 20–1 Supervisory Procedure for Employees with Personal Problems

dentiality because the information obtained is considered a medical record. Encourage your reports to seek assistance on their own initiative before problems affect their work. Generally, time off for counseling is treated as that for any other disability.

A Recommended Procedure

- Hold a frank and firm performance counseling session:
  1. Make certain the employee knows what is expected and that documentation is complete.
  2. Describe the unacceptable behavior or results, not what you think the underlying problem is. Say, "Joe, your daily reports have been one to two hours late every day for the past week" rather than "Joe, you often have alcohol on your breath. You've got to get off the stuff."
  3. Do not accuse the employee of having a personal problem, but encourage such an admission with a statement such as "I've noticed that you seem tense recently. Is something bothering you that we can help with?"
- Put these four questions to the employee:
  1. Are you aware that your performance has dropped below our standards? If yes, ask when he or she first observed this.
  2. Is it possible that a personal problem may be at the root of this? If yes, ask what he or she has done about it.
  3. Are you aware of our employee assistance program?
  4. Is there anything I can do to help?
- If the employee's performance fails to improve, hold a second counseling session:
  1. If the employee still does not admit that there is a personal problem, say, "If you have a personal problem, I suggest counseling help. We have an excellent employee assistance program here that is completely confidential and free."
  2. Emphasize that his job may be in jeopardy if performance does not improve.
- If the employee cooperates and progress is satisfactory, continue your support:
  1. As with any medical condition, expect occasional backsliding.
  2. Make sure that you acknowledge good work.
  3. Resist any temptation to lighten the employee's load. Treat the employee as any other employee, but allow a reasonable transition period after the employee has sought help before expecting job performance to return to an acceptable level.
- If the employee refuses to seek help or if rehabilitation fails, take disciplinary action.

Precautions

- Use only job performance to initiate disciplinary procedures.
- Do not apologize for bringing up performance deficiencies.
- Do not try to be a diagnostician. You are an expert in the area of performance. Other people can better determine the nature of personal problems.
- In your counseling interview, do not discuss personal problems in depth.
- Do not moralize. There should be no stigma attached to personal problems.
- Be tough, but do not take punitive action until counseling has been suggested.

TWO EMPLOYEES FEUDING

There are many reasons why two people do not get along at work. Besides cultural, age, political, and gender differences, there may be competition for attention, promotion, recognition, turf, or resources. Personality differences get blamed most. However, before you attribute the problem to personality clashes, look for external causes. There may be ambiguous position descriptions that do not show who does what or who has what authority. Sometimes bystanders are provoking the situation.

The three basic strategies for coping with this situation are discussed below:

1. Avoidance. This is best when it is not your problem or when you lack the authority to act.
2. Arbitration. This is analyzing the situation and then taking sides or dictating a solution. This approach often fails, and there can be serious side effects.
3. Mediation. You encourage the pair to solve their problem, keep the pair from exploding, and guide them into mutually agreeable solutions. You must be perceived as neutral by both parties. Never take sides.

Sometimes the problem is solved simply by telling the feuding duo that they do not have to like each other to work together and that you expect them to act as adults and to treat each other civilly on the job.

If that approach doesn't work, talk to each person individually, looking for an underlying cause of the animosity. A solution may emerge during one of these conversations. Job redesign, clarification of limits of authority, or revising of territorial boundaries may provide the remedy.

If the problem is still not solved, hold a joint meeting. The intent of this meeting is to convert them from adversaries to problem solvers.

Follow This Sequence:

1. Warn them that if they do not work out a solution, you will take administrative action that may not please either party.
2. Seek some common ground or area of agreement (eg, "You both agree that our goal is to improve customer service, right?").
3. Listen to both sides impartially. Do not tolerate interruptions, blaming, or name calling. Make each person summarize what the other person said to clarify any flawed communication.
4. Ask each person what he or she wants changed. Review areas of agreement and disagreement.
5. Discuss the pros and cons of each alternative, and get them to agree to one.
6. Clarify future behavior (eg, "What are we going to do differently?" or "What are we going to do if . . . ?").
7. Congratulate them for reaching an agreement. Say that you have confidence in their ability to resolve their differences.
8. Follow up. Hold additional sessions if necessary.

If they cannot solve their differences, you must decide whether you can live with the flawed situation. If not, take whatever administrative action is necessary (eg, reassign them so that they no longer work together).

UNETHICAL BEHAVIOR

Organizational ethics defines the boundaries of good behavior. Ethical considerations may relate to performance appraisals, promotions, and disciplinary actions. They may involve the protection of personal privacy, discrimination, or the release of information. Nowhere is the practice of ethical behavior more important than in relationships between employees, superiors, and colleagues.

Ethics represent what we *should* do, not necessarily what we *must* do. Ethical standards are higher than the standards in civil and criminal laws. The easiest ethical violations to recognize are those that also violate laws. The pilfering of supplies comes under the rubric of theft and is therefore both illegal and unethical. More controversial, and within the realm of ethics, is the "borrowing" of workplace equipment for personal use.

Ethical decisions are based on legal, corporate, moral, cultural, and personal values. What we consider ethical depends largely on our core beliefs and values. These are determined early in life based on the teachings of parents, teachers, and role models. Life experiences modify or enforce these beliefs about what is right and what is wrong. Complications often arise in the workplace because employees are asked to merge their values with the organization's values. Sometimes these sets of values are discordant. Value differences readily explain why people frequently disagree about what is ethical and what is not.

Examples of Unethical Behavior in the Workplace

- Telling people to "do whatever is necessary" to achieve results
- Taking credit for other people's ideas or shifting blame
- Playing favorites
- Lying or falsifying records
- Billing for work not performed
- Making false or misleading statements
- Divulging personal or confidential information
- Failing to report violations of legal requirements
- Failing to report health and safety hazards or accidents
- Stealing

Three of the most common ethical violations are lying, falsifying records, and stealing.

Organizational Climate

Employees are more likely to make unethical decisions when their employer or manager makes it difficult for them not to do so. Many employees feel pressured to act in ways that violate their organization's codes of behavior.

Ethics Programs

Most programs consist chiefly of "snitch-lines" in which people are encouraged to report on others. Most of these calls concern petty complaints, such as people taking long lunch breaks.

Good programs provide a code of ethical conduct, employee training, a monitoring system, and an ethics "hotline." The hotline is used less for snitching than for getting expert advice as to whether or not something is unethical or on how to respond to certain situations (eg, the appropriateness of accepting a gift from a vendor or hiring a member of one's family).

An additional benefit of calls for advice is that they suggest what kind of information should be presented in training programs or discussed at staff meetings.

To be effective, calls for advice must be answered promptly and skillfully. Experienced advisors walk the person through the thought process so they can reach the right decision by themselves.

The major three reasons people give for not reporting unethical acts are:

1. they doubt that anything will be done,
2. they fear retaliation, and
3. they do not trust the organization to keep the information confidential.

Ethics training may consist of special courses that are given periodically and included in orientation programs. In these sessions, case studies involving ethical dilemmas can be presented.

Supervisory Actions To Enforce Ethical Behavior

With all the downsizing, restructuring, reorganizing, and increased workloads, many employees feel pressured to "cut corners." Tell your employees to come to you when they are running behind schedule so you can provide them with help or modify their schedule.

Encourage employees to inform you, in confidence, of their concerns about unethical acts by their coworkers. Tell them that there are times when they must choose between betraying colleagues and being loyal to their organization.

Make your pronouncements of intolerance with unethical behavior strong and your disciplinary reactions fast.

When you observe a colleague engaging in minor unethical behavior, it may be appropriate to tell him or her that you are aware of what is going on and will report these transgressions if they continue. If the acts are illegal or represent major ethical violations, go directly to the authorities.

In other situations, discuss the situation with your superior or a member of the human resources department. It helps to be familiar with your policy manual concerning unethical behavior. Refer to it before you make any waves. If you're a member of a professional organization to which the person belongs, consult with a representative of that organization.

NOTES

1. P.I. Morgan and H.K. Baker, "Do You Need an Absenteeism Control Program?" *Supervisory Management 29,* no. 9 (1984): 1–2.
2. M.M. Markowich in a letter to participants in United Hospitals, Inc., Pennsylvania, October 13, 1987.

RECOMMENDED READING AND LISTENING

R. Brinkman and R. Kirschner, *How To Deal with Difficult People* (Boulder, CO: CareerTrack Publishers, 1988), two videocassettes.

M. Solomon, *Working with Difficult People* (Englewood Cliffs, NJ: Prentice Hall, 1990).

W. Umiker, *Coping with Difficult People in the Health Care Setting* (Chicago, IL: ASCP Press, 1994).

Chapter 21

Employees with Bad Attitudes or Habits

- negative attitude
- coaching and counseling for behavioral change
- employees who are too critical of their employers
- colleague with a bad attitude toward you
- negativists
- know-it-alls
- uncooperative silent ones
- supersensitive ones
- moody ones
- jealous ones
- gossipers
- incessant talkers and socializers
- ones whose appearance you dislike

The employees who give supervisors their biggest headaches are not the incompetent ones (they can be trained). They are not the ones who brazenly violate rules (they can be fired). They are the ones who meet work standards but drive supervisors up the wall with their idiosyncratic behavior. These people are usually charged with having a bad or negative attitude.

THE NEGATIVE ATTITUDE

A person with a bad attitude may be a negativist, a goof-off, a hot head, or a disloyal subordinate. We can't get into the heads of these people to see what a bad attitude is. We know that this term is universally used to excess and lacks a concise definition. What we do see are various kinds of behaviors that we find annoying. The line between bad attitude and outright disloyalty or unethical behavior can be fuzzy.

Negative attitudes may be reflected in:

- low productivity,

- high error rate,
- repeated minor violation of rules and procedures,
- lack of team spirit or lack of cooperation,
- public criticism of the organization and its officers,
- constant threats to resign, or
- foot dragging and resistance to change.

If supervisors had the courage to document what they really thought about their people with bad attitudes, one or more of the following adjectives would appear in their performance appraisals: uninterested, inflexible, pessimistic, complaining, indifferent, change resistant, unenthusiastic, and nonsupportive.

COACHING AND COUNSELING FOR BEHAVIORAL CHANGE

Before taking any action, find out if there really is a problem. If there is a problem, how pervasive is it? In the previous chapter we posed the crucial question that comes up whenever we face a difficult person. It is worth repeating: Does the behavior affect to a significant degree the department's output, the employee's teammates, or you? If not, and you think you can live with it, your best move may be no move.

It is best not to accuse a person of having a bad attitude. If you feel that you must, provide specific behavioral examples that led to that subjective conclusion. Failure to do that elicits defensiveness or anger or at best only confuses the person. It is not likely to achieve the desired change. What you really want is for some behavioral change to occur. If the new behavior meets your standards, you need not be overly concerned about attitude. Early in my Navy career, Marine Corps trainers proved to me that when you changed the behavior of trainees, that led to pride in the service and in themselves. The bad attitudes disappeared.

Often a bad attitude can be modified to a satisfactory extent by vigorous coaching and skillful counseling. Discuss the problem with the person candidly. Explain how the behavior affects you, the department, or others. Give specific examples of how you see the person's behavior affecting services and people, especially customers and coworkers.

When the results of your coaching and counseling are not effective, start keeping more detailed performance records. Cutting these folks loose may prove to be the best solution, but you will need concrete proof of how the bad attitude affected performance or other employees.

EMPLOYEES WHO ARE TOO CRITICAL OF THEIR EMPLOYERS

Occasional criticism of the organization or its managers is to be expected. When you think an employee is overdoing it, you can often silence it with a remark such as, "For someone with your ability, I can't understand why you would stay with this organization. Don't you find it demeaning?"

There are two instances in which you must take vigorous action before serious harm is done:

1. when these people badmouth the organization in front of patients, visitors, clinicians, or other customers, or
2. when they are starting to affect the attitudes and performance of other employees.

These two situations justify charges of disloyalty. In most organizations these are grounds for dismissal.

THE COLLEAGUE WITH A BAD ATTITUDE TOWARD YOU

There are times when you must work with a colleague who seems to have a bad attitude toward you. This results in little (or not so little) daily skirmishes that are not conducive to team efforts. Rapport is the key to getting along better. It begins with a genuine desire to improve the relationship.

Throughout this book we mention the importance of risk taking. Here is a good example of a risk that is well worth taking. Grab the bull by the horns. Ask the other person what it is about you that irritates him. You may be in for a surprise. The irritating factor may be as simple as sending caustic memos or e-mail messages. It may be calling him by a nickname.

If you get a frank response, thank the person, and promise to modify this behavior. Then ask the person if you can be candid about what change you would like to see on his part. Do not unload a stack of complaints. This candid approach may fail or even make matters worse, but it's often worth the risk.

THE NEGATIVISTS (PESSIMISTS, CYNICS, AND WET BLANKETS)

Negativists may be hard workers who are competent, productive, and even loyal but who have a bleak outlook toward most things and people. They lack excitement in life and happiness at work. If you hang around them long enough, you get infected.

Negativists are convinced that the people in power do not care or are self-serving. In meetings, when any new idea is proposed, Pessimist Polly can always be counted on to come up with "The trouble with that idea is. . . ."

Negativists may be confused with devils' advocates. Both voice concern or ask challenging questions, but the devil's advocate does so with an open mind and is prepared to join a consensus if convinced. The negativist persists in finding reasons for opposing whatever is being proposed. Even when they lose arguments or are outvoted, they remain unconvinced.

Avoid acceptance of the contrary outlooks expressed by these individuals. Their resistive persuasion not only is depressing and self-defeating but can be infectious. On the other hand, do not dismiss their comments too quickly. They could be right, or they could turn the group against you.

When a known pessimist is present at a problem-solving, do not rush into making suggestions. Call on others, including the pessimists first. Pessimists are often silent while a problem is being explored or when decisions are asked for. They like to spring into action after solutions have been proposed.

Project realistic optimism. Give examples of past successes of the action now being proposed. Concede that every action carries some element of risk. Using a worst-case scenario, show that the possible consequences are not threatening and that the chances for success are great. Explain that current conditions are not like those that were present before when a similar project was unsuccessful.

Avoid arguing with the person. Say that he or she may be right, but that you still want to run with the idea. If the person persists, insist that he or she come up with a better alternative. When a person questions the wisdom of a change, assign him or her information-gathering chores relating to the change.

Keep an open mind. Occasionally employees are right. Occasionally use their negativism when you get to discussing pitfalls and contingency planning. They can tell you everything that can go wrong.

If the pessimist is a colleague and the work situation does not demand that you work together, avoid him or her if you want to maintain your optimistic attitude.

THE KNOW-IT-ALLS

These individuals want you to recognize them as superior. They try to maintain control by accumulating large bodies of knowledge. They are condescending if they know what they are talking about, pompous if they do not. If you object to what they say, they take it as a personal affront.

Do not pose a threat or argue. Remain respectful, and avoid direct challenges. Resist the temptation to debate with them. Do your homework. Be certain that you know what you are talking about. Present your ideas tentatively using phrases such as "What would happen if . . ." or "I wonder whether. . . ."

THE UNCOOPERATIVE SILENT ONES

These people are not those who fail to speak up because they have nothing to say or because they are listening intently. They are not the polite ones who fear that they will say something wrong or will hurt your feelings. The silent ones discussed here are those who reflect fear or suppressed anger by their silence.

Their silence may be preceded by a perfectly congenial conversation until you suddenly touch a sensitive area. You are most likely to encounter this glum silence during counseling or disciplinary sessions. If you encounter one of these clams in a counseling session, use Bramson's technique.[1] When it is Irene the Clam's turn to speak but she remains silent, lean forward and counter with your own silence plus eye contact and raised eyebrows. Maintain this silent, expectant stare for at least 10 seconds. If she remains silent, say "You haven't answered my questions, Irene. Is there some reason for that?" If her silence persists, say "Irene, I'm still waiting." If there is still no response, state the consequences of her inappropriate silence (eg, "Irene, you may have a good reason for not talking. I'm concerned about where this is taking us"). If Irene still remains silent, terminate the interview with, "Irene, since we still must resolve this problem, I want to see you here tomorrow at the same time."

THE SUPERSENSITIVES

These individuals take offense at whatever they perceive as put-downs. They're extremely sensitive to criticism, often bursting into tears, shouting, or dashing off to the restroom. When this behavior is effective for them, these people have a potent tool for manipulating colleagues and superiors—and they make full use of it.

Handle with care, but do not be manipulated by these reactions. Never withhold negative feedback because of previous overreactions. Do not apologize for what you said or did (eg, "Gosh, I'm very sorry that I hurt your feelings").

If, when receiving a reprimand, an employee breaks into tears, say, "Sue, I find it hard to discuss this when you sob like that. Take a few minutes to compose yourself." Most of the time you can simply hand Sue a tissue and go on with the discussion.

If Sue jumps up and runs out of your office, do not run after her or demand that she return. Instead, reschedule the meeting. At that meeting make no mention of the previous episode. Sue has learned that her inappropriate behavior was not effective.

If an employee loses his or her temper and starts shouting, silently wait for a minute or two while maintaining eye contact. If the employee does not calm down, leave your office. In the chapter on safety and violence, we discuss this problem at greater length.

MOODY PEOPLE

Normal people have some mood swings. It is the degree and circumstances that are important. Transient moodiness, such as that during a grieving period, seldom requires supervisory action other than offering a helping hand. A persistent or markedly depressed state, however, calls for professional help. Between these two extremes are a variety of moods manifested by sorrow, sullenness, irritability, or other personality changes.

Ignore mild transient moods. If they persist, ask questions, and listen with empathy. Do not flood these folks with sympathy. Sympathy may prolong the moods, or lead to the martyr syndrome. Empathy is more effective than sympathy. If the situation does not improve, suggest professional counseling.

JEALOUS COWORKERS

Jealousy is common when employees compete for merit pay, promotion, or recognition. Frustrated people may try to undermine your position by starting ill-founded rumors, publicly berating you, becoming a bottleneck, or turning others against you. When any of these disloyal activities occurs, you must take firm action.

First, discuss the problem with your manager and get support. Then confront the envious one. Lay it on the line. Say what you have seen or heard and that you want it stopped. Describe your future expectations (eg, "I do not want arguments in front of staff, patients, or physicians. If you have a gripe, see me in my office"). If the undesired behavior persists, remind the person that it is affecting a future performance rating and possibly continued employment.

THE GOSSIP

A little benign gossip is harmless, but when character is attacked or misinformation affects work or morale, something must be done.

Gossips want attention, so supply it in healthy ways. Spike their misinformation by insisting on validation or correcting false comments. Explain how their gossiping is affecting the team. Add that people are withholding information from them because they fear it will be repeated in distorted forms. Do not encourage gossips by listening intently to their messages. Sometimes it's best to shun these people.

THE INCESSANT TALKERS AND SOCIALIZERS

These folks suffer from verbal diarrhea. Monday morning finds them rehashing weekend sports or their recreational activities. They repeat their broadcasts as long as they find listeners. You must know and act when these time wasters become bottlenecks.

Break up the little group discussions in the hallway. Give the verbose ones extra assignments. When they learn that too much talk and too little work results in extra assignments, they will usually modify their abuse of time. If possible, isolate them from willing ears. Encourage them to do their socializing during breaks. See Chapter 34 for advice on coping with them at meetings.

THE ONES WHOSE APPEARANCE YOU DISLIKE

Ask yourself these key questions:

- Does this person's appearance offend customers or interfere with the orderly conduct of business (eg, cause people to stop work and stare)?
- Does it violate any policy or rule?
- Is it a safety hazard (eg, wearing shoes with high heels that are dangerous on slippery or uneven floors)?

Try not to hire these people in the first place. Applicants who show up for employment interviews looking like something the cat dragged in are exhibiting their best appearance. It will get worse when they report for work.

During orientation of new employees, emphasize the importance of appearance, especially if they have direct contact with customers. Discuss the dress code and your personal expectations. Remember that forewarning is proactive; criticizing is reactive.

THE ONES WHOSE WORK AREA IS MESSY

Messiness is in the eyes of the beholder. Before you can get employees to clean up their act, you must convince them that there is a problem (parents know that this is not easy). Some fastidious supervisors make a big fuss over a little disorder. The key point is whether a disorderly desk or work area negatively impacts performance, coworkers, or customers. A receptionist's desk in full view of visitors has more significance than a beat-up desk in the corner of the maintenance department.

There may be barriers beyond the employee's control. For example, visiting VIPs may drop their coats on a receptionist's chair or delivery people may place large cartons in doorways. Do what you can to help your staff eliminate such problems.

We will discuss hostile people, sexual harassers, and chronic complainers in subsequent chapters.

NOTE

1. R.M. Bramson, *Coping with Difficult People* (New York, NY: Random House, 1981), 73.

RECOMMENDED READING AND LISTENING

R.M. Bramson, *Coping with Difficult People* (New York, NY: Simon & Schuster, 1986), six audiotapes.

R. Brinkman and R. Kirschner, *How To Deal with Difficult People* (Boulder, CO: CareerTrack Publishers, 1988), two videocassettes.

M. Solomon, *Working with Difficult People* (Englewood Cliffs, NJ: Prentice Hall, 1990).

W. Umiker, *Coping with Difficult People in the Health Care Setting* (Chicago, IL: ASCP Press, 1994).

Chapter 22

Coping with Hostile People

- three kinds of hostile people
- Sherman Tanks
- exploders
- snipers
- passive-aggressives

Your unspoken assertive message to hostile people is that you respect their right to have feelings and to speak their minds, but that you also have those rights. In addition, regardless of the rank and power of the other person, you do not have to listen to profane, intimidating, or obnoxious language.

To achieve freedom of expression, be assertive without being belligerent. If you lack assertiveness, none of the advice provided here will work. Passivity will prevent you from using it. Fortunately, there are many readily available publications, seminars, and audiotapes on the subject of assertiveness.

The hostile big three are called, according to Bramson,[1] Sherman Tanks, Exploders, and Snipers. We will use his terminology in this chapter. I highly recommend that you read Bramson's original publications or listen to his fascinating tapes (see Notes and Recommended Listenings).

SHERMAN TANKS (BULLIES, DICTATORS)

Of the hostile groups, Sherman Tanks are the most difficult to handle. They often have power, usually are professionally or administratively competent, and they know exactly what they want. Sherman Tanks have had years of successful intimidation. Their victims are too numerous to count. Sherman Tanks may be superiors, customers, inspectors, staff coordinators, or even colleagues. Every executive suite and every medical staff has at least one of these characters.

Sherman Tanks have permanently adopted that style because it is so effective. They may be physically intimidating, and they are always psychologically threatening. They are aggressive, abrupt, arrogant, and autocratic. Sherman Tanks are contemptuous of their victims.

218

When Sherman Tanks attack, they expect their targets either to fight back or to capitulate—they enjoy either response. The most successful strategy is to stand up to them, but without fighting.

How To Handle Sherman Tanks

When they launch a tirade, do not get defensive or try to counterattack. Be assertive enough to get their attention. To express your opinions while remaining emotionally neutral, try the following:

- Hear them out without interruption. Hold your ground. Equalize eye level as much as possible by asking them to be seated. Stand up if they won't sit.
- Maintain eye contact, but do not try to stare them down.
- Hold yourself erect; do not hunch your shoulders or cower.
- Instead of counterattacking, urge them to continue or ask them some open-ended questions.
- When they start repeating, break in with, "Pardon me." Then deliver your reply, turning up your voice volume enough to be heard, but not quite as loud as theirs.
- Each time they interrupt, say "Please, you interrupted me," and go on.
- Be tentative or noncommittal. Use words such as it appears, it seems, perhaps, and possibly.
- Focus on solving the problems that brought them in. Remember that their behavior is designed not only to grind you into the ground, but also to get a complaint taken care of. Since you have taken the fun out of the former, they're ready to deal.
- When their complaints are legitimate, apologize briefly and move to solutions quickly.
- Do not put up with offensive language or profanity. Walk away. If the person has great influence, tell your manager what you did and why.

EXPLODERS (VOLCANOS, GRENADES, BOMBERS)

Like Sherman Tanks, Exploders manifest anger, but there are significant differences. Sherman Tanks always exhibit the same overbearing attitude, whereas exploders are usually quiet folks between attacks. The anger of Sherman Tanks is contrived and under their complete control, while the anger of exploders is real. They are partially to completely out of control. They sometimes get physical, so handle them with care.

The Exploder suffers from childlike temper tantrums. Exploders learned early in life that people often did not take them seriously or give them what they wanted unless they got mad. As children they often had temper tantrums.

These people have a tremendous need for respect. They explode when their self-esteem is threatened. Precipitating episodes may be when they are the targets of jokes, are kept waiting or are ignored, or when their competency or integrity is questioned.

How To Handle Exploders

Coping is a matter of helping them regain their self-control. Exploders are like wind-up toys. They wind down if you can wait them out. After their explosions, they may become pussycats. Often they become apologetic. Some break down and sob.

If they are out of control, respond as you would to a hysterical person. In a loud voice call out "Stop! Stop!" or "O.K.! O.K.!" or keep shouting their name. Try waving your arms to get their attention. While you are going through those motions, edge around closer to an escape lane just in case.

A clever tactic is to say that you need a piece of paper to write down what they are saying because you know that it is important. This buys still more time for them to wind down. It also boosts their self-esteem.

If they continue to rant and rave, their speech will be loud and fast. Say that you can't write fast enough when they speak so fast, then ask if they would please slow down. When people slow their speech, the pitch and volume of their voice also plummet. Anger drains energy. Often, they will now sit for the first time.

Listen carefully for what it is that has set them off (their "hot button") and what it is that they want. You may hear a word clue repeated (ie, policy, schedule, recognition, consideration, or fairness).

Do not get involved in a verbal boxing match in which accusations or threats swing wildly back and forth without attempts to compromise. Do not try to explain complicated things while they are still upset—their listening mechanism is out of order. After they have calmed down and become rational, find out exactly what they want. If an apology is in order, make it. But add that you get upset when people act as they just did. Show that you are intent upon helping by stating exactly what you intend to do and when. If you discover what their trigger mechanism is, try to avoid it in the future.

If they remain irrational, say loudly that you want to help, but not when they are in such a state. Call a break (eg, "Julie, let's take a 15-minute break. I'll come back after we both have calmed down"). Leave immediately if they become abusive. Over your shoulder, call back that you will talk to them later.

Do not forgive them for their behavior, even when they return all apologetic. Forgiveness reinforces the explosive behavior. Repeat, "I'm always willing to listen to you, but not like that."

How To Handle The Employee Who Explodes

Some employees have an explosive temper on a short fuse, and they become angry with the slightest provocation. These individuals often are job hoppers. They stay on a job only until they blow up, tell the boss off, and quit or get fired. Emotional immaturity, low self-esteem, and marginal competence are characteristic of these firecrackers. They have intense feelings of frustration, fear, prejudice, or guilt.

Thorough employment screening and reference checking weeds out most of these people. If you are stuck with any of these powder kegs, keep them away from customers. They can get you in real trouble—and in court.

Do not take personally what they say in fits of temper. Reply "I'm sorry you said that. I would think that over if I were you. You've nothing to gain by offending me." If the session continues to degenerate, end it. Do not judge, criticize, or moralize; just end it. Simply say that the meeting is no longer productive and that you will continue later.

Professional counseling often is ineffective in chronic cases, but it's worth recommending, especially when you must keep the employee. If they resign during one of their rages, do not let them change their minds later.

SNIPERS (FOXES, SABOTEURS, NEEDLERS)

Snipers would like to be in control, like Sherman Tanks, but they lack the boldness. The sniper's weapons are sarcasm, snide remarks, and sick humor. They throw snowballs with rocks in them.[2] Snipers have discovered that verbal darts can be thrown without assuming any responsibility. They do most of their dirty work in front of other people, who provide their cover.

Snipers use innuendoes, sotto voce remarks, not-too-subtle digs, and not-really-playful kidding. Their remarks usually drip with sarcasm. They often talk behind your back, knowing that what they say will reach you. When you respond angrily, they retort, "Can't you take a joke?"

Many victims do not fight back because they do not want to make a scene. They smile weakly, look confused, and later find out that they have taken some hits. They lie awake thinking of what they should have said or done.

How To Handle Snipers

Your goal is to flush them out and blow them away.[3] Recognize the zingers when you hear them. Say to yourself, "Well, here comes one of Larry's little zingers." Do not laugh, even if it is a little funny or if the other people giggle or snicker. Do not ignore it either.

Bypass your sense of politeness. Stop what you are doing or saying—even in the middle of a sentence. Turn toward the sniper, and repeat exactly what you heard. These darts lose their zing when repeated.[4] Then add, "Larry, that seemed to be a barb aimed at me. Is that what it was?" or "Are you making fun of what I just said?" You have just blown his cover. Now he must either confirm what he said or try to weasel out of it with something such as, "I was only kidding" or "Where's your sense of humor?" Respond with a sour smile and something such as, "Well, it didn't sound funny to me." If he backs up what he said, you may learn something important. Critical feedback can be worthwhile. If he backs down, you have turned the tables on him.

Alternatively, ask the sniper what his or her remark has to do with the subject under discussion (the relevance question). Question the purpose of the remark (the intent question). For example, "What do you mean by that?"

Look for help from your associates. When you overhear the sniper say "What a stupid idea, she's in a dream world," say to the group, "Anyone else see it that way?" If the sniper gets support, you can search for more information about the situation. When the others do not agree with the sniper, follow with "I guess there is a difference of opinion" (not "See, you're wrong").[5]

After a dart-throwing episode, take the sniper aside and make a direct accusation. Snipers do not function well in one-on-one situations; their camouflage is missing. Do not buy their "Oh, you're just too sensitive." Reply that you enjoy a good joke like everyone else but that what you are hearing are not good jokes.

PASSIVE-AGGRESSIVES

Passive-aggressives represent a subset of snipers. Like snipers, they conceal their antagonism. Passive-aggression does not mean fluctuations between passivity and aggressiveness. The behavior is constant. Wetzler[6] aptly calls this behavior sugar-coated hostility. Passive-aggressives are manipulators who pretend to be helpless while they infuriate their superiors and associates.

Passive-aggressives believe that they are getting a raw deal by their supervisors, whom they perceive as dictators; this causes them to feel angry and resentful. They lack the confidence to challenge authority directly, so their resistance surfaces indirectly and covertly. They play many psychological games. Typical things they may do to try your patience are showing up late for meetings, submitting late reports, getting angry with you but refusing to tell you why, or fouling up a procedure.

They apologize superficially, give you endless excuses, or just clam up. Inwardly they enjoy your anger or discomfort.

How To Handle Passive-Aggressives

You are are not likely to change their personality; it is even resistant to psychological help. Your goal is to insist on behavior that meets your expectations and not to let them get you upset when they play their mean psychological games. Do not accept their excuses, and never give them the satisfaction of witnessing the anger or frustration you feel when they upset you.

NOTES

1. R.M. Bramson, *Coping with Difficult People* (New York, NY: Random House, 1981).
2. R.M. Bramson, *Coping with Difficult People* (New York, NY: Simon & Schuster, 1986), 26.
3. R. Brinkman and R. Kirschner, *How To Deal with Difficult People* (Boulder, CO: CareerTrack, 1988), video program.
4. Brinkman and Kirschner, *How To Deal with Difficult People.*
5. Bramson, *Coping with Difficult People,* 30.
6. S. Wetzler, "Sugarcoated Hostility," *Newsweek* (October 12, 1992): 14.

RECOMMENDED READING AND LISTENING

R.M. Bramson, *Coping with Difficult People* (New York, NY: Simon & Schuster, 1986), six audio-tapes.

R. Brinkman and R. Kirschner, *How To Deal with Difficult People* (Boulder, CO: CareerTrack Publishers, 1988), two videocassettes.

M. Solomon, *Working with Difficult People* (Englewood Cliffs, NJ: Prentice Hall, 1990) .

C. Tavris, *Controlling Anger* (Boulder, CO: CareerTrack Publishers, 1989), four audiotapes.

W. Umiker, *Coping with Difficult People in the Health Care Setting* (Chicago, IL: ASCP Press, 1994).

Chapter 23

Complaints and Grievances

- the supervisor's role
- the seven essential steps in handling complaints
- complaints about salary
- when complainers gang up on you
- when an employee goes over your head
- chronic complainers
- grievances
- sexual harassment

Complaints represent a major source of customer feedback, and employees are among our most important internal customers. Legitimate or not, complaints are signs that somewhere something is wrong and demands attention. Most worker complaints are related to policies and rules, working conditions, compensation and benefits, leadership, and relationships with other employees.

THE SUPERVISOR'S ROLE

The supervisor's role is to respond effectively and promptly to both legitimate and imagined complaints. This avoids formal, and often costly, grievances. Increasing numbers of lawsuits are being registered by disgruntled employees, often after disciplinary action has been taken against them.

Gripes may be articulated during staff meetings, performance reviews, exit interviews, and daily contacts. Observant supervisors suspect a problem when they note that an employee is unusually silent, irritable, or depressed. Managers who practice management by wandering around usually return to their offices with a bag of assorted complaints.

Caring managers engage in naive listening. Naive listening is nothing more than listening as though one is meeting these people for the first time, without preconceived notions. Insightful supervisors readily admit that they have a tendency to tune out long-term patients, loquacious colleagues, or boring supervisors.

SEVEN ESSENTIAL STEPS IN HANDLING COMPLAINTS

1. Listen carefully. The initial complaint is often only a trial balloon to see how you will react. You may have to dig deep to find what is under the surface.
2. Investigate. Is the complaint legitimate? Are there less obvious but more serious ones trailing behind? Are other people affected? Is the situation getting better or worse?
3. Choose what, if any, action is needed. Get help if you need it. Ask the complainer what he or she would like done. Make certain that your solution will not make matters worse.
4. Inform the complaining employee about your findings and what you propose to do. Do this without undue delay. If your remedy is not satisfactory to the employee, seek alternatives.
5. Implement your decision.
6. Check the effectiveness of your action.
7. Record what has happened.

COMPLAINTS ABOUT SALARY

Every supervisor has faced these complaints. They surface whenever salary changes are announced, or when people in other departments get larger raises. Employees are usually well informed as to what competitors pay their employees and are quick to point that out to their supervisors. The greater the difference between the expected and the actual salary increases, the more strident are the voices. Tempers flare when favoritism is thought to be at play.

Pay-for-performance strategies exacerbate salary dissatisfaction. Employees who do not receive the maximum merit increase gripe about their performance ratings. Even more unhappy are those who were told that their work has been outstanding and then found a minuscule increase in their paycheck.

Suggestions for Avoiding or Handling Salary Controversies

- Do not overrate employees or make unrealistic promises.
- Know what competitors are paying.
- Try to get more pay for your outstanding performers by other means, such as promotions, title changes, or revision of position descriptions.
- Let employees blow off steam. Be empathic.
- Refuse to discuss salaries of other employees.
- Do not be guilty of favoritism.
- Know exactly how salary increases are determined in your organization.

Here is an example of how to cope with a salary complaint: "Dolores, although salary increases are based largely on performance, other things must be considered. These include market factors such as the availability of certain specialists and what competitors pay. Other considerations relate to how critical each position is to the organization, budgetary restrictions, and projected costs for other activities."

If a raise is not deserved, state the reason very clearly. The person should know exactly why he or she was passed over and how the deficiency can be overcome.

WHEN COMPLAINERS GANG UP ON YOU

When confronted with a group of highly vocal complainers, Bernstein and Rozen[1] practice what they call creative ignoring. The supervisor just sits still and looks thoughtful. This response gets the group to quiet down and become more manageable. If it is a group of customers or colleagues, the supervisor asks for each person's individual input before responding, calling on the least hostile person first. If it is a bevy of angry subordinates, the supervisor tells them to pick one spokesperson. The rest must leave.

WHEN EMPLOYEES GO OVER YOUR HEAD

Ideally your manager sends complainers back to you as soon as he or she realizes that the employee has not given you an opportunity to respond. Unfortunately, some managers are all too willing to lend an ear to employees who bypass their supervisors, especially when the manager and the supervisor do not get along very well.

When you become aware of one of these occurrences, confront your manager. Present your side of the situation. Before you leave the office, suggest that in the future you would appreciate it if he or she would send for you while the complainer is still in the manager's office.

Let the employee know that you know what is going on and how you feel about it. Illustrate how such activities are counterproductive and ultimately backfire on the bypasser.

CHRONIC COMPLAINERS

A characteristic of chronic complainers is that most of their complaints lack validity. These people are more interested in registering feelings than in getting problems resolved. They rarely participate in finding solutions, and their daily conversations consist predominantly of negative comments. Chronic complainers constantly use words such as never and always. They frequent start their negative comment with "Why doesn't someone . . . ?"

The occasional griper can often be stopped with a "Well, what are you going to do about that?" Unfortunately this does not stop certified chronic complainers. They bounce right back, claiming that they have no influence in the organization and that their suggestions are never taken seriously.

The typical chronic complainer is a conscientious and competent worker. Their work is usually acceptable, sometimes above average. This also makes it difficult to get rid of these annoying people.

The Best You Can Hope To Accomplish

While you seldom cure chronic complainers, you can often achieve the following:

- Their complaining decreases to a tolerable level.
- They limit the complaints that they bring to you to those that you can do something about.
- They bring solutions with the problems.
- They spend more time working and less time griping.
- They develop a little more confidence in their own ability.
- They refrain from complaining in front of customers or your superiors.

Practical Suggestions

- Active listening is essential, and that is not easy. If you ignore their complaints, you may divert the complaining to customers or competitors. If their complaints get to your superiors, your reputation as a leader will suffer.
- Listen to their main points. Jot down the complaints in their presence. This is good for their self-esteem. Sometimes simply listening can silence the complainer. Do not agree or disagree with them. Maintain a noncommittal facial expression, avoiding approval nods or sympathetic grimaces.
- Direct your attention more at their feelings than at the object of their complaints. Chronic complainers are insecure. They are reassured when their feelings are validated (eg, "I can understand why you're upset about that"). Validating feelings is different from agreeing with them. It is only acknowledging the right to have those feelings.
- Stop them when they start repeating or if they try to move to another topic. Rein in a rambling discussion by asking, "What's your point?" Acknowledge

that you understood what they said by paraphrasing and summarizing their main points.

- Avoid arguments. Trying to argue them out of their negative stance, trying to placate them, or explaining things in detail seldom work.
- Force them to help solve the problem. After acknowledging that a problem exists, move quickly into problem solving. Ask specific, open-ended questions: who, when, where, and how questions. Avoid the whys because they get you into deep water. True chronic complainers are not comfortable with problem-solving questions; they just want you to agree with their complaints.
- Encourage them to research the problem. If they say that they do not have the time, respond with, "Well, if you change your mind, let me know."
- Be honest when you say what you can and will do or what you cannot do. Ask them what it is they want you to do. When they say that what you propose won't work, ask them what's the worst thing that can happen. Then say you're not worried about that outcome. Another ploy is to narrow the options to two and to ask which they think is the lesser of the two evils.
- When solutions are beyond your control, say so. At times you must make statements such as, "We've simply got to make the best of it."

GRIEVANCES

A grievance is a formal complaint by an employee for which redress or relief from management is sought. Grievance procedures are needed to ensure fair treatment of employees, to maintain good morale, and to avoid costly court litigation.

Employers must abide by the limitations placed by collective bargaining agreements, antidiscrimination legislation, civil service regulations, and employment contracts. Grievance procedures are spelled out in every union contract. Most nonunion organizations have a formal grievance protocol, and supervisors must be familiar with it.

Supervisors who are vigilant for conditions that induce employee dissatisfaction and who handle gripes expeditiously and fairly seldom have grievances filed against them. When these supervisors are faced with grievances, they can counter the charges effectively because they have documented all exchanges with the employee and can justify any measures they took that led to the grievance. There is a direct correlation between the number of disciplinary actions taken and the number of grievances filed.

When an employee is not satisfied with a supervisor's response to a complaint, the supervisor should make the employee aware of the appeal process, even though most employees who file charges will have investigated their rights and studied the organization's policy manual before filing the grievance.

Employers frequently lose litigation cases because supervisors have been guilty of inconsistent rule enforcement, unreasonable application of rules, or excessive penalties in terms of policies. Poor documentation is the most common cause.

SEXUAL HARASSMENT

Sexual harassment is a serious problem because of the legal costs, reduced productivity and morale, and increased absenteeism or turnover that it may cause. However, it is even more serious because it indicates that management has been negligent in protecting its employees or others for whom it is responsible.

Sexual harassment is prevalent in health care institutions because of the many power differences among its members (eg, physician-nurse), and the close customer-caregiver contacts (eg, patient-nurse). Most nurses have experienced or witnessed many episodes of harassment.

Two Major Forms of Sexual Harassment

1. Quid pro quo. This is when an employee is expected to grant unwanted sexual demands or suffer the loss of job or some tangible job benefit.
2. Hostile work environment. This is when an employee is exposed to a work environment that is hostile or abusive because of sexually oriented verbal, visual, or tactile activities. Verbal abuse includes sexual language, innuendoes, epithets, or jokes. Phone calls are frequently mentioned. Visual offenses consist of provocative gestures and sexually oriented posters, letters, notes, or graffiti. Tactile harassment can be sexually oriented touching, patting, pinching, rubbing, or pressing.

Legal Issues

The 1991 Civil Rights Act, an amendment to the 1964 Civil Rights Act, has given plaintiffs the right to recover compensatory and punitive damages when discrimination is found to be intentional. Cases can be tried before a jury, or plaintiffs may appeal to state civil rights agencies for relief. The 1980 Equal Employment Opportunity Commission (EEOC) guidelines stated that employers are responsible for the acts of their agents, supervisors, and employees and other people on the premises (eg, patients and visitors).[2]

To prove a case of sexual harassment, plaintiffs must establish that they were subjected to unwelcome sexual conduct that caused them severe harm.[3]

Organizational Policies and Procedures

The presence and effectiveness of policies and procedures impact the prevalence as well as the control of harassing behavior. These policies must be clear and understandable. Employers and managers must affirm that sexual harassment will not be tolerated and that violations of policy will be treated harshly. Sanctions range from verbal or written warnings to reassignments, demotions, suspensions, or dismissals.

Employers should provide training directed at both potential harassers and victims. This training should include explanations of policies and procedures and illustrations of the kinds of statements or actions that comprise sexual harassment. Confrontational techniques for potential victims is emphasized, and role-playing is recommended.

Supervisor's Role

Insightful managers are aware of the policies and procedures relating to this form of discrimination. They enforce these vigorously and promptly and with fairness, sensitivity, and confidentiality. They do not forget the rights of the alleged harassers. They find solutions that are satisfactory to the victims. In some cases they provide security for these victims.

All supervisors must be aware of the policies and procedures relating to this form of discrimination and must enforce them vigorously and with sensitivity while not forgetting the rights of the alleged harasser. Supervisors should ensure that the workplace environment is free of sexual jokes and inappropriate informality. Nursing supervisors should be alert to violations by patients and visitors and should take appropriate actions.

Investigation of Complaints

In some instances victims turn to their immediate superior. If that person is the alleged perpetrator or if they feel uncomfortable dealing with that person, they seek help from their manager's boss or a specialist in the human resources department.

The procedure for receiving and investigating complaints of sexual harassment must be prompt, fair, and confidential.

Procedure for Handling a Sexual Harassment Complaint

1. Listen carefully to the complaint. Ask the accuser to put it in writing and to include dates, places, names of witnesses, and the exact statements or behavior of the alleged harasser. Note: If the complainant later decides to withdraw the charge, get that decision in writing.
2. Investigate as soon as possible. Interview witnesses and other alleged victims.
3. Confront the harasser, and inform him or her of the complaint. Listen carefully to the rebuttal. If appropriate, tell the alleged harasser that this must stop immediately. Often you find that they simply were not aware that what they were doing constitutes sexual harassment.
4. Document what transpired at the meeting, including the exact words the person used in his or her defense.
5. Get back to the complainant and relate what happened. If no supporting evidence is found, explain this. Reaffirm the commitment on your part and that of the organization to the preventing of sexual harassment. Tell the complainant to report any further incidents.
6. Report the affair to your superior and to the human resources department.

When You Are the One Who Is Sexually Harassed

- Do not encourage the person or remain silent.
- Clarify your position and what you expect out of the relationship (eg, "I prefer to keep our relationship on a strictly professional basis").
- If the solicitations continue, review your personnel policy and follow the recommended procedure, or seek the advice of a senior member of the human resources department. If you belong to a union, complain to your union representative.
- Warn the person that if he or she persists, you will regard the activities as sexual harassment and will report it.
- Document each episode. Get witnesses if possible. Remember that a single incident rarely suffices to make a case.
- If you filed a complaint and it was not handled to your satisfaction, notify the human resources department that you intend to take the complaint to the local EEOC representative, a legal service agency, a state discrimination agency, or an attorney. When legal action is threatened, things usually start happening.
- If you are still dissatisfied, do what you threatened to do!

NOTES

1. A.J. Bernstein and S.C. Rozen, *Dinosaur Brains* (New York, NY: Wiley, 1989), 74.
2. *Discrimination Because of Sex under Title VII of the Civil Rights Act of 1964 as Amended: Adoption of Final Interpretive Guidelines,* U.S. Equal Employment Opportunity Commission Part 1604, *Federal Register,* November 10, 1980.
3. S.E. Burns, "Issues in Workplace Sexual Harassment Law and Related Social Science Research," *Journal of Social Issues 51* (1995): 193–207.

RECOMMENDED READING

P.J. Decker, "Sexual Harassment in Health Care: A Major Productivity Problem," *Health Care Supervisor 16,* no. 1 (1997): 1–14.

Chapter 24

Personnel Retention

- role of loyalty in personnel retention
- why employees go elsewhere
- how to analyze a retention problem
- retention strategies
- recruiting and selecting personnel
- orienting
- coaching
- team building
- morale

---

*"The deadly enemy of great performance on the
front line is high turnover."*[1]

W.H. Davidow

As work processes become more complex and employees assume more responsibilities, work force stability becomes more essential. Vulnerable to the impact of
loss of experienced workers, employers recognize the importance of personnel
retention. People who remain on the job create efficiency and effectiveness by
sustaining productive business relationships with customers, suppliers, and associates.

When unemployment rates are low and there is a limited talent pool, attracting
and keeping the best people are difficult. The people who resign are often among
the top performers.

The dollar cost of replacing an employee is high, often more than the annual
salary of the person who must be replaced. It's more difficult to estimate the cost
of loss of morale, quality, and service continuity. Each departing worker takes
with him or her valuable knowledge, skill, and a piece of a network that may
include important contacts within and outside the organization. Angry departing
employees can wreak havoc. For example, a terminated employee of an oil company erased its computer database that was worth millions of dollars.[2]

High personnel retention translates into high productivity, fewer mistakes, less stress, greater customer satisfaction, higher employee morale, and large direct and indirect cost savings.

The old response to personnel shortages was to step up recruiting. Administrators finally realized that retaining employees is less expensive and less disruptive than replacing them. They also found that the measures they took to improve retention had many other beneficial effects. These included increased productivity, customer satisfaction, and reduced absenteeism.

A fundamental retention strategy begins at the time of selection and continues through to the time an employee attempts to leave the organization.

ROLE OF LOYALTY IN PERSONNEL RETENTION

Corporate loyalty—that traditional bond between an organization and its employees—is rapidly becoming an obsolete concept. Formerly we measured the loyalty of employees by how long they remained with their organization. When workers left for whatever reason, supervisors complained about their lack of loyalty. On the other side of the coin, when a downsizing occurs, employees accuse their employer of the flaw.

Divided loyalties abound in our increasingly complex health care institutions. Employees often find it easier to be loyal to their professional specialty group or union than to their managers. Supervisors also have a built-in split loyalty. They're expected to serve both their superiors and their subordinates. If they lean too far in either direction, they're accused of being disloyal by the aggrieved side.

The first casualty of disloyalty is productivity. Sloppy work, mediocre quality, and poor service follow. Apathy takes over. Disloyal employees lower work standards, withhold information, conceal problems, file grievances, and create ill will.

The causes of loss of loyalty are principally those that destroy morale. Major factors relate to working conditions, compensation, and leadership skills. Other factors are job elimination, limited labor availability in some sectors, and an increasingly mobile work force.

New Paradigm of Loyalty

According to some observers, corporate loyalty—that traditional bond between an organization and its employees—is rapidly becoming an obsolete concept. Loyalty may range from resigned acceptance to fanatical commitment, and it is closely related to work ethic and duty—an unwritten contract that requires employees to be faithful to their profession, their employer, and their colleagues.

The loyalty of employees has all too often been measured by how long they stay with an organization or by blind compliance to those in authority. When workers leave for a better job, their supervisors often complain about a lack of loyalty. On the other side of the coin, when a reduction in force occurs, employees voice the same complaint against their employers.

Divided loyalties abound in health care institutions. Workers often find it easier to be loyal to their work group or union than to administrators. Scientifically trained employees often exhibit more fidelity toward their profession or to their technical societies than to their managers. Supervisors have a built-in split loyalty. They are expected to serve both their superiors and their subordinates. If they lean too far in either direction, they are accused of being disloyal by the aggrieved side.

The first casualty due to absence of corporate loyalty is productivity. This is followed by sloppy workmanship, apathetic employees, mediocre quality, and poor service.

The causes of loss of loyalty are principally those that destroy morale. These include poor working conditions, compensation, and leadership skills. Other factors are job elimination and our increasingly mobile work force.

What Is Needed Is a New Paradigm

The new employer/employee model is based on two realities: (1) employers cannot guarantee permanent employment, and (2) resigning from a job is not a sign of disloyalty.

Enlightened executives realize that workers no longer buy the passivity and humbleness that in the past was regarded as loyalty. They know that loyalty is founded largely on trust, and trust must be earned. Corporate loyalty is providing a safe work environment and opportunities for advancement. It is offering first-class benefits, rewards for high performance, and demonstrated respect for ability.

Better organizations replace the career ladders that disappeared with reengineering and that flattened most organizations with new roles, challenging assignments, and other opportunities for individual growth. They replace job security with new opportunities for their employees.

Supervisors earn worker loyalty by representing workers' interest to higher management and by doing this effectively.

Supervisory Loyalty

The most important action that supervisors can take is to find a substitute for guaranteed employment. The best substitute is the safety net of *employability*. Managers who encourage employees to learn skills and who provide the means to accomplish that lower the rise of unemployment and increase their employees' opportunities for more rewarding careers. Other measures for strengthening loyalty include the following:

- Be honest with employees. Tell them the truth about policies and plans that may affect their jobs.
- Make your expectations clear. Position descriptions, performance standards, orientation, and training are the essential tools.
- Expect the best. Look for strengths. Either eliminate weaknesses or make them irrelevant.
- Be perceived as a supporter, defender, and facilitator rather than a judge, bottleneck, or nit-picker.
- Be consistent, fair, impartial, and trustworthy. Live up to your promises, and earn their respect.
- Practice participative management.
- Show that you value every employee.

Employee Loyalty

Some employees feel guilty offering anything less than absolute loyalty. A more rational approach is to accept the proposition that if employees are reliable, can be trusted, and meet their employment obligations, they are loyal. Loyalty is refraining from castigating one's organization, colleagues, or boss—at least in public. It is not revealing confidential information to competitors or to the press. It is behaving ethically and morally, reducing criticism, and respecting confidences.

Loyalty is making superiors look good and doing everything one can to help them meet departmental goals and deadlines. It is defending superiors against false witnesses or attacks made when those superiors are not present to defend themselves.

Communality is important from a loyalty standpoint. This is a sense of belonging to a work group. It concerns issues of interdependence, mutual respect, and a sense of responsibility for other people. The core of loyalty is genuine caring for the well-being of the others involved in a relationship.

WHY EMPLOYEES GO ELSEWHERE

Employees are plucked away by competitors who offer higher salaries or better benefits. What management often fails to realize is that many departing employees were not lured away by competitors but leave because they cannot stand their supervisors or managers. Other factors are boring work, dissatisfaction with career development, or lack of appreciation for their efforts. Many overworked employees feel that they are being taken advantage of, are neglecting their families, or are experiencing burnout.

In today's job insecurity, employees are looking for the skills, information, and knowledge they can take with them in case of another downsizing. Insightful organizations provide those security blankets, but many hesitate to provide development programs for fear that their employees will leave with their newfound skills and credentials.

Organizations that base their retention initiatives entirely on compensation find themselves in bidding wars with competitors. The more insightful corporate leaders identify morale problems and correct them. They assess workplace environment and make needed improvements, often based on the findings of their periodic employee morale surveys.

Since supervisors have little control over salaries, they feel absolved of the accountability for the departures and identify the employer as the bad guy. Managers often are misled by what they find in letters of resignation or at exit interviews. It's easy to challenge the validity of exit interviews. For several obvious reasons, departing employees are reluctant to reveal the real reason they are leaving. Instead they simply say that they have been offered better jobs elsewhere. Often the real reason for their leaving is how they were handled by their immediate supervisor.

Few employees are assertive enough to confront their superiors. Instead, they sublimate their feelings by directing their ire at top management. When employees say they do not get recognition, they're usually talking about lack of recognition and praise from the person to whom they report.

HOW TO ANALYZE A RETENTION PROBLEM

Gather information from the following sources:

- records of rates of turnover, grievances, and requests for transfer;
- exit interviews;
- recruiters and recruitment-retention committees;
- focus groups;
- employee attitude or morale surveys;
- performance reviews, coaching, and counseling interviews; and
- personal observation.

Ask yourself these questions:

What attracts employees to your organization? What do they like or dislike about their jobs and the workplace? Is there really a problem? When did it start? Are only certain shifts or job categories affected? (Normally, rates are higher for night shifts and nonexempt workers.) How bad is the problem? Is it getting better or worse? Are there manifestations that suggest a general morale problem? What has been our response to date, and how effective have these measures been?

Consider these possible causes:

- lack of competitive pay, benefits, work environment;
- location of facility, parking, and other external factors;
- weak recruiting and selection process;

- inadequate orientation and training program;
- lack of supervisory support;
- lack of opportunity for promotion, advancement, or education; and
- mothers returning to work who may be unable to adjust to changes.

RETENTION INCENTIVES

Cash-Oriented Compensation Plans

The retention tools of choice for most organizations are still based on compensation. They include:

- retention bonuses,
- gainsharing and merit performance pay,
- premium for employees logging long hours, and
- salary adjustments or above-market pay for key positions.[3]

Career Development Offerings

Ambitious employees prize career development programs. Many employees leave employers when such a program is lacking. The kinds of programs offered include:

- career ladders,
- internal job transfers,
- a job-posting program,
- tuition reimbursement,
- a career planning/development center,
- formal succession planning,
- career planning training, and
- outsourcing assistance.[4]

Health Promotion Initiatives

These initiatives are becoming increasingly important to health care workers. They include:

- education training,
- health-risk appraisals,
- health-risk assessments/screening,

- special programs, and
- on-site fitness facility.

RECRUITING AND SELECTING PERSONNEL

Today's health care organizations want employees who share the values and goals of the organization and best meet the requirements of the positions being filled. Candidates recommended by employees have better retention records.

You can often spot potential quitters by reviewing their past employment histories and by asking provocative questions (see Chapter 7). People who change jobs frequently are not likely to be with you for a long time either.

ORIENTATION OF NEW EMPLOYEES

The skillful orientation of new hires has a powerful positive bearing on employee retention. Texas Instrument Company reduced its turnover by 40%, and Corning Glass Works slashed theirs by 69% by improving their orientation program.[5] See Chapter 8 for more on orientation strategies.

COACHING

In the absence of competent and compassionate coaching, most retention efforts will falter. In Chapter 12 we wrote that great coaches are out where the action is and where they are needed. Their attitude is "How can I help?" not "You're not doing that correctly." They know the difference between delegating, assigning, and making busywork, and they delegate often. They also know when and how to praise. They cheer loudly and publicly when an assistant comes up with an innovative suggestion. Good coaches support and defend their staffs. They intercede when their coworkers are confronted by angry customers or administrators.

This kind of coaching and shared governance are powerful factors in retention efforts. Coaches are able to practice situational leadership because they know the disparate motivational and educational needs of each subordinate and respond appropriately.

TEAM BUILDING

Personnel retention creates closely knit groups. Since loyalty locks people into place, it follows that team building can be a powerful force in any retention strategy. Two major motivational needs satisfied by team membership are the affiliation (social) need and the actualization (achievement) need. Trainees and employees with limited skills derive much of their satisfaction from team achievements.

MORALE

"All other things being equal, the best people will stay with the company that pays them the most."[6]

Frederick F. Reichheld

Critical to any retention program is maintaining high morale. Morale and recognition were discussed in Chapters 13 and 14. Key morale factors in personnel retention include:

- management style changes from command and control to coach, counsel, and lead cheers;
- employees who are treated and compensated as professionals;
- benefits and rewards that are selected carefully;
- a safe and comfortable workplace;
- career development that is encouraged and supported;
- employees who know what is going on in their organization;
- work schedules that are flexible and equitable; and
- mentoring programs.

NOTES

1. W.H. Davidow and B.K. Uttal, *Total Customer Service: The Ultimate Weapon* (New York, NY: Harper & Row, 1989), 121.
2. A. Farnham, "The Trust Gap," *Fortune Magazine* (December 1989): 66.
3. J. Condodina and L. Erme, "Compensation Packages Changing Shape," *HRFocus 74*, no. 10 (1978): S1.
4. B. Davison, "Strategies for Managing Retention," *HRFocus 74*, no. 10 (1978): S3.
5. R. Zemke, "Employee Orientation: a Process, Not a Program," *Training 26* (1989): 33–40.
6. F.F. Reichheld, "Loyalty-Based Management," *Harvard Business Review 71* (1993): 64–73.

RECOMMENDED READING

B. Ettorre, "Keeping the Cream," *HRFocus 74*, no. 5 (1997): 1, 45.

Special Report on Recruitment and Retention, *HRFocus 74*, no. 10 (1997): S1–16.

W. Umiker, "Workplace Loyalty in the 1990s," *Health Care Supervisor 13*, no. 3 (1995): 30–35.

M. Yate, *Keeping the Best* (Holbrook, MA: Bob Adams Publishers, 1991).

PART III

Cost Control

Chapter 25

Managed Care

- features of managed care plans
- kinds of managed care arrangements
- new challenges
- strategies of care providers
- strategies of managed care agencies
- outcomes management and benchmarking
- education
- reactions of professional and supervisory employees
- new opportunities in the managed care industry

"Managed care is changing our health care delivery system as radically as the computer chip has changed telecommunication."[1]

The nation's health care system has been reinventing itself with breakneck speed. Employers and consumer groups have mounted major efforts to evaluate how well health insurance plans, hospitals, and doctors provide care. The growing dominance of managed care has disrupted the lives of consumers and providers alike.

In the 1990s managed care focused on cost control. The big question is, "Can costs be reduced without reducing the quality and availability of services?" We have not heard much on this score from the major health maintenance organization (HMO)-accrediting organization, the National Committee for Quality Assurance. We do know that patients express unhappiness with the availability of care, lack of choice of providers, restrictions of services, and various inconveniences. It remains to be determined whether these are simply complaints because of change or whether they represent a real decline in benefits.

HMOs boast about their preventive care initiatives aimed at keeping people healthy. This could be a real plus for managed care if illnesses can be minimized and life prolonged without incurring large medical expenses. These preventive measures must be more than measures to prevent infections and make maternity care more available.

Chronically ill people present managed care with a crucial test. It is these folks and those who need the very expensive diagnostic procedures or therapies who are turning to lawyers to help them with everything from reading contracts to taking insurers to court when they are denied care. Patients feel vulnerable and perceive that advocacy can help them.

Since the major thrust of managed care is to manage costs, it would have been appropriate to include this topic in the next chapter on cost control. We could also have included it in the chapter on change, since it is the most profound change that the health care industry has faced in recent years. However, because it involves more than dollars and cents, and brings into play so many factors, we thought it deserved a chapter of its own.

FEATURES OF MANAGED CARE PLANS

Managed care is a system of care delivery in which the care provider receives predetermined compensation for delivery of a service. According to Lohr,[2] managed care plans exhibit some or all of the following features:

- complex organizational arrangements between institutions and clinicians,
- explicit financial incentives for providers and enrollees,
- defined access to the physician panel and/or services,
- strong controls on use, especially the use of health care specialists,
- coordination and integration of services, and
- accountability for an enrolled population and for quality of care.

Providers strive to reduce utilization rates by offering health promotion programs that target the most costly diseases such as acquired immunodeficiency syndrome, cardiovascular disease, and cancer. They try to limit use of hospitals in favor of outpatient and home visits. One result is that many nurses and other health professionals who worked in hospitals find themselves working elsewhere.[3]

Capitation Reimbursement

One special feature of managed care is capitation reimbursement, a prospectively determined payment system. This transfer of financial risk from the insurer to the provider is based on some level of activity. The set amount of monthly reimbursement fluctuates only as the size of the enrollment population changes. Providers influence profitability only through controlling costs.[4]

KINDS OF MANAGED CARE ARRANGEMENTS

Managed care arrangements include the following:

- HMO,
- Independent practice association,
- Preferred provider organization (PPO),
- Point of service (POS) plan,
- Physician-hospital organization, and
- Physician management company.

NEW CHALLENGES

The overriding challenge is to ensure that managed care delivers high-quality service at an affordable price to all enrollees. The organizations that will survive are those whose leaders continually respond to changing needs. The survivors know how they are positioned in relationship to competitors. They are knowledgeable about who the customer is and what the customer expects.[5] As rival organizations become more aware of and more responsive to the needs of their enrollees, competition heats up.

Providers must be skilled administrators of resources while still delivering quality care. To provide quality services within the parameters of fixed budgets, extensive restructuring and reengineering of the delivery systems of care are mandatory. Simply limiting diagnostic and therapeutic modalities is not enough.

Many traditional physician services are now delivered by clinicians who are not physicians. There is active delegation of responsibilities from professional to technical personnel. Technical personnel turn over many of their functions to employees who are less qualified or have less education. The challenge here is to select these delegates carefully and provide them with the necessary training. Employers seek workers who are proactive, autonomous, and creative and have interpersonal skills.

Since the introduction of managed care, there has been a decrease in certain services and an increase in others. Benge and his associates[6] report a sharp fall in the number of laboratory tests per inpatient. There has been a marked increase in the number of hospitalized patients who are sent home to recover. Although early discharges require more nursing care than they did in the past, insurance agencies are allocating fewer funds for home service.

Additional challenging factors include the following:

- current patients show less trust and respect for care providers;
- care providers are more stressed and often show lower morale;

- work units must adjust to frequent organizational changes;
- rightsizing and outsourcing has reduced job security;
- emphasis may shift from quality improvement to cost cutting (more errors are anticipated by some observers);
- cutbacks of space and budgets may restrict services; and
- new, rapidly growing bureaucracies add to the confusion and frustration.

STRATEGIES OF CARE PROVIDERS

Health care institutions have an obligation to redefine and clarify their missions and values. Then they must put in place the kinds of people who can and will carry out those missions and support the values. Their missions should include vigorous efforts to prevent as well as to treat disease.

Making the transition to managed care requires a blend of well-timed and coordinated strategies. Chief executive officers reengineer many of their systems and processes. Initiatives such as bedside testing, expanded computer systems, outsourcing, and modifying locations and hours of service help to ensure economic survival.

Providers display many innovative and diverse modalities for meeting these new challenges. Clinical enterprises are restructured to compete for the managed care dollars and to develop strategies to capture lost clinical revenue. Sometimes these initiatives are controversial. For example, the practice of using nurse practitioners in place of primary care physicians has come under fire from both patients and physicians.

Providers must overhaul costs and procedures without alienating the staff or letting quality suffer. This involves trimming nurses, adding aides, revising treatment procedures to achieve faster discharges from the hospital, and employing more outpatient treatment. Even a simple mechanical change such as pneumatic tubes to shoot laboratory specimens around the hospital saves time.

Hospitals that have purchased physicians' office practices must align the financial incentives of their physicians with their own. They may appoint incentive compensation committees to achieve these alignments.

Clinical Pathways

A clinical pathway is a written template of expected interventions and outcomes for selected groups of patients. Clinical pathways allow health systems to standardize care and to improve the process and outcomes of care where possible. These pathways provide multidisciplinary health care strategies that optimize patient care by streamlining and coordinating care delivery. Clinical pathways involve collecting patient-treatment data from doctors to compare cost of service and to devise the best methods for standard treatments. This provides standardized service for specific illness or procedures such as pneumonia, hip replacement, and coronary artery bypass surgery.

Patient Focus Care Model

This is a health care delivery structure that seeks to streamline care by restructuring hospitals into delivery units that are more self-sufficient. A premise of this type of system is to provide care to each patient by using fewer providers with a greater number of skills and responsibilities.

Integrated delivery systems put more care into the hands of interdisciplinary teams and coordinate care across many workstations. Computerized clinical assessment systems and automated performance appraisal systems can increase efficiency.

Study of critical patient care paths is critical for managed care environments. Supervisors must know how to develop clinical paths that create excellence in outcomes. There must be emphasis on avoiding errors of both commission and omission. Errors result not only in increased costs because of repeated diagnostic tests and delayed patient discharges, but also in worse medical outcomes. Some of these mistakes can be life-threatening.

STRATEGIES OF MANAGED CARE AGENCIES

Managed care agencies and their providers spend considerable time finding out what their enrollees want. Responses to what is wanted and what will be paid result in termination of some services and addition of others.

Insurers resist reimbursement for treatments they deem investigational. Sophisticated drugs and improved disease-monitoring techniques will remain no more than medical-journal jargon if health insurance fails to pay for these advances under the cost-cutting ethic that dominates much of today's health care.

Although the coupling between managed care organizations and their affiliated health care facilities is a loose one, and there is little face-to-face communications between these two groups, both parties are now attempting to get to know each other better and to meet each other's expectations.

Managed care has exacerbated the reimbursement wars between insurers and hospitals, physicians, and other care providers. The impact of cost-cutting measures may make the commitment to primary nursing too difficult to maintain. The concept of "primary nursing" is that each nurse is responsible for a small number of patients.

According to Kongstvedt,[7] managed care has imposed quality management principles of measurement, customer focus, and statistically based decision making. He writes that there are three sets of criteria:

1. Structure criteria including certification of personnel, licensure of facilities, compliance with safety codes, recordkeeping, and physician network appointments.
2. Process criteria to evaluate the way care is provided. Clinical algorithms, health screening rates, and evaluations against national criteria (benchmarks) are essential.
3. Outcome criteria such as infection rates, morbidity, and mortality.

OUTCOMES MANAGEMENT

Relying principally on benchmarking, advocates of outcomes management seek to reduce medical costs while preserving or increasing quality. Outcomes managers develop appropriate descriptors to determine where resources are under-utilized or overutilized and where professional skills need upgrading. Outcomes management depends on quantitative indicators that compare one health care entity against another—benchmarking. The comparisons may be between hospitals or medical staffs. For benchmark comparisons, practitioners of outcomes management usually use financial and administrative data.

There are two types of benchmarking. The first is clinical benchmarking in which physician practice patterns are matched. The second is operational benchmarking, which compares organizations from the standpoint of staff productivity, staffing mix, and the use of space and resources. Clinical benchmarking systems indicate how well one group of physicians performs against other groups. Process indicators like length of stay, variability in practice patterns, and the impact of clinical pathways are assessed. Quality indicators, such as mortality, complications, functional status, and patient satisfaction, are tracked.[8]

Operational benchmarking programs are critical tools in reengineering processes in institutions. These programs allow administrators to evaluate the productivity of staff, and to determine where the areas of greatest opportunity lie. There are two types of operational comparisons. The first is an internal comparison that allows trends of key indicators over time (eg, cost per billable test). The other operational programs allow for external comparisons—against peer facilities or best-in-class.[9]

EDUCATION

Utilization experts provide practical advice. Physicians and administrators are broadening their focus to include patient education, disease prevention, and health maintenance. Medical staff leaders help management in reprogramming physicians to practice more conservative, cost-effective medicine.

Current educational efforts must be bolstered and orientation programs upgraded. Educational and training programs should be based on needs assessments in which management determines what supervisors need to know. Appropriate topics include meeting enrollees' expectations, cost-effectiveness, time management, and personal empowerment.

For employees to feel empowered, they must have kinds of information that in the past was available only to upper managers. Computerized information systems make this a simple matter to summarize and disseminate. Supervisors and team leaders should have, at the least, access to their unit's financial data. All employees should be kept informed of the financial status of their organizations.

At a time when organizations focus on economic survival, patients and employees are all too frequently lost in the shuffle. Management must promulgate a value system of patient service, articulate clear standards of care, and provide practical guidelines. Managers must motivate care providers at all levels to put the patient first. and to be personally responsible for maintaining appropriate ethical standards of care.

Managers and supervisors should insist on educational programs on managed care. Management should provide supervisors with training in developing budgets that reflect clinical realities, cost accounting, and strategic planning.

Examples of Special Training Programs

Cerne[10] reports that small groups of employees in the Henry Ford Health System attend one-day training programs. These programs cover marketing, human resource needs and strategies, barriers to success, and competitor strategies.

Voluntary Hospitals of America helps its members (nurses, pharmacy, nutritional managers) by providing satellite programs. These programs cover capital environment, models of managed care, restructuring of clinical care, managing continuous quality improvement, and how to manage change.[11]

REACTIONS OF PROFESSIONAL AND SUPERVISORY EMPLOYEES TO MANAGED CARE INITIATIVES

Survival in these turbulent times is greater when every employee thinks in terms of what is best for the patients and the payers. It helps where there are collegial relationships between various care providers, payers, and suppliers.

Employees and their leaders who understand the implications and make the necessary changes are well positioned in this era of managed care. Insightful supervisors develop partnerships. These partners are in finance, utilization review, human resources, and departments that control the resources needed to manage job performance outcomes.

Health professionals must stay abreast of the dynamic knowledge base within their specialties. They must take responsibility for explaining to their patients the processes and expected outcomes of care. Management must insist on maintaining high standards for licensure, certification, and recertification for all individuals and units.

The supervisor's challenge is to develop a responsive work group that can change quickly to meet the ever-changing requirements of the health care workplace.

Stucky and Waltrip[12] have listed four competencies that can help providers survive in managed care settings:

1. *Clinical management*: resource allocation, productivity measurement, disease management;
2. *Financial management*: budgeting, management of variance, cost analysis, statistics;
3. *Information management*: communication flow, medical records, quality improvement; and
4. *Leadership:* personnel management, communication skill, team building, time management.

EMPLOYMENT OPPORTUNITIES IN MANAGED CARE INDUSTRY

Landry and Knox[13] believe that there will still be ample opportunity for health professionals to secure employment in a managed care environment. What will change is the location of the job site and setting. The hospital will not be the dominant employer.

With focus on the provisions of managed care programs, observers have not paid enough attention to the burgeoning growth of the organizations that control these programs. Like all rapidly growing industries, this one has new buildings, multiple hierarchical levels, internal politics, and the usual growing pains associated with massive change. On the positive side, many opportunities are there for the asking if professional and management personnel look for them and are willing to adjust to new roles and responsibilities.

New opportunities are also available in the hospitals and other provider institutions as they undergo radical changes in their missions, goals, and values. Attractive positions are available for health professionals and supervisors who are multiskilled and are willing to master new competencies.

Many employers are looking for multidisciplinary professionals, managers, and supervisors to replace highly specialized personnel in certain settings. Within hospitals, the restructuring process often includes reducing the number of leaders of departments. For example, the technical director of a laboratory may be in charge not only of the laboratory, but also of radiology, electrocardiography, and respiratory therapy.

Within the laboratory, the microbiology supervisor may be asked (or told) to direct the histology and cytology sections in addition to the microbiology section. In these instances, the leaders must learn much about services they could ignore in the past.

Many challenging opportunities lie ahead in quality improvement within the managed care systems. Expertise is needed in data management, profiling, administration of patient surveys and satisfaction questionnaires, and other techniques.[14] Health professionals will also fill new positions in case management, utilization review, quality assurance, and programs that emphasize disease prevention. Examples of positions in managed care organizations are discussed below.

Case Managers

Case managers are found both in health care institutions and in payer institutions. They function through third party administrators or self-administered programs. They may also work for a patient or family member. Case managers deal with managed care patients that have extensive medical problems or are expected to receive care over an extended period. These managers determine whether the care being received is appropriate for both fiscal and quality assurance purposes.[15] Kongstvedt[16] lists the following activities of case managers:

- Coordinate, facilitate, and educate.
- Collaborate with physicians, medical equipment providers, home care agencies, therapists, and other providers.
- Make certain that patients follow the treatment plan prescribed by the physician and that the equipment delivered to the home is what was ordered.
- With benefits personnel, pursue alternatives to the plan package in the best interest of the patient and the payer.

Utilization Reviewers

Evaluations are conducted by health care administrators and other professionals to determine resource usage patterns in patient care. The objective of this process is to provide cost control, promote quality of care, and guarantee enrollee satisfaction. These administrators submit their findings to the appropriate authorities for remedial actions.[17]

Advice Nurses

Many plans use 24-hour nurse advice lines. Nurse advice lines provide members with access regarding medical conditions, the need for medical care, health promotion and preventive care, and many other advice-related activities. These nurses are also called triage nurses.[18]

Enrollees are encouraged (or required) to call nurse advice lines before going to emergency departments. The nurse uses a clinical protocol to evaluate the member's complaints and then renders advice about what the member should do.[19]

Authorizing Authorities

In PPOs, hospital treatment authorization may require the approval of a primary care physician, a so-called "gatekeeper." In other PPOs and in managed indemnity plans, the authorization for elective hospitalization and procedures may be given by plan personnel, not from physicians. These authorizing people are usually nurses.[20]

Marketing and Sales Agents

Marketing staffs gather data on what to sell and how to sell, and they play a role in product development and market research. Sales representatives sell the product and may also serve as service representatives. There are also product specialists who specialize in specific products (eg, HMOs, PPOs, and POSs).[21]

Claims and Benefits Administration Personnel

These employees do not require any special medical training.

Actuarial Service Personnel

Actuarial services deal with financial risks, budgets, and other financial aspects. The employees set budgetary targets and prepare fee structure analysis and models to determine levels of clinical efficiencies and quality improvement.[22]

NOTES

1. C. Landry and J. Knox, "Managed Care Fundamentals: Implications for Health Care Organizations and Health Care Professionals," *American Journal of Occupational Therapy 50*, no. 6 (1996): 413–416.

2. K.N. Lohr, "Measuring and Improving Quality and Performance in an Evolving Health-Care Sector," *Clinical Laboratory Management Review 11*, no. 4 (1997): 265–272.

3. Landry and Knox, "Managed Care Fundamentals."

4. Landry and Knox, "Managed Care Fundamentals."

5. K. Kerfoot, "Today's Patient Care Unit Manager," *Nursing Economics 12*, no. 6 (1994): 340–341.

6. H. Benge et al. "Impact of Managed Care on the Economics of Laboratory Operation in an Academic Medical Center," *Archives of Pathology & Laboratory Medicine 121* (1997): 689–694.

7. P.R. Kongstvedt, *The Managed Health Care Handbook,* 3d ed. (Gaithersburg, MD: Aspen Publishers, Inc., 1996), 402.

8. R.P. Vance, "Resource Utilization and Outcomes Management: Opportunities for the Entrepreneurial Pathologist," *Clinical Laboratory Management Review 11,* no. 5 (1997): 318–321.

9. Vance, "Resource."

10. F. Cerne, "Learning to Survive," *Hospitals & Health Networks 11* (1995): 47–50.

11. Cerne, "Learning to Survive."

12. S. Stucky and L. Waltrip, "Managed Care: Are Your Middle Managers Ready?" *Caring Magazine 14,* no. 10 (1995): 94–98.

13. Landry and Knox, "Managed Care Fundamentals."

14. Lohr, "Measuring and Improving Quality and Performance."

15. Landry and Knox, "Managed Care Fundamentals."

16. Kongstvedt, *The Managed Health Care Handbook*, 274.

17. Landry and Knox, "Managed Care Fundamentals."

18. Kongstvedt, *The Managed Health Care Handbook,* 250.

19. Kongstvedt, *The Managed Health Care Handbook*, 336.

20. Kongstvedt, *The Managed Health Care Handbook*, 470.

21. Kongstvedt, *The Managed Health Care Handbook*, 577.

22. Kongstvedt, *The Managed Health Care Handbook,* 659.

RECOMMENDED READING

P.R. Kongstvedt, *The Managed Health Care Handbook*, 3d ed. (Gaithersburg, MD: Aspen Publishers, Inc., 1996).

C. Landry and J. Knox, "Managed Care Fundamentals: Implications for Health Care Organizations and Health Care Professionals," *American Journal of Occupational Therapy 50,* no. 6 (1996): 413–416.

Chapter 26

Cost Control

- the functions of budgets
- principles and rules of budgeting
- revenue budgets
- preparing forecast budgets
- capital expenses
- wages, benefits, and overhead
- variances and control
- cost cutting
- rightsizing
- process reengineering
- benchmarking

The cost-containment measures imposed on health care providers have intensified the importance of cost control. Supervisors are key people in the control and reduction of expenses. They participate in the preparation of departmental budgets, suggest cost-cutting measures, and direct the application of control measures.

FUNCTIONS OF BUDGETS

Planning Function

The preparation of a budget is part of the planning function. A budget provides a financial map of future activities. It also contains data vital to the determination of new charges.

Budget planning normally starts at executive levels and trickles down to first-line managers. It should coincide with the review of major policies and the reassessment of plans and goals.

Controlling Function

"A tight budget brings out the best creative instincts. . . . Put him under some financial pressure. He will scream in anguish. Then he'll come up with a plan that, to his own amazement, is not only less expensive, but is also faster and better than his original proposal."[1]

Robert Townsend

The administration of a budget is part of the control function. The most powerful tool for controlling costs is a budget. A budget creates a greater awareness of costs by employees. It also helps them achieve goals within stated cost expenditures.

The accounting department usually provides supervisors with weekly or monthly cost reports. These reports highlight variances that serve as red flags for remedial actions.

Evaluating Function

Performance ratings of supervisors include determinations of how accurately they forecast their expenses and how well their expenditures match the monies allocated. Variances reflect poorly on financial skills, unless the deviations result from factors that are not under the supervisors' control. Staying under budget is not always a cause for celebration. Having funds left over at the end of the year often shows poor budget estimations, not efficient management of resources.

Principles and Rules of Budgeting

- Expenses are charged to the department or cost center that incurs the expenditures.
- Every item of expense is under the control of someone in the organization.
- Managers responsible for complying with expense budgets participate in their preparation.
- Supervisors are not responsible for expenditures over which they have no control.
- Unused funds may not be carried over from one annual budget to the next.
- Unused funds for capital expenditures may not be transferred to operating expenses or vice versa.
- Requisitions for individual expenditures require approval by some authority.
- Slush funds are disallowed, but supervisors should try to allocate some monies for unexpected needs.

Revenue

Revenue figures may come from accounting or from data-processing departments. Computerized patient billing makes it possible to calculate revenue figures for each department or section.

Supervisors are usually not directly accountable for revenues, but they can be helpful in computing charges for the services that their departments render. Without the supervisors' cost data, finance departments have no legitimate basis for figuring out charges or for forecasting profit or loss. In predicting revenue and costs, consider not only historical growth trends, but also changes in the anticipated workload because of the introduction of new services, procedures, or equipment.

Preparation of Budgets

A breakdown of expenses charged to a department by categories, such as salaries, benefits, and supplies, is essential (see Table 26–1). Record expenses on an ongoing basis.

A budget cannot be adequately prepared the week before it is due. To prepare an itemization of expenses, collect expense figures for several months. Annualize the figures by dividing the year-to-date expenses by the number of months recorded, then multiply by 12.[2]

During the year, suggestions or proposals may turn up that involve additional expense or cost-cutting opportunities. Record all these. Take into account increases in supply expenses, service contracts, and continuing education expenses when planning a forecast budget.

Capital Equipment

There is usually a separate budget, or part of a budget, for capital equipment. Most organizations now project their capital equipment budgets for a five-year span.

Supervisors who must find the rate of obsolescence of major pieces of equipment often seek this kind of information from manufacturers or suppliers.

Replacement items and new equipment are among the most expensive budgetary items for some cost centers (eg, laboratory or radiology services). The capital equipment budget should reflect the costs of these items.

Wages, Benefits, and Overhead

The figures for salaries, benefits, and overhead are added to the budget by the finance department, not by the operating section. This is appropriate because su-

Table 26–1 Example of a Forecast Budget: Chemistry Section

Item	Annual Expense ($)
Medical/surgical supplies	300
Employee welfare	20,640
Pension	2,112
Postage, freight, express	408
Salaries and wages	281,572
Departmental supplies	367,800
Quality control	28,667
Travel	672
Publications	100
Education	336
Repairs and maintenance	12,000
Total Direct Expense	714,607

pervisors have no control over these items and cannot be held responsible for them.

Salaries represent more than 60% of operating expenses for most cost centers. Therefore when administrators want to cut costs, the first area to scrutinize is usually the personnel expense. It is essential to keep detailed records to justify work hours and overtime.

Management is loath to approve requests for additional staff, even when there is a projected increase in the workload, unless records prove the need. Reports of crises that have occurred because of personnel shortages can help in the justification process. This also holds true for equipment problems and requests for new apparatus.

THE CONTROLLING PROCESS

Always be prepared to defend the figures you submit. With or without modifications by higher authorities, the budget revisits supervisors at least monthly in the form of a responsibility summary (see Table 26–2). This report shows the budget estimates by month and year to date. It pairs the estimates with the actual expenses for the month and the year to date. It shows the variances for each item. When variances exceed a certain amount, supervisors generally must submit a written or verbal explanation.

Review these reports soon after you get them. If an item is not clear or may be in error, seek clarification from the accounting or data processing department. Be prepared to discuss the variances with your immediate superior.

Table 26–2 Responsibility Summary

	Current Month			Year to Date			Total Budget	Budget Balance
	Actual	Budget	Variance	Actual	Budget	Variance		
Inpatient revenue	160,414	167,081	6,667*	349,943	348,275	1,218	2,186,346	1,837,621
Outpatient revenue	106,591	78,129	28,462	233,294	169,937	63,357	1,021,120	851,183
Total patient revenue	267,005	245,210	21,795	583,237	518,662	64,575	3,207,466	2,688,804
Medical/surgical supplies	207	25	182*	289	50	239*	300	250
Employee welfare	2,299	1,663	636*	3,875	3,319	556*	20,640	17,321
Pension	1,059	1,059	0	2,112	2,112	0	2,112	
Postage, freight, express	31	34	3	55	68	13	408	340
Salaries and wages	25,166	23,263	1,903*	50,084	46,423	3,661*	281,572	235,149
Departmental supplies	43,788	30,650	13,138*	69,925	61,300	8,625*	367,800	306,500
Quality control	211		211*	211		211	28,667	28,667
Travel		118	118		318	318	672	354
Publications					50	50	100	50
Education		59	59		159	159	336	177
Repairs and maintenance	49	1,000	951	3,115−	2,000	5,115	12,000	10,000
Total direct expense	72,810	57,871	14,939*	123,435	115,799	7,636*	714,607	598,808
Total patient revenue	267,005	245,210	21,795	583,237	518,662	64,575	3,207,466	2,688,804
Direct expense	72,810	57,871	14,939*	123,435	115,799	7,636*	714,607	598,808
Operating gain or loss	194,195	187,339	6,856	459,802	402,863	56,939	2,492,859	2,089,996

*Unfavorable variances (i.e., low revenue or high expenditures).

CUTTING COSTS

When there is a severe financial crunch, organizations take multiple remedial measures. When drastic action is not imperative, managers introduce changes one at a time to find each change's effect before undertaking the next measure.

Cost control involves more than staff reduction and doing things more efficiently. It involves better inventory control and seeking price relief from suppliers. Reductions of salary overtime and benefits may be necessary but are often counterproductive.

Typical hospital responses are the laboratory responses reported by Jahn.[3] These included freezing or limiting expenditures for filling vacancies, capital spending, salary increases, and cutbacks of continuing education. If these were not sufficiently effective, there were layoffs.

RIGHTSIZING

Rightsizing is matching staffing to workloads to become more efficient. It differs from downsizing, which is simply laying off people to save money. Restructuring, acquisitions, mergers, and financial reverses result in reductions in force (RIFs). Employers can accomplish RIFs by early retirements, attrition, hiring freezes, voluntary separations, or reduced work hours. These measures are often insufficient, however, thus requiring involuntary separations.

The best time to begin this process is before financial constraints demand major staff reductions. The first step for executives is to analyze the workload and find out what can be done to reduce it without decreasing services or turnaround times. The second step is process reengineering or restructuring.[4]

Chief executive officers must decide whether to base furloughing on seniority or on a person's value to the organization. If the latter, supervisors play an important—and often painful—role in the selection process.

Responses to Call for Lower Personnel Costs

Determine if you can increase efficiency or reduce costs by transferring or merging activities within your section. If you must transfer tasks from professional or highly trained technical employees to less educated workers, insist that the latter be trained first, or that they are closely supervised. Tap into the observations and recommendations of the persons who do the work. They have practical ideas on how work flows can be streamlined. When people participate in the planning, they're less likely to object to changes, even when the changes involve staff reductions.

If the mandate you receive is to reduce the payroll to a certain level, hold brainstorming sessions with your employees. Get their ideas for reducing salary costs without laying off anyone. Some senior people may decide that this is a good time for them to end their careers. Some full-time employees may opt for part-time employment, and part-timers may be willing to reduce their hours, especially if they have greater schedule options.

Handling Those Who Leave

Supervisors must face the anger of those who leave and the apprehension of those who remain. The reaction of people who are laid off is much like that of patients when they are told that they have cancer. First, there is disbelief, then anger or depression, and finally acceptance.

Be tolerant of their anger, bitterness, and hostility, and be empathic when the tears flow. Console yourself with the knowledge that most of these people will recover and find new and sometimes more satisfying positions.

Answer their questions honestly, and make sure that they get the information they need about benefits and eligibility for unemployment benefits.

If outplacement services are available, encourage employees to take full advantage of them. These may include placement services, help with job applications and interview techniques, psychological testing, and training for new vocations. Use your personal network to try to find new jobs for them, or at least to steer them in the right direction. Do not give false hopes for recalls. If the likelihood of re-hires is high, keep in touch with them.

Handling Those Who Remain

Layoff survivors often feel guilty and depressed because of losing friends and colleagues. They may experience a drop in self-esteem and morale. In the back of their mind is the fear of future layoffs. Remain visible. Do not hide in meetings or bury yourself in paperwork. Share their concern about their buddies who are laid off.

Distance yourself from idle gossip, but keep yourself informed. Share that information. Explain the rationale for the changes. Answer questions honestly, and listen to expressions of frustration and fear. Do not wait for staff meetings or newsletters to keep your team informed. Call special meetings whenever you learn new things.

You and your staff must pick up the slack. Ask for your staff's participation and cooperation in closing ranks and getting the job done with fewer people. Point out the increased need for teamwork and for everyone to make a special effort. Prepare a list of duties and responsibilities that others must assume. Announce assignment changes, and provide any additional training that may be needed. Use your reward and recognition system to reward your team or individuals who make special efforts.

PROCESS REENGINEERING

Reengineering may prove to be the most cost-effective mechanism in health care institutions. Without reengineering, cost-reduction initiatives will achieve only modest results. The major savings will not come from departmental reengineering, but from those initiatives that address interdepartmental functions and that break down compartmentalization. These include abandoning obsolete systems, forming cross-functional, self-directed teams, amalgamating jobs, discarding old rules and assumptions, introducing new technologies, and creating new principles for task orientation. Reengineering was discussed in detail in Chapter 4.

BENCHMARKING

Benchmarking is the search for best-in-class by comparing current systems or processes with highly successful ones. Your goal is to increase efficiency, cut costs, or improve service. The comparisons may be with standards reported in the literature or with observations at the facilities of recognized leaders. Benchmarking usually leads to some form of process, system, or structural reengineering. It is an essential tool in cost control and quality improvement with improved patient and fiscal outcomes at stake.

Benchworking strategy usually requires data searches, networking, and creation of cross-functional teams. When national standards are unavailable, your external networks can be crucial to establishing standards. Questionnaires and other survey tools are often employed to locate the best benchmark sources.

The usual approach consists of (1) a data-collecting phase that may include literature searches or site visits, (2) an analyzing phase, and (3) an action plan. The planning process may involve use of flowcharts and other problem-solving tools. You want to dissect the work flows to find problems or weaknesses.

Kreider and Walsh[5] reported a highly successful benchmarking project that ensured decreased ventilator-associated pneumonia and intensive care unit costs.

With a cost-restructuring plan based on benchmark information, one hospital reduced its operating budget by $33 million dollars.[6]

Rotondi et al.[7] benchmarked their preoperative patient routing system. After they identified causes for variation, they created multidisciplinary improvement teams to improve the pinpointed areas.

Mitchell[8] found that the national benchmark for turnaround time between surgical cases was 13.5 minutes, while their hospital's time was 19.9 minutes. A quality improvement team carried out solutions that produced an 18% improvement. The cost-benefit analysis showed a potential enhanced revenue of about $300,000.

NOTES

1. R. Townsend, *Up the Organization* (New York, NY: Fawcett, 1971), 173.

2. J. Sattler, *Financial Management of the Clinical Laboratory* (Oradell, NJ: Medical Economics, 1980), 124.

3. M. Jahn, "Laboratorians Speak Out on Benefits, Managed Care, and the Bottom Line," *Medical Laboratory Observer 27,* no. 5 (1995): 29–33.

4. P. Medvescek, "Rightsizing the Right Way," *Medical Laboratory Observer 29,* no. 7 (1997): 102–106.

5. C. Kreider and B.A. Walsh, "Benchmarking for a Competitive Edge," *Medical Laboratory Observer-supplement,* September 1997: 26–29.

6. E. Cohen and E. Anderson-Miles, "Benchmarking: a Management Tool for Academic Medical Centers," *Best Practical Benchworking in Healthcare 1,* no. 2 (1997): 57–61.

7. A.J. Rotondi et al. "Benchmarking the Perioperative Process. I. Patient Routing Systems: a Method for Continual Improvement of Patient Flow and Resource Utilization," *Journal of Clinical Anesthesia 9,* no. 3 (1997): 159–169.

8. L. Mitchell, "Benchmarking, Benchmarks, or Best Practices? Applying Quality Improvement Principles To Decrease Surgical Turnaround Time," *Best Practical Benchmarking in Healthcare 1,* no. 2 (1997): 70–74.

PART IV

Developing Employees

Chapter 27

Job Redesign: A Paradigm Shift

- the paradigm shift to a sociotechnical model
- job satisfaction and enrichment
- meeting motivational needs
- job fit
- quality of work life
- job redesign

This chapter could be called the "See previous chapter" chapter because we refer to so many previous chapters. What we want to do in this chapter is tie together many different aspects of job design or job modification. We felt that this would be helpful for supervisors who are creating a new position or changing an existing one.

Health care is undergoing a paradigm shift from a technical model to a sociotechnical model. Advances in instrumentation and automation are not enough any more. To please our most important external customers, our patients, we need more high-touch. To satisfy our major internal customers, our employees, we need job enrichment. To appease third party payers, we need low costs.

Job enrichment is not a project. It is a continuous process of encouraging employee participation in multiple activities. It capitalizes on and makes full use of all available professional abilities and individual skills. This requires taking a second look at how we assign people and how we design jobs. Each employee perceives job satisfaction and enrichment a bit differently. One person's meat is another person's poison. We must know the motivational needs of individual team members (see Chapter 13). For employees who want more control, we provide delegation and empowerment (see Chapter 31). For those who want more task satisfaction, we provide training, challenge, and job enhancement. For those who have a strong affiliation (social) need, we provide increased opportunities for team efforts (see Chapter 9).

JOB FIT

Before embarking on cross-training and other job enrichment measures, place the right people in the right jobs. Start with accurate position descriptions (see Chapter 5) and comprehensive recruiting and selection of new hires (see Chapter 7). Assign people tasks that take advantage of their strengths and make their weaknesses irrelevant (see Chapter 4). Ensure that employees are not handicapped by oppressive or restrictive policies and rules (see Chapter 6).

QUALITY OF WORK LIFE

The physical work environment, social relationships, kind of supervision, and other morale factors determine the quality of work life. Employees now take these for granted. They and their unions fight to maintain them. These generic factors must be favorable before we can achieve significant sociotechnical break-throughs.

Quality-of-work-life programs and Japanese-style management represent macro models of organizational design. We turn to job redesign for micro models.[1]

JOB REDESIGN

"An effective job design meets both the requirements of the tasks and the social and psychological needs of the workers.[2]

Job Redesign Measures

- cross-training
- rotation of workstations, departments, or shifts
- job transfer
- changed work hours (flextime)
- switches from full time to part time, or vice versa
- deletion or addition of specific duties
- new locations of workstations
- improved instrumentation, flow patterns, communication, and methodology
- changed team membership or roles
- support of creativity and entrepreneurship
- delegation or more challenging assignments
- appointments to committees, quality circles, or other work groups

- involvement in research or development
- assignments to teaching or training roles

When Should Changes Be Considered?

Anytime! The considerations may be formal or informal, planned in advance or on the spur of the moment. There are several more opportune times, such as:

- during the latter phases of probationary employment,
- at the time of performance reviews,
- when salary discussions are initiated by employees,
- when new services are contemplated,
- when employee cutbacks are necessary, and
- when organizational expansions, mergers, acquisitions, or other restructuring take place.

Key Questions To Be Answered

- Does this employee want more authority or autonomy?
- Does this employee prefer to work alone or on a team?
- Will both the organization and the employee benefit?
- What can be achieved without an immediate change in the job classification?
- Will the budget and current staffing permit changes?
- How will the changes affect work flow and other people?
- Will the results improve customer service, costs or charges, or employee morale?
- Will the changes enhance total quality management (continuous quality improvement) measures?

Guidelines or Cautions

- Do not attempt to use job redesign or enrichment as a cure-all.
- Tailor the changes to the needs and wants of the employees and the organization.
- Know the motivational drive of each person.
- Consider the effect of any change on other people.
- Ensure that the employee endorses the new measures.
- Be certain that the employee has a reasonably good chance to succeed.
- Make the goals and plans flexible and reversible.
- Update position descriptions as appropriate.

- Provide feedback and support.
- Do not promise what you cannot deliver.

NOTES

1. J.B. Cunningham and T. Eberle, "A Guide to Job Enrichment and Redesign," *Personnel 67* (1990): 56–61.
2. Cunningham and Eberle, "A Guide," 56.

Chapter 28

Adjusting to Change

- the three general kinds of change
- the essentials of change
- barriers to change
- employee concerns
- preparing for change
- carrying out the plans
- helping people through the stressful phase
- employee responses to change
- how to overcome resistance

*"Directing and controlling change in an
organization has been likened to managing in
white water."*[1]

Nothing is as constant as change. We hear about a technological advance or another medical breakthrough almost weekly. New areas of specialization spring up, and older ones phase out. Acquisitions, reductions-in-force, mergers, reorganizations, and the change to mandated care stir tremors throughout the health care industry. In addition, every few years another "revolutionary" management concept surfaces, only to sputter and die a few years later. How about Theory X and Y, management by objectives, guest relations, and the various permutations of quality improvement.

There are significant differences between the ways that the successful and the not-so-successful organizations cope with change. A change culture requires flexibility, rapid responsiveness, and adaptation. Employees must master new technologies and adjust to new systems and procedures.

Effective supervisors are change specialists who know what their clients want and how well these wants are being met. Too many managers at all levels make changes based on their own perceptions of what is best for the customers without finding out what those customers really want or need. The three general kinds of change are:

1. Organizational changes, in which departments are altered, interdepartmental relationships or reporting relationships are changed, or new management takes over.
2. New systems, structures, procedures, or equipment are introduced.
3. Jobs are restructured.

ESSENTIALS OF CHANGE

- *Motivation.* Motivating people to change is a major challenge of leadership. Managers must understand why people resist change and cope with that resistance.
- *Competencies.* These are the technologies and expertise that enable organizations to satisfy customers and meet new standards. Competencies are affected most by hiring and training systems.
- *Creativity.* Brainstorming is often needed. Change also requires the skills needed to turn ideas into entrepreneurship.
- *Employee commitment.* Employees must "buy-in."
- *Adaptability.* Learning and retraining are the orders of the day. Some employees must be completely "recycled."
- *Stability of work force.* Stability requires low personnel turnover.
- *Patience.* While everything is rush and more rush, supervisors must show a modicum of patience with those people who learn or adjust a little slower than others. They must couple patience with persistence.
- *Rewards and recognition.* People who must adjust to change expect some kind of a payoff.

BARRIERS TO CHANGE

- Dysfunctional teamwork
- Satisfaction with status quo
- Unjustified pessimism about the ability to change
- Ego or personality problems
- Territorial imperatives
- Lack of vision or support by upper management
- Inflexible systems, policies, or procedures
- Work overload
- Lack of confidence in leaders

EMPLOYEE CONCERNS

Change experts know what employees who are affected by change may experience, and they anticipate a spectrum of emotional responses. Even changes that individuals hope for can be upsetting. For example, a promotion elicits mixed feelings. The pride and paycheck are gratifying, but the altered relationships with former coworkers may be upsetting.

The more that a change affects established habits and relationships, the greater the stress produced. Fear is the strongest stressor. There are many kinds of fear: fear of the unknown, fear of failure or reduction in one's influence, and fear of job loss, demotion, transfer, or reassignment. The most common personal fear is probably that one cannot cope with new tasks or responsibilities.

Loss of control is another factor. Reactions are more intense when changes reduce employees' control over their daily tasks. People who worked hard to achieve influence are likely to oppose, overtly or covertly, any threat to this status.

Mindsets are significant. People can perceive changes as threats or as opportunities. There may be pervasive perception that the change is either impossible or not practical. This is most likely when employees have witnessed failures in the past.

People with low self-esteem and a great need for basic security are reluctant to commit to change. Others balk because they receive too little information or may not participate in the planning process.

PREPARING FOR CHANGE

Role of Supervisors

Supervisors carry out changes mandated by upper management or outside agencies, and they introduce some of their own. Through networking, they find out as much as they can about current and rumored change. Then they train, support, and monitor results. If they drag their feet, stonewall, or do much griping, they cannot expect exemplary behavior by their employees or to win points with upper management.

Goals and Plans

A well-defined goal is a prerequisite for productive action and arches over four critical objectives:

1. selecting the right people,
2. preparing and motivating people to change,

3. obtaining the other necessary resources, and
4. carrying out the change.

Every successful initiative requires a workable, clearly defined master plan—committed to writing. The plan answers the following crucial "W" questions:

- What is the proposed change? Is it customer oriented, quality conscious, and cost-effective? What do we hope to achieve? What are the risks, constraints, and barriers? What additional data do we need? What resources are essential? What did we do wrong last time? What additional training will be necessary? What will be the impact on existing power and status relationships?
- Will the change fit the existing organizational culture? Will the people affected see a payoff or a setback? Will the change increase or decrease profit, morale, quality, and productivity? Will the change provide an opportunity to use available skills better? Will people have more autonomy over how they do their work? Will the changes make employees' jobs (and mine) easier or harder?
- Who wants the change? Why? Who will benefit and who will be affected adversely? Who will resist? Who will support it?
- When should serious planning begin? Will there be sufficient time? When must we get official sanction? When will the work start and when must it be completed?
- Where will we find the space, funds, and people?

Assess the compatibility of the proposed change with the current organizational culture and goals. The change should not violate cultural norms.

Gather information about previous successes and failures. Experience is still our best teacher. Focus on activities that strongly influenced success and those that were barriers.

Set a timetable with checkpoints and completion dates. Install a feedback system so people know how they're doing. Be flexible. Successful plans are usually revised often over the course of implementation.

Test your plan by asking these questions:

- Is it concise and clearly written? Does it include action steps?
- Was it distributed to the right people?
- Has there been sufficient input from others?
- Are there formal and informal networks to lend credence and support?

Communicate

Alert your people about upcoming changes as soon as possible. Outline the challenges and the opportunities they present. Involve them early while evaluating new technology or procedures. This also gives them time to adjust to the idea of a major change.

Explain the need for change in pragmatic terms, then patiently listen to them blow off steam. Reassure them about things that are not going to change.

When they report rumors, tell them as much as you can. Once they know that they know what you know, they will gain confidence. The very act of talking about the change reduces fear and resistance, especially if you acknowledge their concerns and anxieties as legitimate. Tell them that what they feel is perfectly normal and that those feelings will pass.

When you must champion a change that you feel is inappropriate, avoid making remarks like "the idiots upstairs issued these orders." This only increases resentment, lowers morale, and delays implementation. You do not gain any points either.

The Name of the Game Is Commitment

Obedience is good, but commitment is better. We succeed only when we get commitment from the people who carry out the change or who are affected by it. Ideally you invite this participation when change is first contemplated. We all support what we create and may even be ecstatic over our own ideas. It takes a lot more effort to get enthusiastic over another person's brainchild. When a team lacks ownership of a plan, getting commitment is more difficult. If you demand it, all you get is "lip service."

If it is not possible for employees to participate in the planning sessions, it is even more important for them to be involved in designing or scheduling the implementation process. Follow through on as many of each person's suggestions as possible.

Explain the rationale behind the change. Articulate the reasoning in terms that make sense to the workers. Does it improve customer service, profits, or competitiveness? Detail the shortcoming of the old way. Show them how the change will affect them. What is in it for them if they do well—or when they do not?

If the history of change is one of failure, explain the new change fully, and point out how this change is different. Provide examples of how the plans succeeded elsewhere.

Upgrade Your Employee Selection Process

In Chapter 7 we discussed how to select job applicants. Pick people who have displayed their ability to adjust to change. You want the ones who have the willingness and ability to participate in planning.

Train—Train—Train

Since fear of the unknown is the source of the most anxiety, eliminate the unknown. The dual approach is to hold enough discussions before the change and to provide sufficient training to ensure confidence.

Clarify training objectives using a thorough needs analysis. Ask the learners what they want, and incorporate their suggestions into the program. Design training that provides the needed job-related skills.

Enroll the highly motivated and influential end-users first. Provide the training just before it is needed and to those who are going to use it first—"Just-in-time training."

CARRYING OUT THE PLANS

It's important not to fail at the start. Introduce changes by using pilot projects and highly motivated teams. This increases the likelihood of quick and favorable results.

Take change one step at a time. Resist the urge to carry out every aspect of a change at once. Empower employees to make changes happen. Build in incentives for using the change. Stay in touch with workers' daily efforts.

The Seven Keys to Successful Implementation

1. Clarify strategy and plans.
2. Mobilize resources. Choosing the right people is especially critical.
3. Introduce new practices slowly.
4. Provide needed education.
5. Give and get feedback continuously.
6. Run interference for the team members.
7. Do not nit-pick or be a bottleneck.

Monitor Progress

Major change efforts require constant monitoring. Things do go wrong. Unexpected situations develop. Some resistance is due to certain aspects of the plan that were wrong to begin with or were carried out poorly. As people are forced to break familiar routines, performance weakens, confusion follows, and job stress increases. People see and hear things that disturb them. They are often disappointed and frustrated by all the problems or bottlenecks that develop.

Some people reach hasty conclusions that the plan is not working. The grumbling grows louder unless leaders have made it clear that the change will not be trouble free. When they complain, showcase the benefits or the progress made. Make it easy and safe for them to express new concerns.

Talk to people. Track results. Look for symptoms like slippage in timetables, productivity downturns, and increased customer complaints. Be aware of signs of uncooperativeness, complaining, or criticizing the folks in charge. Workers may start regressing to the old way of doing things. If you pay attention, you can address the problems before they get out of hand.

Use weekly meetings to discuss modifications and problems. Continue the group meetings throughout the implementation process. Interactions include give-and-take exchanges. Accept, even welcome, appropriate critical comments. For the first 15 minutes of these meetings, let the complaints and frustrations hang out. Then switch to a brag session where individuals talk about their little victories. Pay close attention to what is said out in the corridors after the meetings break up.

Monitoring performance and tracking results also enables you to identify the role models who are contributing most to the change effort. Honor them and celebrate their achievements.

Reward

Hanging on to established habits makes sense to employees when their old reward system stays in place. Therefore try to restructure the way people are compensated. While money is a limited and transient motivational force, the lack of a fair compensation system is a strong *de*motivator.

Autonomy is a powerful reward for some people, so delegate authority to those who show the interest and the ability to use power judiciously. For achievers who relish challenges, the strongest reward may be to get involved in another change—maybe a bigger or more difficult one. Most employees feel rewarded to some extent if they perceive that the change will enable them to get their work done faster, more easily, or more enjoyably. See Chapter 14 for more on rewards and recognition.

HELPING PEOPLE THROUGH THE STRESSFUL PHASE

Employees are relieved when told that their concerns are normal and will pass. The principles of stress management apply here. The earlier you take remedial measures, the better results you will get. Workers appreciate reassurance that their jobs or their teams will not be altered.

You may be able to reassure employees whose positions are in jeopardy by:

- promising new positions,
- offering retraining opportunities,
- recommending early retirement packages,
- reassuring that jobs will be eliminated only by attrition.

Vital elements of coping include the following:

- using active listening skills, isolation avoidance, and empathy;
- legitimizing their feelings and expressions;
- ensuring that training measures meet their needs;
- showing understanding, but holding firm on the need for the change;
- searching for specific needs and problems and bringing them into the open;
- exploring ways of achieving desired changes through conflict management skills and win-win negotiation;
- expertise;
- being patient; and
- not promising what you cannot deliver.

EMPLOYEE RESPONSES TO CHANGE

Individuals vary widely in their openness to change. Some thrive on change, but most people do not. Some employees sense that they will be affected. Others convince themselves that they won't be involved.

People often go through the stages of anticipation, denial, anger, bargaining, depression, and, finally, acceptance. The first opposition to change may take place when news of possible change surfaces.

While most employees show a degree of support, others take a wait-and-see attitude, and some actively reject the process. The two undesirable responses are resistance and the development of stress. There may be increased absenteeism, turnover, and grievance filing. Hostility, moodiness, and slowed output may result.

Fortunately most employees settle down and accept the change. Later, many fight to prevent any return to the old system. A computer breakdown that requires a temporary return to the old manual system causes consternation in the ranks.

Happy Campers

A minority of a work group embrace new marching orders enthusiastically. The better the preparation for change, the larger this percentage of people will be. Alert managers make full use of these eager beavers. Assign them to pilot programs and have them discuss successes during the early phases of a new initiative.

Fence Sitters

Most employees are fence sitters. Fence sitters are not obstinate or uncooperative, but they do fret about how a change may affect them. While not hostile to change, they are not enthusiastic either. They want proof that the change will work. They ask where the change was tried before, and what the outcome was. Most will join in the endeavor when they see colleagues commit themselves and when they witness early successes.

When people believe that they will be unaffected by a change, some of them become amused bystanders. They show little sympathy for the people who are involved. Sometimes they taunt those who are struggling with the new initiative. Do not tolerate these snide remarks.

Cynics

One highly vocal cynic can infect an entire department. Cynics often have some truth to support their pessimism. There may have been failures in the past, or there are formidable barriers ahead.

When you hear grumbling, investigate the problem and address it without delay. It helps to have some team members relate successes during the early phases of the change.

Rational arguments, such as pointing out that this change is unlike old, failed initiatives, may not achieve the desired effect. In that situation the best strategy may be to admit that we also have concerns but decided to risk going ahead with the change. We add that we hope the cynic will also make the same choice. When this does not work, you may have to spend your efforts trying to limit the influence of the cynic on other employees.

Occasionally you can convert cynics by giving them more of the action or getting their ideas for expediting the process.

Resistors

Resistance can be overt or covert, active or passive, well intentioned or subversive. People fight change in ways that best fit their individual personalities, so expect a wide range of tactics at work when resistance emerges.

Managers often mistake the lack of overt opposition for support. Covert resisters disguise their resistance to make it safer or more politically correct. People in this category are cunning. These saboteurs operate under cover, resisting on the sly, fighting change carefully to reduce their chances of being caught. They may claim that they did everything in their power to support the change.

Subtle sabotage is expressed in a myriad of ways, for example:

* intentionally "forgetting" to do things;
* inciting resistance;
* doing exactly what their supervisor requests when they know that such action will be detrimental; or
* setting up roadblocks.

Your job is to blow their cover. Look for signs of passive resistance—foot dragging, quiet uncooperativeness, or malicious compliance. When you spot these people, corner them and give them an earful. If counseling is not effective, disciplinary measures must be taken.

Among the resisters are a few firebrands who are loud and outspoken in their opposition to change. One or two highly vocal critics can rock the boat, so it is hazardous to ignore them. Usually you have to get rid of such obstructionists. Pritchett[2] expresses the opinion of most of us when he writes, "Make an example of someone who resists. If this sounds ruthless, remember that it is their choice to resist. Something has to suffer, either them or the change effort."

HOW TO OVERCOME RESISTANCE

Resistance to change is not all bad. It can be valuable, sometimes keeping leaders from making critical mistakes. However, for the most part, resistance is a roadblock that you must remove.

When employees do not accept change, it may be because they do not understand it. They may think that it will be bad for them. Some employees lack confidence in the ability of their leaders or their team to make it work.

Chances for success decrease when change occurs without proactive analysis, planning, or direction. The likelihood of success increases when you understand how your people react to change and use that awareness to help navigate them through the process.

Participation by Stakeholders

We've already discussed the importance of getting employees involved in the planning and implementation processes. By involving people before specific changes, a leader confronts deep-seated, negative attitudes before they become barriers.

Education

Do not overlook the knowledge gap that changes create. There is usually much to be learned. Make certain that people have the necessary understanding. They must handle new kinds of equipment and face unfamiliar methods. Once workers realize that they will be retrained, their resistance often plummets. When they receive instruction manuals, hands-on training, and the time to use new equipment, they quickly develop self-confidence.

Communication

Earlier we discussed the importance of communication when laying the ground work for change and when anticipating employee concerns.

In the implementation phase, get developing resistance out into the open. Make it safe and easy for people to express their feelings. Be patient enough to get beyond superficial answers so you can reach the true issues. Try to understand their positions. Evaluate the legitimacy of their resistance. You might discover that some of their reluctance keeps you from doing something dumb. At the very least, they can educate you about why they are resisting and how you can elicit their support.

When people say that things were better before a change, remind them of the problems that existed then. We all forget many of the negative aspects of "those good old days." For example, while people may have griped about a new computer system, few would elect to go back to the old one.

Supervisor Commitment

Your actions speak louder than your words in this regard, so "walk the talk." Be obvious and passionate in your determination to follow through. Do not try to reduce resistance by softening your position. It will only stiffen the resistance. Employees will fully commit only when they trust their superiors. Each of us must earn this trust.

NOTES

1. G.P. Boe and C.G. Hudson, "Managing Change in Troublous Times," *Medical Laboratory Observer 23*, no. 9 (1991): 24.
2. P. Pritchett, *Resistance: Moving Beyond the Barriers to Change* (Dallas, TX: Pritchett & Associates, 1996): 21.

RECOMMENDED READING

J.A. Belasco, *Teaching the Elephant To Dance* (New York: Crown Publishers, 1990).

A.J. Bernstein and S.C. Rozen, *Dinosaur Brains* (New York: John Wiley & Sons, 1989).

R. Maurer, "Transforming Resistance," *HRFocus 74*, no. 10 (1997): 9–10.

C.R. O'Connell, "After Reduction in Force: Reinvigorating the Survivors," *Health Care Supervisor 14*, no. 4 (1996): 1–10.

W. Umiker, "How To Prevent and Cope with Resistance to Change," *Health Care Supervisor 15*, no. 4 (1997): 35–41.

Chapter 29

Encouraging Creativity

- the creative process
- intuition
- characteristics of creative people
- the innovative supervisor
- stimulating creativity in your staff
- communication precautions
- rewards for creativity
- barriers to creativity

*"Innovation is the practical application of a
creative thought."*[1]

Employers with tunnel vision think that all worthwhile ideas are generated in
executive suites or in research departments. But the front-line worker has the best
opportunity to see how that job can be improved. Employee input results in better
cost control, quality, productivity, and customer service.

Organizational infrastructures are shifting to make room for people who are
innovative. Innovative potential now outranks graduate degrees in some progressive institutions. The fundamental driver of continuous quality improvement and
cost reduction is innovation. Failure to promote innovation leads to lower quality
or more rationing of care—two equally undesirable results.

Downsizing, with its adverse impact on morale, has greatly affected employee
creativity. However, it has stimulated foci of creativity where economic survival
is at stake or competition is keen.

Although workers at all levels have ideas on how to improve things, some are
blessed with greater innovativeness, intuition, or entrepreneurship. These creative
employees are among the most valuable members of an organization if their super-

visors treat them well. Your goal as supervisor is to keep these people flooding you with ideas—without letting them get out of control.

THE CREATIVE PROCESS

Innovative creativity is the ability to come up with really new ideas (eg, the artificial lens for cataracts). Inventors have innovative creativity. Just as a kaleidoscope forms new patterns from many disconnected pieces, the creative person forms new patterns from many seemingly unrelated ideas. The process usually starts with a problem. Problems are opportunities in disguise. Edwin Land invented the Polaroid camera after his young daughter asked him why she could not see pictures as soon as she took them.

Adaptive creativity is shown when people find better ways to do their work. This may be putting old ideas together in a new way or simply putting creative ideas of others into practice. Entrepreneurs exhibit adaptive creativity. Because creative people are often unable to work out the details of their ideas, we need both types of creative people, the inventors and the entrepreneurs.

When you challenge employees to think creatively about their work, they seek to learn more about their jobs. In the process, they become more competent and efficient. It is creativity that leads to new services and products.

When supervisors suppress creativity in favor of conformity, the creativity resurfaces outside the workplace in hobbies, recreational activities, and artistic endeavors. Back on the job, stifled operational creativity may be expressed in unique ways to annoy bosses or to bypass policies and rules.

INTUITION

Intuition has long been regarded as a mystical power that originates below the conscious level. We refer to it euphemistically as flashes of insight, hunches, and gut reactions. Intuition is knowledge gained without rational thought or logic. Think of it as experience stored in the unconscious mind.

> *Intuition + Logic = Common Sense*

Intuition is a sixth sense. Everyone is born with it, but it declines with disuse. The more attention we pay to our intuition, the more useful it becomes. For example, before you sign a contract, make a checklist of pertinent questions, then take time to identify completely your feelings about each of those questions. This combination of rational and intuitive decision making is more effective than either process alone. The same holds true for selecting new employees.

CHARACTERISTICS OF CREATIVE PEOPLE

People who are creative have a sort of restlessness. Confident that there is always a better way of doing things, they challenge systems, processes, procedures, tradition, practices, policies, and rules. Most share the following characteristics:

- They have innumerable bits of information (the pieces in the kaleidoscope) that relate to the focal point of their interest.
- They blot out what to them seems irrelevant or unimportant, sometimes to the annoyance of their supervisors.
- They are curious, open, and sensitive to problems. They may bombard their supervisors and others with questions, many starting with "why," "why not," or "what if. . . ."
- They are optimistic risk takers who like challenges and rarely talk about failure.
- They often appear preoccupied. At times they work furiously. Their ideas usually come in spurts.
- They dislike rigid routines, monotonous tasks, restrictive policies, and bureaucratic interference.
- They tolerate isolation and ambiguity.
- They value independence and autonomy.
- They often enjoy the innovative process more than the results of the innovation.
- They sense when things are right and when they are not.
- They bounce ideas off others and build on the suggestions of their associates.
- They are voracious readers.
- They are often nonconformists, regarded by their peers as different. At meetings they are likely to play the role of devils' advocate.
- They may like to hang out with other creative people. Many are loners.

THE INNOVATIVE SUPERVISOR

Effective supervisors strive to increase their own creativity and that of the people who report to them. To avoid job blindness, they occasionally step back and take a new look at processes, systems, and people. They seek fresh insights into nagging problems.

Innovative supervisors:

- believe that there is always a better way, and are always on the lookout for that better way;
- overcome ideonarcissism—the egotism of thinking that your idea is unique;
- view problems as challenges rather than annoyances;
- chalk up failures as learning experiences;
- utilize brainstorming techniques for making decisions and solving problems;
- are tolerant of ambiguity or the idiosyncrasies of teammates;
- cut red tape;
- set aside some time each day for reflective thinking;
- inject humor into situations (some of the best ideas originate as jokes); and
- are willing to stick their necks out in support of their ideas.

STIMULATING CREATIVITY IN YOUR STAFF

Creativity flourishes only when employees feel secure and free of the fear of failure. Insightful employers establish corporate cultures that support new ideas. To switch from a culture that endorses conformity and compliance to one that fosters innovation is not easy. Here are some suggestions for stimulating creativity in your unit.

- Identify your innovative people, and strive to know them better. Focus on each person's unique expertise.
- Emphasize creativity during the orientation and training of new employees. Present problems as challenging opportunities. Be alert for and encourage employee statements that begin with "Maybe we could . . ." or "What if . . .?" These flash the message that a creative idea is about to be born.
- Give people a loose rein to pursue and develop new ideas. Tolerate some daydreaming. They need this to fire up their creativity or to retrieve information stuck in the catacombs of their unconscious minds. Use idea traps, such as quality circles, brainstorming sessions, incentive awards, and suggestion boxes.
- Do not nit-pick or demand perfection. When employees start to neglect their routine duties in favor of pet projects, you may have to tighten the reins. But do not say, "You can't do that." Instead, say, "You can get back to your project when. . . ."
- Let them take some risks and make mistakes without risking their jobs. Tolerate failure and mistakes as the costs of innovation and progress.
- Provide the necessary resources and psychological boosts. Give them some discretionary time for nondirected research. The ones who are already spending weekends so engaged are the most deserving.
- Expose them to in-house and outside learning, including:
- seminars and professional meetings;

- consultants and guest speakers;
- publications, audiotapes, videotapes, and computer programs;
- customer input; and
- vendors and sales representatives.
- Protect them. Employees and managers may harass people who are different.
- Expect some creative ideas from everyone and tell them that. For those supervisors who complain that their people never come up with creative ideas, let me pose this question: If you walked around your department with a roll of $100 bills and offered one for each idea, would you get any suggestions? You bet you would!
- Give lots of praise and rewards.

COMMUNICATION PRECAUTIONS

Do not say yes or no too quickly. A quick no leaves the employee feeling that you have not given his or her idea serious consideration. When you say yes too quickly, you may find yourself in hot water or forced to renege on your promises.

Use the PIC Response to All Ideas

P = Positive: If you find an idea worthwhile, say "Great idea, let's try it" or "What can I do to help?"

I = Interesting: If there may be merit, say "That sounds interesting. Tell me more."

C = Concern: If you cannot find anything of value in the idea, say that you have some concerns, and express those concerns. Avoid killing the suggestion directly.

Avoid statements such as:
  You've got to be kidding.
  That would never work here.
  The trouble with that idea is . . . .
  I'm paid to do the thinking.

Substitute the following:
  Keep talking, you may have something.
  How can I help?
  Let's give it a try.
  Can you get me the figures for that?
  Wow!

REWARDS FOR CREATIVITY

Because creativity is usually expressed in bursts, rewards of all kinds are best delivered in bursts. Bonuses that follow specific accomplishments are more motivating than end-of-year bonuses. Do not save recognition for the next performance appraisal.

Base recognition and rewards on outcomes of their value to the organization. These values may relate to teamwork, quality, new services, and customer satisfaction. These systems demand factual and fair performance appraisals.

Give prizes not only for suggestions but for criticisms that lead to improvements. Creative people are likely to have reward values that differ from those of their colleagues. For example, they usually value financial support of their projects more than they value salary increases.

Shower them with recognition. Encourage them to publish. Let them attend meetings where they meet other creative people.

Other rewards are:

- increased work space, equipment, resources;
- personal library;
- appointments to teaching staffs of academic institutions; and
- relief from tedious tasks and bureaucratic time wasters.

BARRIERS TO CREATIVITY

The following situations can stymie creativity:

- Prejudging ideas. We accept ideas more readily from authority figures or people we respect and reject those from marginal performers or individuals below us in the hierarchy.
- Fear of failure. This is a great inhibitor of creativity.
- Restrictive policies, rules, rituals, and procedures
- Strict controls and limited budgets
- Complex or slow approval procedure for suggestions and projects
- Demands for a consensus
- Understaffing and excessive work group assignments
- Long chain of command
- Group norms
- Disparaging remarks

NOTE

1. B. Filipczak, "It Takes All Kinds: Creativity in the Work Force," *Training 14,* no. 5 (1997): 32–40.

RECOMMENDED READING

R. Davidhizar, "Intuition and the Nurse Manager," *Health Care Supervisor 10*, no. 2 (1991): 13–19.

P. Preston, "Breaking Down Barriers to Creativity," *Clinical Laboratory Management Review 9*, no. 6 (1995): 449–455.

W.T. Weaver, "Championing New Ideas: Whose Job Is It?" *HRFocus 72*, no. 1 (1995): 22, 23.

Chapter 30

Staff Development

- the benefits of staff development programs
- the planning process
- who is accountable for the program?
- needs assessment
- the staff development program
- mentoring

Career development is a combination of education and experience. Employees may have to reinvent their careers numerous times and must continuously update their technical skills to stay employable. Unfortunately employers cannot even tell their workers what skills will be needed in the future. A paradigm of lifelong education and training must replace short-term consideration of an education completed at the end of college.

BENEFITS OF A CAREER DEVELOPMENT PROGRAM

Development programs for employees benefit the employees by making them more eligible for promotion, increasing their self-esteem, and injecting more interest into their jobs. The programs keep employees abreast of fast-changing skills needs so they can maintain their employability and marketability.

Employers benefit by having a more talented and flexible roster. To remain competitive, organizations must help their employees adapt to the fast cycle of change. Career development enhances morale and motivation and increases personnel retention, productivity, and service quality. Recruitment is stimulated when candidates learn about the educational advantages offered by the institution.

Some executives express concern over the loss of talented employees who leave for better jobs. This disadvantage, however, is balanced by the enhanced expertise of those who do not leave. There is also the goodwill of the people who have resigned. That often benefits the organization indirectly.

As employees become more highly qualified, supervisors can delegate more and therefore have more time to spend on other high-priority responsibilities. They also have the pride and satisfaction that all coaches and teachers derive from watching their charges mature.

THE PLANNING PROCESS

Planning is most effective when it is tailored to fit individual needs. Some health care workers seek promotions to managerial positions; others eschew supervisory responsibilities. They prefer to climb a professional ladder if it is available. All employees want some growth within their current positions. It adds spice to work and prevents boredom.

Some of you will be reviewing the position descriptions of your employees to ensure compliance with various laws (eg, the Americans with Disabilities Act). This is a good time to consider revisions that will establish the criteria necessary for employee advancement. These revisions usually address titles, responsibilities, and the amount of supervision that the incumbent requires.

When interviewing job candidates, include a brief explanation of your career development program. This can be a strong incentive for the more ambitious candidates.

Discuss goal changes or modifications at performance reviews. Action plans for helping the employee work toward these goals should be a major agenda item at these meetings. Affirm your confidence in the employee's ability to achieve these goals. Employees are motivated more strongly when their desire to move up in the organization is accompanied by an expectation of success.

WHO IS ACCOUNTABLE FOR CAREER DEVELOPMENT?

Top management is accountable for the educational facilities, staff, and resources. Supervisors are partly responsible for developing and implementing the programs for their units. They share this responsibility with the educational or personnel department of their institution.

Career development is primarily self-development. Many health care professionals wail about not being trained for supervisory jobs before they assume those roles. Most of these people knew for a long time that this opportunity would be available. They often had years to get the necessary training but failed to do so, assuming that management was responsible for this. This is a hangover from our public educational system, in which the programs and schedules are prepared for the students, who quickly learn that if they pass a few tests they will be promoted—sometimes without passing the tests.

After accepting supervisory roles, some professionals continue to focus their educational efforts on the clinical aspects of their job. They often limit their managerial training to the mandatory programs provided by their organization.

In organizations where promotions have stalled, supervisors can encourage employees to consider lateral moves or cross-training. These moves have motivational value and increase the employees' marketability.

NEEDS ASSESSMENT

Any training program worthy of the name should be preceded by a needs assessment. This assessment should consider the following:

- The expertise needed by the department, now and in the future. This involves obtaining product or service forecasting information from top management. Skills-inventory charts list the employees who are qualified to handle each major job component. These charts are invaluable for planning skills enhancement, cross-training, and workstation rotation.
- What is needed by individual employees to meet or exceed the requirements of their jobs or to be ready to assume greater responsibilities?
- What is needed to bring old-timers up to date? Job obsolescence occurs at an ever-increasing rate, and because women play a major role in health care institutions, many positions are filled by employees who have interrupted their careers to start or raise families.
- What is needed to energize stalled or marginal workers whose work interest needs rekindling?
- What is needed to make you dispensable? The highest order career development program is succession planning. Supervisors who make themselves dispensable by training successors are more eligible for, and worthy of, promotion.
- How does the knowledge of the employees compare with the skills demanded in their field?

Bartsch[1] offers the following tips for determining training needs:

- Ask your human resources department to give you a list of performance deficiencies that are frequently documented in performance appraisal reports.
- Review your department's performance appraisals looking for specific problems or training needs.
- Observe the behavior of people at work, especially their interactions with customers and coworkers.

- Study patient and employee satisfaction surveys.
- Keep abreast of legal and legislative issues that could lead to performance problems (eg, the Americans with Disabilities Act).
- Review your organization's mission statement and values to find out what kinds of training can contribute to long-term goals.

To help decide how well your current training program meets basic needs, answer the questions in Exhibit 30–1.

Exhibit 30–1 Questions Related to Skills Enhancement of Your Staff

1. Do you have an in-house educational program for each staff member? Does it include a minimum number of hours of participation or some results evaluation method? Are records kept? Are you satisfied with the results?
2. Are training materials (books, journals, tapes, and other teaching tools) easily available? Do you know how frequently these are used? Are they frequently updated?
3. Is there an ongoing professional and/or management training program readily available?
4. Do your employees have the time to make use of the training materials? to attend lectures, demonstrations, and other educational sessions?
5. Is there financial support for continuing education? Are schedules flexible enough to permit employees to attend programs of educational institutions?
6. Do your employees get intellectual stimulation through problem-solving sessions?
7. Do your employees have the opportunity to cross-train? to rotate workstations? to assume greater responsibilities? to serve on committees, quality circles, task forces, and other work groups?
8. Do you delegate tasks that provide valued educational experiences for your employees? Do they assume greater responsibilities? Do you empower them sufficiently to carry out these responsibilities?
9. Are educational subjects presented at routine staff meetings?
10. Are there real opportunities for promotion? Do you have dual career tracks? Can your employees be promoted within their current grades?
11. Does each employee have an individualized career growth plan that is jointly formulated?
12. When employees plan to attend outside seminars or workshops, do you jointly establish practical goals for that experience? Are these discussed when the employee returns? Do you provide opportunities to put those new skills to work?

THE DEVELOPMENT PROGRAM

The major goal of any program is self-reliance. Employees are taught a lifelong process dedicated to learning and development. Trainers make available a variety of self-assessment instruments such as the Myers-Briggs Type Indicator.

With the guidance of career counselors, employees use benchmarking techniques with which they learn how to identify the best and the brightest in their organization and field and to determine what makes them successful. They then compare their preferences and skills to those of the top performers. The skills gaps are used to identify development goals when the employees put together action plans for continuous learning.

Other modalities include:

- orientation and on-the-job training of new employees;
- in-service education, including the use of guest speakers and consultants;
- workshops and seminars;
- formal programs at educational institutions;
- job rotation and cross-training;
- self-education:
- books, journals, computers, audiotapes, and videotapes;
- participation in any educational endeavor;
- special assignments;
- committees and other special work groups;
- assignments as trainers, instructors, or lecturers;
- duties as coordinators or facilitators (eg, quality assurance, safety, or data processing);
- "horizontal promotions";
- temporary assignments at satellite facilities or elsewhere; and
- substituting for absent employees.

Practical Career-Building Tips

- Work on easier skills first to ensure early success.
- Ask others to help.
- Maintain a high ratio of praise to criticism.
- Correct errors before they become habits.
- Be patient. Expect plateaus in progress.
- Serve as coach, facilitator, advisor, and cheerleader, not as taskmaster.
- Use adult training methods. Employees are not school children.
- Encourage mentorships.

MENTORING

In mentoring, an experienced or influential person guides and nurtures individuals or small groups of employees. Mentors teach protégés how to survive, thrive, and progress within an organization or a profession (ie, to attain their full potential).

Mentoring may begin shortly after a new employee comes on board. During the orientation of new hires, the latter have an excellent opportunity to spot a manager or senior team member they would like to have as a mentor.

Corporate Mentoring

Some organizations provide formal mentoring programs. They assign mentors to new employees, and provide training to mentors and protégés. In the past employers crafted special programs for women and minorities as part of affirmative action. However, this may expose employers to charges of reverse discrimination. So for now, most programs are available to all employees.

Mentor

A mentor can be someone on the same team, in another department, a retiree, or an outsider. He or she may be a senior manager or an expert in the same field. An employee's immediate supervisor is not the ideal choice because protégés will be more reluctant to ask questions for fear of appearing ignorant or irritating the supervisor.

A *counselor* mentor:

- helps protégés make career decisions,
- introduces them to the intricacies of political savvy,
- enhances their sensitivity to organizational culture, and
- helps them in enlarging their personal network.

A *coach* mentor is an experienced professional or technical expert who shares knowledge and skills that help protégés fine-tune their expertise.

Mentors teach their protégés how to be successful in a particular organization or profession. They suggest ways to (1) cut bureaucratic red tape and (2) how to avoid troublesome people, policies, or practices. They point out cultural sand traps, rituals that must be followed, who has the clout, and how decisions are made. They highlight pitfalls such as leaving work before the chief does.

Mentors share visions of their protégé's future, perceive their potential, and challenge them when they are not living up to this potential. They detect real and potential hindrances, and recommend ways to eliminate or reduce these.

Mentors take an active interest in the employee's continuing education. They recommend literature and seminars or workshops. They are readily available for questions, and are open, authentic, and receptive. They provide appropriate affirmation and offer opinions in a way that promotes the protégé's feelings and self-worth and competence.

Mentors help individuals to enhance their careers by removing obstacles, teaching team skills, advising on career development strategy, and serving as role models. In brief, they may teach, sponsor, advise, coach, counsel, guide, motivate, or critique.

Great mentors are empathic and inquisitive. They listen more than they talk and avoid excessive direct advice. They avoid remarks such as "Let me give you a piece of advice," or "You ought to. . . . " Instead they relate their experience (eg, "What I've found helpful in that situation is. . . . ").

Mentor-Protégé Relationships

Protégés must respect their mentors and must not disclose confidential information. A little deference is appropriate. Most mentor-protégé affiliations are similar to doctor-patient or attorney-client relationships. Protégés must have a sincere desire to assimilate information and reconceptualize ideas. They should keep their mentors informed of their progress but not make pests of themselves. Associations may end quickly or gradually. Some change into collegial relationships or social friendships.

Recent Developments in Mentoring

With managed care programs and various organizational changes, mentoring programs are showing up with innovative twists. One of these is *reciprocal mentorship*, in which peers exchange expertise. For example, a laboratory supervisor who has a master's in business administration, but lacks laboratory experience may help a lead technologist prepare for a supervisory role. The technologist, in turn, helps the manager understand the intricacies of laboratory procedures.

Another form is *team* or *big-brother* mentorship. Here, senior team members offer assistance to struggling junior colleagues.

Group mentorship, where a mentor serves a group of protégés, can save time and elicit broader discussions. The proteges develop the agenda, and the mentor responds to their needs.

NOTES

1. M. Bartsch. "Go Beyond Surveys To Assess Needs," *Training 33,* no. 5 (1996): 15.

Chapter 31

Delegation and Empowerment

- assigning versus delegating
- why some supervisors are reluctant to delegate
- the willingness of employees to accept delegated activities
- "dumping"
- how to delegate
- when delegation falters
- horizontal delegation
- reverse (upward) delegation
- hopscotch delegation
- empowerment

ASSIGNING VERSUS DELEGATING

Assigning is telling a person what to do, how to do it, and when the task must be completed. The tasks are usually of a nonsupervisory nature and are found in the position descriptions for particular jobs. There may or may not be a consignment of authority. Delegation is the transfer of authority, responsibility, and accountability. The tasks are those that the delegator was doing. Delegation is usually negotiable or optional and requires a commitment by the delegate.

WHY SOME SUPERVISORS ARE RELUCTANT TO DELEGATE

There are a number of reasons why some supervisors are loath to delegate. The most common ones are:

- They are workaholics or perfectionists.
- They are insecure because they are afraid that:
  1. the delegate will fail,
  2. the delegate will do it better than they did, or

3. they will be accused of dumping.
- They do not like to turn over what they enjoy doing.
- They do not think their employees are ready or willing.
- They have had unpleasant experience with delegation.
- They do not know how to do it.

Reluctant managers say things such as:

- "I do not have the time."
- "Do you know what happened the last time I tried that?"
- "If you want things done right, do them yourself."
- "I can do it faster and better."
- "When I try to delegate, the employees say that it's not in their position description, or they ask what's in it for them."

WILLINGNESS OF EMPLOYEES TO ACCEPT DELEGATED ACTIVITIES

The willingness of employees to accept delegated responsibilities is determined by whether or not:

- they think they are qualified,
- their previous efforts have succeeded,
- they are concerned about what their teammates may say or think,
- they think they have the time,
- they like what is delegated or see some reward in it,
- they think they will have enough authority,
- they think the delegator will support them, and
- they think they are being manipulated or dumped on.

DUMPING

Delegation is a two-edged sword. It can be the key to increased productivity, time management, and motivation, or it can be a wet blanket that squelches initiative and lowers morale. The latter outcome is usually because of "dumping."

Dumping is loading people with repetitive, mundane work that has little value to the organization or to their career.[1] Because dumping is often done on the spur of the moment, the recipient feels like an errand runner, the proverbial gofer.

The response to dumping is resentment or anger. The perception of being dumped upon is just that: a perception. One person's meat is another person's poison. Delegation is more likely to be perceived as dumping when delegates:

- have poor working relationships with their superiors,
- have been dumped on in the past,
- know that others have refused to do the same task,
- fail to see any personal advantage in carrying out the assignment,
- have not been told that occasionally they will be asked to do things that are not in their position description, or
- see the delegator wasting time while they do all the work.

If you have good rapport with a subordinate and rarely take advantage of your authority, the subordinate will not mind some of these kinds of assignments.

When you assign a task to an employee, and another employee asks "How come you never ask me to do that?", what you have done is probably delegation. When an employee says "How come you always ask me?", that is probably dumping.

HOW TO DELEGATE

Four Simple Ways To Pick What To Delegate

1. As you go about your daily routine, just before you tackle a task, ask yourself whether this is something that someone else could do.
2. When you return from a vacation, list your duties that subordinates took care of while you were away. Some of these temporary assignments could become permanent.
3. At performance reviews, when you discuss future career plans for your associates, ask them whether they would like to take over any of your responsibilities.
4. Select tasks from those listed in your position description (see below).

Delegate Using Your Position Description

1. List 10 or more of your tasks, excluding any that may not or should not be delegated.
2. Select those that someone could assume now, and those that a member of your group could learn to do.
3. Prioritize each task according to:
   - how much time you would save by delegating the task,
   - how significantly it would benefit or be acceptable to the delegate, and
   - the degree of difficulty (usually you should start with simple tasks, ones that relate directly to the delegate's current assignments or ones that are segments of a complex task).

What May Not Be Delegated

- *Accountability*: Delegators are still accountable to higher authorities for delegated work.
- *Powers other than authority*: Only formal power, or authority, can be delegated (see Exhibit 31–1).
- *Functions forbidden by law, regulation, or policy* (licensure, certification, special training, qualification, or education is required for some duties).

What Should Be Delegated Only with Caution

- Sensitive or high-leverage activities dealing with people:
  1. interviewing, selecting, and orienting new employees
  2. approving new hires
  3. coaching, counseling, and disciplining
  4. evaluating employee performance
  5. resolving personal conflicts, complaints, or grievances
- Activities that involve too great a career risk for the delegator or the delegate
- Activities perceived as dumping by the delegate
- Special administrative responsibilities:
  1. formulation of mission statements, goals, objectives, strategies, and plans
  2. making, publicizing, explaining, and enforcing policies
  3. presiding over important meetings
  4. preparing or approving budgets and reviewing fiscal variances
- Tasks assigned by your superiors to be done by you personally
- Some functions that you find very pleasurable

Exhibit 31–1 Kinds of Power

Authority—Delegated power: "You all now report to me."
Competency—Expertise: "See Louise, she's the specialist."
Knowledge—Information: "Ask Joe, he's on the committee."
Physical—Brute force: "If you want to stay healthy. . . . "
Connections—Whom they know: "His mother is on the board."
Fiscal—Who has the bucks: "He who gets grant money gets promoted."
Union—Selected by peers: "Nora will get action, she's the union rep."
Charisma—Persuasiveness: "He can talk you into anything."

Select the Delegates and Get Their Acceptance

Select delegates who have the necessary competence and willingness. The most qualified person for a particular responsibility may not be the one who will benefit from it most. A less experienced employee may try harder and do a better job in the long run.

Seek cooperation. Avoid petulant compliance. Consciously or unconsciously, delegates ask you or themselves, "What's in this for me?" If their perception is negative, the delegation is in trouble. Be wary if you hear:

- "Is that an order?"
- "Do I have to?"
- "That's not in my position description."
- "Nobody told me I must do all that."

People are more willing to take risks if they know for certain what is involved. Perhaps in the past they took a small step, and Pandora's box opened. Tell them exactly what they are getting into, and give them possible outs. Start by telling them:

- why you decided on the change;
- why you picked them;
- whether or not they have a choice;
- what you expect;
- what resources and authority are available to them;
- what you are going to tell other members of the group if they are affected;
- what, if any, modifications there will be in their current assignments; and
- the checkpoints and, when appropriate, a target date or timetable.

When employees object because they do not have the time, agree to share some of the work. At other times you can relieve them of other responsibilities. Usually you can promise them that the delegation is reversible (ie, you will relieve them of the responsibility with no loss of their prestige). This is seldom necessary if you picked the right task, selected the right person, and prepared the delegate sufficiently.

How To Implement the Delegative Action

- Select the right task and the right delegate.
- If this is a major change, get permission from your superiors.

- If you are serving in a team mode, discuss the change with your team.
- Provide essential training, resources, and authority.
- Agree on an action plan. Listen carefully to delegates' ideas about how to get it done.
- Set up checkpoints. Checkpoints enable you to monitor progress and to give some pats on the back.

Monitor Progress

Be patient and persuasive, not demanding. Avoid statements such as "Do not worry," "You should have . . . ," or "I wish you had. . . ." Help delegates when they get stuck.

Periodically stop by and ask how things are going. Avoid constantly looking over their shoulders or asking too many questions. Questions should reflect your interest in their approach rather than exhibit nervousness you may have about their ability to finish the job.

WHEN DELEGATION FALTERS

Avoid the temptation to abandon ship when there are problems. Allowing people to make some mistakes is the best way to encourage meaningful growth. Although a delegator accepts responsibility for a failure, confidence in the delegate is not readily restored. When employees have done their best but failed, have them prepare a balance sheet in which they identify what went well and what did not. Always let them criticize themselves first. Ask how you could have helped more, because when your delegate fails, you too have failed.

HORIZONTAL DELEGATION

Truly skilled delegators can delegate to people over whom they have no authority. These individuals may be colleagues or volunteers. Horizontal delegation increases in importance as health care institutions feature more cross-functional activities and make greater use of volunteers.

Success depends largely on factors such as:

- persuasiveness,
- influence,
- interpersonal skills,
- rapport,

- degree of teamwork,
- past favors for the other person,
- the strength of one's network, and
- rewards and recognition for past cooperation.

REVERSE (UPWARD) DELEGATION

Upward delegation is the art of passing along to superiors what employees do not want to do. They are often successful in this because their bosses just cannot say no. Managers who seldom delegate are especially susceptible to upward delegation. Drucker and Flower[2] write: "Every subordinate is good at delegating upstairs. It's hard to resist because it's very flattering. You must learn to say 'no'."

Reverse delegation often follows attempts by a manager to delegate. The delegate reluctantly accepts a task. At the first obstacle he throws up his hands and tries to pass the buck back to the manager. The manager thus becomes the reluctant delegate.

Sometimes upward delegation is necessary. For example, a supervisor may delegate so much work to an assistant that the assistant cannot complete her routine work. It is then up to the delegator to consider various options: take back some work, establish new priorities, or transfer some tasks to another employee.

HOPSCOTCH DELEGATION

When your manager bypasses you and gives assignments directly to your subordinates, that is hopscotch delegation. To correct this, it helps to have good rapport with your superior. If you confront your superior when he or she is in a belligerent mood, you may get a response such as, "Well, you're never around when something has to be done." If this shunting of authority rarely happens, it is probably best to ignore it. However, if you feel that a confrontation is necessary, take a positive approach by playing down the issue of authority. As you negotiate with your manager, focus on the advantages of your knowing what he or she wants done or of how your people get confused when they get conflicting orders from different managers.

If you cannot get action through your boss or if you want to avoid a confrontation, try acting through your staff. Instruct them to hold up action on nonurgent orders from other people until they have checked with you. Another tactic is to have your associates ask your boss in a polite way to please make the request directly to you because they are working on a priority item of yours.

EMPOWERMENT

Empowerment does not mean that employees may do as they please without any orders, monitoring, or control. Empowerment means providing an environment and opportunities for employees to enhance their competencies and accept more responsibility.

External empowerment is giving people the authority to do what they are capable of handling. It encourages people to make judgments, form conclusions, reach decisions, and then act. It liberates workers from rigid oversight and direction.

Internal empowerment or *self*-empowerment is what individuals generate intrinsically, like they generate enthusiasm or optimism. It reflects competence, experience, assertiveness, character, personality, and charisma.

Benefits of Empowerment

Empowerment enhances feelings of self-efficacy—a state of mind that causes people to believe they can cope effectively with situations and people. Empowerment reduces or eliminates feelings of helplessness. The more that people feel that they are in control of their work and their lives, the greater their enthusiasm, optimism, self-confidence, and energy.

With empowered staffs, leaders can mobilize stronger forces when responding to crises, and with less risk of chaos. The leaders can also set higher performance goals and standards.

Excellent health care service requires empowered care providers, especially when they interact directly with customers. Patients and other customers want providers who respond with confidant empathy—not calloused indifference, apathy, or plastic smiles.

Empiric Empowering Actions

Employees must know more than how to do their daily tasks if they are to maximize their contributions. They feel more empowered when they learn about organizational financial matters and their role in providing excellent services.

Ten Steps That Empower

1. Know what each of your reports does and how well the tasks are done. Review position descriptions, performance standards, and previous performance appraisal reports.

2. Decide what additional authority they can handle right now. In their performance reports, look for notes regarding competencies, experience, and training needs.
3. Ascertain what preparation each of your employees needs to achieve the competencies and mental toughness that will empower them. Such preparation may involve training, coaching, psychological support, and incremental delegation.
4. Conceptualize a new supervisory role that reduces micromanaging and matches the level of supervision with the ability, maturity, and motivation of each employee.
5. Ensure that workers know the purpose (mission) of their jobs. Is this stated in their position descriptions, and stressed during their orientation? If necessary, clarify each job and your expectations of what outcomes should be.
6. Delegate activities that involve decision making and problem solving.
7. Review your education and training program. Empowered organizations are learning institutions. Design a cross-training and job rotation program so that people become more flexible and more aware of customer problems and their solutions.
8. Make tasks more challenging. Assign complete rather than fragmented tasks. Assign progressively more difficult tasks starting with ones that ensure success—an essential aspect of situational leadership.
9. Provide sufficient resources, time, and psychological support.
10. Emphasize commitment rather than conformity.

Potential Problems of Empowerment

We previously noted that delegation involves risk. With pervasive empowerment, this risk is even greater. It is also greater than forming autonomous teams because you do not have teammates exerting a tempering effect on other members.

Some empowered employees do silly things; a few abuse their new authority.

When employees are ill-prepared, or when they think you have not adequately rewarded them, they may rebel—actively or passively.

Many workers are uncomfortable with more power, especially if they are passive or have victim mindsets. They prefer conformity and safety to entrepreneurship and risk. An often heard comment from these folks is "I just want to do my work and go home."

Employees may lack confidence in their leaders. Those who have been jerked around during a series of failed management initiatives are not likely to join in the celebration of still another program-du-jour. Instead, they hunker down and wait for it to pass as most of the previous ones have.

Some managers do not want to share power. They feel they worked hard to earn the power they have, and are reluctant to give up any of it.

NOTES

1. W.B. Werther, Jr., *Dear Boss* (New York: Meadowbrook, 1989), 162.
2. P. Drucker and J. Flower, "Being Effective," *Health Care Forum Journal 34* (1991): 52.

RECOMMENDED READING AND LISTENING

W.C. Byham, *Zapp! The Lightning of Empowerment* (New York: Harmony Books, 1988).

S.R. Lloyd and T. Berthelot, *Empowerment: A Practical Guide for Success* (Menlo Park, CA: 1992).

D. Lohr, *How To Delegate Work* (Boulder, CO: CareerTrack Publishers, 1987), two audiotapes.

W. Umiker, *The Empowered Laboratory Team.* (Chicago, IL: ASCP Press, 1996).

PART V

Special Supervisory Skills

Chapter 32

Verbal Communication

- the informal communication system
- sending more powerful messages
- barriers to verbal communication
- listening skill
- telephone courtesy
- what all phone users should know

*"The most difficult obstacle the new technical
supervisor needs to surmount is the immediate
acquisition of communication skills."*[1]

As technical experts, supervisors provide scientific information and technical advice, usually verbally. As leaders, supervisors use communication skills to discharge their management responsibilities. Communication is, by far, the most important managerial skill. Without it, all other skills are inoperative. The importance of verbal communication in daily work becomes very apparent when we suffer from acute laryngitis.

Communication systems form the cornerstone of cultural shaping and participative management. To improve quality, customer service, and productivity, we must take a second look at these systems and how we use them.

Most employees feel that bosses hold back things that employees should hear. Subordinates may withhold important information from their superiors if they dislike or mistrust them or if they fear that the information will adversely affect their relationship.

Effective information sharing must be:

- multidirectional (up, down, lateral, and diagonal),
- objective, factual, and true,
- comprehensive, but not excessive,
- credible, and
- timely.

309

INFORMAL COMMUNICATION SYSTEM

There are serious limitations to formal communication systems. These systems depend largely on written messages and formal meetings. Supervisors who depend entirely on this source are soon out of touch with what is going on in their organization. Watered-down newsletters or notices on bulletin boards are not enough. Electronic bulletin boards, voice mail, and one-on-one contact are more effective.[2]

When managers tune into the grapevine, they realize that the information they receive via formal systems is often late or incomplete. A common managerial problem is placing too much reliance on the computer. Not all important information gets into the computer, and not everyone knows how to extract all the information that is there.

The informal communication network, or "grapevine," flourishes when information is scarce or delayed or when organizational changes take place. The grapevine is rapid, up to date, and pervasive and distributes information quickly. Network senders translate complex directives into understandable language. Like other communicators, the senders add their personal spins to these messages. Managers who tap into the informal communication systems learn what is bothering their employees and how their leadership is perceived by the workers.

On the negative side, much of what is transmitted is rumor and gossip. Rumor mills are subject to distortions and omissions. Many reputations and careers have suffered as the result of misuse of this channel. The grapevine is a major time waster and often sends shock waves through organizations that turn out to be unsubstantiated.

Supervisors must know who the grapevine's principal receivers are and keep tuned into them. Secretaries of VIPs, for example, are excellent sources of current information.

When you hear distorted or false news, put out corrections promptly via both formal and informal channels. This aborts false rumors and discredits the rumor mongers. Set aside part of each staff meeting to verify, discredit, or clarify rumors.

Use the grapevine to counter misinformation and to distribute good news. You can make pronouncements that are not appropriate for newsletters or memos. You can also test the waters for the reactions to controversial projects.

SENDING MORE POWERFUL MESSAGES

"How well we communicate is determined not by how well we say things but how well we are understood."[3]

Effective care providers command respect by displaying self-confidence and poise. Their unspoken message to customers and subordinates is, "I can help you because I know what's going on and can make things happen."

This unspoken message is transmitted through words, voice tone, facial expressions, and body language. Mehrabian[4] in his studies at the University of California, Los Angeles, found that words convey only 7% of the feeling in spoken messages. Thirty-eight percent comes from voice characteristics, and 55% from facial expressions and body language. Every message consists of two parts, the content and the emotional component. When the words do not jibe with the emotional message, the words lose their power. Picture a distraught supervisor yelling at a subordinate with, "I'm in control here." The subordinate inwardly grins, knowing that the supervisor has lost control and the encounter.

Avoid the assumption that your message has been received and understood. Do not rely on a positive response to your "Do you hear me?" or "Do you understand what I said?" Do not think that because no one asks a question that everyone knows what you said. While you cannot give a quiz after each communication, you can ask people to paraphrase important things you say or ask for comments on specific points. Watch their body language as they respond. The knitted brow or the blank stare speaks louder than the words.

Practical Tips

- Speak with conviction. Remember the power of voice quality and body language.
- Substitute strong responses for weak ones: Instead of "I wonder if you would send . . . " say "Please send me. . . . "
- Call something a misunderstanding instead of a disagreement.
- Say what you can do, not what you cannot do.
- Shake hands with enthusiasm, and smile.
- Be assertive. Maintain your right to be recognized and to state what you think.
- Use people's names often and pronounce them correctly. People feel validated when we do that. It says "You're important to me." Insist that your receptionist and telephone answerers use each caller's name at least once.

BARRIERS TO VERBAL COMMUNICATION

Electronic Barriers

We could not get along without our computers, electronic mail, faxes, and answering machines. However, they can adversely impact friendship with customers and collegiality with colleagues. Because managers can get masses of data instantly, they often feel that they have a complete handle on things. Unfortunately, not all significant information gets into the computer. Still more gets buried in the trivia.

Semantic Barriers

Each day we speak in at least five languages:

1. English,
2. body language,
3. professional and technical jargon,
4. organizational and bureaucratic talk, and
5. "computerese."

We often fail to consider the educational, cultural, and mental status of each of our customers and employees. A nurse who uses the same phraseology when conversing with a mentally challenged patient as she does when she talks to a physician confuses the patient or angers the doctor. Garbled messages, jargon, acronyms, and computer language may befuddle even our fellow professionals. Mixed messages—when words do not match body language—confuse everyone.

The graduates of inferior schools usually need help in basic communication. We must encourage them to eliminate slang, street talk, and fillers like "ya know . . . right on . . . and ya gotta be kidding."

Psychological Barriers

These are the most pernicious barriers. They include:

- Interrupting, arguing, blaming, talking down to, kidding, or being sarcastic;
- inflammatory utterances—name calling or threats;
- patronizing words, such as "you girls";
- statements indicative of indifference or apathy such as:
  1. "You must realize that we're understaffed";
  2. "I don't know" (without offering to find out or refer);
  3. "We can't do that";
  4. "You'll have to . . . ";
  5. "That's not my responsibility";
  6. "That's not our policy"; or
  7. "It must be a computer error."

LISTENING SKILL

Most of us are terrible listeners. Our spouses and children usually will affirm that. If your training program accomplishes nothing more than improving the listening skills of your staff, it will have been well worthwhile.

Body Language

Listening is visual as well as auditory. Make certain that your facial expressions, posture, and movements match your words. You can learn a lot about a person's thoughts by observing things such as the following:

- *Signs of attentiveness or interest:* Person rubs chin, rolls eyes upward and to right or left, maintains eye contact, leans forward, and smiles.
- *Signs of disinterest or disagreement:* Person touches or rubs nose, rolls eyes straight up, leans backward, tugs on ear, folds arms across chest, frowns, shakes head, drums fingers, starts avoiding eye contact, or rearranges papers.
- *Signs of concealment or deception:* The person puts hand partially over his mouth, avoids eye contact, exhibits nervous fingers, blinks eyelashes quickly, squirms, blushes, or acts like his shirt collar is too tight. When you hear many expressions such as "to tell the truth" or "honestly," be suspicious.

> *A caveat: People who are just nervous or insecure may also exhibit these signs.*

Touching Is Tricky

Touching is powerful, but it must be done in a way that the person cannot interpret the touch as having sexual or aggressive overtones. Important factors in the appropriate use of touching are the anatomical location, the kind, and the context. Safest touch zones are the forearm and elbow. Use light, transient touches. Do not hold, pat, or massage. The context of the conversation is important. The touch should reinforce the verbal response. Touch is especially appropriate when one is expressing appreciation or support.

People like to get handshakes unless those handshakes produce pain (arthritics dread them), are prolonged, or make one think they are handling a dead fish.

Watch Your Phonetics

How one says something is just as important as what one says. Voice tone, volume, and rate vary with one's emotional state. For example, a subordinate may say "I'm O.K," but the phonetics say "I feel miserable." Verbal patterns that reduce your power include the following:

- posing questions to make requests or demands: "Would you like to get me a cup of coffee?"
- using disclaimers: "I know this sounds silly, but . . . ."
- using weak qualifiers: "sort of," "maybe."
- tolerating interruptions.

Three Keys of Successful Listening

1. *Look* like you are listening—face the person. If sitting, lean forward toward the person. Establish eye contact. Good eye contact is not staring down the other person. It's shifting your gaze from the person's eyes to other parts of his or her face or occasionally glancing away entirely. Nod, smile, or frown at the appropriate times. Avoid a poker face. Let your facial expressions show your feelings. Your body language must be congruent with your verbal messages.
2. *Sound* like you are listening. Use expletives such as "please go on"; "I see"; or "Uh-huh."
3. *Provide feedback.* This is the most effective of the three. Only when you provide feedback does the speaker know that he or she has received the right message. Paraphrase what you heard and saw—the message content and the associated feelings.

Kinds of Responses

- Defensive: "That's a lie!"
- Judgmental: "You're too sensitive."
- Advisory: "I'll tell you what I would do."
- Questioning: "Be more specific."
- Empathic: "You seem upset. I can understand that."

Skilled listeners make frequent use of empathic (supportive) responses and they avoid defensive, judgmental, and advisory ones. Questioning is appropriate unless it sounds like cross-examining. They also listen carefully for underlying feelings.

Avoid the following:

criticizing	diagnosing	falsely praising
ordering	name calling	advising
moralizing	threatening	cross-examining
diverting	feigned listening	insincerely reassuring

Naive Listening

We tune out mentally confused patients, orderlies, members of the housekeeping service, and even some colleagues, friends, and family members. To overcome this, stop occasionally and listen as we did the first time we had any contact with that person. That is naive listening.

USE OF THE TELEPHONE

Telephone etiquette appears to be a low priority item in many health care organizations and physicians' offices. That is unfortunate, since it affects client satisfaction and time management. Managers should be choosy when hiring a receptionist. They should insist that receptionists and others who handle many incoming calls attend a training session on telephone courtesy.

How your telephone is answered says a lot about you and your department. An answering voice may express an affirmative, helpful attitude or an "I-don't-really-care" one. Callers mirror how they are treated. If we sound friendly, our callers respond in kind.

A Test for Telephone Etiquette and Helpfulness

Anonymously call your unit after regular hours and ask a complex question about an aspect of your service. Be prepared for a shock.

Tying up telephone lines with personal calls angers callers. So does transferring callers to a series of departments.

Everyone assumes that they know how to use the telephone. When you suggest that an employee attend a workshop on telephone courtesy, that employee may get very upset. A somewhat manipulative trick is to tell the person that you want someone to attend the training session and then come back and teach what they learned to the rest of the staff. This sensitive issue can be avoided if the organization mandates periodic training programs for the entire staff or includes this training in its orientation protocol. An added benefit is that such group education promotes uniform telephone etiquette, which, in turn, has a reinforcing effect.

WHAT ALL PHONE USERS SHOULD KNOW

Answering the Phone

Answer within three rings, or apologize for the delay. Sit up straight. Project helpfulness. A smiling face helps—smiles do travel over telephone lines. To remind employees how important customers are, put stickers next to each phone that read, "The CEO is calling."

Identify self and unit; then offer to help. Sound enthusiastic and helpful. If the person states his or her name, use it at least once. If they do not offer a name, ask for it.

Take messages when appropriate. The message should include the person's full name, organization, phone number, any information they would like to leave, time and date of message, and your initials. (Note: A special phone log is helpful.)

Placing on Hold

Being put on hold is a frequent complaint. Apologize when you cannot connect a person to their party. Avoid saying "Just a second, I'll be right back." This is rarely true and is annoying. Offer a choice of waiting or being called back. When on hold, check every 30 seconds, and repeat the offer. If the caller says that she prefers to be called back, make sure that this is done. Also, avoid use of call waiting. Call waiting forces a choice between which caller is the more important. One or the other is offended.

Screening Calls

If it's necessary to screen calls, do it politely and tactfully. An effective screener helps callers by trying to answer their questions or by directing them to someone who can answer them. To avoid transfers to wrong parties, the screener must be knowledgeable about departmental matters. People who screen calls should know which callers are always to be put through immediately and those who should not be put through at all. They should also know the questions or problems they may handle and the ones they refer to other people.

Phraseology used is important. Here are some overused or rude phrases:

- "Alice hasn't come in yet."
- "Joe just stepped out."
- "She's in a meeting." (Few callers believe this these days.)
- "I never heard of her."
- "You'll have to call back."
- "What's your name and what do you want?"

What you should hear is:

- "Dr. Jones is out of his office right now. May I ask him to call you?"
- "He's not available at the moment. May I tell him who called?"
- "Doctor, Miss Smith is meeting with our supervisors. The meeting usually ends by 0900. May I have her call you then?"
- "That name doesn't sound familiar. Can you give me more information?"
- "He's not in right now. I expect him back about 1400. Will you be available then?"
- "Yes, she's in. May I tell her who is calling?" (Do not ask for callers' names before telling them that their party is not in.)

Some consultants recommend that special customers be given the unlisted phone numbers of key personnel—with the latter's permission, of course.

Transferring Calls

Before you transfer a call, ask if you can help or if the caller would like to be called when the person becomes available.

Being transferred from one extension to another is a frequent source of irritation. A courteous transfer requires a brief explanation of why the caller is being transferred. The caller is reassured that his or her questions will be answered. To avoid the consequences of a disconnection, give callers the name, title, and extension number of the person to whom they are being transferred. Do not hang up until the connection has been made.

Taking Messages for Someone Else

Walther[5] recommends getting rid of the "little pink slips" in favor of forms that have enough space for the following information:

- Name of caller (phonetic version if the name is difficult to pronounce);
- caller's organization or department and phone number;
- time, date, and purpose of call;
- impression of caller's mood (eg, upset, angry or euphoric?);
- any promises made to caller;
- callers' unwillingness to talk to anyone else;
- any known previous important contacts with caller. (If so, it may be appropriate to attach copies of that prior correspondence.)

Recommendations for All Employees

- Use the caller's name frequently.
- Say what you can do, not what you cannot do.
- Diffuse anger by answering empathically.
- For outbound calls, state your business first and save the small talk for last.
- Answer promptly and identify yourself.
- Sound enthusiastic and cooperative.
- Keep person focused on the reason for the call.
- Keep personal calls short and infrequent.
- End conversations on a positive note and thank person for calling.
- Make sure that the callers know what you are going to do. Do it promptly.

Forbidden Phrases

"I don't know."
"That's not done in our department."
"There's nothing I can do about that."
"You have to."
"You should have."
"Why didn't you."
"I'll try."
"You can't have."
"Our policy is."

Ending Conversation

In telephone conversations, as in interviews or written correspondence, the beginnings and the endings make the strongest impressions. Conclude calls with a verification of key points covered. You want to be remembered as a pleasant, efficient person to deal with. Therefore take the time to thank the person for calling; say you were glad to be of service (or sorry that you could not help). End the conversation on a pleasant upbeat note, but refrain from using that tiresome cliché, "Have a nice day" or, even worse, "Bye-Bye." Instead, say "goodbye" in a pleasant voice or with an appropriate comment such as, "It was nice hearing from you again," or "Thank you for filling me in—I appreciate it." Let the caller hang up first.

Phone Tag

We all know the frustration of calling people when they are out and you are not available when the calls are returned. This can go on for hours, even days. It can also be expensive when the calls are long distance ones.

Effective ways to avoid phone tag:

- Pick the best time to call. People are most likely to be in their offices just before lunch and late in the afternoon. Ask when it is a good time to call. You can say when you will call again, and ask that this information be placed on the person's desk.
- Ask the person to page your party, or ask if there is another number at which you can reach the person.
- Ask if there is someone else who can answer your question.
- Leave a message.
- Use an answering machine or e-mail.

Tips for Outbound Calls

- Have an up-to-date telephone directory nearby. Keep a list of frequently called persons and their phone numbers. Add the best time to call and any other helpful information.
- Set aside a period each day during which to make outbound calls. Avoid calls before 0900, after 1700, or between 1200 and 1330 hours.
- Most people do not like to be called at home when the subject is one that can be handled during the workday.
- Keep in mind any time differences when you make long distance calls.
- Plan what you are going to say. Retrieve any documents you might need.
- Let the phone ring at least five or six times before hanging up. If a secretary initiates the calls, make certain that you remain close by. It's irritating to the person being contacted and embarrassing to a secretary who has to hunt for you.
- Start conversations by stating your name. Do not wait to be asked.

- If you're not well acquainted with the person, ask the switchboard operator how the person's name is pronounced, the name of her secretary, and her extension number—in case the first call does not get through.

Voice Mail

Train employees in technotalk (e-mail, voice mail, and cellular telephone technology). After all, management has held classes for telephone use for years.

Many callers are irritated by voice mail. Some refuse to leave messages. When used well, however, voice mail can eliminate frustrations for both caller and call recipient. Deeprose[6] provides the following excellent advice for using voice mail effectively:

- Change your greeting regularly to let callers know your situation (eg, "I'm on another call right now," "I'll be back in my office at noon," or "I'll be out of my office until Monday, February 12").
- State—in addition to your name, organization, and phone number—the time and date, the nature of your call, when it is convenient for you to be called, or when you will call back.
- Substitute a message for a request to be called back.
- Suggest a fax response if a response is needed; provide your fax number.
- Let your callers know when you make call-backs (if you screen calls as a time management technique).

Ubiquitous Answering Machine

Many people hate talking to an answering machine. Many refuse to. For those of you who refuse to respond to these machines, I urge you to give the gadgets a fair shake. It's like pumping your own gas—as you grow familiar with these, they become less irritating. These machines have these advantages over human contacts:

- They force you to be brief.
- You do not get any negative feedback or long-winded conversations.
- There is less likely to be misinterpretation, since the person can listen to the message as often as he or she likes.
- They're great for reducing phone tag.
- If you do not want interruptions during interviews or other critical times, the answering machine can be as effective as a secretary.

NOTES

1. D. Shandler, *From Technical Specialist to Supervisor* (Menlo Park, CA: Crisp Publishers, 1993), 31.
2. F. Sonnenberg, "The Essentials of On-the-job Information," *Supervisory Management 37* (1992): 8.
3. D. Smith and H. Sutton, *Powerful Proofreading Skills* (Menlo Park, CA: Crisp Publishers, 1994), 29.
4. G.R. Walther, *Phone Power* (New York, NY: G.P. Putnam & Sons, 1986), 74.
5. Walther, *Phone Power*, 50.
6. D. Deeprose, "Making Voice Mail Customer Friendly," *Supervisory Management 37* (1992): 7, 8.

RECOMMENDED READING

D. Arthur, "The Importance of Body Language," *HRFocus 72,* no. 6 (1995): 22, 23.

R.W. Lucas, *Effective Interpersonal Relationships* (New York, NY: Irwin Publishers, 1994).

D. Tannen, "The Power of Talk: Who Gets Heard and Why," *Clinical Laboratory Management Review 10,* no. 3 (1996): 209–220.

Chapter 33

Written Communication

- selection of an appropriate communication channel
- steps in preparing a document
- the anatomy of a memo
- how to edit a staff member's document
- facsimiles and e-mail

Some employers are not pleased with the writing ability of today's graduates. Ricks,[1] for example, states, "The secondary schools have disgorged a generation of workers who cannot write a three-sentence memo."

Trainers at health care institutions recognize the importance of helping employees to upgrade their writing skills. However, they lack the time to focus on grammatical errors or to look for split infinitives. They must limit the little time they have to barebones writing competencies. Trainers depend on supervisors to define the writing skills their employees need on the job (eg, writing memos and preparing reports).

Customer satisfaction is involved when we address writing skills. Customers want simple and clear messages that they can understand. A lot of "thank-yous," "pleases," and other stroking words are less important than tact and helpfulness.

Writers of memos and letters should consider the level of education of their readers. Courtesy is shown by making it easier for people to respond. For example, invite readers to return your letter with their responses on the letter, thus eliminating the need to compose and print a new letter.

SELECTION OF AN APPROPRIATE COMMUNICATION CHANNEL

On a daily basis, we must pick the most appropriate channel of communication. These selections affect efficiency, expense, and client satisfaction. Verbal communication is usually faster. It allows complex exchanges and transmits feelings better. Use it when you want immediate responses or reactions or when discussion or lengthy questioning is needed.

Written messages can mute hostility or emotion, are permanent, and usually— but not always—are less susceptible to misinterpretation. A big advantage is that they do not interrupt the recipient's work like verbal exchanges and phone calls do. The writing choices include memorandum, letter, facsimile, posted notice, electronic mail, or a computer bulletin board.

It pays to know the preferences of one's superiors and clients. Some folks prefer verbal messages; others like everything in writing. We all know people who refuse to leave messages on answering machines. Those commercial recordings can be irritating. How often does a recorded voice tell us that our message is very important, and then we are placed on hold for interminable periods.

Letters are for external, private, or formal purposes. Memos—"messages in shirt-sleeves"—are more suitable for in-house, informal messages. Most of these are now transmitted via e-mail. Use letters when transmitting extensive data or information that will be retained as a permanent record. One useful rule in deciding between memo and letter is that any message that requires a stamp should be a letter.

The Anatomy of a Memo

To: Usually it's best to send it to a position rather than to an individual. If the person is on extended leave, the memo may reside in his or her incoming basket for weeks.
From: This is the originator of the message, not the person who types it or an assistant who prepares it for an executive.
Date: The date the memo leaves the department, not the date dictated or typed.
Subject:
Message:
Action: What are you going to do or what do you expect the receiver to do?
Copies: Send copies to everyone whom you want to take action or be informed.
Attachments: These may be references, copies of previous reports, or special precautions.
Other: Name or initials of the typist may be appropriate.

STEPS IN PREPARING A DOCUMENT

1. Define the purpose and means of the message. What do you hope to accomplish? Is the message really needed? Do you expect the receiver to take

some kind of action or do you merely want to inform? What is the best sending channel to use? Must it be typed? Should it be a memo or a letter? Do you have all the information you need?

2. Freewrite a rough draft. Picture the reader sitting across from you. Start with the person's name or with a "you." Frontload the opening paragraph with the core of the message. The first paragraph gets the most attention and is what readers remember best. Use a verbal hook to stimulate the reader's interest (eg, "You're going to like what we are doing about your recent suggestion").

   • Prepare a strong closing statement. The last paragraph gets the next most attention.

   • Do not waste time correcting grammatical errors or spelling in the first draft. Concern yourself only with content and clarity.

3. Rewrite. Check the rough draft for brevity, clarity, and personal touch. Does it answer what, who, when, where, why, and how? Improve readability by:

   • using stroking words (eg, the reader's name, "you" and "we," compliments, or expressions of appreciation);

   • converting negative or impolite statements into positive, tactful, and courteous ones:

     – *"You receive late reports because your requests are usually late."* (bad)

     – *"When we get requests before 0700, our reports are rarely late."* (The accusatory "you" has been eliminated, and the focus is on the activity and a solution.)

   • strengthening vague or abstract wording:

     – *"We're going to try to decrease the turnaround time."* (imprecise)

     – *"We're going to decrease the turnaround time by an hour."* (precise)

   • using gender-inclusive language. If you want to incur the wrath of women, use all male pronouns. Stereotyping women as secretaries and men as managers is even worse. While we cannot eliminate "man" from all words (eg, *mankind, penmanship, and manager*, we can neuter most words or find appropriate substitutes).

   The simplest way to neuter sentences is to use "he or she," but this gets cumbersome. Substitute titles, such as "the employee" or "they." You can also balance the gender by using "he" in one paragraph and "she" in the next.

4. Edit carefully. Observe the following rules:

   • Keep the message simple and specific.

- Check the paragraphs. Keep them short, with one major thought for each.
- Use lists, columns, headings, and alphanumerics.
- Highlight key words or phrases by using different fonts.
- Allow plenty of white space: wide margins, double space, and limited numbers of lines per page.
- Check the sentences. Vary their lengths to avoid telegraphic sound; break up the long ones.
- Convert passive to active voice.
  - *"Our monthly meeting has been discontinued."* (passive)
  - *"We elected to discontinue monthly meetings."* (active)
- Convert some active to passive voice for diplomatic reasons. It softens statements and avoids finger pointing.
  - *"Dr. Jones objected to your appointment."* (puts Dr. Jones on the spot)
  - *"An objection to your appointment was raised."* (diffuses responsibility)
- Convert -ion nouns into verbs: *"It is my intention."* *("I intend")*
- Check punctuation, spelling, and grammar. This has been simplified by the speller, thesaurus, and grammar software now available with most computers.
- Eliminate the following kinds of words and use the substitutes (in parentheses).
  - –Archaic, pompous, or overused phrases:
  - *"Upon receipt of your reply . . . "* *("When we hear from you.")*
  - *"Please advise us."* *("Please tell us.")*
  - –Unnecessary words, phrases, or modifiers:
  - *"The consensus of opinion"* *("The consensus")*
  - *"It is a grey color and has a round shape."* *("It's grey and round.")*
  - *"Filled to capacity"* *("Filled")*
  - –There are:
  - *"There are too many people arriving late."* *("Too many people arrive late.")*
  - –Weak words (Substitute strong ones):
  - *"We think that we give good service."* *("We strive for outstanding service.")*
  - –Excess pronouns and prepositions:
  - *"The decrease in profit is of great concern to us."* *("We're concerned about decreased profit.")*
  - –Slang, jargon, or acronyms
  - –Buzzwords or hackneyed phrases:
  - *"down the tube" "out of this world" "belly up" "bottom line."*

HOW TO EDIT A STAFF MEMBER'S DOCUMENT

Do not return a your staffer's document marked up like a school paper. Never, never use red ink for your comments. Review it with the person. Focus on major defects. Is the piece organized logically and supported by data? Does it clearly state its purpose? Give specific examples of what you want. If you find too many minor flaws, they will either think you are nit-picking or they will get discouraged. End with an encouraging comment about how the person's reports have improved in content, readability, or promptness.

FACSIMILES

Avoid long or irrelevant documents. The faxed document should contain all the information needed for the recipient to reply. Include your fax number, phone number, and address. Do not fax a confidential document unless confidentiality is assured at the other end (eg, if the recipient is standing by the fax machine or has a secure, private fax mailbox).

ELECTRONIC-MAIL (E-MAIL)

E-mail is great but has risks. Stored messages can become evidence against an organization if it is sued. There have been suits charging sexual harassment, race or age discrimination, and other violations. On the other hand, trying to police e-mail can expose employers to charges of invasion of privacy.

E-mail has put new strength into our "open-door" policy. E-mail enables all employees to access just about anyone in their organization. They do not even need to knock on the door. On the one hand, executives are more receptive to e-mail messages because they can read them when convenient. On the other hand, when they return to their offices and find hundreds of messages, they may be less responsive.

Explain your security system to all your employees. They must know what data are sensitive, and must restrict e-mail usage to business purposes. There should be a procedure for disposing of computer backup after it has served its purpose.

NOTE

1. D.M. Ricks, "Why Your Business-Writing Courses Don't Work," *Training 31* (1994): 49–52.

RECOMMENDED READING

D. Booher, *Send Me A Memo: A Handbook of Model Memos* (New York, NY: Facts On File Publishers, 1984).

K. Davis, "What Writing Training Can and Can't Do," *Training 32,* no. 8 (1995): 60–63.

Chapter 34

How To Hold More Effective Meetings

- major purposes of meetings
- components of a meeting
- preparations by the chair
- the meeting
- important "do nots" for chairs
- postmeeting activities
- tips for members
- problem members
- committee meetings
- conference calls

Despite their tainted reputation, meetings are one of our most valuable communication tools. We use them for team building and coordination, cross-functional activities, dissemination of information, training, problem solving, and decision making. Committees, task forces, and focus groups could not function without meetings. Ad hoc problem-solving meetings conducted in a brainstorming mode are often the most valuable ones.

Let us not forget the departmental and staff meetings. I know of no health care institution that does not have a problem of shortage of places to meet. Only vehicle parking space is in greater demand.

The amount of information flowing out of computers has made meetings even more important because there are more data to be shared and discussed.

Most managers think they spend too much time in meetings and that most meetings are a waste of time. They are right! Nevertheless, the higher people rise in organizations, the more time they spend in conferences. Insecure managers call meetings for the sole purpose of getting moral support or sharing responsibility. Perhaps the biggest time waster is the regularly scheduled meeting, often held when there is nothing important to discuss.

MAJOR PURPOSES OF MEETINGS

- To explain new policies, laws, services, protocols, systems, restructuring—anything that involves change.
- To accept reports or recommendations.
- To get help in making decisions, solving problems, allocating resources, preparing plans, establishing priorities, generating ideas, or assigning tasks.
- To persuade or obtain commitment for an idea, program, or proposal.
- To teach, train, demonstrate, or explain tasks and procedures.
- To congratulate or reward.

COMPONENTS OF A MEETING

Purpose: The reason for the meeting.

Input and Content: Leader, members, agendas, visual aids, handouts, meeting room facilities, objectives, facts, and opinions.

Process: Presentation, discussion, consensus, voting, negotiation, information exchange, expression of feelings, planning, problem solving, and decision making.

Product: Problems solved, decisions made, compromises, commitment obtained, schedules, assignments, priorities, resources allocated, action plans.

Responses and Follow-up: Actions taken. Information to meeting constituents and other people affected by the decisions.

MEETING PREPARATIONS BY THE CHAIR

Besides preparing an agenda and ensuring that meeting space and facilities are available, chairpersons improve their effectiveness by getting ideas, opinions, and information before the session. They encourage the members to submit suggestions for topics. Talking to members before a meeting often eliminates the need for that meeting. This is also a technique of getting opinions from passive members who may be reluctant to speak up at the meeting. Let the participants know what you expect of them. Designate whom you will call on to discuss certain points.

Morning meetings when everyone is awake and fresh are ideal. After lunch, people fall asleep. Many people like to hold meetings at 4 pm. By that hour, they have taken care of most of their major daily problems, and still have a little time to return to their office for last-minute details after the session.

The selection of members is important. You can reduce costs and avoid displeasure if you limit attendance to people you need and are willing to serve. The members should collectively have the necessary knowledge and experience. They should be the kind of people you can depend on to show up and participate.

The larger the number of attendees, the slower the meeting progress, and the more difficult it is to stick to the agenda. A group of five to eight people is ideal for most action meetings. To help reduce meeting size, consider part-time attendance; that is, ask people to be present only when you need them. Encourage them to leave when they have made their contributions (busy people are grateful for this).

If your meetings tend to drag on, schedule them just before quitting time. Many supervisors prefer Friday afternoons because they can review the week's progress. They also prevent the premature departure of folks who like to leave work early on Fridays.

> *A caveat:* You do not win popularity contests with this practice.

Select a Competent and Conscientious Recorder

Meeting records are important, so you want a recorder who takes clear and concise notes. The recorder summarizes and condenses the information into the minutes and submits them to the chair for review and approval. Recorders (or chairs) often use flipcharts to record progress, or to check off agenda items as they are disposed of.

Seating Arrangements

Most meetings are held around a rectangular table. A circular one is preferable, especially if there is no designated leader. Classroom or auditorium arrangements are fine for distributing information, but not for problem solving or committee meetings. Circular, semicircular, and U-shaped configurations of chairs have their advocates. Seminar leaders and discussion panels like hollow square groupings with the leader or panel of discussants seated on one side.

Do not seat antagonists facing each other at rectangular tables (typical union-management arrangements) where they can glare across the table at each other. If you can, seat them on the same side of the table.

Agenda

Think of the agenda as the rudder of your discussion boat. The agenda is to a chairperson what a recipe is to a cook. Encapsulate the topics in action or goal-oriented statements. Avoid the word discuss when the purpose of the meeting is to recommend action. Discussions that do not lead to actions are usually just a lot of hot air. After each item on the agenda, show the expected kind of result (eg, "to prepare the final draft of our mission statement").

Indicate the time allocated for each topic and the names of the people you expect to report. Use a computer to prepare your personal copy of the agenda. You can leave enough space between each item for notes. You eliminate puzzling over your scribbling in the margins. List everything you want to cover, then cut the agenda in half. Always include a start and end time for each topic. Use action phrases like "to recommend" or "to make a final decision" rather than "to discuss" or "to consider."

Distribute the agenda several days before the meeting. If you issue the agenda too long before the meeting, some of the people will lose their copy and forget its contents. If you do not give them enough time to read and digest its content, they lack time to prepare for the session. You must know where to send each copy. Some people like to get their copy at home, others at work. A bad practice at many hospitals is that board members pick up their copies as they enter the meeting room, or the agendas are handed out at the start of the session.

THE MEETING

Get Started

Arrive early to ensure that everything is in readiness. For quick sessions, remove the chairs and hold stand-up meetings.

Memorize your opening statement. The opening statement establishes the direction for the meeting.

If this is the first meeting of a group, establish some ground rules before any discussions start. Here are some good guidelines:

- We will start and end the meetings on time.
- We will listen to others without interrupting.
- We will not allow sarcasm, ridicule, or intimidation.
- Everyone gets a chance to talk, and is expected to do so.
- We will seek consensus rather than majority voting.

Sound and look enthusiastic as you review the highlights of the previous meeting and ask for any comments or corrections. Note any progress made since that meeting.

How To Encourage Participation

- Go around the table, calling on each member by name.
- Respond enthusiastically to all suggestions.

- Split into breakaway groups.
- Let others lead some questioning or chair the session.
- Reinforce participation from reserved members, e.g., "Thanks, Erica, for speaking so candidly."
- Use non-threatening, open-ended questions, e.g.,"How do you think someone opposed to that idea will respond?"
- Withhold your opinion until everyone else has spoken.
- If a person's suggestion cannot be accepted, try using part of it.
- Encourage members to build on the ideas of others.
- Preserve the ego of all members.

Avoid the Abilene Paradox

The Abilene Paradox is the inability to manage agreement.[1] It occurs when members approve an action that is contrary to what they really want. The reason is that they fail to express their true opinions and vote for something they object to but feel that the group is in favor of. This scenario is common when chairpersons are domineering. When the result turns out unfavorably, members either accuse each other, or give lame excuses for not speaking up. This paradox is avoided when participants have courage, or a devil's advocate is present.

Maintain Control

Keep people from going off on a tangent. When they stray, say something like, "Jessica, that's interesting. We'll look into that. Now about. . . ." Summarize progress periodically by using a flipchart or blackboard. Call for a break when things stall.

Force Decisions

Ask if anyone needs more data before a decision is made. Ask a proponent to sum up her view. Do the same for an opponent. Go around the table and ask each person for his or her position; then try to achieve a unanimous decision. Call for a vote only when a serious effort for a consensus has failed or you need a record of how each member has voted.

Ensure that recommendations are phrased in specific terminology. For example: "To improve emergency room service" is too general. "Decrease average waiting time in the pediatric clinic to less than 15 minutes" is more specific.

Close the Meeting

To avoid confusion, summarize the discussion and decisions. Indicate the areas still requiring consideration. Review assignments, and select the date for the next meeting.

When you must leave a meeting that is still in progress, provide a brief explanation and turn the chair over to an alternate. Before you do that, assign any special responsibilities or tasks to members.

Important "Do Nots" for Chairs

- Do not try to dominate the meeting.
- Do not state your opinion before others have given theirs.
- Do not tell a participant that he or she is wrong.
- Do not instruct or lecture unless that is the purpose of the meeting.
- Do not argue (disagreeing is acceptable).
- Do not ridicule, kid, or use sarcasm.
- Do not take sides early in the discussion.
- Do not fail to control problem members.
- Do not allow the meeting to run overtime.
- Do not try to accomplish too much at one meeting.

POSTMEETING ACTIVITIES

Notify the convening authority of the outcome if appropriate. Send thank you notes to individuals who made outstanding presentations, clarified remarks, supported you, or agreed to carry out postmeeting tasks.

Prepare minutes without delay. Copies should be available within 24–48 hours. The minutes should include the following:

- time of start and adjournment
- who was present and who was absent
- statement that previous minutes were read and approved
- brief discussion or presentation of each item on agenda
- record of agreement or disagreement, record of vote or decisions made
- follow-up on actions to be taken
- date, place, and time of next meeting

TIPS FOR MEMBERS

- Ask yourself why you are there, and come prepared to participate.
- Arrive on time.
- Listen thoughtfully to others and try to understand their points of view.
- Look for hidden agendas.
- Ask for clarifications.
- Respect the opinions of those with whom you disagree.
- Offer honest opinions, even when these are unpopular.
- Try to separate facts from perceptions, assumptions, or opinions.
- Disagree without being disagreeable.
- Remain rational and assertive, even when harassed.
- Seek win-win solutions, and be willing to compromise.
- Accept special assignments such as searching the literature or serving as recorder.
- Avoid being a problem member.

Advice for Nonassertive Members

Some individuals hesitate to speak up at meetings, thus depriving the group of their knowledge and opinions. Ideally, these people should obtain assertiveness training via seminars, workshops, or books.

There are also tactics for bolstering one's courage to speak up. One is to come prepared. Another is to use escalating dialogue. Here you break your silence by asking questions—starting with benign requests for information or clarification—followed by more challenging queries. Finally, you start to express your opinion.

Another technique is to maintain a state of interest and active neutrality during controversies. Opposing members try to convince fence-sitters who then become centers of attention. Simply listening to both sides and asking appropriate questions provides the neutral observer with clout.

Use power language by avoiding discounters like "I know this sounds silly, but . . . . " Do not use clichés like "It goes without saying." Eliminate those dreadful fillers such as "Ya know" or "Uhhhhhh."

Sound enthusiastic, speak clearly and forcefully. Do not tolerate interruptions. Say "I wasn't finished, Lou." Then go on without waiting for an apology.

Support your vocal expressions with appropriate body language. When a speaker looks at you, give a head signal that shows your reaction. If you nod agreement or shake your head, the person will give you more attention.

PROBLEM MEMBERS

There are all kinds of participants: incisive thinkers, impatient doers, chronic objectors, speech-makers, shoot-from-the-hip decision makers, and ultraconservatives; you can probably name others. Let us take a closer look at the ones who give chairpersons the most difficulty.

Latecomers

It is sometimes best to declare an intermission and brief the latecomer during that interval. Encourage chronically tardy members to arrive on time. Do not reward their tardiness by reviewing what transpired before they appeared. This encourages more tardiness.

Members Who Offend Others

No member has the right to mock or insult others. The leader should immediately interrupt the errant behavior and apologize to the person who has been ridiculed. Admonish the offender (eg, "Jack, that is uncalled for, and I'm sure the rest here agree. Let's keep this on a professional level").

Intimidators

Intimidation is a common method for trying to force opinions. The three tactics are: appear to be angry, assume a superior attitude, or to ridicule. The chair must stop this quickly.

Hostile or Angry Members

If you know who these people are, plan what to say. Practice by saying it aloud several times before the meeting. Visualize a successful confrontation. At the meeting, encourage venting. The more anger that pours out, the less there is left. Do not interrupt the person, and insist that he or she not interrupt you.

Nonparticipants

Their thoughts are elsewhere. You should not have invited some of these people. Bring their minds back on track by posing questions or asking for their opinions.

Side Conversationalists

Some private conversation is natural. Timid members may be afraid to speak up, so they whisper to each other. They may be bored or just discourteous. If you stop in the middle of a sentence and glare at them, this may work. If not, ask them to share their conversation with the group.

Comics

We all enjoy a little humor, but individuals who overdo this can be disruptive. Stop them in their tracks by not laughing, giving a wry smile as you shake your head, and say that you want to get on with the business.

Motor Mouths

These people are enthralled by their own voice and never seem to run out of gas. Their comments are endless, and their questions are really just more comments.

Jump in when they pause for breath. Say: "Just a minute, Rita, let's hear what others have to say," "We're getting bogged down, Rita, please make your point," or "Please put that in the form of a motion."

Some of these folks cannot get enough air time. They try to engage you in repeated one-on-one conversations, usually by asking many questions. Ask them to stay after the meeting to discuss these. They rarely do.

Destroyers

Some participants become emotionally rather than rationally involved. They play psychological war games and demand attention by criticizing, interrupting, or taking offense at innocent remarks. One of them may say "I resent that" or "If you people approve that, I'm walking out." Ignore their outbursts. Do not argue or get excited.

Let them say their piece, and then go on.

COMMITTEE MEETINGS

Committee meetings are subject to the same rules and conduct as other meetings. Standing committees are permanent and meet regularly. The Joint Commission on Accreditation of Healthcare Organizations requires many of these committees. Standing committees deal with matters such as quality, safety, infections, ethics, and credentials. Bylaws, union contracts, and operational procedures or protocols list the functions and responsibilities of standing committees.

Ad hoc committees are temporary, created to deal with a single issue such as a threat of unionization. A task force is a special kind of ad hoc committee.

It is unfortunate that so many health care workers dislike committee assignments because committees are constantly growing in number and importance.

Managers at any level can appoint ad hoc committees. When you appoint a committee, be specific about what you expect. Answer the following questions:

- Who is to be the chair, and does that person have the power to appoint members, schedule meetings, and prepare agendas? Select the chairperson carefully.
- Is membership voluntary?
- What is the goal or mission of the committee?
- When is a report due? Are there to be interim reports? If so, at what intervals?
- If it is only a decision-making committee, what are the alternatives to be considered?
- If it is a problem-solving committee, do you want only what is deemed to be the best solution or do you want a list of all the alternatives?
- Will you carry out whatever the committee recommends, or only the parts you like?
- What facilities and fiscal support are available?
- If the committee is to serve permanently, have terms of tenure and plans for rotation of membership been provided?

TELEPHONE CONFERENCE CALLS

There are disadvantages to these calls. It may be difficult to identify all the voices. Participants lack the opportunity to watch body language, and it's easier for individuals to dominate the conversation. Finally, some people are simply not comfortable with this form of communication. Despite all these disadvantages, the use of conference calls has been increasing because of their convenience and the saving of time and expense. They are ideal for obtaining a vote or getting quick opinions from key people.

NOTE

1. J.B. Harvey, "The Abilene Paradox," *Organizational Dynamics 17* (1988): 35–80.

RECOMMENDED READING AND LISTENING

C.W. Burleson, *Effective Meetings: The Complete Guide* (New York, NY: John Wiley & Sons, 1990).

G. Carson, *Making Meetings Work* (Boulder, CO: CareerTrack Publishers, 1992), two audiotapes.

Chapter 35

Decision Making and Problem Solving

- why decision making is now more important
- decision making and leadership
- when to avoid making decisions
- the essential trinity for effective decisions
- the dual cognitive functions
- coping with daily problems
- the logical process: key steps in solving large problems
- steps of rational problem solving
- the computer and other problem-solving tools
- your intuitive process: key to creative problem solving
- group problem solving

Problems are inevitable when people work together. The hallmark of a well-managed team is not the absence of problems, but whether the team resolves problems effectively. Managers still blame their employees for most problems, but the real villains are faulty management decisions.

WHY DECISION MAKING IS NOW MORE IMPORTANT

The rate of organizational, technical, legal, and operational change constantly increases. Many of the decisions related to these changes have great impact on financial or job security, role alterations, assignments, and customer satisfaction.

Supervisors are forced to make decisions that were less common previously (eg, downsizing, reassigning, cross-training, and replacing professional employees with less qualified personnel). Critical shortages of certain specialists demand quick hiring decisions before competitors snatch these persons.

Our society is more litigious. Flawed decisions lead to legal nightmares (eg, harassment and discrimination issues). Employee safety, satisfaction, and ethics are more numerous and complex.

People decisions are by far the most important. Hiring, training, disciplining, promoting, and discharging of employees demand careful consideration.

DECISION MAKING AND LEADERSHIP

Autocratic leaders make decisions without soliciting help from others. *Consultative* leaders get input from others before deciding. *Democratic* leaders participate with their staffs in making decisions. *Delegative* leaders turn the process over to others.

Upper management deals chiefly with decisions that relate to major outcomes or long-range strategies—the what. Supervisors deal principally with operational processes—the how.

AVOID MAKING DECISIONS WHEN . . .

- it is not your problem;
- the problem will probably correct itself or interference is likely to make matters worse (if it ain't broke, don't fix it.);
- you or the others are emotionally upset or there are serious attention distractions;
- more information or advice is needed; and
- the problem should be delegated. Most decisions should be made at the lowest organizational level—as close to the scene of action as possible—if the delegates are capable and willing.

THE ESSENTIAL TRINITY FOR EFFECTIVE DECISIONS

An effective decision must be:

1. the most cogent decision.
2. timely, both when made and when carried out. Professionals often procrastinate because they are looking for more data available. They fall prey to "paralysis from analysis."
3. acceptable to the people affected. Many managers are adept at making decisions but fail to persuade people to carry them out.

THE DUAL COGNITIVE FUNCTIONS

There are two cognitive approaches to decision making and problem solving: analytical and intuitive. Analytical, or left-brain function, provides rational, logical, scientific thinking. Intuitive cognition, or right-brain function, provides creativity and inspiration.

Left-brain thinking is a flowchart process. Analytical people rely on algorithmic processes, plans, reports, computer printouts, and step-by-step procedures.

They exercise judgment at each step and exclude anything that is irrelevant. Managers and investigators who treat problem solving as a science often fail to come up with creative ideas because they depend entirely on this rational approach. In an earlier chapter we mentioned that managers tend to use more left-brain thinking while leaders rely to a great extent on their intuition.

Intuitive thinking depends on data buried in our unconscious minds, which are like computers with almost unlimited memory storage capability. Unfortunately, what we file in these cerebral banks may be difficult to recall—like a computer program for which we lost the password. Unlike computer-stored data, brain information is constantly and unconsciously analyzed, synthesized, and reformatted.

Innovative people have deeper insight or stronger gut reactions. They visualize more than their rational counterparts. They prefer diagrams to printouts. They often throw logic out the window. An intuitive thought process can seldom be flowcharted; rather, it is hop, skip, and jump.

> *Common sense is a combination of logic and intuition,*
> *the left and right brain working in tandem.*

COPING WITH THE MANY MINOR PROBLEMS

Supervisors face innumerable little problems and decisions every day. Solving problems is the supervisor's most important responsibility. If there were no problems, we would not need any supervisors. Their subordinates bring problems into their office by the carload. Better training, planning, coaching, delegating, and policy making do wonders in cutting down on the number of these daily interruptions.

The Stop-Look-Listen Approach

Approach these daily questions or problems like you approach a railroad crossing:

- Stop what you are doing.
- Look interested.
- Listen carefully.

If the problem is still unclear, ask pertinent questions. Then ask the folks who bring you the problems what they think should be done. Most of the time they will have thought through the problem and may have a better solution than you can offer on the spur of the moment. If you agree, approve their suggestion and congratulate them. If they keep bringing in the same problem, tell them that they do not need your decision each time.

Tell your people that you expect them to practice completed staff work. Explain to them that the military term, completed staff work, means that whenever a staff member comes in with a problem, they must also bring in their ideas on how best to solve the problem. Participative management requires much completed staff work.

If the problem is one that only you can solve, give them your answer on the spot, or get back to them without undue delay. Follow up when appropriate.

THE LOGICAL PROCESS: KEY STEPS IN SOLVING LARGE PROBLEMS

Step 1. Prepare a problem statement. Diagnosis is the most important part of problem solving, and it is often the most neglected part. Too often, people offer solutions before they really understand the problem. Poor problem statements can lead people astray. For example, the problem statement "Lack of clear policy relating to sick leave" is not likely to lead to solving a problem of excessive absenteeism due to poor enforcement by the supervisor.

Step 2. Obtain and interpret the facts or data by asking the following questions:
- When was problem first noted?
- How serious is it?
- Is it getting better or worse?
- Is it more complicated than first appeared? In what way?
- What is the cause? (This is the most important question.)
- How was this handled in the past? What were the results?

Step 3. Generate alternatives (as many as possible).

Step 4. Formulate criteria to evaluate the alternatives. There are two types of criteria:
- *Absolute criteria:* criteria that must be met by an acceptable solution (eg, "No increase in costs or personnel")
- *Differential criteria:* criteria used to compare and contrast the various alternatives (eg, turnaround time, schedule convenience, availability of supplies, and degree of expertise required)

Step 5. Evaluate the alternatives and select the best one.

Step 6. Look for flaws in the choice.
Ask many "what ifs." Avoid the jigsaw puzzle fallacy. The jigsaw fallacy is based on the false assumption that there is only one good solution (ie, a jigsaw puzzle must have four straight edges). Often there are several

equally satisfactory solutions: The edges of life's puzzles are seldom straight lines.

Step 7. Develop an action plan.

Step 8. Carry out the plan. If there is hesitation about implementing the plan, ask what would be the worst possible thing that could happen if the plan is carried out. Also ask what the worst possible thing would be if you do not take the risk.

Step 9. Follow up. If what you are doing is not working well, make the needed changes.

USEFUL TOOLS FOR PROBLEM SOLVING

Bar Graphs

Bar graphs (Figure 35–1a) display a series of numbers (eg, the number of patient visits on each day of the month). When a bar graph shows the distribution of a variance, it is called a histogram (Figure 35–1b).

Pareto Diagrams

Pareto diagrams (Figure 35–1c) display the frequency of occurrences listed in order of importance or frequency.

Scattergrams

A scattergram (Figure 35–1d) shows the correlation between two variables.

Run Charts

Run charts (Figure 35–1e) plot data over time. They exhibit trends, cycles, or other patterns in a process (eg, attendance records, turnover, or customer complaints).

Control Charts

Control charts (Figure 35–1f) illustrate values that are either in control or out of control. In Figure 35–1f, the solid horizontal line represents an average or normal value. The spaces between the solid line and the dotted lines are acceptable values, usually plus or minus two or three standard deviations. Any value outside the dotted lines is an out-of-control value.

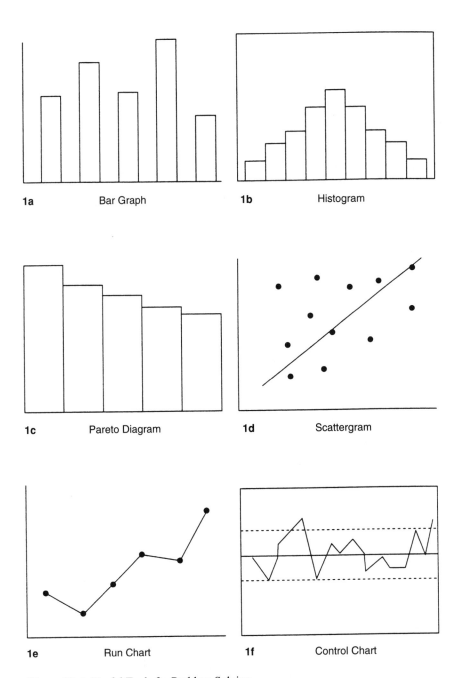

Figure 35–1 Useful Tools for Problem Solving

Flowcharts

A flowchart (Figure 35–2a) represents a series of steps or events arranged chronologically.

Cause and Effect Diagrams

Also known as fishbone charts, these devices are useful in an early stage of problem solving or when one is considering potential problems (Figure 35–2b). A cause-and-effect diagram forces a focus on potential causes. On each leg (each bone), possible factors are recorded and grouped according to different categories (eg, process, human, equipment, or policies).

Pie Charts

Pie charts (Figure 35–2c) illustrate relative numbers or percentages.

Gaussian Curve Charts

The bell-shaped curves show frequency distributions. These are among the most common quality control charts (Figure 35–2d).

Force Field Charts

These are useful when considering the advantages and disadvantages of a new service, process, procedure, or piece of equipment. The opposing considerations can be illustrated and quantified by a force field chart[1] (Figure 35–2e).

Checklists

Checklists (Figure 35–2f) are used as reminders or for documentation of activities. Shopping lists, daily "to do" schedules, and validation of records are just a few uses for this ubiquitous tool. Figure 35–2f is a partial list of tests that a new laboratory technician must be qualified to do.

Gantt Charts

The Gantt chart[2] (Figure 35–3) is a graph with activities listed on the vertical axis and time units on the horizontal axis. It is used to find the shortest total time required to reach a goal by showing how much time each activity requires and which activities can and which cannot be done simultaneously. In Figure 35–3, note the overlapping of several activities.

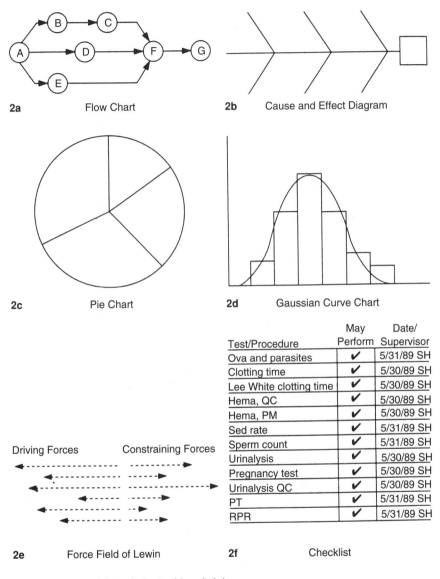

2a Flow Chart

2b Cause and Effect Diagram

2c Pie Chart

2d Gaussian Curve Chart

Test/Procedure	May Perform	Date/ Supervisor
Ova and parasites	✔	5/31/89 SH
Clotting time	✔	5/30/89 SH
Lee White clotting time	✔	5/30/89 SH
Hema, QC	✔	5/30/89 SH
Hema, PM	✔	5/30/89 SH
Sed rate	✔	5/31/89 SH
Sperm count	✔	5/31/89 SH
Urinalysis	✔	5/30/89 SH
Pregnancy test	✔	5/30/89 SH
Urinalysis QC	✔	5/30/89 SH
PT	✔	5/31/89 SH
RPR	✔	5/31/89 SH

2e Force Field of Lewin

2f Checklist

Figure 35–2 Useful Tools for Problem Solving

PERT Charts

Program Evaluation and Review Technique (PERT) charts (Figure 35–4) were developed to reduce and control the time required for large projects. The PERT

Activities \ Weeks	1	2	3	4	5	6	7	8	9	10	11	12	13	14	15
1	x	x													
2			x	x											
3					x	x	x	x							
4					x	x									
5							x								
6								x							
7									x						
8									x						
9									x						
10											x	x	x	x	
11														x	
12													x		
13															x

Total time: 15 weeks

Figure 35–3 Gantt Chart

chart is composed of activities and events. Events are represented by circles. Arrows show the time necessary to complete events. When there are steps carried out simultaneously, different times are needed for each of these parallel steps. In Figure 35–4, the lines could represent the following steps:

A-B	=	time for a request to reach a workstation
B-C	=	time for blood collection and delivery to a laboratory
C-D	=	time for serological testing
C-E	=	time for immunohematological testing
E-F	=	time for delivery of blood product to patient

The critical path represents the sum of the times for individual steps in the path that require the most time. In Figure 35–4, the critical path is A-B-C-D-F because it takes longer to do the serological tests than to do the routine compatibility tests.

Breakeven Charts

This chart is a scattergram in which the Procedures and the Expenses—variable and fixed—are plotted with diagonal lines representing total revenues and total costs (Figure 35–5). The point at which the diagonal lines cross represents the

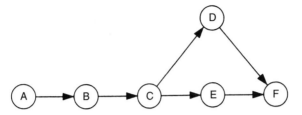

Figure 35–4 PERT Chart with Critical Path

financial Breakeven Point. The number of procedures performed below that crossing show a loss; those above that crossing show a profit.

Likert Charts

Likert charts[3] (Figure 35–6) are useful when one is comparing and contrasting multiple factors of performance at two different times (eg, before and after a change).

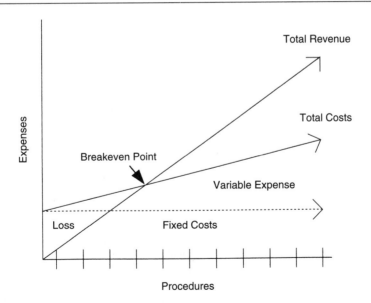

Figure 35-5 Breakeven Chart

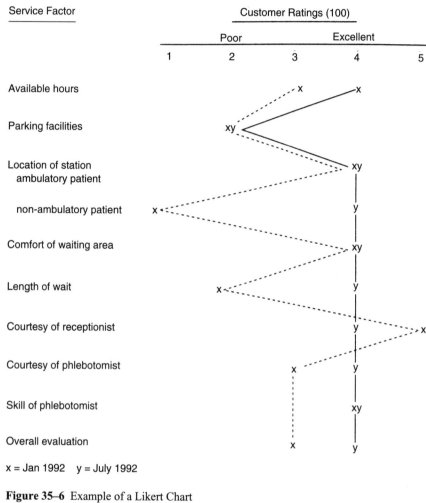

Figure 35–6 Example of a Likert Chart

Computer Applications

Computers have been used for a long time to file data, to reassemble information into new formats, and to perform logical operations and calculations. An exciting trend available to computers in problem solving is in the area of expert systems. These rely on stored facts and rules of thumb to mimic the decision making of human experts. This has been successful when applied to narrowly defined tasks, but we still lack a system that possesses common sense.

YOUR INTUITIVE PROCESS: KEY TO CREATIVE PROBLEM SOLVING

Give your intuitive process time to act. Set aside some think time each day. Capture thoughts as they occur, like the ringing of a muted telephone. These are most likely to pop up when your logical thought process is on hold. Turn off conscious cerebration to let your cerebral energy flow into your unconscious mind. Daydreaming, relaxation, and meditation help. Walking, jogging, and other kinds of exercise increase cerebral blood flow, and this improves the thought generation process. Solitude can be effective, particularly when it is enhanced by listening to ocean sounds (real or recorded) or background music.

Pay attention to the nagging doubts you get when you are trying to make a decision. They may represent experience stored in your unconscious mind. A strategy espoused by Dr. Joyce Brothers, the well-known television psychologist, is to think about a problem just before dropping off to sleep.[4]

A Simple Way To Stimulate Your Intuitive Process

Document your problem at the top of a sheet of paper. Under this heading, number the lines 1 through 20. Now force yourself to write down 20 solutions. The first few will come easily (these are usually the ones that you have already considered and discarded). Subsequent alternatives surface with increasing difficulty and are more likely to have originated in your unconscious mind and are more inspirational.[5]

GROUP PROBLEM SOLVING

A problem is like a world globe. From any one spot, you cannot see all of the globe. Neither does any one person have an all-encompassing view. In group problem solving, more ideas are generated. An added bonus is that a group is more likely to support the choice it made.

Group discussions increase the likelihood of serendipity—the fortunate situation when two events accidentally come together to create an opportunity. When people put their heads together, they come up with more solutions than when they work individually. With this synergy, $1 + 1 = 3$.

The Importance of Consensus

A group often makes decisions before all the opinions of the members have been explored. Participants who are not heard from may leave a meeting angry.

They may not support the activation of the decisions. A few will even sabotage the initiative. A consensus prevents this.

A consensus is a genuine meeting of the minds. It is not reached by voting. Even a unanimous vote does not represent a consensus if some members are denied an opportunity to speak up. With a consensus, some members may prefer different solutions, but after full and fair discussion, they agree that they can live with what the group decided.

The Basics of Consensus Decision Making

- Ensure that each person expresses his or her viewpoint fully.
- Avoid hasty conclusions or agreements.
- Explore the positive features of each alternative.
- Expose and analyze each alternative's negative features.
- Resolve disagreements.
- Avoid techniques of voting, averaging, or bargaining.
- Insist that each member agree that he or she can live with the solution. If any member balks, you do not have a consensus.

Be wary of the Abilene Paradox described in the previous chapter.

CREATIVE PROBLEM-SOLVING GROUPS

Unstructured Brainstorming Groups

Unstructured meetings are little more than beer-and-pretzel gab fests—lots of talk, lots of wandering off the topic, and not much action. All too many committee meetings degenerate into these kinds of sessions. There are exceptions, of course, especially when a group of entrepreneurs or creative people gets together.

Structured Brainstorming Groups

These groups generate ideas guided by certain rules. Here is one technique[6]:

1. A problem is presented to the group.
2. Each member thinks about the problem and records his or her ideas on a sheet of paper. No comment or discussion is allowed at this time.
3. Each member reads one item from his or her list. Each of these is recorded on a flipchart. No comment or discussion is permitted at this time either, but members may piggyback on the ideas of others.

4. This sequence is repeated until all the ideas are displayed on the chart.
5. Each item is then discussed, amplified, or modified. The originator of each item may be asked to leave the room while his or her idea is discussed. Criticism is now encouraged.
6. Each member ranks the items, and the votes are recorded on the chart.

Note that there are two phases in this approach: the generation phase (steps 1 through 4) and the evaluation phase (steps 5 and 6).

To get the maximum benefit of the brainstorming, make certain that participants know beforehand what is going to be discussed and are encouraged to come loaded with ideas. Set a good example by bringing a large packet of your own suggestions, including some really wild ones. Lead off with your wildest one.

NOTES

1. K. Lewin, *Field Theory in Social Science* (New York, NY: Harper & Row, 1951).

2. H. Gantt, *Industrial Leadership* (Easton, PA: Hive, 1973).

3. R. Likert, *New Patterns of Management* (New York, NY: McGraw-Hill, 1961).

4. D. Sullivan, *Work Smart, Not Hard* (New York, NY: Facts on File, 1987).

5. E. DeBono, *Lateral Thinking: Creativity Step by Step* (New York, NY: Harper & Row, 1970).

6. A.L. Delbecq, et al. *Group Techniques for Program Planning* (Glenview, IL: Scott, Foresman, 1975).

Chapter 36

Negotiating Skill

- the four basic forms of negotiation
- preparation for a negotiation
- major steps in a negotiation
- barriers to successful negotiation

We all engage in negotiations at work and at home on a daily basis. Many of us start our day negotiating with offspring over what they will wear to school. Supervisors negotiate with vendors; workers negotiate over vacation schedules. When we hold a performance review, a counseling session, or moderate a problem-solving meeting, we often wish that we were better negotiators. A characteristic of effective leaders is that they are persuasive negotiators who obtain commitment rather than obedience from their people.

FOUR BASIC FORMS OF NEGOTIATION

1. The Power Play or "Gotcha." This authoritarian approach is based on marshaling enough power to overwhelm opponents. People who play this game may have prestigious titles, powerful friends, or weighty professional expertise. They think it naive to believe that cooperation works. These attempts at dominance often meet counterdominance and become less effective as people learn how to cope with them. The Sherman Tanks we described in a previous chapter like to play "Gotcha."

    There are several ways to cope with power plays:

    - Develop a thick skin. Do not take the nasty things you hear personally.
    - Do not be intimidated. Be assertive without being aggressive.
    - If someone tries to intimidate you with technical jargon, don't hesitate to speak up (eg, "I need you to put that in one syllable words").
    - Request a third party mediator.
    - Respond to threats with "Why would you want to do that?"

2. Taking fixed positions. In this "take it-or-leave it" approach, both sides adopt rigid positions and are reluctant to compromise. They become locked into defending those positions to save face, and negotiations become contests of will rather than problem-solving exercises.

3. Haggling. Experienced hagglers ask for more than they expect to get. They offer options that are only favorable to them. They try to create an obligation by giving the other party a little something—or make them feel guilty (eg, "I take that remark personally"). They promise more than they know they will deliver.

   Avoid the high-low dollar game. In that game sellers quote figures that are much higher than they expect to get. Buyers respond with figures much lower than they expect to pay. The expectation is that the agreed-upon amount will be somewhere in the middle. While that game may be appropriate in some instances, the outcome depends too heavily on the persuasiveness of one party or on how badly the buyer wants the product or service. If you are the buyer and you have done your homework, make one honest offer and stick to it. You have the option of turning around and walking away.

4. Collaborating or value adding. This approach is more likely to result in win-win outcomes. You achieve your goals while helping others achieve theirs. Collaboration is based on the premise that you make the pie bigger rather than fighting over the size of each party's slice. The negotiators add value to the package rather than seeking concessions from each other. The more creative they are, the better the results. For example, an employee seeks permission to leave work early each day so she can pick up her child at school. Her supervisor balks. When the employee proposes to make up the time by accepting more weekend assignments, the supervisor readily agrees. They both win.

PREPARATION FOR A NEGOTIATION

Prepare Your Wish List

Since each person has different interests, being prepared helps you understand these different interests. At least you must know what you want and what you are willing to concede. Sometimes it helps to have not only a specific goal but also several fallback positions or alternative goals. For important negotiations, put these goals in writing.

Before the meeting, try to find out what the other side wants. . . and how badly. What are they likely to propose? What advantages do they have?

Collect Data

The data may be copies of laws, policies, protocols, or guidelines. Get up-to-date information through your formal and informal communication channels. Organize information so it is concise and understandable. Include handouts, graphs, charts, and other visual displays.

Take Action

- Sketch out the options you can offer.
- Prepare your opening remarks.
- Ready the arguments you can make to maximize the positive aspects of your interests and to counter the other person's arguments.
- Role play what you plan to say or offer with a friend or mentor.
- Pick the best time and place for the meeting.

MAJOR STEPS IN A NEGOTIATION

Step 1. Clarify interests. Ask the person how she views the situation and what is important to her. Paraphrase her message and ask if you have interpreted her view correctly. Then state yours. Do not go on until these viewpoints and desired outcomes are clear.

Step 2. Focus on points of agreement. Center on what you perceive as areas of agreement. Work from there. Get into the problem areas later.

Step 3. Formulate possible options—the more the better. Articulate the benefits of each option to the other person. Do not get stuck believing that your solution is the only good one. Be gracious. If the person has a valid argument, say so.

A common mistake that novice negotiators make is to think that something is not negotiable. This may be based on past experience or what you have been told by others. These assumed constraints are often just that—assumed. You may later regret not exploring such possibilities.

Instead of presenting your idea as a proposal, test the waters by stating your case as a question (eg, "I wonder what would happen if we...?"). If it gets a cool reception, you can easily drop the subject with a simple "Yeah, that's right." It you think your idea has great merit and has a good chance of being accepted, the above approach may lead to others taking it over by adding an additional twist. To prevent that, have a written outline of your proposal and introduce it into the discussion.[1]

Step 4. Agree on the best option. If you cannot reach complete agreement, be willing to compromise—but not until you have explored all possible win-win solutions.

Step 5. Be prepared for an impasse. Keep the meeting going even though your initial efforts are unsuccessful. The longer the discussion continues, the more likely the other party is to give in. He or she is reluctant to invest a lot of time in a negotiation without achieving any result. If things continue to stall, call for a break or a postponement. Each of you may need more information, or to consult with other individuals.

Step 6. Perfect the deal. Refine the selected deal to ensure that each of you is comfortable with it.

Step 7. Wrap it up. Review what is agreed and document that fact. If it was a long or rigorous negotiation, compliment the other party on being a tough negotiator. This helps to end on a positive note.

NEGOTIATING WITH YOUR BOSS

Unless you are a clone of your manager, the two of you will have disagreements. Most of the time, you reach amicable solutions. On rare occasions, your boss will reject something you feel very strongly about (eg, an ethical problem or a raise for you or one of your employees). After the first rebuff, try a second verbal approach at a more convenient time or place and bring more ammunition with you. If that visits stalls, put your request in writing. Emphasize that you feel very strongly about the request. If that does not work, you must decide whether the matter is important enough to challenge your boss, and possibly to risk your career. If you think it is worth pursuing, tell your manager that you would like the two of you to discuss the problem with his superior. If he declines to accompany you, but tells you to go ahead, do so after telling him exactly what you plan to say to his boss. If his response is to threaten you in some way, you must be prepared to react appropriately.

In Chapter 39 we will discuss salary negotiation in more detail.

BARRIERS TO SUCCESSFUL NEGOTIATION

Fear

There may be fear of loss of friendship or future cooperation. Some people cave in quickly because they do not have the stomach for any kind of disagreement. Others are inflexible or demanding because they fear that people will take advantage of them.

When you are negotiating a salary increase and you feel that the organization or your manager is taking advantage of you, there are times when you must threaten to resign. Never do this unless you are willing to follow through. Still better, wait until you have a bona fide offer elsewhere.

Secrecy

Some negotiators mistakenly think that they will win more often if they withhold information.

Ultimatums and Deadlines

Avoid making threats yourself unless they are absolutely necessary. However, sometimes the threat to walk out of a bargaining session will get results. Once you make such a threat, be willing to do it. If you do not, your bluffs will be called in future negotiations.

Anger, Guilt Induction, Ridicule, or Tears

These emotional responses or attempts to manipulate are seldom indicated. Experienced negotiators are not moved by these gimmicks, but admittedly some novices are.

The Team Approach

While team efforts have some advantages, such as augmented expertise and mutual support, there are problems. Showing up with a cadre of supporters may suggest that you lack the ability to handle the process by yourself. Sometimes one member of your group makes a remark that hurts your case, or reveals disunity among the group's members. The team approach also takes longer and is more likely to end without a consensus being reached.

Reliance on Data

Statistics are useful if valid and not redundant. However, too much reliance on them backfires when the other party finds flaws in your data or comes up with more impressive data of his or her own. You rarely convince people with facts and figures. Search for something in your proposal that appeals to them, and then keep pushing that hot button. For example, during a bargaining, the other person frequently mentions paperwork. When negotiation stalls, repeatedly come back to your offer to help with the documentation and reports.

Delaying Tactics

Repeated and unnecessary delays often postpone needed action. They also erode the spirit of cooperation and can be very frustrating to both parties.

NOTE

1. J. Salzman, *How To Get Results with People* (Boulder, CO: CareerTrack Publishers, 1987), four audiotapes.

RECOMMENDED READINGS

K. Albrecht and S. Albrecht, *Added Value Negotiating: The Breakthrough Method for Building Balanced Deals* (Homewood, IL: Business One Irwin, 1993).

A.R. Cohen and D.L. Bradford, *Influence without Authority* (New York, NY: John Wiley & Sons, 1990).

R. Dawson, *Secrets of Power Persuasion* (Englewood Cliffs, NJ: Prentice Hall, 1992).

R. Fisher and W. Ury, *Getting to Yes: Negotiating without Giving In* (New York, NY: Houghton-Mifflin, 1988).

H.S. Rindler, *Managing Disagreement Constructively* (Los Altos, CA: Crisp Publishers, 1988).

Chapter 37

Time Management

- supervisors who have time problems
- your office or workstation
- planning and scheduling
- delegating
- procrastination
- time wasters
- visitor control
- meetings
- one-on-one communication
- more tips for saving time
- time thefts

Supervisors are well aware of the value of their time. Deadlines, turnaround times, emergencies, and interruptions constantly challenge them. Seldom are there enough hours to complete all their tasks. Most managers put in long hours on the job and often take home unfinished work. Then there are the hours that conscientious supervisors spend at home worrying about problems back at work.

Time management programs, like weight reduction programs, succeed only if one commits to reaching a goal. Experts can tell you how to save time, but you must supply the necessary discipline. To lose weight, people sacrifice things they like to eat. To gain time, people give up some activities they like to do, especially when they do those tasks so well.

There are two aspects of time management: managing your time and eliminating the waste of time by the people who report to you.

SUPERVISORS WHO HAVE TIME PROBLEMS

Managers who practice management by crisis have major time problems. They react rather than anticipate and plan. They spend large chunks of time running around trying to solve crises instead of preventing them.

There are the perfectionists. They are not satisfied with excellence. They strive for perfection. Perfectionists check and double check everything. They get more data and opinions than they need.

Leaders who cannot or will not delegate are always running out of time because they try to do things that others could do for them in addition to the things that only they can do.

Passive people have the same kind of time problems as the nondelegators. Because they cannot turn down requests for their time, they too are constantly struggling to keep up with their own work while serving on numerous committees, doing favors for colleagues, and listening to people problems that belong elsewhere.

YOUR OFFICE OR WORKSTATION

The best place to start a time management program is in your office. Here is where you can see results quickly. To avoid distractions, move your desk so that it does not face the door, or keep your door closed. Arrange filing cabinets and other furnishings to provide ready access to documents.

A messy desk does not necessarily mean a messy mind. If you can quickly find what you are looking for, and other folks, such as secretaries, do not need access to items strewn about in your office, keep your organized clutter. Ignore the jibes from your associates. On the other hand, most supervisors spend loads of time looking for things in their office. Instruct your secretary and others on how you want papers, manuals, office supplies, and other items stored. Revise your filing system. Use a desk drawer file for papers you refer to often. Put other papers in cabinets. Sort and batch your documents, using folders that you label appropriately. Set aside a drawer as a slush file for documents that you are not likely to need, but are reluctant to discard right away. Clean out that drawer each month.

Paper Flow

Supervisors feel overwhelmed by the volume of information they face. We thought that the computer would alleviate the paper overload, but it seems to have added rather than subtracted.

Filing begins when you sort your incoming mail. Try to handle each item only once. Practice the 3D idea: Do, Delegate, or Discard. When you hesitate to discard, ask yourself "What is the worst thing that could happen if I do not have this?"

Do not let your hold basket or folder get out of control. Review the items there daily, and act on as many as you can. Jot down a throw-out date on major filed items. Clear off your desk every night to avoid chaos when you arrive on the next day.

Additional Ways To Cope with Information Overload

- Be ruthless about what to read and what not to read. Reduce your "to read" pile after screening for relevant information.
- Check the messages you are sending out. Do they improve customer service or provide essential information?
- Answer memos by writing your responses on the memos rather than preparing another memo.
- Purge your e-mail of nonessentials.
- Let your computer replace your address/telephone book, Rolodex, "to do list," calendar, and appointment book.

Maximize the Value of Your Reading Time

- Scan articles, memos, journals, newspapers, or documents.
- Read the introductions and last paragraphs to decide if you need to read the rest.
- Highlight or underline key passages. Use a scanner to transfer information into your computer.
- Prepare and file summaries for important books or lengthy documents.
- Take reading material with you when you have appointments or travel.
- Set aside blocks of time for reading.

PLANNING AND SCHEDULING

When you fail to plan, you are planning to fail. Establish goals, priorities, schedules, and deadlines for all major undertakings. The more time you spend preparing for meetings, the less time is wasted at those meetings.

Most supervisors have little slack time these days. Make good use of what you have to catch up on correspondence, inventory, files, and low-priority items (busywork). Get your administrative tasks out of the way early or late in the day when there are fewer people around to take up your time. Leave some time for unexpected things. Differentiate between real deadlines, such as payroll data, and less urgent ones, such as the minutes of meetings.

Our physiological clocks are different. We each have hours of the day when our productivity and ability to concentrate are greater than during the rest of the day. Use those hours to work on major items (eg, presenting ideas to your manager, high-priority discussions, and important correspondence). During periods of low productivity, do things that are less mentally challenging, such as reading mail, making routine telephone calls, filing, and other routine chores.

Be sure that projects have priorities, due dates, and time estimates. Set realistic time frames. Review long-range goals frequently with superiors.

Use "To Do" Lists

Group similar things together on a "to do" list. Number the actions in order of importance and urgency. Label each item as must, should, or maybe. Do not expect to accomplish everything on your list every day. Remake or update the list daily. At the end of your workday, the items you did not get to should be low priority ones that you can transfer to the next day's list.

DELEGATING

The greatest time saver of all is delegation. Every hour that someone else does something that you previously did is an hour of your time that is saved. See Chapter 31 for a discussion of delegating.

PROCRASTINATION

At the very least, procrastination results in spending your time doing tasks that have a lower priority than the one you should be working on. This is compounded when you are immobilized because you have placed the topic on hold.

Practical Suggestions for Minimizing Procrastination

- Use daily prioritized task lists.
- Start the day with the high-priority or unpleasant tasks.
- Avoid the temptation to stall.
- Do not get involved with trivia.
- Block out enough time to complete time-consuming tasks.
- Slice a big task into thin slices that are more easily completed.
- Convince yourself that the task needs doing.
- Challenge your excuses.
- Do not reward procrastination. Do not allow yourself to engage in pleasant activities while you delay action. Sit in a straight chair without coffee or conversation.
- Set a timer for 5 minutes, and force yourself to start when it goes off.

TIME WASTERS

Use a time log to find out how you spend your time. This enables you to ferret out your wasted time and to alter your time schedules. It takes 21 days to establish a habit. Select your top five time wasters, and work on them for three weeks. Here are the principal offenders:

- Doing things you do not need to do:
  1. things that could be delegated
  2. trivial things that could be eliminated
  3. excessive socializing
- Inefficient planning, organizing, and scheduling
- Unnecessary or poorly run meetings
- Interruptions
  1. visitors
  2. unexpected problems
  3. the telephone

Do Not Let People Take Advantage of You

To avoid overcommitment of your time and other resources, say no diplomatically but emphatically. With subordinates, this often means not allowing them to delegate their work to you. That is not easy if you are easily flattered or manipulated.

Offer alternatives to colleagues. When a superior makes a request that creates a serious time problem for you, nail down priorities (eg, "Should I stop working on the. . . ?" or "Will someone handle my....?")

VISITOR CONTROL

Do not refer to visitors as annoyances or time wasters—even though many are. Most visitors are external or internal customers, and you should treat them as such. Efficient managers save time elsewhere so that they can spend more time with their visitors.

Techniques for Controlling Visitors Who Abuse Your Time

Unfortunately, we all have to deal with people who are excessively verbose or have lots of time to kill. Certain sales representatives and casual acquaintances may be high on your list of pests. The worst of the lot are those who cannot take hints that you are very busy and would like to end the conversation. Here are some suggestions for handling these folks:

- Train and empower your staff so they have less need to consult with you or to get your permission on routine matters.
- Train your staff to help visitors when you are not immediately available.
- Meet people in their territory. You then control the time of the meeting. Managing by walking around reduces the number of people who walk into your office.
- Shut your door when you really need privacy.
- Intercept visitors outside your office. Once people get into your office, transaction time increases.
- Remain standing and do not invite the visitor to be seated.
- Use verbal and nonverbal language to signal that you wish to end the meeting.
  1. Reduce eye contact.
  2. Glance at the clock or your watch.
  3. Start shuffling papers, tapping a pencil, or drumming your fingers.
  4. Put your hand on your telephone.
  5. Say "Could we continue this later when I'm not so swamped?" or "I won't take any more of your time."
  6. Stand up and extend your hand.
  7. Come out from behind your desk and walk toward the door.

GROUP MEETINGS

Try to limit group meetings to 45 minutes. People get restless after that. If you must go on, call a break.

If you are not the chair and the meetings always start late, come late or bring busywork with you.

Send members of your staff to represent you. For more on meetings, see Chapter 34.

ONE-ON-ONE COMMUNICATION

Apply all the communication skills we discussed in previous chapters. Communication competency prevents misunderstandings, mistakes, and the need for repeats—all of which are big time wasters.

If you tend to be verbose on the telephone, put an egg timer next to the phone.

When windy talkers trap you in a corridor, wait until they pause for breath. Then summarize what they said and start edging away. If they continue to talk, ask them to excuse you and leave. Say that you have an appointment (you can always have an appointment with your inner soul, can't you?).

TIPS FOR SAVING TIME

We have already given you these:

- Avoid procrastination or perfectionism.
- Delegate what others can do or can be trained to do.
- Plan, schedule, and set priorities.
- Improve your communication skills.
- Learn to say no.
- Reduce wasted time at meetings.
- Use margin replies for informal written correspondence.
- Keep your desk ready for action.
- Select the most appropriate channel for communication.

Here are more:

- Express as much appreciation to people for saving your time as you do to people who help you save money.
- Reduce interruptions by coming to work early or staying late, by finding a good hiding place, or by using a "Thank You for Not Disturbing" sign.
- Monitor your time usage. Keep a log.
- Use waiting times to read or do short tasks.
- Make phone calls in bunches.
- Refer calls and visitors to others.
- Decrease your socializing time.
- Study and streamline your work flow patterns.
- Use videotapes for repetitive teaching (eg, orientation and training of new hires).
- Use dictation instead of doing the typing yourself.
- Use the telephone for conference calls.
- Ask for help when you need it.

Ten Major Time Blunders

1. Tolerating abuses of your open-door policy
2. Overuse of memos, reports, and electronic messages
3. Unnecessary or poorly run meetings
4. Lack of assigning and delegating
5. Too much socializing
6. Doing other people's work and solving their problems

7. Accepting too many unimportant assignments
8. Lack of planning
9. Inadequate paper flow and storage
10. Procrastination

TIME ABUSES BY OTHERS

Time theft may be America's biggest crime. Robert Half, a personnel expert, writes, "The average worker in the United States has an average of 7 to 12 unscheduled absences each year. He wastes 18% of the time he is supposed to be working. That equals nine 35-hour weeks . . . a "vacation" of more than two months per year at work."[1]

Major Time Thefts

- unjustified sick days
- tardiness or leaving early
- long breaks or meals
- leaving one's post for personal trips (eg, shopping)
- doing personal tasks on the job
- excessive socialization and idle conversation
- interrupting others
- wandering around the building
- excessive personal phone calls
- personal or family visitors
- daydreaming

Nip bad habits in the bud by better coaching and counseling. Remember, however, that your subordinates are your customers and should be treated with kindness and consideration. Show compassion for employees who have latchkey children or who have other special situations.

The first step in eliminating or decreasing this time waste is to be aware of it. Our old strategy of managing by wandering around pays off handsomely. Merely appearing on the scene squelches idle conversations and lets people know that you are aware of their inappropriate absences from the work area.

Changes in workstations can often help. Some employees accomplish more when they work alone. Others get more done when working in a group.

Study work flow patterns and other systems to find out whether you can achieve more efficiency.

NOTE

1. R. Half, "Management Roundup," *Management Review 73* (1984): 7.

SUGGESTED READINGS

R. Bittel, *Right on Time: the Complete Guide for Time-Pressured Managers* (New York, NY: McGraw-Hill, 1991).

M.E. Douglass and D.H. Douglass, *Time Management for Teams* (New York, NY: AMACOM, 1992).

D. Scott, *The Telephone and Time Management* (Los Altos, CA: Crisp Publishers, 1988).

PART VI

Self-Enhancement for Supervisors

Chapter 38

Coping with Stress and Burnout

- external causes of stress
- internal factors
- responsibilities of supervisors
- how to reduce stress in your department
- departmental stress programs
- burnout
- your personal stress managing

One of every three workers in the United States who call in sick has a stress-related problem. According to a report in *Time Magazine* [June 6, 1983], the cost of stress-related illnesses in the United States was $50 to $75 billion a year back in the early 1980s. It is probably several times that now. In this country, the four most used drugs—headache remedies, tranquilizers, anti-hypertensive agents, and ulcer medications—are for stress-related conditions.

EXTERNAL CAUSES OF STRESS

Most of us have limited control over the external factors that contribute to stress. External stressors at work include:

- *Work environment:* parking difficulties, uncomfortable or noisy working environment, equipment failures, and safety concerns. Infection and safety concerns are especially prevalent in health care institutions.
- *The job itself:* too much work, time pressures, organizational and procedural changes, job insecurity
- *Work relationships:* harassment, threats, personality incompatibilities, difficult patients or patients' families, competition between departments and workers
- *Hierarchical factors:* lack of goals, mission or objectives, confusing or difficult policies, lack of support from management

- *Poor leadership:* flawed communication, favoritism, discrimination, insufficient authority to fulfill responsibilities, nit-picking, unclear responsibilities
- *Outside factors:* family, financial, legal, or health concerns

INTERNAL FACTORS

These causes dwell within ourselves. They act as multipliers of the external factors that besiege us:

- Lack of confidence or self-esteem due to lack of expertise or experience.
- Health problems resulting in decreased immunity and frequent illnesses.
- Irrational thinking. False perceptions of powerlessness and flawed assumptions may be rampant. Some people set unrealistic goals and aspirations. Employees often stretch virtues into evils (eg, trying to be a perfectionist, being too emotionally involved in patient care, or making work the most important thing in life).
- Clash of actions with values. Stress occurs when our actions are not congruent with our values. For example, when we spend long hours at work (action) and neglect our family responsibilities (value).
- Emotions. Being buffeted by a negative emotion such as fear, guilt, anger, or resentment is like trying to drive a car with the emergency brake on. Movement is limited and there is a great strain on the parts.
    1. Fears. We are beset with all kinds of fear—with or without real basis: fear of job loss, fear of failure of rejection, and fear of getting acquired immunodeficiency syndrome or hepatitis. These fears are compounded by the ever-increasing rate of technological and organizational changes, and lack of job security.
    2. Guilt. Guilt is characterized by feelings of inadequacy and inferiority. It makes us indulge in self-criticism, and in the criticism of others. People who feel guilt use "victim language" like: "I should," "I have to," or "It wasn't my fault."
    3. Anger. The stress produced by daily contact with difficult people is often associated with anger. When this is not resolved, frustration sets in. There is usually an underlying hurt or fear, especially the fear that you cannot cope with the situation or that you are regarded as unimportant. Resentment is a subtle, continuous, seething anger that is seldom expressed directly to the person or persons who are resented.

RESPONSIBILITIES OF SUPERVISORS

Since leadership plays an important role in the amount of stress within a group, supervisors have much accountability for stress control. Their four major responsibilities are:

1. to reduce the stress that they cause;
2. to protect their reports from stress induced by other people;
3. to empower their employees and raise their self-esteem; and
4. to recognize the signs and symptoms of burnout and take remedial steps.

HOW TO REDUCE STRESS IN YOUR DEPARTMENT

Hire Stress-Resistant People

Select employees whose needs and abilities correspond with the demands of the job. See Chapter 7 for the kinds of questions that help to spot the susceptible people during employment interviews.

Orient and Train Thoroughly

Well-designed orientation and training programs reduce anxiety, create realistic job expectations, and provide the skills needed to work effectively. Clear and unambivalent policies and procedures, when enforced uniformly and fairly, reduce hierarchical pressures. Active mentoring provides additional stress resistance.

Empower Employees

Individuals who feel that they are in control of their work and their future are better able to handle stress. When they are competent and their skills are marketable, they become more burnout resistant. Self-empowerment and empowerment by management are essential to the development of this mindset (see Chapter 31).

Counsel Stressed Workers

Support your employees by word and action, especially when performance drops off. Get them to express their concerns and frustrations. Help them to reinforce the good things about themselves by reviewing their past successes. Encourage them to adopt realistic goals. Refer them to professional counselors if this seems indicated. Eliminate specific stressors when possible without interfering with the work flow or imposing on other workers.

Ensure Time for Breaks

Make certain that your people get their breaks. Encourage them to use the time in a healthy way (eg, socializing, exercising, relaxing, and meditating). If possible, provide health food such as fruit instead of donuts and coffee.

Modify Assignments, Team Compositions, Management Style

Rotating assignments or shifts may be appropriate in specific instances. Transfers or changes in work schedules may be therapeutic.

DEPARTMENTAL STRESS PROGRAMS

Support groups are most effective when they function under their own leadership. Participants can talk openly about their personal responses to the demands of their work. They find common problems and search for remedial measures. At their meetings, they may use guest speakers, audiovisuals, reading materials, and brainstorming.

Coping Methods for Departmental Stress Programs

- relaxation or meditation techniques
- exercise
- diet adjustment
- review of job designs, policies, and procedures
- solving of communication, ethical, and work-flow problems
- conflict resolution

There is increasing interest in wellness and disease prevention. Exercise, healthy diet, and supplemental vitamins and minerals appear to increase immunity and counter the harmful physiological effects of stress. Health stores feature many herbs and neutraceutical combinations that are alleged to help cope with stress. Employees appreciate talks from dietitians and health experts.

BURNOUT

Burnout is the condition of emotional and physical collapse caused by unchecked escalation of stress. Everyone has their breaking point, but most emotionally stable people protect themselves intuitively by focusing on current tasks while shutting out most past or future problems.

The most vulnerable employees are the perfectionists, workaholics, overachievers, insecure job holders, and people who have low self-esteem.

Signs and Symptoms of Burnout

Anxiety or depression
Chronic fatigue
Insomnia and nightmares
Headaches, backaches, premenstrual
  syndrome
Loss of appetite

Waking up tired
High blood pressure
Cardiac irregularities
Duodenal ulcers
Elevated cholesterol
Compulsive eating

What Colleagues and Families Notice

Emotional outbursts
High-pitched, nervous laughter
Increased use of sick leave
Resistance to change, inflexibility
Avoids making decision
Increased use of alcohol or drugs
Talks a lot about escaping
Increased irritability and complaints
Decline in work performance
Trembling, tics, or stuttering
Lack of enthusiasm and energy

The Four Typical Stages of Coping with Burnout

1. Doing nothing, hoping it will go away.
2. Seeking fast relief from alcohol, drugs, and/or pharmaceuticals.
3. Taking it out on others.
4. Seeking professional help.

When an employee is ravaged by full-blown burnout, continued employment is impossible, and the person must receive extended professional counseling. In its early stages remedial measures can reverse the illness.

It is the responsibility of supervisors to be alert for the signs and symptoms of burnout and to persuade the person to get professional help. They can modify or eliminate major stressors and provide psychological support during the employee's therapy.

YOUR PERSONAL STRESS MANAGING

Self-empowerment is the key to immunizing you against stress and preventing burnout. You have more power than you realize. You have some degree of control over each of your major stressors. For example:

- You can eliminate your job insecurity by making your services more marketable.
- You can fire (with cause) that employee who makes life miserable for you.
- You have the power to make most of the daily decisions you face.
- You can make people smile, laugh, frown, and even cry.
- You do not need permission to do most of the things you do (eg, thank someone, hold a meeting, ask for help, say "no," or pack up and leave).

Augment Your Competencies

- Keep up to date technically and professionally.
- Fine-tune your interpersonal skills.
- Make yourself more marketable.
- Request more educational support.
- Train for alternative jobs or vocations.

Eliminate Perceived Barriers

Separate what is only a perception from that which is reality. Challenge each of your assumptions.

Improve Your Self-Talk

Shower your subconsciousness with positive affirmations. Affirmations are simple statements that proclaim positive facts about yourself or someone else. Articulate them plainly and emphatically. They are clear, brief, strong, and positive, and they grow more effective with repetition. Some examples are "I will" (instead of "I should" or "I will try"), "I am in control here," "I am a worthy person," "I feel good about that," or "I earned that." Affirmations have a way of becoming reality.

Kick the habit of putting yourself down. Instead of criticizing yourself and telling yourself what you cannot do, congratulate yourself for the things that you can do. Do not compare yourself unfavorably with others. When criticized unfairly by a superior, say to yourself "That's only her opinion." Neutralize negative data by saying "cancel" when negative thoughts start to flow into your consciousness. Say it aloud instead of just thinking it—the sound provides double reinforcement. Follow the "cancel" with an affirmation.

Surround Yourself with Optimistic, Enthusiastic Doers

The people you associate with affect the way you feel and how you ultimately behave. Examine your friendships and relationships at work and during your leisure hours. If you have been lunching with negative and critical people, find more upbeat folks. Eat with a different group each day. Put some limits on the time you spend with negative friends and relatives.

Join social and community organizations. Most organizations feature optimistic, energetic people. Become a leader in one of these organizations. Almost anyone can be elected to an office in a professional group. All you have to do is attend the business meetings, sit up near the front, and ask an occasional question or make a few comments. On the other hand, do not get bogged down by social or professional activities that are stressful or take too much time away from work or family.

Practice Success Imaging

There are two kinds of success imagery. In *results imagery*, you visualize a highly successful outcome of a future event. For example, when preparing to give a talk, you picture your audience giving you a standing ovation. In *process imagery*, you visualize every step of the activity and feel each emotion. For example, in the above scenario, you visualize the moderator introducing you. You feel your heart pounding. You see yourself taking a deep breath and forcing a smile. You hear your introductory remarks.

Laugh More

> *When the going gets tough, the tough lighten up!*

The simple act of laughter increases our body's endorphins—the stress fighters. People who watch a video comedy have higher levels of endorphins and lower levels of adrenaline and cortisol—the stress producers. Snicker when you make a little mistake. Enjoy a hearty laugh, and actively seek humor. When you visit a work site, notice the differences in the amount of joking and smiles. You can sense the reflection of stress.

- Escape, literally or mentally. Take a walk on your breaks. Find a quiet place to relax and daydream.
- Learn relaxation or meditation techniques.
- Expand your supportive network (see Chapter 41).
- Keep a log of your successes.
- Behave assertively (see Chapter 41).

RECOMMENDED READING AND LISTENING

M. English, *How To Feel Great About Yourself and Your Life* (New York, NY: AMACOM, 1992).

R. Mellott, *Stress Management for Professionals* (Boulder, CO: CareerTrack Publishers, 1987), four audiotapes.

B. Sommer, *Psycho-Cybernetics 2000* (Englewood Cliffs, NJ: Prentice Hall, 1993).

B.E. Statland, "Caught in the Web: Combating Work Stress in the Information Age," *Medical Laboratory Observer 29*, no. 8 (1997): 82–89.

Chapter 39

Career Development For Supervisors

- the five criteria of success
- characteristics of achievers
- who is responsible for your career?
- worthwhile careers involve taking risk
- the winds of change blow in opportunities
- increase your promotability and marketability
- nine steps to success
- how to negotiate for more compensation

"Luck is where you find it—but you have to find it.
Meanwhile, get as much experience as you can, so
you'll be ready for luck when you run into it."[1]

Henny Youngman

FIVE CRITERIA OF SUCCESS

Most of us would be happy if we could meet the following five criteria of success:

1. peace of mind,
2. health and energy,
3. a loving relationship,
4. freedom from financial worry, and
5. a perception of personal fulfillment.

CHARACTERISTICS OF ACHIEVERS

- Achievers have a winning attitude.
- Achievers are enthusiastic about their work.

- Achievers adjust quickly to change.
- Achievers accept ambiguity and uncertainty.
- Achievers are rapid learners and invest in lifelong education.
- Achievers hold themselves accountable for outcomes.
- Achievers manage their own morale and empowerment.
- Achievers are problem solvers, not complainers.
- Achievers set goals.
- Achievers use their time wisely.
- Achievers have a reputation for innovativeness.
- Achievers are technically or professionally competent.
- Achievers are assertive and stress resistant.
- Achievers are great communicators.
- Achievers are customer oriented.

WHO IS RESPONSIBLE FOR YOUR CAREER?

You are!!! See Chapter 30.

WORTHWHILE CAREERS INVOLVE TAKING RISKS

Excellence requires, by definition, deviance from the norm. That deviance involves career risks. You achieve excellence by making unpopular or risky decisions that are avoided by others. Courage is needed.

Risk taking is essential if you want to advance. Even sitting pat involves risk because a job may become obsolete. Preparing for the future requires making decisions, some of which involve considerable time, expense, and sacrifice. Risk takers exhibit the flexibility that today's employers appreciate. Self-confident, enthusiastic, and optimistic, the risk takers regard mistakes as learning experiences.

We are not recommending that people take foolish risks or neglect to get sufficient information to make good decisions. Risk taking can be overdone, even foolhardy. Avoid making the same mistake twice. Do not disregard your intuitive warnings and past experience. Reduce risks by adding safety measures. For example, find a new job before putting your present one on the line.

Answer These Questions Before Taking a Major Risk

What is my goal or objective?
What is the best and the worst outcome?
What additional information do I need? From what sources?

What are the alternative measures?
What are the relative rewards and risks of each alternative?
What barriers must I overcome?
What support is available?
What contingency plan is available?
How can I eliminate or reduce amount of risk?
How will delay affect the benefit and the risk?

Eliminate Your Fears

Two of our most powerful fears are fear of failure and fear of the unknown. You must be willing to take career risks and to regard failures as learning experiences.

WINDS OF CHANGE BLOW IN OPPORTUNITIES

The myth that opportunity only knocks once is ridiculous. Opportunity is knocking all the time, if people would only listen. Because opportunities often present themselves without any warning, always be prepared to grab the brass ring when it comes around.

Investigate Opportunities in Your Workplace

New services such as patient-focused care present new challenges. Consider projects or new assignments that solve problems for your employer or your leader.

Do not forget all the administrative roles needed to carry out various organizational changes. Reporters comment on the loss of jobs at various institutions. However, perceptive observers note that while employers are eliminating some positions, they are offering many new ones. The parking lots are still full. Reengineering, alliances, new services, and adjusting to the mandates of state and federal regulations create fissures that require new positions.

The best new jobs in your institution are not those you find in the local newspaper or in the company newsletter. They may not appear on the bulletin boards outside personnel departments. They reach you via the grapevine or your personal network. Now is a critical time to expand that network and to latch onto mentors who are at the forefront of your organization's initiatives.

Learn all you can about your organization's initiatives. What initiatives are your employer or your manager contemplating? Reflect on how you can benefit from these changes. Still better, suggest some changes of your own. Maybe you can create a new and better job for yourself. Consider possible new services or customers, marketing strategies, satellite operations, or restructuring. Look, sound, and act as someone who is already qualified to assume a new role. You want your boss to feel comfortable when he or she tries to picture you in that slot.

Organizational restructuring creates opportunities for people who are willing and able to move into new careers. Supervisors who dislike controlling others are usually happier when they revert to nonsupervisory roles. Alert professionals are always on the lookout for new positions created by any restructuring in their institutions or elsewhere. Organizations in crises are always in need of capable leaders who can help their employer survive.

Design a new position for yourself that will make your work more satisfying for you and more valuable to the organization. Before you discuss your proposal, outline a comprehensive plan. What do you want and what do you need to get there? In these negotiations be assertive, but not demanding, about changing your position description or assignments. Be willing to compromise.

Be Alert for Outside Opportunities

Do your own market research. What are current and future trends in the industry or in other areas where you may have career interests? What skills do you need now and in the future? Consider the advantages and disadvantages of each type of position or employers. For example, professionals who are bored by working in the same environment may find more satisfying roles as on-call employees for multiple medical facilities.

Consider a vocational change. Many nurses and other health care supervisors are finding their niches in managed care organizations. See Chapter 25 for a description of some of the positions available in the managed care industry.

Many people use career changes to do things that they never had time for or to develop previously latent talents. Consult with your mentors. Career counselors are just as close as the yellow pages of your phone book.

INCREASE YOUR PROMOTABILITY AND MARKETABILITY

Hard Work Is Not Enough

Hard work alone rarely earns promotions or gets big raises. Employers applaud excellent past performance and usually base rewards and recognition on that basis. Nevertheless, they have even a greater incentive to promote people who have the potential for doing still more for them in the future. When managers consider promoting someone, they are thinking "How will promoting this person help me?"

Employability requires keeping up with the literature, attending educational and professional meetings, and expanding your personal network. Question mentors and other people in your network about opportunities in your present field or in a new one. Ask them for advice on whom to contact.

In the final chapter we discuss the importance of workplace politics and networking in job advancement and rewards.

What Current Employers Look For

Employers look for people who can make good and quick decisions, who can come up with solutions to problems, and who have enthusiasm and initiative. They want leaders who can coordinate new teams, integrate new technology across department lines, and accept supervisory roles created by workforce reductions.

Knowing that front-line supervisors and their staffs can spot opportunities for improvement before executives do, employers want leaders who are observant, proactive, and innovative. They value flexibility and adaptability more than ever.

Review Your Present Status

Take a second look at your career as it now stands by asking yourself the following questions:

- Am I doing what I want to do?
- Do I spend most of the workday doing things I enjoy?
- What aspects of my present situation am I reluctant to change?
- What changes in my present job would decrease the amount of time I spend doing what I dislike doing, and/or increase the time spent on enjoyable tasks?
- Should I move in the direction of generalist or specialist?
- Would I like to switch from full time to part time, or vice versa?
- Are my actions congruent with my personal values? Is my present career hurting my family life?
- To reach my new goals, what must I sacrifice? Am I willing to make that sacrifice?
- How do my family members feel about a change?
- Should I look for a different job within this organization or elsewhere?

Clarify Your Values

Values should weigh heavily in career decisions. A value is what in life is important to you. Without having first established your values, you may lack a clear idea of why you seek a particular goal. With respect to work, do you value challenge, interesting assignments, recognition, involvement, control, or innovation?

Is the absence of stress important? Do you prefer independence to teamwork? With respect to outside values, do you want more time with family, friends, hobbies, or recreational activities. Financial considerations are important. Is a higher income a top priority, or can you postpone monetary rewards while preparing for a new career?

Expand Your Competencies

Each individual must make up his or her own mind about whether to specialize or generalize. Some employers are practically begging for people with a hard-to-find skill, while still more employers want people who can broaden their area of competency when occupational needs change. Having one's ear to the ground helps to know which direction to take. The important action is to continue with education and training.

All health care supervisors must continue to balance their educational efforts between those that are professional or technical with those that are supervisory. In the past health care professionals tended to neglect the latter and concentrate on teachings learned at the meetings of their professional societies or in the professional journals. This is changing as supervisors realize that their performance ratings depend more on their leadership ability than on their professional expertise.

Develop a Reputation for Innovativeness, Flexibility, and Customer Service

Directly or indirectly, customers' evaluation of service determines the success of care providers. Hospitals and managed care organizations are soliciting more feedback from patients, physicians, and other external customers. More of them seek the perceptions of internal customers such as departments that service other departments.

When departments fail to live up to expectations, their work may be reassigned to other in-house departments or contracted with outside providers. Heads often roll.

Do your best to build rapport with people outside your department, especially those that you serve—your internal customers. Accept invitations to sit in on their meetings and social functions. Volunteer for special assignments that provide interdepartmental contacts. Socialize with them at organizational training or informational meetings. Invite them to your department.

Promote Your Capabilities

Make yourself more visible, but do it with class. Be assertive, but not pushy. Come to meetings prepared, and participate actively. Ask questions and make suggestions. Volunteer to make department presentations or to represent your unit at management meetings. Look like someone who is on the way up. Appearances still count.

When you get compliments, ask the givers if they would put them in writing and send a copy to your manager.

Get personal calling cards and use them. Keep a file of your accomplishments and bring them up at your performance reviews.

Expand Your Personal Network

Some people complain that "It's not what you know, but who you know." They are right, but you invariably find that the complainers have made little or no attempts to get to know people who can help them. When it comes to promotions and finding jobs elsewhere, mentors are among the most important people in your network. We address mentoring and personal networks in the final chapter.

STEPS TO SUCCESS

Most people spend more time planning a vacation than they spend planning their career. Do not be one of these folks. Try these nine steps to success.

Step 1.   Start with a vision. Martin Luther King Jr. had a vision ("I have a dream"). Do you? You can accomplish what you want, but be sure that you know what that is. Visualize the scene when you have reached your main goals in life. What do you like about that vision? Fame and fortune? Being in charge of a large department? Being highly respected because of your technical expertise? What would you like a speaker to say about you at your retirement ceremony? The answer to that question helps you to elucidate your vision.

Step 2.   Select your mission statement and major goals. A mission statement is the "why"—the reason for your goals. It is a declaration of direction that has the power to design your activities for the rest of your life. A good mission statement is one that has meaning for you. It may be to improve the medical care in your community by serving as a top official in a health care institution or to spend your retirement in Florida. The final statement may not be as important as the time you take to reflect on your life and what is important to you.

Mission statements provide the motivation to accomplish our goals. Hal Lancaster,[2] who writes an excellent column on career managing in the *Wall Street Journal,* invited his readers to submit copies of their mission statements to him. While he found a great divergence in what the responders regarded as mission statements, he came up with a personal statement that could serve as an example for you with some simple modifications. Hal's mission statement is, "My mission is to enlighten and entertain people through my writing and to help provide a life for my family that is emotionally and financially secure, loving, learning and fun."

A goal is the "what." A person without a goal is like a ship without a rudder. Once you've tuned in to your goal, you will find that the workings of your unconscious help you to reach it. You become open to sources of information that you were not aware of and you gravitate toward people who can help you.

Besides career goals, consider your family and personal life goals. Because of limitations of time and money, you may have to sacrifice some goals to promote others. We all know of broken homes that result from neglect of family goals. There are many early deaths because a high-powered professional sacrificed his health on the altar of a career.

If one of your goals is to get promoted, take a piece of paper and jot down all the advantages and disadvantages of that change. You may decide that at least for the present, this is not a good choice. Before you finalize your goals, discuss them with your family, close friends, mentors, and your manager. You will probably need their help along the way.

Document your mission statement and goals. Studies have shown that people who do so are much more likely to succeed. Some people carry their mission statement with them in their wallets. Others review their statements periodically to provide inspiration and motivation.

Step 3.   Prepare a list of objectives for each major goal. Objectives are steps to achieving goals. For example, if one of your goals is to be promoted to a higher management position, one of your objectives may be to earn a master's degree in business administration. A good objective should be specific, challenging, realistic, achievable, and measurable.

Step 4.   Take an inventory of your strengths and weaknesses. Be honest and forthright about weaknesses. You will not correct them if you refuse to admit that they exist. Review your last performance appraisal and discuss this with your manager. Activities that supervisors frequently feel they do poorly include writing letters and job descriptions, holding disciplinary and employment interviews, delegating, budgeting, and resolving employee conflicts.

Step 5.   Prepare a needs analysis. Catalog your development needs using the list of weaknesses you prepared. Break them down into smaller categories if necessary.

The acquisition of new education, skills, and experience is imperative. The people with the most intellectual capital and experience find new opportunities with their current employer or with other organizations.

Step 6.   Document potential barriers and how you plan to cope with them. Common barriers are time, finances, and resistance from family.

Step 7.   Chart your action steps and add target dates.
Begin your initiative with a small first step (eg, Getting a catalog of educational courses or signing up for a seminar). See Exhibit 39–1 for an example of goals, objectives, and actions.

Step 8.   Implement the process. Transfer your action plans to daily "to do" lists.

Step 9.   Monitor, evaluate, and reward.
Your motivation is stronger if you enjoy the process as well as reaching your goal. For example, it is much more difficult to continue with a long educational program if you dislike taking the classes.

Exhibit 39–1   Example of Goal, Objectives, and Actions

Goal: To be promoted to unit manager
Objectives: To meet professional requirements by [date]; to meet administrative requirements by [date]; to meet supervisory requirements by [date]
Actions:
  1. Complete courses needed to get MBA:
   • get support of family
   • seek financial support
   • enroll in local university
  2. Study administrative functions of unit:
   • computer information system
   • quality improvement program
   • budget preparation and use
   • routine and special reports
   • anticipation of next inspection by Joint Commission on Accreditation of Healthcare Organizations
   • procedure manuals and employee handbook
  3. Educate self about supervisory functions
   • read at least one book on supervisory skills for new supervisors
   • attend at least one seminar, workshop, or college course on the topics of leadership, planning, counseling, interviewing, writing skills, delegating, negotiating, empowering, and career development
   • volunteer to serve on a cross-functional team or a quality improvement committee
   • find a mentor and expand professional network by at least one new person each month

Reward yourself for what you accomplish. Self-evaluation and self-reward decrease your need for approval from other people. The advantage of praising yourself instead of waiting for others to do it is that you can lay it on thick and in the right places. Do not wait until you have reached your goal or achieved an objective. Do it on a frequent basis.

Watch Out for the Career Killers

People who fail usually blame other people, society, or fate, but most cases represent self-destruction. (See Exhibit 39–2).

HOW TO NEGOTIATE FOR MORE COMPENSATION

There is an old myth that if you work hard you will be rewarded. Many employees earn big raises, but few get them. In a typical health care institution, a person whose performance is rated as outstanding receives a salary increase that is 2% to 3% above that of the average worker. Big deal! What is even worse is that if you have been getting those kinds of raises for several years, you may find that your salary is lower than that of new people in equivalent roles.[3]

If you never ask, you are not likely to get what you are worth. To receive a substantial salary increase, you must earn it, AND you usually must negotiate for it. If you are as good as they say you are, your superiors should take your requests seriously.

Exhibit 39–2 The Career Killers

- Lack of, or inappropriate, goals, objectives, or priorities
- Fears and inability to make decisions or to take action
- Poor time management
- Lack of motivation or enthusiasm
- Drifting into obsolescence
- Too many diversions or outside interests
- Lack of self-control, trustworthiness, or integrity
- Lack of flexibility or ability to adjust to change
- Ineffective leadership or followership
- Lack of interpersonal skills
- Problems with alcohol or drugs
- Passivity and negative self-talk
- Poor team player

Important Do Nots When Negotiating for More Pay

- Do not tell your manager that you deserve a raise because you have been with the organization for umpteen years. Seniority does not count much anymore. It's how valuable you are to the organization and what your potential is.
- Do not try to convince your manager that you should get a raise because you need more money. You may get some sympathy, but not much more in your pay envelope.
- Do not rely on your manager giving you more money because you are doing a terrific job and your performance rating is outstanding.
- Do not threaten to resign—at least not early in the process or in haste.

Your manager probably has the power to get you more money despite his or her strong protestations to the contrary. Employees who resign when told that funds were not available often learn that their replacements started at higher salaries than they were being paid.

Preparation for Walking into the Lion's Den

As in all negotiations, preparation, confidence, and sales ability are critical. The first prerequisite is knowing your market value and using that value to decide the figure you will shoot for. Research the pay scale for your kind of work. Know what competitors are paying, and be sure that these comparable jobs are available.

There are several sources for finding your market value. Lancaster[4] claims that few managers know their market value, despite a wealth of salary information. He suggests researching business publications, professional groups, cyberspace, alumni, and your alma mater to see what recruiters are offering. You can also check with your mentors and other members of your personal network, and see what you can find in the library. There is a telephone service called "PinPoint Salary Service" (773-472–5279) that will do research for you and provide a print-out of your competitive range.

If your coworkers all receive about the same compensation, factor in the functions, responsibilities, and special competencies that only you possess. If you are directly instrumental in producing value (eg, finding customers or obtaining grants that can be expressed in terms of dollars), add that information to your presentation.

Do not be passive in your approach. Equally bad is to stalk into your manager's office and demand more money. You must use a little finesse. Despite that squeamish feeling about a confrontation over salary, you must be assertive. The meek may inherit the earth, but they seldom get substantial raises. If you're a worthy recipient, your manager will feel just as uncomfortable about your request as you do.

The timing of your pitch is critical. When your employer is in financial difficulty or your manager is experiencing work, health, or family problems, do not expect a favorable response. Never approach bosses when they are very busy, emotionally upset, or in the middle of an important project or crisis. Sometimes a good opportunity is right after you have received a glowing performance appraisal.

Be prepared to compromise. There are many things other than salary. Would you be satisfied with a better benefit package? How about funds for continuing education or a research project? Would a work schedule change enable you to earn money elsewhere? In academic centers, professionals value the opportunity to carry on a private practice, do research, write a book, consult, or teach elsewhere.

If you are turned down, ask what you must do or achieve to earn a raise. Use the response to make appropriate modifications of your career development program (or to start looking for another job). Check back periodically with your manager to find out how you are doing.

NOTES

1. H. Youngman, "Lessons in Life from Henny Youngman," *Bottom Line-Personal 18,* no. 18 (1997): 13.
2. H. Lancaster, "It's the Thoughts That Count in Putting Missions in Writing," *Wall Street Journal,* Tuesday, October 28, 1997, B1.
3. H. Lancaster, "How Do You Know What You're Worth in a Job Marketplace?" *Wall Street Journal,* Tuesday, September 30, 1997, B1.
4. Lancaster, "How Do You Know What You're Worth?"

RECOMMENDED LISTENING

L. Milteer, *Success Self-Programming* (Boulder, CO: CareerTrack Publishers, 1987), two audiotapes.

D. Waitley, *Dennis Waitley Live: Powerful Strategies for Reaching Your Potential* (Boulder, CO: CareerTrack Publishers, 1987), six audiotapes.

Chapter 40

Succession Planning

- benefits of succession planning
- risks in picking and training a successor
- selection and training plan
- grooming your successor
- monitoring your successor

"If you haven't prepared someone to step into your shoes, you're not ready to take a successful step upward."[1]

In today's uncertain times, the need for succession planning is more vital than ever. Everyone in charge of a work unit should answer these four questions:

1. If my services are suddenly not available, how would my responsibilities be discharged?
2. How long would it take to find and train my replacement?
3. Who is on board right now who could take over?
4. What have I done to prepare a successor?

BENEFITS OF SUCCESSION PLANNING

The strength and adaptability of an organization are linked to how fully it has developed the talents of its personnel. This development depends largely on the willingness and capability of supervisors to share their expertise with potential successors.

After you have mastered your job and are looking for advancement within your organization, make yourself dispensable. Not to do that freezes you into your present job because your superiors regard you as indispensable in that position.

There are other benefits. When you have a trained backup, you can do the things you did not have time for previously. This increases your value to the organization and enhances your career.

You can be absent from the work scene with the assurance that your unit will function smoothly in your absence. You can skip those calls back to work to check on how things are going.

RISKS IN PICKING AND TRAINING A SUCCESSOR

There is always the possibility that you pick a lemon, but remember that the only people who never fall down are those who keep sitting in their chairs. Every leader worthy of that title has made poor decisions and choices, but they regard such mistakes as learning experiences, and they move on. Careful planning and thorough preparation minimize this risk.

A more frequent risk is that your protégé gets promoted out from under you or is enticed away by a competitor. While this elicits pangs of disappointment proportional to the effort you made in developing the individual, you still get important benefits: a reputation as a career builder, the gratitude of the person you trained, having a supporter (your former protégé) in other units or organizations, and the ability to repeat the process with greater competency.

Some supervisors worry that a protégé may prove to be a more effective leader than they are. Maybe they would be putting their job in jeopardy. These supervisors usually have already displayed this fear by their reluctance to delegate. These concerns are based on false assumptions. It is rare for supervisors to lose their jobs because a protégé outperforms them. On the contrary, because they will have more time to expand their own expertise, their security will increase.

SELECTION AND TRAINING PLAN

Finding the appropriate understudy can be simple or complicated. You do not have far to look if you already have an assistant and are satisfied with that person's potential. In that situation, you have probably already trained that person to handle supervisory tasks and to demonstrate leadership ability. You already know his or her strengths and where additional training or experience is needed.

If you do not have an assistant and must choose from several employees who have the same potential, this can be a more delicate matter. Do not take for granted that all these people are interested in your job. This is something you should have learned during performance reviews, or during your daily contacts.

Do not waste your time preparing reluctant successors unless they have such impressive leadership talents that it is worth trying to recruit them. Do not be in a hurry to designate a single candidate as the anointed one. The moment such a move becomes apparent, others stop striving for the job. Some may see the handwriting on the wall and leave.

When you have several prospects, treat them as equal contenders. Delegate supervisory and administrative responsibilities to each and document how they handle them. Let them take turns moderating staff meetings or representing you at interdepartmental meetings. When you are going to be absent, appoint different substitutes. Pay close attention to how they handle these situations. Does the work get done? Do they try to do everything themselves, or do they get the cooperation of other team members? How did their fellow workers perceive their performance?

The fairness of these delegated responsibilities and the documentation of performance may later save you the embarrassment of being charged with discrimination or favoritism.

Any effective program of supervisory development begins with an appraisal of a person's strengths, weaknesses, and potential. It sets attainable development goals. The program usually includes practical on-the-job coaching, formal educational courses, attendance at management seminars, and selected readings.

GROOMING YOUR SUCCESSOR

How you prepare the chosen one is very important. The process consists largely, but not exclusively, of a series of delegations and special assignments. Ensure that the person does each of these tasks often enough to become competent and comfortable. Make certain that he or she has enough time to handle daily responsibilities.

Besides these delegations and assignments, take your protégés to some of your meetings. Let them sit in on interviews you hold and accompany you as you "manage by walking around." Work jointly on things like budgets or plans.

Developing a successor involves much mentoring. Provide opportunities for meeting senior managers and important customers. The latter include internal customers—those units that serve or are served by your department. Provide visibility by letting your successor give reports to the bigwigs and chair meetings.

When your chosen one does something worthy of mention, let your boss know about it. In your performance appraisal reports on your protégé, use phrases such as "shows leadership ability" and "is developing into an excellent facilitator."

A worthy protégé will do most of the planning and energizing on her own. He or she will:

- decide what seminars to attend, what courses and workshops to take, what books to study, and what periodicals to read;
- set goals and develop action plans; and
- make the extra effort needed to work on career development while still discharging daily responsibilities.

An outline for a training plan is seen in Exhibit 40–1.

Exhibit 40–1 Action Plan for Skill Enhancement

SUBJECT:	(Skill to be enhanced)
PURPOSE:	(Why this is important)
OBJECTIVES:	(How success will be measured)
RESOURCES:	(Funds and other materials needed)
OBSTACLES:	(People, time, other) (How they can be removed)
IMPLEMENTATION:	(List in sequence the steps to achieve the desired change. If possible, assign target dates.)

MONITORING YOUR SUCCESSOR

The true test of managerial ability is not only that the people know how to do things they were taught. It is also how they do the things that they were not taught. Meet regularly with the person to discuss progress. Do not wait for the annual formal performance review.

NOTE

1. M. Feinberg, "Succession Planning," *Wall Street Journal,* November 12, 1990: A14.

RECOMMENDED READING

C.R. McConnell, "Succession Planning," *Health Care Supervisor 15,* no. 2 (1996): 69–78.

Chapter 41

Networks and Organizational Politics

- benefits of networking
- potential participants in your personal network
- computer networks
- characteristics of great networkers
- politics and the informal organization
- negative politics
- positive political scripts and tactics
- coping with the person you report to

PERSONAL NETWORKS

> *"A wise man knows everything, a shrewd man*
> *knows everybody."*

> Old Chinese Proverb

Developing outside relationships is largely a matter of networking. Luebbert[1] defines a network as "an informal group of contacts that share advice, facts, techniques, job leads, plans and dreams, and who lend each other moral support." We still hear the old (and true) cliché, "It's not what you know, but who you know that counts."

Fortunately, there is abundant opportunity to get to know people who can help us if we are willing to make the effort. Networking is largely a matter of knowing how to be helpful to your contacts and how to ask them for help.

BENEFITS OF NETWORKS

Networking is invaluable to teams for improving daily productivity, efficiency, and achievement. It is also a fast track to personal growth for individual members. People who build connections within and outside organizations are much more likely to succeed. The benefits of active networking are:

- technical, professional, legal, or fiscal advice;
- advance information about trends, new projects, or organizational changes;
- opinions on proposals, ideas, speeches, or reports;
- moral support;
- mentoring or counseling help;
- learning about job opportunities;
- becoming aware of the availability of job candidates;
- soliciting recommendations or support; and
- sharing experiences—successes and failures.

POTENTIAL NETWORK PARTICIPANTS

External Customers

Patients, physicians, and other outside customers can provide a constant source of suggestions for improving your service. When you satisfy these clients, you gain enthusiastic supporters.

Internal Customers

These are departments or individuals within your organization that you provide services for or who provide services to you.

Coworkers

These are employees who precede or follow you in work flows, and colleagues who serve with you on committees, task forces, or problem solving groups.

Former Professors and Instructors

These people take pride in responding to your requests to tap into their knowledge bank.

Vendors

Your suppliers are loaded with valuable information and very willing to share it.

Community Associates

Fellow members of civic, service, and social or religious organizations comprise this category.

Gatekeepers

These are people who provide access to important people, services, or knowledge. When a gatekeeper is part of your network, you are operating on the inside track.

Competitors

Keep in touch with "friendly" competitors. You can teach each other how to save costs and avoid problems. If a cross-town competitor warns you about hiring one of his or her former employees, your friendly relationship has proven its worth.

Family Members

Never forget the special people in your life. They serve as your publicists and supporters. Wives and husbands have their own networks. Even when they are not in the same profession, their spheres of influence overlap. Most successful people owe much of their success to their mates, whether they remain at home or have their own professional careers.

HOW TO MAKE AND MAINTAIN CONTACTS

Use your Rolodex or address book, files of correspondence, business cards, membership rosters of organizations you belong to, alumni associations, and Internet rosters. Establish contacts at professional and social meetings, seminars, workshops, committees, churches or synagogues, schools, clubs, hobby groups, and among your neighbors. Your present network can provide contacts with people you would like to include in your network.

The omnipresent lapel name tags on attendees are signs of networking in action. The networking at a meeting may be more valuable than the program itself.

Raise your visibility by giving talks, holding office, or becoming a spokesperson. Earn a reputation as a recognized expert in some professional or technical aspect of health care. Constantly expand your professional and social network. Do this by getting people obligated to you rather than asking favors.

Gain the respect of your colleagues. Become a resource person and troubleshooter. This goes a long way toward developing a power base. Do not shift blame or point fingers. Never take credit for something others have done. Instead, lead the cheers for their accomplishments. Acknowledge their support, especially to superiors.

With all the current restructuring and realigning, many employees have new contacts with personnel in other departments and institutions. Employees in health care institutions have dealings with people in managed care organizations. There is less stress when people know each other's expectations and strive to collaborate. Ideally these relationships are supportive as well as cordial. This is easier said than done. Many situations are conducive to antagonistic positions.

**Tips for Building Rapport with People
Outside Your Work Unit**

- Accept invitations to sit in on their meetings or to visit their work areas. Invite them to your meetings and facilities. Ask them to sit with you in the cafeteria.
- Be visible. Introduce yourself to others when you are in the same room.
- Volunteer for assignments that provide interdepartmental contacts.
- Attend organizational social functions.
- Take advantage of training sessions and seminars where you meet people from other departments or agencies.
- Participate in extracurricular activities.

COMPUTER NETWORKS

Computer networking is the sharing of computer resources among various users. These resources may be the computers themselves, databases, printers, or even human expertise. Communication may be one-to-one electronic mail between individuals, message sending to a distribution list, and group participation in electronic forums or conferences. Document sharing, central databases, and computer forums now play a vital role in sharing knowledge and expertise. Electronic distribution lists enable managers and professionals to broadcast information or to address concerns to many people. E-mail is rapidly replacing memos and has the advantage over telephone conversations in that the responder can look up information and get back to the sender when it is convenient.

Computer networks enable employees to obtain information directly from sources without having to contact supervisors and middle managers. This computer capability has been a factor in the elimination of many middle manager jobs.

People are learning through their computers how to do things for which they formerly needed the help of staff specialists. For example, supervisors can gather and process their own budgets without the assistance of their accounting department. Greater access to accounts and files enables front-line employees to answer questions and serve their clients better. Personnel on after-hour shifts and those stationed in satellite facilities feel more in touch with each other and with their organization.

CHARACTERISTICS OF GREAT NETWORKERS

- They know how to interact with people. They ask good questions and listen attentively.
- They keep in touch with their contacts.
- They are great joiners.
- They circulate at parties and meetings and introduce themselves rather than wait for someone else to do the honors.
- They are cordial and courteous to all but are selective about the people with whom they develop special rapport.
- They use coffee breaks and lunch times to chat with different people.
- They volunteer for committees and other group functions.
- They teach, coach, and mentor.
- They serve as officers in social and professional organizations.
- They go out of their way to establish relationships with newcomers.
- They share clippings, reports, articles, and other information.
- They send out many thank you notes, and they remember birthdays and other special occasions.
- They express their appreciation for favors in special ways.

WORKPLACE POLITICS

Politics is the pursuit of power. The original meaning of the word was to act in the service of society. It meant a high form of public service. Politics has been reinterpreted to mean service to oneself—self-empowerment with a negative connotation. What winners call interpersonal relationships, losers call politics. Career failures can result from political as well as professional incompetence. Unwillingness to address the political components of a job has snuffed out many a promising career. Losers make no effort to find mentors or to build personal networks. They grow resentful toward their employers, their superiors, and their colleagues. Often they become chronic complainers or shrill negativists.

Corporate politics is gamesmanship—using other than good performance to improve one's stance in an organization. This includes trying to influence superiors and gaining a competitive edge over one's peers. If your political script is a positive one, you play the game fairly and ethically.

At one end of the scale, politics is selfish, unethical, or illegal. At the other end, political behavior supplements professional competency. It is often beneficial not only for the political person but also for his subordinates, superiors, teammates, and employer.

POLITICS AND THE INFORMAL ORGANIZATION

Every organization has an informal structure. Unions are officially sanctioned informal organizations. Cliques represent informal coteries that discriminate against fellow workers. The informal organization selects its own leaders and communicates via the grapevine.

Powerful informal work groups set productivity norms. They may introduce initiation rituals that sometimes include such severe hazing that new hires quit. The culture of the informal organization may allow disloyalty, insubordination, and even sabotage.

Politics overlaps the formal and the informal organizations. Political scripts are flexible because there are few, if any, documented guidelines. The first rule of politics is that nobody will tell you the rules.

NEGATIVE POLITICS

Negative politics may be dysfunctional, unethical, or even illegal. It gets blamed for almost everything: bad communication, inappropriate behavior, unpopular promotions, discrimination, and favoritism.

Block[2] claims that organizational politics is partly based on the time-honored bureaucratic wish to be blameless and safe. Terrell[3] identifies the following factors as the breeding grounds for negative politics:

- lack of clear organizational goals or lack of communication of the goals,
- autocratic or bureaucratic leadership,
- multiple layers of management (the more layers, the more politics),
- little upward communication,
- frequent changes,
- controversial management shifts of power, and
- poor relationships between workers and managers.

Political Games That Subordinates or Colleagues Play

- taking advantage of being indispensable
- abusing friendships

- probing for weaknesses of others and revealing those weaknesses
- undermining operations or new services
- starting unfounded rumors or providing misleading information
- creating crises or discord
- displaying undue emotional distress to achieve selfish gains
- discrediting teammates in public or undermining them in private
- intimidating new employees and provoking sensitive people

Political Games That Managers Play

- stealing ideas or credit
- excluding others from meetings or information
- eliminating or downgrading the jobs of employees whom they dislike or distrust
- assigning unpleasant tasks
- delegating work that places delegates at risk or that prevents them from handling their regular work
- pitting one employee against another
- giving unfair or false performance appraisals
- not hiring anyone who could be threatening to them

Manipulation

Manipulators invoke the names of high-level people to get their way. They curry favor of those who outrank them, sometimes to a degree of obsequiousness. They take advantage of friends and colleagues. Threats or even bribes may be part of their strategy. They usually forget their promises. Political savvy to these folks means passing the buck, procrastinating, and saying what they do not mean. They are always cautious about speaking candidly.

You know someone is manipulating you when they lead off with: "You don't value my service anymore, do you?" or "You owe me one," or "The boss will back me on this."

POSITIVE POLITICAL SCRIPTS AND TACTICS

Assertiveness

Assertiveness is standing up for one's personal rights and expressing those feelings and beliefs in direct, honest ways that do not violate the rights of others. The assertive person's theme is "You're OK, I'm OK." Lack of assertiveness chips away at one's self-image and self-respect.

Ask yourself these questions:

- Do you often say yes when you should say no?
- Do you allow people to interrupt you?
- Do you use self-deprecating comments? For example: "I know this sounds stupid, but. . . . "
- At meetings, do you want to speak up, but seldom do?
- Do you always avoid controversial issues?
- Are you doing work that others should do?
- Are you the one who always gives in?
- Do others take advantage of you?
- Do you find it difficult to negotiate?

If you answered yes to many of these questions, follow the recommendations in the box below:

Increase Your Assertiveness

- Attend a workshop or read a book on assertiveness.
- When others say something negative about you, reply, "Are you trying to make me feel guilty?" Watch them turn red!
- Appreciate the fact that you have more power than you realize!
- Set boundaries or limits. Learn to say "no."
- Rehearse expressing yourself or engage in role-playing with a close friend.

Rapport With People Who Report to You

One thing that employees notice quickly is whether "the score" is being kept equitably. The score refers to how you evaluate performance, how you treat each employee, and how you enforce the rules.

Political power is short circuited when employees feel that they are being manipulated or hoodwinked. Negative political statements and unfulfilled promises lead to resentment, anger, and loss of trust. On the other hand, if there are mutual trust and respect and if your people perceive you as their champion, your personal power will skyrocket.

COPING WITH THE PERSON YOU REPORT TO

It is not likely that your employer will ask you to select a manager. However, if you are job hunting or transferring within your organization, one of your considerations should be the person to whom you will report.

You want someone with whom you can get along. You also want to know as much as you can about the leadership style, morale, and turnover in the new unit. This information is not found in any handout. However, you can learn much with some probing. Question some of the employees who work in the unit.

Get To Know Your Manager's Expectations, Likes, and Dislikes

Managers are often insecure because they do not really know much about what you do on the job. Clarify this by reviewing your goals and priorities with your manager and by asking the manager if he or she agrees with the goals. In this way the manager will also be in a better position to offer more specific support.

We have already mentioned leadership styles. Communication preferences are also important. Learn how the manager wants to receive messages. Some like to read them, as President John Kennedy did. Others prefer to listen to them, as President Harry Truman did. Keep your manager informed. Never hide problems, and when you report them, offer solutions. Do not waste his or her time with trivia or gossip. Learn when to speak up and when to remain silent.

Avoid disagreements in public, and never embarrass the boss in front of others. Pick the right time and place for presenting your ideas. Some managers like input first thing in the morning so they can get a handle on operations. Others do not want to hear or see anyone until they complete their morning chores.

Other considerations are the manager's likes and dislikes, decision-making style, stereotyping, or other hangups. Most importantly, what are his or her expectations and priorities concerning your performance? Ask the manager to review your position description and work standards with you.

Discover the problems that your manager has with his or her superiors and provide whatever support you can. Do everything you can to make your manager look good to upper management.

Accept delegated responsibilities with enthusiasm. Better still, seek out additional responsibilities. For example, volunteer to chair a committee or to lead a focus group. When you pinch hit for your manager, consider this as a chance to "try out the job." Remember that promotions are based not so much on what you have done as on what your superiors think you can do for them in the future.

Direct Your Manager's Behavior by Using the Carrot

This can be done verbally or by means of thank you notes or e-mail. When one of your requests is granted, a thank you message is appropriate. Do you respond enthusiastically and gratefully when your manager approves your request to attend a professional meeting or to take a long weekend? Depending on how important the favor is, a small gift is not out of order.

Group expressions of appreciation are even more acceptable. Handing out the carrots of praise are much more effective in channeling behavior than using the stick (threats or complaints).

Be Loyal and Show Respect

This means making your boss look good. You can display loyalty by defending your manager when he or she is criticized, arriving on time at meetings, making extra effort, and by expressing enthusiasm.

Most important is a tone of respect in daily communications. Know when and how to dissent. Most managers accept disagreement if it is done tactfully. Learn how direct you can be, and be diplomatic. Remember that what you think is a bad decision by your manager may be one that had imposed on him or her. Share credit for your accomplishments with your manager.

When You Have More Than One Immediate Superior

Today, many health care employees report to two or more superiors. This can lead to conflicts of time sharing or priorities or even of conflicting orders. When you get competing assignments, inform the junior member of the pair of the conflict and ask for his or her advice.

Tips for Coping with Your Manager

- Say complimentary things about your manager to other people—your boss will get the message.
- Act as a devil's advocate occasionally, then yield gracefully (bosses like to persuade people).
- Develop a reputation as a problem solver. Be willing to risk your reputation by offering innovative suggestions or introducing new techniques in your unit.
- Have the courage to stand up for what you think is right.
- Deliver on your promises.
- Protect and defend the reputation of your organization and your boss.
- Keep your frustrations and negative thoughts to yourself.
- Know when and how to resign or ask for a transfer.

Do not:

- do anything that would lead your boss to regard you as a threat;
- say "That's not in my position description" or "I wasn't hired to do that";
- let pessimism or negativism creep into your attitude;

- steal credit;
- knock your boss, coworkers, or organization in public;
- distort the truth;
- develop an amorous relationship with your boss;
- threaten to resign when you do not get your way; and
- sacrifice your professional and ethical values.

Never go to your manager's superiors with problems or complaints before discussing them with your boss. These end runs are usually the beginning of the end of a work relationship. The most serious end run is when someone keeps going up the chain of command until he or she finds someone who gives the answer he or she wants. If you are frustrated over not getting satisfaction from your superior and want to talk to a higher authority, disclose your intention to your manager first and suggest that you both make the visit. If the manager refuses, tell him or her exactly what you are going to say to the higher up.

Difficult Bosses

Look at the bright side. Inevitably most of us must deal with an unpleasant or incompetent boss. When you have one of these early in your career, you have a wonderful opportunity to fine-tune your skill in getting along with someone who has power over you. I shall always be grateful to one of my first superior officers in the U.S. Navy. He was a real tyrant, but I learned how to tolerate him. All my subsequent chiefs seemed like pussycats.

Before you put all the blame on your manager, examine your own behavior. Are you doing anything that irritates him or her? Is your work area a mess while his or her office is orderly? Do you show up at his or her meetings late and without excuses? Are you occasionally careless about your appearance while your manager always dresses impeccably? Do you get frequent personal phone calls or visits or have to drop things and run home? Do you routinely get to work after he or she has arrived or leave before he or she does? Have you been insensitive to things you say or do that you know annoy him or her?

Procrastinators

These are usually agreeable, well-intentioned folks with perfectionist tendencies. They avoid or put off decisions for fear of making mistakes or offending others.

Try to find the reasons for their hesitancy and eliminate them. Praise them when they do make decisions or take action promptly—"Louise, we really appreciate it when you are so proactive. It helps us meet our schedules and get home on time."

Be reassuring of and optimistic toward procrastinators. When you need to get something approved, have all the supporting data ready. Tell them that you have checked out your proposals carefully. Instead of asking permission, send a memo stating what you intend to do unless you hear to the contrary. Make sure that you give them sufficient time to get back to you.

Unfair Bosses

If you are getting more than your share of unpleasant assignments, instead of accusing him or her of sticking it to you, state exactly what it is that is bothering you. You will usually find that the manager is not aware of the situation or that you are upset about it. If the boss is dumping excessive busywork on you or is delegating too much, ask him or her to help you to set your work priorities or to provide additional help.

If you think that he or she is discriminating against you, point it out to him or her in behavioral terms. If the discrimination gets out of hand, blow the whistle after you are certain that your evidence is firm and specific. Be prepared to give examples and have corroborative evidence. Check with your mentors and local governmental agencies.

Bosses Who Bypass You

These managers frequently give orders to your subordinates without your knowledge, usually when you are not right on the spot. You can eliminate most of these intrusions if you discuss the problem with them. Point out how this undermines your authority and confuses your staff. Give specific examples.

Tell your staff that they are to keep you informed about requests from others. Except in emergencies they are not to carry these orders out until they have consulted you. If you feel that your employees can diplomatically tell certain of these order givers that they must get your approval first, try that approach. You may want to authorize your team members to decide when they should honor extrinsic orders. You can provide a discretionary task list.

You must have the courage to protest when a superior repeatedly issues orders to your people in your presence. Try diplomacy first. Tell him or her that results will be better if requests are made to you. If this practice continues, point out that your employees are confused about some of his or her orders and that they are afraid to ask for clarifications. If this behavior continues and results in real problems for you and your people, you are justified in going over the superior's head with your complaint.

Laissez Faire Leaders

These people are not really leaders; they just have the title. They have abdicated their responsibility. They are never around when you need them. When they are on site, they provide no help.

Know what your authority is, and use it. Revise your position description to include more control over your areas of responsibility. Seek broad approval for your objectives, plans, and schedules, and then go ahead with them. Pin him or her down when vague directives are issued. Gradually assume more responsibility and control.

NOTES

1. P.P. Luebbert, "Networking for Survival and Success," *Medical Laboratory Observer 19*, no. 6 (1987): 39–42.
2. P. Block, *The Empowered Manager: Positive Skills at Work* (San Francisco, CA: Jossey-Bass, 1987), 45.
3. R.D. Terrell, "The Elusive Menace of Office Politics," *Training 26*, no. 5 (1989): 48–54.

RECOMMENDED READING AND LISTENING

S.M. Crow and S.J. Hartman, "Improving the Political Skills of Health Care Supervisors," *Health Care Supervisor 14*, no. 4 (1995): 35–42.

S. Dellinger, *Political Savvy: The Unwritten Power Skills for Professional Women,* (Boulder, CO: CareerTrack Publishers, 1987), four audiotapes.

Index

About the Author

William Umiker, M.D., is Adjunct Professor of Clinical Pathology at the Hershey Medical Center of Pennsylvania State University. He holds an M.D. from the University of Buffalo and received his postgraduate training at the University of Michigan.

Dr. Umiker is a health care administrator with more than 40 years of experience. Subsequent to service in U.S. Navy and Veterans Administration hospitals, he was laboratory director at St. Joseph Hospital in Lancaster, Pennsylvania until his retirement in 1985. He has served as an inspector of blood banks, clinical laboratories, and schools of medical technology.

Dr. Umiker has been widely published and is author of six books about health care management.